I0191687

OUR JACKIE

KAREN M. DUNAK

Our Jackie

PUBLIC CLAIMS ON A PRIVATE LIFE

NEW YORK UNIVERSITY PRESS

NEW YORK

NEW YORK UNIVERSITY PRESS
New York
www.nyupress.org

© 2024 by New York University
All rights reserved

Please contact the Library of Congress for Cataloging-in-Publication data.

ISBN: 9781479830565 (hardback)
ISBN: 9781479830602 (library ebook)
ISBN: 9781479830589 (consumer ebook)

This book is printed on acid-free paper, and its binding materials are chosen for strength and durability. We strive to use environmentally responsible suppliers and materials to the greatest extent possible in publishing our books.

Manufactured in the United States of America

Also available as an ebook

CONTENTS

AUTHOR'S NOTE

Those writing women's history often find that as their subjects age and change, so, too, do their names. And as historians know, names matter. A name communicates something fundamental about a person's identity.

As I moved through each chapter of this book, and as Jacqueline Bouvier Kennedy Onassis's context—and her name—evolved, I had to consider the best way to refer to her. I am not interested in referring to Mrs. Onassis (her preferred address at the end of her life) as just "Jackie." Using a first name alone is not the standard practice when writing about male subjects, and so, with a few exceptions, I have not done that here. In using the name of her preference, I aim to pay her the respect so many failed to afford her during her lifetime, when they ignored the Onassis surname and continued to call her "Jackie Kennedy" or, assuming claim to her and adopting a familiarity she did not necessarily welcome or return, called her "Jackie O." Or, just "Jackie" (see the title of this book).

In the pages that follow, I refer to Jacqueline Kennedy Onassis in a number of ways. Before her first marriage, it is easy. She was Jacqueline Bouvier. Afterward, it is more complicated. To avoid confusion, rather than using on its own either of the last names she shared with either of her husbands, when I write about her, I use "Mrs. Kennedy" or "Mrs. Onassis," her full name, or her initials. Her husbands' names became hers, and in many ways, their influence on her perceived identity lasted well after their unions had ended. But my goal is to privilege JKO as an individual in her own right, to put her at the center of the stories told about her. In navigating what name to use, that has been my priority.

Many scholars—as evidenced in the titles of the many texts about the former first lady—call her "Jacqueline Kennedy Onassis," and I have largely followed that model. Given the regular usage of "JFK" (John Fitzgerald Kennedy) and "RFK" (Robert Francis Kennedy), both of which I have used in this book, I have also employed the use of initials in my discussion of Jacqueline Onassis and other figures who appear in this text.

JBK: Jacqueline Bouvier Kennedy (used for discussions of her life from September 12, 1953, to October 20, 1968)

JKO: Jacqueline Kennedy Onassis (used for discussions of her life from October 20, 1968, on)

AO: Aristotle Onassis

ER: Eleanor Roosevelt

HRC: Hillary Rodham Clinton

CK: Caroline Kennedy

PROLOGUE

BECOMING A PUBLIC FIGURE

In a personal essay penned in 1951, twenty-one-year-old Jacqueline Bouvier wrote first about her appearance: "I am tall, 5'7", with brown hair, a square face and eyes so unfortunately far apart that it takes three weeks to have a pair of glasses made with a bridge wide enough to fit over my nose. I do not have a sensational figure but can look slim if I pick the right clothes." Living in New York until she was thirteen, she had spent her summers in the country. As a child, she had "hated dolls, loved horses and dogs and had skinned knees and braces on my teeth for what must have seemed an interminable length of time to my family." In the room where she was meant to take naps as a child, she instead hopped down from her resting place and plucked copies of Shaw and Chekhov from the shelves, reading them when they were still "too old" for her even by her own accounting. In boarding school, she had attempted to become grown up by copying the girls who had "callers" every Saturday night. Her pass into adulthood came when she learned to smoke "in the balcony of the Normandie theater in New York," and was immediately asked to leave by the usher, who informed young Jacqueline and her friend that "other people could not hear the film with so much coughing going on." Vassar, where she spent two years, had been fine, but the real turning point had been a junior year in Paris. Of this time, she wrote, "I loved it more than any year of my life." It was during this trip that she evaluated herself critically and "learned not to be ashamed of a real hunger for knowledge, something I had always tried to hide." As for hobbies, Bouvier noted that there were none at which she worked "constantly," but expressed an interest in art and indicated her love for riding and fox hunting.

From this essay, part of her application for *Vogue*'s 1951 Prix de Paris competition, Bouvier emerges as a forthright young woman, self-deprecating in her humor and capable of crafting an intriguing self-portrait. There is evidence of her privilege and her intelligence and her curiosity about the world in which she lived. Indeed, something in her style caught the eye of the prize committee. Bouvier, competing against nearly 1300 contestants from 225 colleges, emerged the winner of the contest. As her prize, she was offered the opportunity to work six months in *Vogue*'s New York offices and six months at the Paris headquarters.[1] Even with an articulated aspiration "to be a top editor at Conde Nast," Bouvier ultimately turned down the opportunities presented as part of her prize, ostensibly at the behest of her mother, Janet, who had promised Jackie and her sister Lee a European summer vacation and threatened to cancel the trip if Jackie moved forward with the *Vogue* post.[2]

Reading Bouvier's essay and considering her self-assessment, there is much to suggest that Jacqueline Bouvier, as she aged and matured, was likely to dedicate herself to art and culture and writing and travel, even without the *Vogue* prize to pave the way to such a life. At just twenty-one, she was sharp and funny and self-aware. With the contacts provided by her elite station, she might well have entered into a kind of professional life where her "hunger for knowledge" could be satiated, even in 1951, when women of a certain standing were not necessarily expected to pursue such a course, and popular wisdom held that those women who did work did so out of necessity rather than any particular drive. Aside from her referenced teenage admiration for girls who had callers at boarding school, the only mention of men in Bouvier's application comes as a list of artists she admired: French poet Charles Baudelaire, Irish writer Oscar Wilde, and Russian ballet impresario Serge Diaghilev.[3] There is no indication of marital ambition. Indeed, rather than spend her college years searching for a suitor, as many women of her generation did, and as noted in her application, Bouvier spent her junior year in France, having first proven her academic merit to warrant acceptance in Smith College's prestigious program. She took an intensive French course at the University of Grenoble, enrolled in the Sorbonne, and chose to live with a French family rather than reside in the American dormitories. While in Paris, she attended chic French parties and salons. She traveled to the Riviera and Italy, Austria and Germany, the south of France, and finally Scotland and Ireland, visiting museums and historic sites but also taking stock of a Europe forever changed by World War II and adapting to a new world order.[4]

But a life such as that offered by the Prix de Paris and sampled as part of her study abroad, though possible, was not to be. At least not initially. And not as a fully independent actor. After graduation from George Washington University, where she matriculated after her Parisian semester, Bouvier continued to live with her mother and stepfather just outside Washington, DC. Following university and a summer of European travel, she entered into and called off an engagement and established herself as the "Inquiring Camera Girl" at the *Washington Times-Herald*, a post she made into a vaunted feature of the publication. While she had met him in the spring of 1951 at a dinner party hosted by mutual friend Charles Bartlett, it was only after a subsequent meeting in May 1952, again dining at Bartlett's home, that Jacqueline Bouvier began a steady courtship with aspiring senator and sitting Massachusetts congressman John F. Kennedy. He sometimes called Bouvier from the campaign trail, scheduling dates in advance of his return to Washington. They double dated with his brother Bobby and sister-in-law Ethel, staying in for dinner and games or going out to the movies. Indicating the seriousness of his intentions, Kennedy invited Jackie to join him at the family's summer home in Hyannis Port, where she got a taste of the "slightly madcap Kennedys." After his election, it was she who accompanied him to the inaugural ball.[5]

In the spring of 1953, when Bouvier traveled to London on behalf of the *Times-Herald* to cover the coronation of Queen Elizabeth II, the two exchanged communication across the Atlantic. He cabled her "Articles Excellent But You Are Missed. Love, Jack" and was there to meet her plane when she returned to the United States. Shortly thereafter the two became engaged, but Bouvier and the Kennedys delayed announcement of the engagement until after the *Saturday Evening Post*'s June 1953 publication proclaiming Kennedy "The Senate's Gay Young Bachelor." Once made public, the news scored a headline in the *New York Times*: "Senator Kennedy to Marry in Fall: Son of Former Envoy Is Fiancé of Miss Jacqueline Bouvier, Newport Society Girl."[6]

The *Times* headline, among the first national coverage Bouvier received, presented readers with a sense of opposites attracting. Kennedy was a senator, son of a diplomat, linked to public service, whereas Bouvier was highlighted as "Society Girl," a frivolous title, and one casting Bouvier in the diminutive. He was well known whereas she was known only in certain circles, designated as elite by the reference to Newport (Hugh Auchincloss, Bouvier's stepfather, owned a summer home there, and it is where she had made her debut). While the *Post* article suggested that Kennedy was not a natural glad hander, he had warmed to the necessities of the campaign trail and embraced the public nature of his chosen profession. Jacqueline's desire to delay news of their engagement suggested an early wariness about how the publicity that followed Kennedy might affect her private life.

Based on the Kennedy overview provided as part of "The Senate's Gay Young Bachelor," readers might assume that with his engagement Kennedy had added to his team yet another devoted woman who believed he "need[ed] looking after." In 1952, the Kennedy women had jettisoned their respective interests in Chicago, New York, and Paris so that now eldest brother and son John might achieve the collective family goal of a Kennedy man in office.[7] Teas and small talk and an element of transparency marked the work they had done to contribute to his senatorial win. Women outside the Kennedy clan willingly had given their time and indicated their devotion to the young man in need of a woman's touch. Jacqueline Bouvier was but one of many women who seemingly wanted to marry John Kennedy. The key difference between Bouvier and other women: she was the one Kennedy wished (or, as those less romantically inclined have speculated, was willing) to wed.[8]

The precise details of Bouvier's background, her interests, education, and elite standing, at this point were largely unknown to a curious public who received only bits and pieces of information about the future Mrs. Kennedy in news stories introducing her on the national stage. And to a large degree, her background and any individual interests she might have held were beside the point. As projected by American media, she was the lucky young woman who had won Kennedy's heart. That was what people needed to know about her. In her nationally syndicated article, Patti Simmons speculated, "Those much publicized 1000 females to every 855 males in Washington are probably dying to know how Miss Bouvier went about this business of snagging the town's most eligible bachelor." Simmons suggested it was Bouvier's good looks, combination of status and common touch, and sense of humor that allowed her to stand out. These qualities, Simmons asserted, would "also go big with voters," alluding to the political calculation implicit in John Kennedy's selection of a mate.[9] Mainstream expectations would have been that securing a relationship with a man like Kennedy had been Bouvier's goal, and even with reference to Bouvier's education and time in Paris, Simmons's text did nothing to combat that notion. Marriage, most people assumed, was a woman's natural state. A young woman might face warring impulses when it came to personal ambitions versus social and familial expectations, but the widespread sentiment of the postwar period was that a woman's primary desires were to secure a husband, establish a home, and start a family.[10] She would have caught him, not the other way around. Coverage of John Kennedy's fiancée suggested that he was what made her distinct. He could have chosen anyone; Bouvier was special because he had chosen her. In the early 1950s, it was not uncommon to assess a young woman according to the man standing beside her.

But copious coverage of Jacqueline Bouvier Kennedy Onassis—historical and that recently produced—has revealed just how distinct she was in her own right. Where the American public did not know the particulars of Bouvier's background, what she had to gain from the union warrants consideration. She had grown up in a world of wealth and privilege but without a promised fortune of her own. After Janet Bouvier's 1940 divorce from John "Black Jack" Bouvier, her means of guaranteeing a secure future was through marriage to millionaire Hugh Auchincloss. Jacqueline Bouvier's conundrum: she was accustomed to a certain standard of living, but her father's money had all but dried up and because she was an Auchincloss stepchild, her mother's renewed source of income was not hers. Bouvier lived in a time when securing such a standard for herself through a means outside or beyond the confines of marriage was an unlikely prospect.[11] Her most immediate model demonstrated that marriage was the path to wealth and status. It is possible that a pairing with millionaire Kennedy was a means to an end. Regardless of whatever romantic attachment the two had, Kennedy had money, and if Bouvier would have to leave behind an interest in professional writing and publishing, she still would be able to pursue her other interests and ambitions in a private context and, even more, in contribution to the career of a man she, by all accounts, found exceptional. To Kennedy's benefit, the private interests of Bouvier could be used to enhance the public image he and his team were so dedicated to crafting.

As her friend Aileen Bowdoin said of the period leading into the pair's marriage, this "was the turning point for [Bouvier] going from private life to public life."[12] Early coverage set a tone for understandings of her public persona. A month after the *Saturday Evening Post*'s celebration of John F. Kennedy's bachelorhood, resulting from a "media day" orchestrated by the Kennedy family, *Life* magazine featured John Kennedy and Jacqueline Bouvier on the cover of its July 20, 1953, issue and offered readers an inside look at "Courting with a U.S. Senator." Photographed on Cape Cod at the Kennedy family compound, John and Jackie are seen together and with the rest of the Kennedy brood, enjoying sun, surf, and rousing bouts of athletic competition. In the very limited text accompanying the photo essay, Bouvier indicated that while at the *Times-Herald*, as she interviewed people in and around the halls of Congress, she and Kennedy had occasionally crossed paths. Upon their engagement, however, she claimed to be somewhat "less inquisitive—'We hardly ever talk politics.'"[13] From this point on, Bouvier largely was understood as apolitical. Popular media regularly framed Jackie as disinterested in her husband's politics, as though emphasizing that that was his preserve and not hers. When coverage did suggest a modicum of interest, it was very much in the form of Jacqueline as fascinated pupil or dedicated helpmate. She would provide Kennedy with emotional support and encouragement or serve as a rapt audience for his ideas and convictions, whichever style suited his needs or desires. His opinions, media suggested, would be hers.

The Kennedy family, led by Joseph Kennedy Sr., had an astute understanding of and close relationship with American media—from film to newspapers and magazines with national reach. From his time managing Hollywood studios to his years as ambassador to Great Britain, Joe Kennedy—with his politically savvy wife, Rose—had managed their family with an eye toward promotion and fanfare, with elite contacts in the world of politics, diplomacy, entertainment, and journalism. His was a family comfortable in front of the camera. So when John Kennedy wed Jacqueline Bouvier on September 12, 1953, theirs was not a modest event as initially imagined by Jacqueline Bouvier and Janet Auchincloss. It was a media extravaganza intended to communicate an idyllic romance between two beautiful young people who would from that point forward regularly appear on pages and screens across the United States.[14]

In its front-page coverage of the Kennedy-Bouvier wedding, the *New York Times* emphasized popular interest in the union as it reported that "a crowd of 3000 persons," many of whom arrived in front of St. Mary's Catholic Church in Newport, Rhode Island, an hour before guests arrived, "broke through police lines and nearly crushed the bride." In describing the bride and groom posing for their well-wishers after the ceremony, the *Times* reported that John Kennedy appeared "with a grin on his face," while "the bride appear[ed] a little startled."[15] Beyond the "society fans," as *Life* magazine called those assembled outside the church, "600 diplomats, senators, social figures" witnessed the wedding and 900 guests attended the reception held afterward at the Auchincloss's Hammersmith Farm.[16] In the text accompanying *Life*'s photo spread of the event, readers learned that "the wedding turned out to be

Jacqueline Bouvier Kennedy and John F. Kennedy on their wedding day, with members of their wedding party. Rivaling Queen Elizabeth's coronation for its glamor, the wedding introduced the couple to the nation. Newport, Rhode Island, by Toni Frissell, September 12, 1953. Glasshouse Images/Alamy Stock Photo.

the most impressive the old society stronghold had seen in 30 years." As "one enthusiastic guest" noted, it was "just like the coronation," referring to the June event Jacqueline had covered. Barbara Baker Burrows, who later became a picture editor at *Life*, called the event "a marriage made in heaven: the Kennedys and *Life*."[17] Whether observers regarded the wedding as a "royal affair" or the cementing of John and Jacqueline Kennedy as a "national celebrity couple," Joe Kennedy succeeded enormously in his orchestration and promotion of the event.

Jacqueline Bouvier became Mrs. John F. Kennedy, an identity that led her to be cast in a different light than the one she had fashioned for her Prix de Paris essay. Instead of an independent figure of interest in her own right, media framed her as a supporting player to her husband's professional ambitions. And this was true when it came to articles published in national periodicals, syndicated columns and stories appearing in "women's pages" of local newspapers, and television coverage and appearances. In the early years of her union to John Kennedy, the press portrayed the far junior Jackie in a manner fairly typical for a young wife, linking her to her husband rather than recognizing the possibility of her autonomy, attributing her public significance to her husband rather than to any individual merit.[18] Initially, she seemed to acquiesce to this image. In public statements for years to come, she would play to the notion of what it meant to be a dutiful political wife. But visions of Jacqueline Kennedy changed over the course of her public life, inspired by shifts in her own life and sense of self and also reflecting amended expectations of women as a whole and the relatedly evolving means by which they were evaluated by American media.

From the time of their September 1953 wedding through his eventual election to the nation's highest office, mainstream media asserted that John Kennedy's preserve would be the public, professional world, while Jacqueline Kennedy would focus on the private world of "culture and character," although, when possible, she would use these elements to assist JFK's professional advancement. Even before they wed, the two, media suggested, were prepared to fulfill the expected marital roles of their time and station: they would be partners, of a kind, but there were differences between men and women. Coverage further suggested that both were satisfied with their roles, and accordingly, formed an idyllic pairing.[19] Jacqueline Kennedy was, first and foremost, a wife, and then in 1957, a mother, with all the obligations assumed of these roles. And for the remainder of her public life, media would return to these components of her identity and assess her largely by how dutifully she fulfilled these positions and their affiliated obligations.

And yet the early years of her marriage and public life reveal something of her individual potential. Response to Jacqueline Kennedy on the 1958 campaign trail suggested the appeal Mrs. Kennedy held in her own right and the means by which she might aid her husband's political career. While she had been a senator's wife for nearly five years, the 1958 senatorial reelection campaign was her first test as wife to a political candidate, and it was a baptism by fire. Traveling to Massachusetts regularly, JBK eventually joined her husband in 184 local communities.[20] She gamely embraced the requirements of campaigning, even if the nature of the campaign trail was the antithesis of her reserved style. "I never can remember sleeping at home for however many months it was. Two months, I guess. But you know, just running, running," she recalled of that time.[21] When JBK addressed voters in the North End of Boston in Italian, William DeMarco, Boston district leader, recalled, "All pandemonium broke loose. All the people went over and started to kiss her, and the old women spoke to her as if she were a native of the North End. And I think her talk is actually what cemented the relationship between Senator Kennedy and the Italian-Americans of the district."[22] As Kennedy stalwart Dave Powers noted, "She was always cheerful and obliging, and to me a very refreshing change from the usual candidate's wife because she did not bother to put on a phony show of enthusiasm about everything she saw and every local politician whom she met. The crowds sensed that and it impressed them." By being herself, despite being very different from the typical Massachusetts voter, Powers suggested, JBK appealed to her husband's constituency. Powers further remarked, "When Jackie was traveling with us, the size of the crowd at every stop was twice as big as it would have been if Jack had been alone."[23]

The Kennedys' time was well spent. In 1958, JFK won reelection with 73.6 percent of the vote, breaking all records for the state and winning a larger plurality that year than any other senator in the country. It was a victory of such magnitude, as Kennedy intended, that party leaders could not ignore it. A December 1958 issue of *Time* chronicled six likely Democratic presidential hopefuls (a list that included John Kennedy) as well as the "Hopefuls' Helpmates." Jacqueline Kennedy was described as hailing from a "socialite Republican family," and her education and early career warranted mention, as did the scope of their wedding (a "big Newport blowout") and her position as mother to "an infant daughter." "Although she traveled with her husband during the last campaign ('Some days we would shake 2,500 to 3,000 hands')," *Time* reported, "Jackie tried to avoid making speeches, prefers a homebody's life." This game willingness but natural reluctance increasingly would become a hallmark of public perception of JBK, and in some ways, would feed the fire of public demand for more and more of her. But even as media often painted her as apolitical, she recalled, "People say he never talked about politics at home with me, but that's all that was talked about." While they may not have engaged in policy debates, "He always talked at home of what he was thinking about, or people."[24] From these discussions, Jacqueline Kennedy became increasingly astute in her understanding of relationships, image, and media, in relation both to her husband's political ambitions and to her own navigation of public life, which would last well beyond her husband's time in public office. For the next four decades, Jacqueline Kennedy's interaction with and framing by American media reflected the opportunities available to women in public as well as the limitations they encountered. *Our Jackie: Public Claims on a Private Life* explores that history and uncovers the complicated expectations that American women contended with then and continue to navigate well into the twenty-first century.

INTRODUCTION

In November 1993, I was in eighth grade. The teacher charged with instructing us on history and civics was an early Baby Boomer, born just as the American youth population began to explode, and a known John F. Kennedy devotee. Each year, as the anniversary of the Kennedy assassination approached, Mr. Steel dedicated multiple days to the teaching and commemoration of JFK's death. Woodrow Wilson School lore held that the lessons were emotional. Previous students forewarned, "People will cry." In presenting the Kennedy assassination, funeral, legacy, and associated imagery, we received a blend of Bill Steel's personal response to Kennedy's death and the broader significance of the assassination and the national mourning that followed. Sure enough, people cried.

I was a women's historian before I ever took a women's history class. I was interested in John Kennedy, certainly, and as an Irish Catholic kid in a fairly Catholic stretch of New Jersey beach towns, I appreciated what Kennedy meant to many of the adults in my life. But in that eighth-grade class, the person who interested me more was the woman veiled in black, who was left to lead a nation in mourning her husband and raise up children whose father had just been murdered in the most public fashion. What was her story? In May 1994, Jacqueline Onassis died, and the imagery presented in my classroom the previous November was back, on television and on newsstands, and I learned a particular version of JKO's story from those representations and interpretations of her life.

When I followed up on my youthful predilections and chose historian as my profession, my interest in American women's lives continued.

What also emerged were interests in celebrity, media, and culture. When I finished my first book and thought about what to do next, I thought of Jackie Kennedy (not yet adding the Onassis to her name) and went searching for her in histories of the second half of the twentieth century. A person who had served as first lady, had been at the center of a national trauma, and then had gone on to live as the most famous woman in the world certainly had to have received some scholarly consideration. What was out there, and what could I contribute? In *Where the Girls Are: Growing Up Female with Mass Media*, Susan Douglas calls Jacqueline Kennedy "a one-woman revolution," an antidote to the stultifying "stuffiness, conformity, and confinement" of the 1950s. Douglas continues, "Jackie was tradition and modernity, the old femininity and the new womanhood, seemingly sustained in a perfect suspension. She was a wife and mother, but she had also worked outside the home. She deferred to her husband, but at times outshone him. The week of JFK's inauguration, it was Jackie's picture, not Jack's, that appeared on the cover of *Time*. . . . Jackie Kennedy, in the early 1960s, was the most charismatic woman in America, possibly in the world."[1] This was a starting point, I thought. Surely, I imagined, the woman who inspired the evaluation offered by Douglas had received consideration of her image and cultural significance more broadly from other scholars. But while Jacqueline Kennedy Onassis has been the subject of an astounding number of books, such assessment of her was largely lacking.

In the years since I began this project, people's responses to the former first lady have run the gamut. In reference, people have called her "Jackie," "Jackie O," and "Jackie Kennedy." Baby Boomers, like Douglas, thinking about JKO across the whole of her life, have marveled at all she endured, seeing her as a singular figure in their life's history. People have been puzzled that I would choose her as the focus of a project, asking, "What did she even do?" Others have linked her immediately to her first husband. "Did they love each other?" they will inquire. Some have focused on the details of her husband's assassination and the trauma she must have endured as the person by his side as a bullet pierced his skull. Or, again tying her to John Kennedy, people have commiserated with her and the humiliation she must have felt as she endured his many infidelities, in real time, and then as they were revealed more publicly. Inevitably people remark on her style. Early on, I presented a paper about Jacqueline Kennedy's cultural politics, and a member of the audience recalled his mother's response to her White House tour: "Well," she remarked, unimpressed. "Isn't she chi-chi." Since I began this project, Natalie Portman received rave reviews in Pablo Larrain's *Jackie*; Kim Kardashian adopted Mrs. Kennedy's style for an *Interview* cover shoot; a cruel portrayal of Jacqueline Kennedy on *The Crown* raised eyebrows; and Google alerts keep me current on the continuous stream of media covering her history, her family, her style, her former real estate holdings, and her continued relevance. As I wrote the final pages of this book, the National First Ladies' Library hosted an online auction of items culled from a recently donated collection of JKO paraphernalia, encouraging bidders to "Own Your Own Piece of Jackie Kennedy!" Even now, thirty years after her death, Jacqueline Kennedy Onassis commands attention and strikes a nerve.

There are, unsurprisingly, traditional biographical treatments of Jacqueline Kennedy Onassis, many of which employ a good deal of speculation, with authors attempting to imagine what JKO may have felt or thought (Christopher Andersen's *Jackie after Jack: Portrait of the Lady*, Edward Klein's *Just Jackie: Her Private Years*, or Barbara Leaming's *Jacqueline Bouvier Kennedy Onassis: The Untold Story*—and there are many other titles that fit into this category, several of which are penned by the aforementioned authors). Then, there are volumes meant to scandalize, tabloid in style, intended to titillate as much as they intend to inform (most notably Kitty Kelley, *Jackie Oh!*). More recently, writers have produced well-researched but relatively traditional biographies, following Jacqueline Kennedy Onassis year by year, in an effort to trace the trajectory of her life (Sarah Bradford's *America's Queen: The Life of Jacqueline Kennedy Onassis* or Donald Spoto's *Jacqueline Bouvier Kennedy Onassis: A Life*) or at a certain stage of her life (Barbara Perry, *Jacqueline Kennedy:*

First Lady of the New Frontier and Tina Cassidy's *Jackie after O: One Remarkable Year When Jacqueline Kennedy Onassis Defied Expectations and Rediscovered Her Dreams*).[2]

JKO is also the subject of more niche histories, such as *Dreaming in French: The Paris Years of Jacqueline Bouvier Kennedy, Susan Sontag, and Angela Davis*, by Alice Kaplan. An excellent text, it is more about the nature of French influence on important American women of the second half of the twentieth century than it is about these women, per se. Recent works have focused on JKO in her particular capacity as editor—such as Greg Lawrence's *Jackie as Editor: The Literary Life of Jacqueline Kennedy Onassis* and William Kuhn's *Reading Jackie: Her Autobiography in Books*. Most recently, Carl Sferrazza Anthony published *Camera Girl: The Coming of Age of Jackie Bouvier Kennedy*, a text that details her life leading up to her engagement to John Kennedy, with particular focus on her college and early career years. What these texts have in common is an effort to uncover something of the inner JKO, endeavoring to reveal something about her heretofore unknown. And in so doing, they take JKO seriously, as a cultural figure and intellectual and a person deserving of the attention and interest she received over the course of her lifetime, outside the bounds of her relationships to two men who in so many ways were larger than life.[3]

But in the world of scholarly consideration of mid-to-late twentieth-century womanhood, Jacqueline Kennedy Onassis is a figure who rarely appears. Mrs. Kennedy's style, of course, was the subject of much discussion during her time as first lady and beyond. In the 1960s and 1970s, copycat fashions abounded. In contemporary media, her look remains a kind of gold standard. She appears in the many volumes dedicated to the life of John Kennedy—penned both by the slain president's intimates and by historians and journalists of subsequent generations as they have reconsidered JFK's time in office and his legacy. While many of these are revealing and sometimes excellent works, the books vary in the treatment of Jacqueline Kennedy. Sometimes she is all but ignored; at other times, she is a key figure, but a supporting figure nonetheless.[4] Within the far-reaching historical scholarship on American women at midcentury and beyond, however, JKO has not been a central character. This book aims to fill that gap.

* * *

Our Jackie: Public Claims on a Private Life assesses the way in which media framed Jacqueline Kennedy Onassis over the course of her public life. The central tension of media's representations of Jacqueline Kennedy Onassis—as Jacqueline Bouvier Kennedy and, later, as Jackie O—fluctuated between her service to others and her perceived self-interest. When JKO projected the image of or was interpreted as a woman dedicated to her family and her country, to supporting those to whom she was linked, she warranted praise from contemporary mainstream media—and praise, too, in popular memory and historical considerations of who she had been and what she had meant to the nation. At these times, media of all kinds granted JKO a measure of authority, communicating a sense that she was competent and capable of knowing her own mind and charting her own course. But when she appeared to reject perceived duties for personal satisfaction and engaged in behavior that seemingly privileged her own wants and needs rather than those of others—and especially if it appeared she was neglecting the needs of others—she opened herself up to critique. At these times, media raised questions about her personal authority and speculated about those to whom she might listen or defer. And, of course, which purposes she was serving and when were not always obvious or agreed upon. Such assessments reveal ongoing cultural antagonism to particular kinds of women's public actions and displays of autonomy. In this way, JKO often served as a barometer for articulated and idealized views about American women—how they should behave, what they should value, to whom they should defer. Considerations of Jacqueline Kennedy Onassis in American mass media and culture suggested particular concerns about women, their place in public life, and the extent of their authority in determining how they might inhabit that space.

This book is neither a traditional biography nor an effort to get at the "real" Jacqueline Kennedy Onassis. I am interested, rather, in what representations of and responses to JKO suggested about views of American womanhood more broadly. I take inspiration from Jo Burr Margadant's concept of "new biography," in which the individual is regarded as a figure "with multiple selves whose different manifestations reflect the passage of time, the demands and options of different settings, or the varieties of ways that others seek to represent that person."[5] The text is dedicated to considering JKO's power as an image—and one open to wide interpretation. Mrs. Onassis was masterful in her self-projection and her attempts at image crafting, but total control of her image, where it appeared and how, eluded her. What is more, cultural conceptions of JKO, strong as they were, could sometimes be diametrically opposed, informed by the perspectives of those framing their chosen subject.

Like David Greenberg's treatment of Richard Nixon, this book is concerned with "the ancient themes of image, reality, perception, interpretation, and meaning."[6] Unlike many public figures, particularly as the twentieth century continued, JKO often refused to explain or justify the motivations behind her actions and decisions, thereby claiming an authority—one regularly denied her by those devoted to chronicling her—to determine a life of her own choosing and one she did not see the need to defend. She did not pen a memoir. She did not share her innermost thoughts. Many of her personal papers remain unavailable to researchers. She projected an image of a public figure committed to maintaining a private life, but her explicit motives often remained known only to her. As a result, culture and media assessed and interpreted JKO neither with nor against a full understanding of her intentions. Those intentions seemed particularly perplexing and resulted in particularly critical assessments when her actions failed to match the idealized model of womanhood at a given time. As Alice Kessler-Harris speculates in "Why Biography?," perhaps, "as historians," we are called "to watch how an unfolding life is called to account in different ways as the social climate changes and political tides turn." In following that life, Kessler-Harris suggests, "we will learn something if we watch the weather change, the value systems shift, the storm descend and retreat: as we observe the engaged life struggle to maintain its balance."[7] This book, a blend of cultural biography and media investigation, a consideration of the public mapping and interpretation of JKO's life, provides the perfect kind of historical consideration for a woman so endlessly chronicled and uncovers what that chronicling reveals not only about her but about the world in which she lived and how women were expected to navigate it. Jacqueline Kennedy Onassis was a person, but she also served as a symbol of broader cultural expectations.[8]

Just as JKO changed over the duration of her life as a public figure, reflecting changes occurring for American women more broadly, the media world in which JKO received consideration fundamentally changed during the years of her fame. Over the course of her public life, as media coverage and reach expanded, the public anticipated a greater constancy of coverage. An expectation that there would be news fed the creation of news items. Rather than their actions, those in public life were likely to be assessed by the image they projected and the subsequent reception and reporting of that image by American media. The public, then, made sense of that representation, or image, in the context of the culture in which they lived. The constancy of reporting on public figures created a sense of proximity or familiarity with these figures, which in turn generated a sense of legitimacy in tracking their moves and assessing their lives. For figures like Jacqueline Kennedy Onassis, a fixture in various kinds of American media for over three decades, such sustained coverage meant that, for many, the person Jacqueline Kennedy Onassis was replaced by their perception of Jacqueline Kennedy Onassis and who they imagined she was and what they imagined she stood for.[9]

When Jacqueline Bouvier wed John F. Kennedy, politicians' wives might be an asset, but they were most often understood as backdrop to a campaign, not a recognized partner in the process, however untrue that may have been. Profiles or features of potential first ladies appeared on the women's pages of local newspapers. Women reporters, assigned to "woman stories," experienced a world in which their evaluations were regarded as soft news, the kind of information one might find likewise in fan magazines committed to sharing the private details of public figures' lives, even as they committed to taking seriously the stories to which they were assigned. During the 1960s and 1970s, the media world evolved in its consideration of what was news—and who might make it. From an unofficial agreement that a politician and his family's life was private, his transgressions not of the material one would report, the press shifted focus to consider what private activities indicated about a candidate, his character, his integrity, his ability to fulfill the requirements of his desired office.

From a world where hard news and soft news were regarded as separate entities, one pertaining to the immediate, the important (as understood by those reporting on the news), and the public and professional worlds, largely dominated by men, and the other related to potentially "interesting" stories that were not time sensitive, often pertained to private roles and relationships, and were not "gathered by interaction with recognized news generating institutions," media practitioners increasingly blurred the boundaries of this fabricated separation.[10] The business of news coverage blended the world of politics and entertainment as politicians (and those adjacent to them) were regarded and assessed in much the same way as were celebrities. It was not enough to learn and understand what these public servants did; the desire was for a sense of who they were. And this shift was legitimized as campaigns aimed to project such imagery (often based on understandings of public opinion and with intent to win public approval and in cooperation with those covering them). Jacqueline Kennedy Onassis's public life and the coverage it received illustrates the blurring of alleged lines between the world of hard and soft news. Mainstream, "respectable" publications like the *New York Times* began reporting on stories of a kind and in a manner that formerly had been the preserve of fan magazines like *TV Radio Mirror*, dismissed for their speculative reporting that was more likely to be labeled gossip rather than news. Beyond newspapers and magazines, there also emerged in the decades following JFK's assassination a host of tell-all treatments about the president and his private life, many of which laid bare just how imagined Jacqueline Kennedy's Camelot may have been. JKO, no longer a politician's wife and no longer protected by an abandoned code, was subject to a different, more invasive kind of coverage and consideration.[11]

It is this world of an altered media, combined with an America in which conceptions and realities of women and womanhood shifted dramatically, that warrants another look at Jacqueline Kennedy Onassis. She has been the subject of numerous biographies, of tabloid-style tell-alls and exposes. She has been a supporting character in the John Kennedy canon. But sustained investigation into media representations of JKO is lacking. What she meant and what she represented reveal a great deal about visions of American sex, gender, and public life across the second half of the twentieth century. The consternation she caused among members of the press, too, suggests something about the limits of media's conceptualization of women at particular moments in their lives and across the life span. How could a woman combine characteristics that were seemingly incompatible? How could a woman behave one way at one point in her life and then behave in a manner that seemed entirely at odds? Or, why was fairly consistent behavior met with such varied reaction? The conundrum Jacqueline Kennedy Onassis presented stemmed not only from her disinterest in justifying or explaining herself; it resulted, too, from a lack of self-reflection by the media and an inability to grant public women the full scope of their humanity, warts and all.

A person writing a book about Jacqueline Kennedy Onassis, even with JKO's reticence to share her innermost thoughts, is privy to an embarrassment of riches. While the chronicling never ceased, the conclusions drawn by those assessing JKO were an exercise in constant evolution. Among the many sources this book draws upon are the women's sections of local newspapers, syndicated columns, and sustained coverage from some of the nation's preeminent newspapers; political and popular magazines; fan and gossip and fashion periodicals; television programs; memoirs of intimates (alleged and otherwise); film; written correspondence; polls and surveys; and public testimony and memorials. This well runs deep. And while my source use aims to be representative of the kind of coverage JKO received, it is hardly exhaustive.

Readers familiar with narratives about JKO will find contradictions in accounts of coverage she received. They should be prepared to dispense with truisms about Jacqueline Kennedy Onassis and expand their sense of her historical significance beyond the time she spent as first lady (not even three years). She contributed to what came to be expectations of the non-office, but she eventually moved on from the role, shifting, in her understanding of herself, from a public figure to a private person. She was as complicated as the decades in which she lived her public life, and those assessing her in real time were not always up to the task of acknowledging or accepting that complexity.

The chapters that follow offer assessment of various media that chronicled JKO from her emergence as a truly national figure in the 1960 presidential campaign to the memorialization of her death in 1994. Following the chronology of her life and arranged by the roles by which she was understood are the chapters "Campaign Wife," "First Lady," "Widow," "Single Woman," "Fallen Queen," "Jet Setter," "Professional," and "Icon." At various times, JKO, like all women, found herself subject to more than one image and assigned role. Expectations and understandings had the capacity to overlap, revealing the complexity not only of a full life but of one lived on an international stage and subject to relentless coverage. That coverage tells us not just about Jacqueline Kennedy Onassis but about views and expectations assumed of and navigated by American women for the better part of a half-century.

* * * * *
* * * * *
* * * * *

[1]

CAMPAIGN WIFE

John F. Kennedy and his team, having actively courted and tracked national interest and media attention throughout the 1950s, received continued and heightened coverage leading up to the 1960 presidential campaign. Even before his announced intent to seek the Democratic nomination, political insiders took as a given that Kennedy would play a key role in the presidential primaries. It was not only the senator who graced the pages of American newspapers and periodicals across the nation, however. Jacqueline Kennedy, emerging as a figure in her own right, attracted a degree of public attention unmatched by any other potential first lady.

JBK not only rated an article but appeared on the cover of the August 24, 1959, issue of *Life* magazine. In the cover image, she gazes directly at the camera, clothed in a pink sheath and adorned in a double strand of pearls, communicating her wealth and privilege. A picture of femininity, she is young and thin and beautiful. Perched on the porch behind her, the figure of her admiring husband is blurred, underscoring how she is the focus of both the cover and the accompanying article. Appreciation for the visual image she presented was reflected in the feature's title, "John Kennedy's Lovely Lady." The article highlighted Jacqueline Kennedy's beauty ("cameo faced," it called her) and her efforts to bring balance to the ambitious young senator's life while also emphasizing her intelligence and autonomy by describing her as a "self-sufficient girl with an intellectual turn of mind." The accompanying photographs projected the glamorous image for which the Kennedys increasingly were known: Jacqueline, keeping fit with daily walks and, as would become a kind of trademark, on horseback; Jacqueline, swinging Caroline in the surf and cuddling her to keep her warm after seaside play; Jacqueline, supporting her husband at various political events and spending time with his extended Kennedy clan. In these images, she was a perfect embodiment of a "helpful partner to a husband on the stump," as the article suggested. The piece emphasized a traditional maternalism, as JBK eschewed fancy theories on childrearing, preferring instead a focus on "love, security, and discipline," and defended her husband against those speculating that he was nothing more than a "glamor boy" by highlighting his "curious, inquiring mind." Anticipating a rigorous campaign season, Jacqueline Kennedy hit all the cues expected of a candidate's wife.

JBK, as presented here, however, also defied easy categorization. She met expectations of 1950s womanhood, and then she subverted them. If women of the long 1950s were meant to kowtow to their husbands' interests—or, even more, to regard their husband as an all-consuming interest—Jackie Kennedy had none of that. She was an antidote to the political world, preferring a small party to an embassy ball or an art gallery to a cocktail party. She was, *Life* assessed, "quiet, cultured, unpolitical." John Kennedy said this: "She breathes all the political gases that flow around us, but she never seems to inhale them." But even if she was irreverent about the world of politics, suggesting that the next Democratic convention take place in Acapulco, the article speculated about her potential contribution to her husband's career: "Out on the stump meeting the public, she has already proved that beauty and quick brains are no handicap in politics." It is in this feature that readers learned about JFK's misplacing of a speech in which he quoted Tennyson's *Ulysses*. Jackie Kennedy, intellect that she was, saved the day "by quickly reciting the appropriate lines." She seemed happy to help in such a manner. But politics was John Kennedy's interest, the article suggested; Jacqueline Kennedy had her own, which kept her, *Life* noted, "happily occupied." She was a helpmeet, but of a different kind than Lady Bird Johnson, wife of Senator Lyndon Johnson, who embraced politics as if it were her own calling, or Pat Nixon, who dutifully followed vice president and eventual 1960 Republican candidate Richard Nixon's lead. While she clearly supported her husband's endeavors, as demonstrated by her willingness to campaign with him in 1958, Mrs. Kennedy held herself at some remove from the public, aloof to a certain extent, giving the impression that she had her own thoughts and interests to occupy her.

There appeared to be some power in this not entirely conventional and not entirely expected model of womanhood. Speculating that JBK could prove to be one of "her husband's strongest campaign assets," *Life* celebrated the effect of her charm on political leaders and voters alike, which requires that we think twice about the labeling of JBK as "unpolitical" and, indeed, expand on who and what we assess *as* political. While JBK's natural inclination was "to remain in the background," the Kennedy team regularly made use of her multilingualism by having her give short speeches in Italian and French. When JBK declined the opportunity to speak, audiences, such as one in Seattle earlier in 1959, "expressed audible disappointment." Even without a penchant for "vigorous handshaking or speechmaking," JBK made "a graceful, refreshing appearance at teas, barbecues, and factory visits," and increasingly demonstrated the "political savvy and coolness" required of a front runner's wife.[1] *Life*'s willingness to describe JBK in this way is particularly striking given how little she was like the wives of most front runners in recent memory. Eleanor Roosevelt (ER) had broken the mold as first lady, embracing an outspoken political role both during and after her husband's administration. Bess Truman and Mamie Eisenhower played well with the American people, but each woman represented a kind of Middle America relatability that hardly could be described as "coolness." Each born in the nineteenth century, their ages marked them as being of a different generation, and their appearances tended toward the matronly. Jacqueline Kennedy was wholly unlike these women. In estimating JBK's appeal, *Life* suggested something of a sea change in what kind of political-spouse imagery and identity would appeal to American voters. Given the propensity to imagine the first lady as the standard bearer for all of American womanhood, such a positive assessment of Mrs. Kennedy further suggested evolving notions of American women as a whole.[2]

Life magazine, the standout mainstream, middle-class publication of midcentury America, thus placed Jacqueline Kennedy onto a particular kind of pedestal. Beautiful, reserved, individualistic, and intellectual, she was neither like the typical woman next door nor was she like women most often featured in American media, popular culture, or politics. Perhaps most significantly: the article was about *her*. Just as her husband's youth and freshness appealed to many Americans, JBK's possession of the same qualities likewise drew attention.[3] John Kennedy may have been a contender for the presidential nomination, but Jacqueline Kennedy was *Life*'s focus. Coming to the close of the 1950s and moving toward a new decade, when there was such hope and optimism about the modern future of the 1960s, JBK, as presented here in 1959, represented a version of womanhood that other American women, of various ages and stations, might recognize, admire, or even aspire to emulate—or, as happened in the 1960 campaign when evaluations of JBK became more critical, against which they might blanch. The suggested importance of her role to her husband's career and candidacy matched prescriptive literature's claims about the power of the woman behind the man, but increasingly, as the 1960 campaign got underway, public demand was for the woman to step out from behind the man and share something of herself. Assessments of JBK suggested recognition of her as a public figure in her own right, beyond her link to JFK.

Jacqueline Kennedy's style, interests, and intellect drew increased attention during her husband's presidential run. So, too, did her roles as wife, mother, and household manager. She represented a woman who served her family but held personal interests unrelated to her domestic obligations; hers was a world not confined to household mundanities. Often an asset, JBK also drew criticism from journalists and potential voters alike for failing to live up to the imagined standards—most often related to age, appearance, style, and public behavior—expected of a prospective first lady. She held tremendous symbolic power, communicating to the American people not only what was true about American women but also what they wished—or feared—to be true. In the varying responses to JBK, she became a kind of lightning rod, not because of her husband's proposed policies but due to evolving ideas of American womanhood at the start of a new decade when conceptions of public womanhood were opening to wider possibilities.[4] Consideration of JBK, pronounced as it was, suggested the American public's awareness of and varying degrees of comfort with a new style of womanhood not only in the White House but across the nation more broadly. She defied neat packaging. This complication intrigued and stymied observers and resulted in a growing fascination with Mrs. John F. Kennedy.

* * *

After his decisive reelection to the Senate in 1958, John Kennedy's political intentions became clear to his wife. As she told Arthur Schlesinger, "After election night in Boston—I think we went somewhere in the sun or something . . . he started speaking all the time. Again, all those years before the White House—every weekend he was always traveling. You know, invitations from all over the country—and then they led up to the primaries."[5] Teams of "Kennedy men" spent 1959 plotting campaign strategies for the next year's primaries. On January 1, 1960, John F. Kennedy sent a letter announcing his candidacy to seventy thousand names on file. On January 2, he made his candidacy known in a Washington press conference.[6]

Jacqueline Kennedy recalled a fall meeting, which took place at Bobby Kennedy's Hyannis Port home. She was not invited, however, and when interviewed by Arthur Schlesinger, she knew little of the details. As she recalled, "When Jack would come home from something like that, I wouldn't ask him, 'What did you plan here and there?' He'd come home, and then it would be fish chowder, or what would he like for dinner, or records, or then someone there to laugh. . . . I would have been a terrible wife if I tried to pick his brains about that." Unlike her sister's husband, who had "love[d] to bring his problems home," John Kennedy "didn't want to talk about the things that were bothering him." Even as JFK expected JBK to be up to date on media and current events, even as he regularly discussed people and relationships, home—one Jacqueline Kennedy beautifully decorated and expertly managed—was expected to provide something of a respite. In a not uncommon and fairly idealized 1950s style, JBK had shaped her wifely role to fit her husband's desires. She suggested this as a fairly typical marital compromise when she spoke to Schlesinger in 1964: "I think a woman always adapts, and especially if you're very young when you get married and, you know, are unformed, you really become the kind of wife you can see that your husband wants. . . . If Jack wanted to . . . talk about things at home—then I'd be asking him questions."[7]

While her description of their relationship, and the sense of a wife's responsibility to create a kind of "port in the storm" for her husband, seems a throwback to the separate spheres allegedly occupied by women and men, this arrangement very likely served JBK's interests as well as it did her husband's. While John Kennedy suggested that his wife breathed the political gases but never inhaled, it is as likely that JBK did inhale, but the fumes that so intoxicated him did less for her. She had become part of the world of electoral politics by association, not personal desire. Her interests, as *Life*'s feature noted, were more artistic, literary, and cerebral. If these were the things that would entertain her husband and take his mind off politics, then Jackie Kennedy's victory was twofold: her husband was happy and she was engaging in her own passions rather than topics in which she had more limited interest.[8] It was this image of JBK, private, cultured, at some distance from the political world, that marked early coverage of her during the presidential campaign.

People close to Jacqueline Kennedy recalled that she was "ambitious for the presidency" even if she was not predisposed to the public life required of a campaign.[9] Leading into 1960, however, others recalled her fear about the strains the presidency would put on JFK's health and on their family as a whole. As she told journalist friend Laura Bergquist, "It isn't the right time of life for us. We should be enjoying our family, traveling, having fun."[10] Regardless of JBK's actual feelings, JFK already had set the wheels in motion. Even before his January 2 announcement of his candidacy, the campaign was underway. While John Kennedy may have desired a separation between home and work, his wife's potential contribution to his career and her power as a political weapon, made clear during the 1958 campaign, was evident even on the first day of his candidacy. His speech, delivered in the Senate Caucus Room, describing his visions for American life, was directly influenced by passages JBK had read aloud from Charles de Gaulle's memoirs.[11]

While Jacqueline Kennedy likely would have embraced a behind-the-scenes role in the campaign, in the age of mass media, more was expected of a candidate's spouse even as spouses responded to expectations in various degrees.[12] Mrs. Roosevelt broke precedent with her political activism and engagement with the press. Hers was—and to a large degree, remains—the standard against which subsequent first ladies have been evaluated. But breaking precedent and setting precedent are different things. Both first ladies of the post–World War II era, Bess Truman and Mamie Eisenhower, took part in their husbands' campaigns but were far less engaged with their administrations. Bess Truman, along with daughter Margaret, accompanied President Harry Truman on a whistle-stop tour across the country as he ran for reelection in 1948. Together, the family traveled 31,700 miles in thirty-five days. While the president proudly introduced his wife to crowds as "the Boss," and she may have served as a political confidant behind the scenes, she was silent before crowds, present only to buoy her husband, demonstrate her support for his presidency, and contribute to the image of the Trumans as a traditional American family. When Bess Truman realized she was under no obligation to hold a press conference, she canceled the one she announced she would hold.[13] Mamie Eisenhower served a similar function as Dwight Eisenhower campaigned in 1952 and 1956. In 1956, she was the first candidate's wife to appear on television, she joined Ike in public appearances, and she lent her name to magazine articles written on her behalf. Mrs. Eisenhower embraced media framing of her as housewife (albeit one who oversaw a staff rather than toiled in her own right) and made clear the differences between herself and her husband: "Ike runs the country, and I turn the lamb chops." Mrs. Truman's and Mrs. Eisenhower's roles in their husbands' campaigns largely aligned with the role they adopted as first ladies, that of "traditional wives and mothers," a direct contrast to ER, who had engaged regularly with the press about matters of her husband's policy and her own particular political interests.[14]

Jacqueline Kennedy was no Eleanor Roosevelt. But neither was she the traditional mother of Middle America projected by Bess Truman and Mamie Eisenhower. The necessity of determining JBK's role concerned the Kennedy team, although both Pierre Salinger and Ted Sorensen claimed recognition of her as a "political asset" in memoirs recounting their time on JFK's campaign. Beyond the potential challenge presented by JFK's Catholicism, his team worried about the challenge posed by the "French-speaking, couture-clad, foxhunting Jackie." Kennedy himself appeared unconvinced about his wife's liability status, given reports that in a private memo to his staff, he scribbled a single line about JBK: "We need to promote her more." Still, advisor Richard Goodwin recalled, "There was a conscious decision, as I remember, to keep her in the background. They wanted to keep her away from the campaign because they were political experts and they thought that the American people's idea of a first lady was Bess Truman—nice, matronly, dowdy, Midwestern American mother." Goodwin recognized the limits of the Kennedy campaign team's vision when he noted their belief "that someone like Jackie would just turn people off, which showed how much they understood the American people!"[15]

If the Kennedy team underestimated JBK's potential appeal, their ignorance reflected the bias of the time. In 1960, women might be important campaign volunteers, and certainly the woman vote had to be considered, but in the world of party politics, candidates and leaders generally were men. Politics was men's work even if that point of view ignored the fundamental role women played in John Kennedy's political rise, from the Kennedy sisters' campaign labor to staff workers like Evelyn Lincoln and Mary Gallagher as essential cogs in the logistics machine to advisors like Joan Braden as savvy evaluators of media and the voting public. Obtuseness to women's broader political contributions reflected prevalent notions and left unquestioned gendered views of public and private life at the time.[16] Journalist Laura Bergquist, who wrote for *Look* during Kennedy's time in the Senate and the White House and covered the Kennedys extensively, recalled of JFK, "He was beguiled by women, he loved being around them. But when it came to serious talk, he preferred talking to the guys about politics or whatever. He was kind of a man's man." Kennedy, she asserted, "liked women very much," but "not somebody in the sense of an equal working partner in the business of government."[17] Jacqueline Kennedy had no ambition to be an "equal working partner in . . . government," but the Kennedy team's seeming obliviousness to potential voter interest in her style, her intellect, and her very difference from other political wives revealed their limited understanding of emergent challenges to the roles of men and women in 1960s American politics and culture. For all the Kennedy team's embrace of youth and newness, they initially overlooked a striking example in their midst.[18]

Just as she had during the 1958 Massachusetts senatorial campaign, JBK attracted crowds whenever she joined her husband in his travels—both before and during the campaign. Hinting at the power she might hold in 1960, an October 1959 trip to Louisiana reaffirmed JBK's appeal to foreign-language voters. JBK attended the crowning of the queen of the Rice Festival, where an estimated crowd of nearly one hundred thousand cheered her arrival. After JBK greeted the crowd in French, campaign worker Edmund M. Reggie recalled, "You could just hear the screaming. When I tell you screaming, it was just unbelievable, the applause, the shouting. . . . She went on to tell the crowd in French that she was very happy to be in south Louisiana because her father had told her as a child that Louisiana was a little corner carved out of France, that she loved France because of her own French ancestry—and that she was glad to see for herself that what her father said was true that this was the beautiful part of France." A spectator concurred: "It sounded like the top of the City of Crowley had exploded."[19] JBK may not have gravitated to politics, but natural reticence failed to diminish her appeal.

As JFK and his team surveyed the political landscape, they committed to widespread but also judicious travel. Kennedy's goal was to arrive at the Democratic National Convention as the clear choice, propelled by primary voters rather than merely backed by like-minded political figures. The Kennedy family's experience with mass media and their related media savvy likewise aimed to present John Kennedy as the Democratic front runner.[20] During the early primary rounds, the plan was for Jacqueline Kennedy to accompany her husband as often as possible. As Ted Sorensen noted of JFK, he traveled sixty-five thousand air miles in more than two dozen states, "many of them in the midst of crucial primary fights, most of them with his wife." In many ways, Jacqueline Kennedy was John Kennedy's early partner in his effort to win the White House. She was young and fresh in her own right, and her presence also communicated JFK's status as a family man, an image his campaign sought to promote.[21]

Kennedy achieved an easy win in New Hampshire (during which the Manchester mayor's overzealous appreciation for Jackie Kennedy led JFK to quip, "The mayor seems somewhat more enthusiastic about my wife's candidacy than he is about mine. Unfortunately he's going to have to take me to get her"). Kennedy's team focused on Wisconsin, competitor Hubert Humphrey's back yard.[22] Rural Protestant voters looked at the Catholic Kennedy with suspicion, and the extended Kennedy family, the senator, and Mrs. Kennedy dedicated long days (and plenty of money spent on radio, television, and advertising) to bringing voters around.[23] If the 1958 Massachusetts Senate race had been a baptism by fire, Wisconsin posed an even greater test. As JBK recalled the primary race in Wisconsin, she noted, "We'd go into a ten-cent store or something, three people in it. They'd back against the back wall. They wouldn't want to shake your hand. You'd have to go up and just grab their hand and shake it. Or little rallies in a town, where you'd have a band and everything there and nobody'd show up. You know, they were really hard."[24] What may have been commonplace when campaigning on the East Coast revealed itself as unwelcome in Wisconsin, as when one La Crosse reporter expressed shock after he saw Mrs. Kennedy walking down the street, cigarette in hand. "This just isn't done up here," he sniffed.[25]

While JBK recalled Wisconsin as a particular low on the campaign circuit, Kennedy insider Kenny O'Donnell remembered JBK's fortitude against the weather and her persuasiveness with a reluctant public: "Jackie would shake hands and talk with people on one side of the sidewalk on the main street of a small town while her husband worked the opposite side. He kept his eyes on her and often muttered to one of us, 'Jackie's drawing more people than I am, as usual.'"[26] When necessary, she operated independently. At a Kenosha rally, she told the crowd, "I'm not in the habit of arriving at a campaign stop before my husband, and as I don't have any speech prepared, I can tell you whom *I'm* voting for in November." When JFK had to return to Washington for a civil rights vote, JBK continued on her own. The "attractive" JBK gave, an article in the *Wisconsin Rapids Daily Tribune* reported, a "creditable pinch-hit performance" to an "overflow crowd."[27] She made speeches across the state where she celebrated JFK's long years of national service and assured voters that a vote for Kennedy would not be vote miscast. At one point, she took over the public address system in a local grocery store, saying, "Just keep on with your shopping while I tell you about my husband." While on her own, game as any politician, "she shook about 2,500 hands and made eight stops, the last at 10 p.m. Along the way, she was taken to a dairy man's farm and dutifully walked out to the cow shed to admire his herd."[28] While Wisconsin's women voters, the *New York Times* reported, repeatedly remarked that Jacqueline Kennedy was "lovely" and "gorgeous," a "typical male reaction" was that "she handled herself well for an amateur at this political business."[29]

Other coverage suggested an alternative kind of "male reaction" and demonstrates just how much JBK's appearance served as her defining quality in early reporting. In writing about the Democratic hopefuls' wives, journalist Relman Morin labeled Muriel Humphrey as a "trim little woman with wavy grey hair," while he described JBK as a "slim, dark-haired woman with a girlish expression." Mrs. Humphrey, in "coo[ing]" her introduction of her husband, charmed everyone, "especially the ladies," while JBK, when substituting for her absent husband, shyly remarked, "My husband couldn't be here today, and of course I can't really substitute for him—not really," charmed everyone, "especially the men." Coverage of this kind suggested that journalists would frame JBK, due to her beauty and her youth, as a different kind of campaign wife than those wed to the other potential candidates and different, too, from political wives of years past. *Washington Star* reporter Isabelle Shelton wrote profiles of the likeliest candidates' wives and described JBK as "by far the most striking in appearance," suggesting that she could "easily be mistaken for a movie star."[30] Such framing appeared in local and national newspapers, in syndicated columns, and across the spectrum of hard news of campaign-event coverage and the soft news of candidate-wife profiles.

JBK's beauty, however, was not regarded as an automatic advantage. Political columnist Fletcher Knebel, who profiled each potential candidate's wife, joined others who speculated that the Kennedys' appearance might pose a problem for the aspiring candidate: "For a couple of eggheads, who read heavy tomes on government and history and bat philosophical ideas about as though they were ping-pong balls, the Kennedys are blessed—or cursed—with an abundance of physical radiance." Her beauty notwithstanding, Jackie Kennedy, Knebel noted, was particularly drawn to reading, the arts, and high culture more broadly, a reflection of her elite social and economic status, which Knebel highlighted in the article. Knebel was not alone in recognizing Mrs. Kennedy as a kind of anti–Mamie Eisenhower and gave voice to the possibilities her appearance might generate on the campaign trail: "What the national reaction would be to Jackie Kennedy as the wife of a candidate is hard to say. . . . Dazzling and youthful beauty in a prospective first lady is an unknown quantity in modern politics. There's a feeling that women voters would prefer a kind of middle-aged neutrality in the wife of the candidate. Others contend the voters will respond favorably to a vision of vitality. The primaries may give a clue, for there is certainly nothing neutral about Mrs. John F. Kennedy."[31] Whereas John Kennedy's campaign promoted his good looks and capitalized on his starlike qualities, when it came to Mrs. Kennedy, attractiveness was not automatically regarded as a positive attribute.[32]

Indeed, Peter Edson, in his "Washington News Notebook," reported on findings by Cowles Publications, an American media conglomerate, published in their "semiconfidential tip sheet," the *Insider's Newsletter*, indicating that JBK was considered "too beautiful" to be first lady. As reported by Edson via the *Insider's Newsletter*, JBK was "the average American's image of an empty-headed beauty." While Edson disputed JBK's empty-headedness by highlighting her impressive scholastic resume, he willingly had floated the idea of her ineptitude to readers. In noting her international travels, Edson suggested that JBK would make "a good international hostess," which, given the academic record he reported, was the tip of the iceberg as to what she might offer as first lady. Widespread prejudices played a role here, from the tired stereotype that a beautiful woman, by definition, must be a stupid woman to the notion that not much would be expected of a first lady, pretty or no, to an undercurrent that suggested another tiresome stereotype: that less beautiful women, as a rule, do not like beautiful women. Thus was the journalistic environment of 1960, when those holding power in the business of American media, especially syndicated columnists and those writing for purveyors of hard news—mainly men—framed stories to reflect their understanding of the world.[33]

In debunking the notion of Mrs. Kennedy as a brainless beauty, Edson attributed to JBK interests beyond her husband and family and opinions on topics beyond the domestic. References to her intellect suggested a kind of gravitas, a depth of thought, the potential for viewpoints and ideas—and controversy. The sitting first lady, Mamie Eisenhower, called Dwight Eisenhower her "whole life." She showed little interest in causes. She refused to speak to the press. Media reported on her public activities but knew nothing of her thoughts beyond those about style and domesticity. She loved the look and things of the 1950s. Her image was largely inoffensive.[34] As Jacqueline Kennedy and the Kennedy team endeavored to craft her image for the 1960 campaign, Mamie Eisenhower's was the sitting model of first lady against which they considered their efforts and against which American citizens would evaluate her potential successor.

Many of the profiles provided about Jacqueline Kennedy appeared on the women's pages of local newspapers, dedicated pages for women with copy largely written by women. Hard news but of the kind made by or related to women often appeared on these pages as well. While relegated to a separate section of the paper, many women journalists used their allotted space on the women's page to write stories to dismantle or challenge limiting expectations of women.[35] And so, even with the attention to and speculation given JBK's looks, profiles of the potential first lady, when they dug into her background and interests, often revealed that there was more to JBK than a pretty face and that a first lady who was something more than inoffensive held a particular public appeal. Isabelle Shelton reported, "She is the only presidential hopeful's wife who had campaigned for her husband in fluent French and Italian. She could hold forth in Spanish too if the occasion demanded." While her looks and background might at first appear a turn-off, Shelton reported, "It should be noted that Jacqueline seems so far to have made a favorable impression on the hustings." JBK's intellect and education are evident in the profile, which highlighted her particular interest in reading (especially texts on eighteenth-century European history) and painting.

But Mrs. Kennedy is not all egghead in Shelton's profile. Both the author and JBK were careful to make the candidate's wife relatable to women voters by emphasizing her devotion to her husband, her family, and her home. Her intellect did not preclude or prevent her ability in her domestic roles. JBK said, "The thing that gives me the greatest satisfaction is making the house run absolutely smoothly, so that Jack can come home early or late, and bring as many unexpected guests as he likes. That takes quite a bit of planning." In imagining what life in the White House might bring, JBK proclaimed,

I think every woman's husband decides what she would do in such a situation. I would do whatever he wanted. Someone noted the other day that

Mrs. Franklin Roosevelt traveled around as the eye of her husband when he was president. If my husband wanted me to go inspect things, I would. . . . I certainly would not express any views that were not my husband's. I get all my views from him—not because I can't make up my mind on my own, but because he would not be where he is unless he was one of the most able men in his party, so I think he is right.[36]

With this self-presentation, JBK limited the potential subversiveness of her elite education and interests, she undercut any possible accusations of selfishness or hyperindividualism, and she revealed herself to be as dedicated to her husband's professional success as any wife in America. The layered evaluation of JBK also revealed the thoughtfulness of those profiling her and their desire to communicate a nuanced point of view.

The April 5 Wisconsin contest yielded a victory, but returns were disappointing. Senator Kennedy won 56 percent of the vote, but he had invested time, volunteer hours, and financial resources into the primary far beyond what Hubert Humphrey had put into the state primary. But the experience proved valuable in West Virginia, another important location. In West Virginia, the Kennedy team capitalized on positive coverage JBK had received during the first months of 1960 and highlighted her campaign role. With the goal being a decisive victory to prove that a Catholic could win even a non-Catholic stronghold such as West Virginia, Ted Sorensen recalled, Kennedy "spoke in every town and hamlet, Jacqueline tirelessly by his side."[37] Jacqueline Kennedy remembered a warmer reception in West Virginia than the campaign had received in Wisconsin. Even with anti-Catholic literature being distributed throughout the state, voters responded warmly to the Kennedys. Charles Peters, a campaign volunteer, speculated that women voters "were drawn" to JBK because she was unlike them; her difference was her appeal. Kenny O'Donnell remembered JBK's West Virginia efforts: "Jackie, then in the early stages of pregnancy . . . visited miners' wives in their ramshackle company houses, handed out bumper stickers at shopping centers, and shook hands on street corners." JBK actively courted West Virginia citizens of all kinds: "One day, driving alongside a stretch of railroad tracks, Jackie saw a gang of railroad laborers sitting on the tracks, eating lunch. She asked [Ed] King [her driver] to stop the car, got out and sat down with the workmen and chatted with them for a half hour."[38]

JBK further alleviated some campaign anxiety about her elite origins with her West Virginia performance. As reported in one syndicated article from West Virginia, John Kennedy encouraged his wife to deliver a speech. The result: "She probably received a bigger ovation than Lincoln got for the Gettysburg address."[39] Whether her glamor attracted voters, as suggested by Peters, or she had more of a common touch than she had been given credit for, JBK was not the liability the Kennedy team once suspected she might be. In addition to public addresses and face-to-face visits, JBK provided interviewers with copy that suggested she was more like a typical or "normal" American woman than not. Coverage of JBK's youth and beauty often was supplemented by praise for her style, which would become a hallmark of her public life. But in an interview given in early May, published in at least one West Virginia newspaper on the day of the primary vote, Jackie Kennedy "admitted detachment for clothes" and rather than a clotheshorse, painted herself as a woman dedicated to "simplicity and comfort." As she discussed how she packed for the campaign trail, she confessed to journalist Claudette Rashid, "The suit I'm wearing is four years old, the evening dress I brought with me is three years old. I never have any time to press anything so I take simple things, my favorites that don't age and aren't dated." Suggesting that there were "a million other ways to spend . . . time" than shopping, JBK maintained that while being well groomed was important, "dwelling on it" was "shallow."[40] Detaching herself from a depiction as rich and idle, JBK suggested both practicality and depth. In indicating a preference for simplicity, she aligned with West Virginia women, who might favor simplicity out of necessity rather than choice but who might very well appreciate this commonality with the potential first lady.

Kennedy efforts in West Virginia produced the victory so desired. Having traveled back to Washington rather than wait out the returns in West Virginia, the Kennedys dined with journalist Ben Bradlee and his wife, Tony, in the Kennedy's Georgetown home and then went to the movies. After they returned home, JBK recalled, "I was in the pantry getting some ice cubes and suddenly I heard this war whoop of joy!" With that, they boarded a plane and returned to West Virginia.[41] For all the attention she had garnered on the campaign trail, Ben Bradlee noted of JBK, "She was then far from the national figure she later became in her own right." Bradlee, journalist and eventual editor of both *Newsweek* and the *Washington Post,* capitalized on the tell-all market of the mid-1970s with his book *Conversations with Kennedy,* an assessment of his friendship with John and Jackie before and throughout JFK's presidency. Of the night they flew to West Virginia, he recalled, "When Kennedy was enjoying his greatest moment of triumph to date, with everyone in the hall shouting and yelling, Jackie quietly disappeared and went out to the car and sat by herself, until he was ready to fly back to Washington."[42] Bradlee read this as evidence of JBK being miserable, ignored by her husband. But one could also read her behavior as a natural response of the more private partner of a public couple, the partner who had been established since the beginning of the union as the figure in the supporting role. It is a move not at all in line with the standard expectation that a wife stay by her husband's side no matter what. JBK may well have believed she had fulfilled her campaign role, as it were, in this case, and seeing that as a duty satisfied, retired to allow her husband his celebration.

During the first half of 1960, JBK traveled with JFK to a dozen states.[43] When she discussed JFK's view of campaigning with Arthur Schlesinger in 1964, she recalled, "He enjoyed it . . . When he got caught up in it, and when it was going well, then he really liked it and responded. . . . And he loved the people who were really glad to see him—the little old ladies, or children, or what." She remembered the frantic pace and the exhaustion of the campaign—and the often less than desirable accommodations: "I remember once there was a whiskey bottle under the mattress because the American Legion had had a convention in that hotel there before and there were whiskey bottles under all our mattresses."[44] But even as the campaign trail was her husband's chosen environment rather than her own, she acquiesced to the requirements of campaigning, even as she did so in her own style. John Kenneth Galbraith remembered the difference between John Kennedy's and Jacqueline Kennedy's preparation for a day of vote getting in Pennsylvania during the 1960 campaign: "He had a briefcase full of speech drafts, political memoranda, biographical material on the politicians he would meet. She had the *Memoirs du Duc de Saint-Simon* in French. She would take no part in the day's political persuasion. It was only important that she be there; she, as much as the candidate, was the one the crowds wanted to see." But Galbraith was adamant about her value beyond public interest: "She had a deeper purpose; it was she, not the more trusting JFK, who would observe, hear and render judgment on the politicians they would encounter."[45]

This detachment from politics could—and did—surface in Jackie Kennedy's unscripted comments. While in West Virginia, JBK was asked what she liked about the state. Her response: "It's so close to Washington." This was not the ideal compliment the Kennedy team would have hoped for. The response, which might have been a blunder, charmed some observers. As noted in the syndicated column "A Letter from Joanne," "People like candor and respond to someone who can give them a chuckle. Politics is so cliché . . . A frank, off-beat answer like Jacquelyn's [*sic*] is good to hear and with it she emerges as a real person. A smooth and careful reply would reveal nothing." In bearing up under pressures of the campaign, JBK revealed not only her sense of humor but a measured response to the campaign and what was at stake. This kind of fortitude and this sense of balance, the column suggested, would be admired especially by women who could understand how a family life outside the national spotlight was not such a bad consolation prize.[46]

Only once the primaries came to their June conclusion did the Kennedys officially announce that JBK was again expecting a child. As recalled by Ted Sorensen, "[JFK] disliked political exploitation of 'motherhood,' but, told early in the campaign that housewives would disapprove of Jacqueline's absence, he reluctantly and self-consciously explained during his two-day train trip through California, 'She's home having a boy.' He never mentioned the subject again." Asked how he knew it was a boy, Kennedy responded that Jackie had told him.[47] After the announcement, reports suggested that JBK would miss early sessions of the Democratic National Convention in Los Angeles but would attempt to attend later sessions.[48] As a whole, however, her campaigning would be limited, given the difficulties she had faced in previous pregnancies. While journalists speculated that the Kennedy team feared JBK "too chic and avante garde for the voting masses," and thus saw the pregnancy as a blessing in disguise, JBK faced very real health concerns.[49] From a historical distance, observers of the campaign can see the draw JBK was for the campaign. But views of women in politics were what they were, and conventional wisdom suggested that JBK was not the image people had in mind when they imagined the first lady. Responses to the 1960 campaign signaled that conventional wisdom was changing, but how fast, for whom, and to what end for the Kennedy campaign, those working on his team could not be sure.

As she would have had there been no campaign, JBK spent most of the summer on the Cape with the other Kennedys. But time at the beach did not mean a respite from the campaign. Whenever Senator Kennedy traveled north for the weekend, their home became campaign headquarters, with politicians, journalists, and even curious voters storming the gates. As John Kennedy traveled to California for the Democratic National Convention, JBK's doctor, John Walsh, encouraged her to remain home and view the proceedings on television. She had delivered a stillborn baby just weeks after the Chicago Convention in 1956, so this advice was no surprise. JBK remembered the tension she felt, being at such a distance from the campaign. At the Cape with mother Janet, stepfather Hugh Auchincloss, sister Janet, and daughter Caroline, she recalled to Schlesinger years later, "Jack would always call me up, usually terribly late at night, or say something would be all right, or not to worry, or this or that. I suppose he was worried about me worrying, having a baby. Oh, but I was panic-struck watching it. But I guess they weren't as worried out there, because Bobby told me that once he got to the convention, he knew they'd get—you know, he'd get the nomination."[50]

Bobby Kennedy was right. Even if JFK's nomination was not as foregone a conclusion as her brother-in-law indicated, *Time* acted as if it were, featuring a Kennedy family portrait on its July 11, 1960, cover— Joseph and Rose Kennedy, John and Jacqueline, with the rest of the family represented in framed photographs hanging from the wall behind them. John F. Kennedy accepted the nomination as the Democratic candidate for the presidency on July 13, 1960. JBK's distance from the Los Angeles convention did not mean a respite from eager reporters. Upon her husband's acceptance of the nod, Mrs. Kennedy went to her front yard and "appeared amazed at the large group waiting to see her." She joked, "I thought I was alone in the country. Little did I know there were so many of you here." She expressed happiness and excitement for her husband's achievement, but visited with reporters only briefly, rushing back inside to watch her husband speak.[51] The presence of reporters on the opposite coast from the actual convention, eager to hear the response of the candidate's wife to his nomination, reveals how, beyond her husband, Jacqueline Kennedy had become a kind of celebrity figure and news maker in her own right and also how the world of news was changing.

John Kennedy had promised a return to Hyannis Port after the convention. While he held true to his promise, his return to the East Coast signaled a relocation of rather than a reprieve from the campaign. Days after his acceptance of his party's nomination, workers erected a stockade fence around the three Kennedy homes on Hyannis Port. Secret Service men and local and state police flanked the house "to halt curiosity seekers." Four telephone trucks arrived to provide new lines necessary for keeping the campaign going from JFK's summer home.[52] Bobby Kennedy's next-door residence became an unofficial campaign headquarters.[53] Whatever limited escape Jacqueline Kennedy had found on Cape Cod had come to a close.

* * *

Jacqueline Kennedy's time away from the campaign trail did not mean that national interest in the potential first lady waned or that the Kennedy team ceased to use her as part of the campaign. Quite the opposite. With the attention JBK had attracted on campaign stops and in national media, she required assistance in responding to voter correspondence and balancing the responsibilities of her private life and increasingly public role. The Kennedys had long employed a staff at their Georgetown home, with a cook, a maid, a driver, and a nurse for Caroline. The daily responsibilities required of running a home were covered. But the responsibilities of a campaign were different. To tackle the labor required of a candidate's wife, Jackie Kennedy enlisted the assistance of a personal secretary, Mary Barelli Gallagher, who had been a secretary in John Kennedy's office since 1952 until the birth of her first child in 1956, and subsequently had worked part-time for Janet Auchincloss, JBK's mother, and JBK herself. During the 1960 campaign, Gallagher agreed to work exclusively for Mrs. Kennedy, four to five days a week.[54]

In her description of the correspondence received by JBK over the course of the 1960 campaign, Gallagher reveals what a lightning rod the potential first lady was for the American public. In their letters to Mrs. Kennedy, Gallagher recalled, many people showed kindness and support for the campaign efforts and for the Kennedy family more broadly. Some requested a photograph, the recipe for Kennedy Fish Chowder, or campaign paraphernalia. Some celebrated the baby on the way. Such feedback indicated the success of the Kennedy campaign's framing of John Kennedy as family man, and the ways in which the candidate's and his wife's media appearances had generated among American citizens a sense of closeness to or intimacy with them.[55] In the kind of correspondence she received, JBK was very much Mrs. John F. Kennedy, linked to her husband, addressed as a candidate's wife rather than an independent figure. Gallagher alerted JBK to friendly, personal letters, and JBK would dictate a response.

But other letters criticized Jacqueline Kennedy directly and at an individual level. Chief among the critiques was her wardrobe, "what she should or should not wear." Some letters "enclosed haircombs, express-ing the wish that Jackie change her hairstyle to one they thought more suitable for the wife of a Presidential candidate." These letters played to the Kennedy campaign team's anxieties about JBK as a liability for her husband's presidential hopes. While Gallagher claimed an effort to keep the negative feedback from JBK, John Kennedy was aware of it; his office received some of the same. As Gallagher recalled, "One day he said to me, 'Oh, Mary, how is the mail running on Jackie's hair?' I said, 'Heavy.'" These "impertinent" letters received a routine acknowl-edgment.[56] Regardless of voters' opinion of JBK, what stands out is that voters responded to the image she projected—and the image promoted by the Kennedy campaign. The vision of Jacqueline Kennedy shared with and by American media struck a nerve with the American public in a way that motivated them to articulate their views. Whether that was a desire to celebrate or emulate the freshness and youth and style of the prospective first lady or whether it was a desire that she should fall in line with standard expectations of how a candidate's wife should look and behave depended upon the individual voter. The divide in opinion revealed just how splintered the nation was when it came to the desired image of the ideal woman in these years before Betty Friedan published her assessment of the *Feminine Mystique* but was hard at work attempt-ing to understand the disconnect between prescription and reality in the lives of American women.

While John Kennedy's first call after receiving the nomination had been to his wife, he forgot to mention her in his acceptance speech, an omission staffers believed could hurt Kennedy with women vot-ers. Joan Braden, a former assistant to Nelson Rockefeller and then to Oveta Culp Hobby during her tenure as Eisenhower's secretary of health, education, and welfare, had, at California Democratic Party leader Paul Ziffren's request, undertaken the task of ensuring that the Los Angeles Coliseum would be filled for the Democratic National Convention, no small feat given its capacity for nearly one hundred thousand spectators. After her successful completion of this assignment, Robert Kennedy, his brother's campaign manager, asked Braden to join the Kennedy team for the remainder of the campaign. Interviewed in 1969, Braden recalled an early conversation with RFK: "'I think one of the most tremendous assets Jack Kennedy has is his wife,'" she told him. "And, you know, people were saying she didn't want to do anything, wouldn't and couldn't and so forth. And I said to Bobby, 'I'm just sure this isn't right,' and 'I would like for everything we do [with Mrs. Kennedy] to [emphasize] Mrs. Kennedy being the leader of it.'"[57] When RFK instructed Braden to draw up a strategy to implement her suggestion, she presented him with the following:

> One: Draw Jackie into the campaign as much as possible. People have criticized the senator for not mentioning her in his acceptance speech. Have her write a weekly "Campaign Wife" column for newspapers. Two: Start a "Calling for Kennedy" operation, asking people what they think are the important problems facing the country, and saying the responses are to be tabulated and given to the senator. And Three: Organize "Coffee for Kennedy" parties. Start by asking women to invite ten friends for coffee; ask each friend to contribute ten dollars; get "Coffee for Kennedy" cups and pour the coffee into these; have campaign workers attend as many of the parties as possible; hand out pamphlets and Frank Sinatra's "High Hopes" campaign record at each party. And at the end of the campaign put John and Jackie Kennedy on television for a half-hour broadcast in which six or seven problems from the "Calling for Kennedy" operation get answered.

Bobby Kennedy gave each suggestion the go ahead.[58]

With Braden at the helm, JBK campaigned more actively from Hyannis Port and the Kennedys' Georgetown home. None of what Braden suggested was particularly revolutionary. The plans suggested that men and women had different political concerns and that women had to be campaigned to as a separate constituency. The "Coffee for Kennedy" parties assumed a population of women who stayed at home and had the space and the means to host parties for at least ten guests, all of whom would contribute money to the campaign.[59] But the events allowed the Kennedy team to keep Jackie Kennedy in the spotlight and

Even though pregnancy largely sidelined Mrs. Kennedy during the 1960 campaign, she joined her husband for a Broadway ticker-tape parade in New York City on October 19, 1960. Images such as these communicated the campaign's confidence and contributed to the couple's celebrity status. Keystone Press/Alamy Stock Photo.

frame her in the manner so desired by the campaign. For all the ways the Kennedys clearly were unlike middle-class, Middle American voters, this was a way to present them in a familiar and recognizable manner. Jackie Kennedy may have spent time studying overseas, and she may have been a "talented linguist," but she was also John Kennedy's wife, reticent to give "big speeches," because "they'd rather hear Jack." The campaign could emphasize her dedication to her husband's political aspirations in a way that situated her alongside domestically inclined women voters.[60]

Braden was right to get Jacqueline Kennedy in on the campaigning and not just because of the attention JBK had attracted to this point. After Richard Nixon secured the GOP nomination, the contest of the potential first ladies was set: JBK v. Pat Nixon. Both young, both attractive, they were ripe for comparison in a media world that eagerly put the women side by side. A July assessment of the two noted that maybe the greatest commonality between them was the difference they presented when held against first ladies of the recent past. As Marie Ridder and Bob Wells wrote, "We are used to first ladies who shun the spotlight. See their husbands are taken care of, entertain competently but not conspicuously, and in general, try to remain in the background as much as possible." Neither JBK nor Mrs. Nixon fit such a description, the authors suggested. Nor should they, given their youth and the world in which they had come of age. Ridder and Wells's article suggested a measure of comfort with this shift as they noted, "Nobody can say that such a homemaker is typical of modern-day America. Bess Truman and Mamie Eisenhower spring from an earlier time and clime, a happy time before suburbia, working mothers and the League of Women Voters." But if Mrs. Nixon and Mrs. Kennedy represented a modern departure from the political wives of previous administrations, they were not cut from the same cloth. Pat Nixon would "represent the values of the solid, thrifty, hard-working middle-class" while JBK likely would "embody the flair, cosmopolitanism and varied interests of the upper classes." According to Ridder and Wells, their differences were all to the good: "Each in her own way would be typical of America. It is our talent and our good fortune that we cannot only afford but tolerate variety."[61]

A suggested tolerance for variety in who would be the standard bearer of model American womanhood was an optimistic view. After JFK secured his party's nomination, the focus on JBK increasingly zeroed in not only on her appearance but on her sense of and her spending on fashion. Her "avant-garde" style was one thing as the wife of a senator, but when faced with the idea that the first lady would outfit herself in such a way, the public reacted and not always favorably. Even worse, according to some, was her "shaggy hairdo."[62] Andrew Tully, who interviewed JBK in the summer of 1960, reported that she was "interested but not annoyed" to learn that some women were "not enthusiastic" about her modern bouffant. But her response suggests a possible undercurrent of annoyance: "My husband likes my hair this way." Discussing how her hair had changed over the course of the campaign, JBK refused to defend her appearance. She revealed feeling anxious about responses to her look, but ultimately asserted her independence, individualism, and unwillingness to change for the sake of public opinion, saying, "I can't just become another person."[63]

But becoming another person was precisely what critics such as syndicated columnist Ruth Millett demanded. In an article titled "Mrs. Kennedy Will Have to Fit into Expected Role," Millet speculated that while Jackie, as she called her, "glorie[d] in her youth . . . brightly colored clothes and the tumbled hairdos . . . popular in the younger set," she soon would have to "say goodby to all that." To have the "strings of her youth rudely sundered" is painful for any wife, but, Millet explained, "it is a universal sacrifice demanded of wives and must be endured." John Kennedy's youth, which Millet argued would not serve him particularly well in office, would need to be underplayed. In support of her husband, JBK would have to downplay her own youth and "start looking more mature in her public appearances" to lend her husband an air of gravitas. Playing on traditional notions of a wife's duty to her husband, Millet asserted, "One of the prices a woman must pay for her happiness as a wife is that she must subordinate her own whims and fancies in dress to the position of her mate." In imagining a wife's contribution to her husband's career, Millet concluded that "the world has made her appearance a factor in judging the capabilities of a rising husband."[64]

While the prevailing view of "serious" journalists was that discussion of potential first ladies—let alone their style—was not "real" news, the September 11, 1960, *New York Times Sunday Magazine* provided a forum for Martha Weinman to consider the importance of political wives' style and its potential effect on their spouses' electability. Before giving an overview of selected first ladies' relationships with fashion and the contemporary feedback they received, Weinman led with Jackie Kennedy: "When Jacqueline Kennedy, then five days the wife of a Presidential nominee, stepped aboard the family yacht in Hyannis Port, Mass., wearing an orange pullover sweater, shocking pink Capri pants and a *bouffant* hairdo that gamboled merrily in the breeze, even those newsmen who could not tell shocking pink from Windsor Rose knew they were witnessing something of possibly vast political consequence." Weinman continued, "Political pollsters may not know precisely what The Women's Vote is, but they know it exists." In this capacity, the woman voter emerged as an enigma. Who knew why she did what she did? In her approach to candidates, she was unscientific (as opposed to male voters, apparently) and driven by emotional or instinctual response.

In addition to voters, the first lady had to please representatives of business and media, too:

> The fashion press, which opens a first lady's closet doors to the public, views her choice of costume for a lawn reception with the solemnity that others reserve for such issues as the National Purpose—and can, indeed, manage to make the two sound synonymous. Further, millions of women throughout the country consider it their constitutional right to know what she wears, where she bought it and whether or not it was a bargain (it seldom is). Further still, thousands of designers, manufacturers and store executives keep a jealous eye on the fashion company she keeps and habitually view with contempt anything she bought at the other fellow's place.

Any number of individuals or institutions might take offense at what the first lady did or did not wear. Beyond censure she might receive at any given moment, there was also the question of what "next election time, would they do to her husband?" As Weinman noted, "One begins to see the gravity of her situation."[65]

In thinking about the most recent first ladies in comparison to the two women who hoped soon to fill the role, Weinman wrote first of Bess Truman and Mamie Eisenhower: "The cozy conjuration of a White House wife who looks just like your neighbor roughly parallels Hollywood's abrupt shift in leading ladies from goddesses to girls-next-door." Truman eschewed fashion as much as possible, although she did "spiff up," as Weinman says, when told it was her "duty to her country." Mamie Eisenhower, wrote Weinman, "looks average, as most women do." Like "most women," she loved clothes and worried about spending too much. These qualities made Mamie "typical, and thus ideal."

But while "most women" could identify with Mamie Eisenhower and "sympathize" with her efforts to achieve a stylish hairstyle, neither Pat Nixon nor Jacqueline Kennedy presented the same kind of "next door neighbor" appeal as the sitting representative did and the previous first lady had. Pat Nixon, while fashionable, was inoffensive, and, Weinman suggests, in a calculated and obvious way. She quoted Mrs. Nixon as having said, "I never buy a dress just because I like it. I think, will it pack? Is it conservative enough?" She kept lists of what she had worn where so as not to repeat. This strategizing did not necessarily play well with voters. Weinman quoted one voter as saying, "Pat Nixon always looks too good to be true. . . . I get the feeling that she never in her life held anything up with safety pins, and it irritates me." On the other side of the spectrum, Weinman suggested that Jackie Kennedy faced censure for being too beautiful, too unconcerned with potential voter response, too concerned with high fashion trends, and too willing to spend vast sums to achieve her desired look. "She is a couturier's dream: she wears clothes as well as any fashion model in the business (a possible handicap), likes avant-garde fashions (another possible handicap) and spends, together with her mother-in-law, Mrs. Joseph P. Kennedy, some $30,000 a year in the Paris salons (a distinct handicap)." Indeed, of Mrs. Kennedy, one Manhattan housewife opined, "She looks too damn snappy. I just don't like women who look that snappy, that's all." In considering the two women side by side, Weinman assessed that JBK's "devil-may-care chic is as troublesome to some women as Mrs. Nixon's conservative perfection."[66] In sum, Pat Nixon cared too much and Jacqueline Kennedy too little. Any woman finding herself in the public eye need tread lightly.

This was the climate JBK navigated when, nearly seven months pregnant, she chose to respond rather than retreat. Agreeing to meet with her husband in New York City, ostensibly to purchase maternity wear, JBK met with reporters on the thirty-seventh-floor suite in the Waldorf Towers and responded to ongoing critiques about her style— and her spending. In this capacity, the Kennedy campaign created a "newsworthy" event with Mrs. Kennedy at its center. Ostensibly, she was campaigning for her husband, but in this event and the reporting it generated, she was the star.[67] Such copy did she provide that the *New York Times* featured the story on page one of its September 15, 1960, issue. Jacqueline Kennedy responded to critiques of her hair, which some likened to a "floor mop." Mrs. Kennedy assured reporters, "I try to keep it neat and well groomed" and then asked, "Do you think it looks offensive?" She admitted to buying "one suit or coat from Balenciaga and Givenchy" when abroad, but insisted, "I hate a full closet. . . . but anybody in public life must be equipped with clothes in advance." JBK labeled critiques against her "dreadfully unfair," and drew Pat Nixon into the discussion by asserting, "I'm sure I spend less than Mrs. Nixon on clothes. She gets hers at Elizabeth Arden, and nothing there costs less than $200 or $300." The dresses JBK tried on and modeled for reporters, delivered from a Fifth Avenue store, ranged from thirty to forty dollars each, clearly designed to combat the rumor, referenced by Mrs. Kennedy, "that I spend $30,000 a year buying Paris clothes and that women hate me for it." Irreverently, JBK continued, "I couldn't spend that much unless I wore sable underwear."[68]

Style was not the sole topic during Mrs. Kennedy's meeting with the press. She also discussed her husband's campaign and her wish that she were better able to support him on the road. When asked what her husband's "greatest contribution" to the presidency might be, she responded that his sense of history, his view of the past, and his care for his country would guide his leadership. She continued, "A terrible, frightening decade is ahead. People are too complacent about this country's power. Someone has to talk to the Russians. If my country were in Jack's hands, to give the decade a start, I'd feel safe."

Jacqueline Kennedy's assertions about her husband's capabilities in governing were not the most remarked-upon parts of the interview. Syndicated columns largely focused on Mrs. Kennedy's racier remarks. Those responding to the interview were shocked that Mrs. Kennedy would dare to reference her undergarments in such a public forum. Such crass talk was not in keeping with the dignity of an American first lady. As noted by columnist James McCartney, such talk "might go over swell at Vassar but won't do much for the female vote in Sauk Center, Minn."[69] And in referencing Pat Nixon, Jackie Kennedy not only invited even greater comparison between the two women; she also positioned Mrs. Nixon to respond. When Mrs. Nixon did address JBK's statement, she took the high ground: "I have no comments about what Mrs. Kennedy wears or what she says." Linking herself to potential voters, Pat Nixon continued, "I shop like an American woman, mostly in Washington and off the rack."[70]

No longer was Jacqueline Kennedy primarily a women's page feature. Her remarks made her a target of editorials published and reprinted across the United States and not just on the Women's Page. When it came to controversy, hard-news journalists responded to the soft-news content of a candidate's wife, thus blurring the alleged boundaries of the journalistic world.[71] Some took the "sable underwear" reference as a great joke. George Dixon's widely reprinted column asked, "Where can you purchase drip-dry sable underwear, and is it serviceable for the woman who has to travel a lot?" In considering the debate over the potential first lady's styles and spending, Dixon noted the media's interrogation of the fashion industry for expert views on the issue. Foolishly, he noted, only women had been interviewed, a decision he "deem[ed] shortsighted because I'm convinced the controversy holds more appeal for men than women."[72] An editorial by syndicated columnist Henry McLemore likewise joked about the issue, noting that whichever wife proved she could dress on thirty cents a year would "carry her husband to victory in a landslide." More seriously, though, he listed a variety of top concerns—"the farm problem; the missle [sic] race; international diplomacy"—and noted, "all have had to take a back seat to which of the candidates' wives spends the most money on clothes, and is the better dressed."[73] It was all well and good to discuss Mrs. Kennedy as John Kennedy's wife, as a kind of supporting figure, but it was unacceptable for her to take focus off actual issues and the real work of politics. Of course, there was nothing to mandate coverage of a candidate's wife's comments. Columnists' impetus to do so indicates just how successful was the Kennedy campaign's projection of style as substance and the ways the world of politics and celebrity had become increasingly intertwined.

The broader disdain for the attention received by both potential first ladies motivated an editorial appearing in the *Charleston (WV) Gazette*. Referencing the questions related to wardrobe, the editorial criticized the "unkind remarks" leveled against Mrs. Kennedy because of her appearance, noting, "many of which probably originated in the minds of women who were all too aware of her attractiveness," again suggesting a kind of competition existing between women. In a plea for voters to focus on the most pressing issues, the editorial read, "We would hope that should the electorate decide on the Republican candidate, it will do so because it feels him the best-qualified man—not because it wants his wife to occupy the White House." The editorial concluded by pleading with members of the press to "devote less time to asking these pointless questions and more time to airing a discussion of the genuine issues that face us."[74] In an open letter to Carrie Lee Nelson, wife of Wisconsin governor Gaylord A. Nelson, Miles McMillin bemoaned the state of current politics, noting the sustained discussion given to "whether Jackie Kennedy or Pat Nixon spends the most money for clothes." He complained, "If this is the high level campaign that was promised, heaven save us from the low." This he saw as a fundamental flaw in modern electoral politics: "We have been inviting it by this orgy of building up politicians' wives to the point where they get more publicity than the politicians." For fear that politicians' wives would be expected to go into greater detail not only about their fashion but also about their domestic perspectives, McMillin revealed something of his views of women's place in politics when he pleaded with Nelson to "lead an exodus of politicians' wives out of politics and back into the home."[75]

But journalists' response to Jackie Kennedy's off-the-cuff "sable underwear" commentary was not her only source of newsworthiness in the final weeks of the campaign. Following Joan Braden's advice, the Kennedy team provided Jacqueline Kennedy an opportunity to address voters in her own voice, uninterrupted, and on topics of her own choosing in the "Campaign Wife" column. Here, JBK (and the Kennedy campaign) could manage the image projected to American voters as Eleanor Roosevelt had in her "My Day" column, which allowed her to promote her interests and her husband's New Deal programs, share elements of her daily life in the White House, and respond to critique or express frustration—uninterrupted and on her own terms.[76] Distributed by the Democratic National Committee, "Campaign Wife" allowed JBK to address the voting public, sharing her campaign contributions and daily activities and highlighting elements of her husband's policy about which she (and the Kennedy team) believed women would be particularly interested.[77] The column also provided the Kennedy team with the opportunity to respond to trending feedback on JBK and to present an image of the potential first lady designed to appeal to potential voters.

In the first column, which appeared on September 16, 1960, Jacqueline Kennedy expressed her frustration at being homebound while her husband entered the home stretch of the campaign. She referenced the time she spent campaigning in West Virginia and Wisconsin and how she would love to see those people again. Subsequent columns likewise celebrated particular locations in the United States, and JBK suggested an acclimation to her husband's trade when she referenced her appreciation "to politics for showing me America."[78] In this capacity, JBK combated her image as an East Coast elite and indicated her appreciation for all of the United States. In so doing, she suggested that as first lady she might understand and represent a diversity of regions and lifestyles.

Mrs. Kennedy also used her first column to address head on the issue of her fashion. Backpedaling from the proclaimed disdain for shopping she had expressed in West Virginia, JBK wrote, "I've always loved clothes, and when I've had the time I've enjoyed the universal feminine sport of shopping around from store to store and looking for new styles in the women's magazines." This, she emphasized, revealed something about her (and about women more broadly) but was irrelevant to the 1960 campaign. Referring to her trip to New York City, she noted, "All the talk over what I wear and how I fix my hair has amused me and puzzled me." Echoing those who were critical of the discussion of the potential first ladies' aesthetic appeal, JBK asked, "What does my hairdo have to do with my husband's ability to be President?"[79] With this line of questioning, Mrs. Kennedy challenged media focus on her look—and insinuated that the media had invented the story rather than endeavored to provide voters with information they actually needed. Mrs. Kennedy's column, geared as it was to women, suggested that issues affected women voters' decision-making process. While the issues she emphasized were fairly traditional, most notably education— framed through her personal interest as a mother—such issues were regarded as more substantive than candidates' wives' hairstyles or fashion and credited women voters with having actual policy concerns.

Moving forward, JBK emphasized both her husband's ability to be president and the ways in which women voters could help make that happen. Media was at the heart of both. In discussing JFK's first debate performance, JBK explained how she had hosted a listening party in Hyannis Port, inviting friends over to bear witness to what she regarded as a historic "encounter," akin to the Lincoln-Douglas debates. Those who attended promised to host a party of their own for one of the remaining debates. She hosted a party for the second debate as well, this time at her Washington, DC, home. She expressed pride in JFK's call for action, calling him "marvelous," and expressing hope that "other Americans felt the same lump in their throat that I did."[80] In her October 13 column, she appealed to women by emphasizing her husband's sense of their importance to the campaign, his view that "one woman is worth 10 men in a campaign. They have the idealism, they have the time to give, and they work without making demands." Of course, JBK was talking about a particular class of women, those with time and those with money, who could volunteer for the campaign without any need for remuneration. Beyond volunteering, these were the women who might have the means and the location to host a viewing party such as JBK had herself. These were also the women who might participate in the "Calling for Kennedy" initiative designed to create a network through which women might reach out to other women, learn women's most pressing concerns, and address the benefits of a Kennedy administration.

JBK's column also attempted to appeal to professional women. Her October 13 column described a recently developed "Women Committee for New Frontiers," intended to give women engaged in occupations related to "cost of living, medical care, education and foreign policy" a direct line to John F. Kennedy. Here, JBK played to another audience of women—those who were professionally minded and wondering about the capacity for change under John Kennedy's leadership. While educated, JBK was no longer established in a profession of her own accord. In expressing admiration for women who were career oriented, in noting that she "profit[ted] enormously from the discussions" she had with the committee, and in particular noting her regard for Frances Perkins, the first woman to hold a Cabinet position during Franklin Roosevelt's New Deal, Mrs. Kennedy indicated appreciation for this populace's desire for a political voice and suggested the potential for women's advancement in her husband's administration.[81] JBK likewise celebrated women as engaged voters when, in her November 1 column, she remarked upon the thousands of Calling for Kennedy forms received by the campaign. If all supporters were "working as hard" as the women sending in the forms, Jacqueline Kennedy confidently noted, "Jack and Senator Johnson are sure to be elected!"[82]

But where JBK's column may have been intended to draw in women voters, encouraging their professional and civic engagement, at least one syndicated columnist, Dick West, saw the column as a vehicle for humor. Noting Mrs. Kennedy's former career as a journalist, West wrote that JBK "resumed her newspaper career this week as an unpaid columnist for the Democratic National Committee." Referring to Jacqueline Kennedy as his "colleague," tongue firmly in cheek, West expressed his hope that "her non-salaried status doesn't start a new trend." Intending to be humorous, West drew attention to the nature not only of political wives' labor but of many women's political work—supportive of male candidates and generally unpaid. Belittling JBK's time as the Inquiring Camera Girl, West reduced her work in that position to going "around taking pictures of truckdrivers and asking them questions like 'What do you think of the new Paris fashions?'" Reporting that Mrs. Kennedy had been "rather shy" back then, West noted that she relied on assistance from "male colleagues," an undertaking he imagined to have been rather "easy," given her status as an "attractive brunette." As a whole, West's column not only made light of JBK's campaign efforts but made her look silly in the process, no match for "real" writers or political operatives. Underneath West's light tone was a hint of the broader unease with the possibility of women's potential political power, as wielded both by figures like JBK and the woman who might vote for her husband because of her influence.[83]

* * *

With less than a month to go until the 1960 presidential election, *Life* magazine published an article entitled "Lovely Aspirants for Role of First Lady." In noting the predominance of women voters in campaign crowds, *Life* claimed that Jackie Kennedy and Pat Nixon played "key roles" in the 1960 election. Celebratory of both women, the article painted a picture of balance between the women's domestic responsibilities (primarily related to their children) and their support of their husbands' political aspirations. In regard to Jacqueline Kennedy, the article referenced her private nature and the appeal of her campaign-trail reticence to voters. Reported upon was her desire to be with her husband and her sadness at being sidelined by her pregnancy, but likewise suggested was her irreverence for politics, or her unwillingness to allow it to come first in her life, as perhaps best illustrated by a description of her scrapbook, which contained "a convention story headlined, 'It's Kennedy!'" followed by another: "Caroline's Turtle Places Second in Pet Show." For all the vitriol surrounding Mrs. Kennedy's image during the campaign, *Life* suggested her importance to her husband's campaign by quoting an unnamed congressman's assessment of Jackie: "She is the ultimate political weapon."[84]

Beautifully illustrated, with pictures of Jacqueline tucking daughter Caroline in for a nap, pouring tea at an event for women journalists in her Georgetown home, and walking along the surf at the Kennedy's Hyannis Port home, the article reveals nothing of the debate over the nature of Jacqueline Kennedy's fitness for the position of first lady. Additionally, absent from these images were Caroline's nurse, Maud Shaw, and Mrs. Kennedy's secretary, Mary Gallagher. Clearly, JBK and her husband's campaign team had a sense of how the potential first lady should appear to voters and were active in crafting the image of JBK seen by the American public.[85] Throughout the campaign, on the pages of the nation's periodicals, local and national, that debate over Mrs. Kennedy raged. In considering whether or not young, fashionable Jacqueline Kennedy was "fit" to be first lady, the nation revealed the contested nature of American womanhood more broadly. A woman should be beautiful, but was Mrs. Kennedy too beautiful? A woman should be educated, but was Jacqueline Kennedy too educated? A woman should support her husband, but did Mrs. Kennedy support him not enough? Or too much? Beyond revealing whether or not JBK was fit to fill the non-office alongside her husband, the conversation revealed the fine line women were expected to walk to achieve social and cultural approval. Jacqueline Kennedy did not walk that fine line, and as a result, served as a lightning rod in the world of public response. When she more actively responded to media, Mrs. Kennedy hit on the expected topics—home, family, fashion—but not necessarily in the expected or ideal way. In this capacity, she not only revealed her own complexity but suggested the complex roles and identities of American women more broadly. The typical frames American media applied to American women failed to contain Jacqueline Kennedy, even as the Kennedy campaign team worked to project an image of Mrs. Kennedy that would appeal to voters and even as those voters were casting ballots for John and not Jacqueline Kennedy. In the aftermath of the 1960 campaign, her position was fixed and campaigning at an end: she was first lady, and she would decide what that role entailed. In that capacity, she would garner even more attention, receive coverage that revealed even more overarching ideas about women in public, and hold even greater influence over conceptions of modern American womanhood.

[2]

FIRST LADY

Following John F. Kennedy's narrow November victory and leading up to his January 20th inauguration, American media reported on any number of elements linked to the president-elect's life, from the professional—his meetings with vice president–elect Lyndon Johnson and various political advisors and his considerations for potential political appointments and administrative priorities, for example—to the personal—his new son's development since his November 25th birth, the Kennedy family's Christmas celebration, and the family's plan for moving into the White House. Anticipation for the inauguration was high. The *New York Times* described the week leading up to the inauguration as "a peculiarly American drama. . . . There is the sadness of farewell and the gaiety of welcome. There is great solemnity, and much mirth; quiet dignity and carnival hoopla." Democrats, overrunning the city and causing a hotel shortage, the *Times* suggested, were responding to this particular inauguration in an especially and "openly jubilant mood." Indeed, the paper reported, "Washington . . . began to resemble a city bent on celebrating a second New Year's Eve."[1]

But for all the anticipation of JFK's administration, it was not the president-elect who appeared on the cover of *Time* magazine's January 20, 1961, issue. The incoming first lady instead adorned the cover. In a multipage feature that offered an overview of Jacqueline Kennedy and what she might expect as she moved into her non-office, Americans learned also what they might expect from her. In an article recounting some of the soon-to-be first lady's personal history, elements of the 1960 campaign, and a general sketch of Mrs. Kennedy's style and personality, an array of themes emerged: her penchant for art and culture and internationalism; an eye for fashionable elegance and sophistication; and a potentially natural—but deliberately unchecked—complexity that suggested Jacqueline Kennedy could be a tough public figure to read. These very themes would serve as hallmarks of her time in her non-office.

In her capacity as first lady, *Time* declared, Jacqueline Kennedy would "live as a cynosure." Every action would lead to a reaction. "Whether she wants to or not, she will influence taste and style," the magazine proclaimed. Aware of her shift in status, of beginning what the magazine predicted to be a "difficult, demanding and often thankless role," JBK noted, "I feel as though I had just turned into a piece of public property. It's really frightening to lose your anonymity at age 31." Although the election made her position as "public property" more official, one might suggest that Jacqueline Kennedy had lost her anonymity as soon as the 1960 campaign began (maybe even before that). During that campaign, *Time* posited, Mrs. Kennedy had received "a full quota of wound stripes." Renewed rumors swirled that Joe Kennedy had, at one point, offered Jackie one million dollars not to divorce John Kennedy. Midcampaign, some had speculated that she was not actually pregnant, "that it was all an elaborate hoax to remove her from the campaign scene." And, of course, there had been "her biggest battle—the affair of the sable underwear."

But in noting these pressures, those already faced and those to come, the article also hinted at a steely resolve beneath the surface of Jacqueline Kennedy's glamorous exterior. In addition to recounting her privileged upbringing and family history, information widely discussed throughout the 1960 campaign, a more personal accounting of JBK in relation to the Kennedy family provided readers with additional insight into the incoming first lady's comportment. Notoriously clannish, loud and brash, comfortable at being the center of attention, the Kennedys were cut from a different cloth than the more reserved Bouviers. True to her family style, Jackie Kennedy had maintained her sense of self and had "flatly refused to be smothered" by the extended Kennedy family.

She withdrew from family football games after breaking an ankle in 1955. She would dine with the entire family once a week while in Hyannis Port rather than every night. She refused to defer to patriarch Joe Kennedy or change her tastes to meet those that prevailed among the extended family. The strong-willed Kennedys, *Time* reported, "stood in awe of her because she had the stamina to stand up for her own tastes." As JBK said, "They seem proud if I read more books, and of the things I do differently. The very things you think would alienate them bring you closer to them."

What had appealed to the Kennedy family had contributed to Jacqueline Kennedy's appeal on the campaign trail, and would enhance her appeal during her years as first lady. In a solidly middle-class America, following a first couple who had been solidly Middle American, relatable and recognizable to the American public, the Kennedys offered an alternative, a vision of wealth and cosmopolitanism and elegance. Perhaps the most obvious flashpoint for her elegance and affluence was Jackie Kennedy's fashion. While JBK's style was derided as avant-garde during the campaign, *Time* quoted a friend who defended it as "completely American." Her style was "classic and simple and terribly chic—not startling." Described as simple, practical, with "very little jewelry," Jacqueline Kennedy's style was essentially the opposite of that of her predecessor, Mamie Eisenhower, who had embraced the cinched waist and full skirt of Christian Dior's New Look and a "more is more" approach when it came to accessories and adornment. *Time*'s cover revealed something of JBK's elegant simplicity: a portrait of Mrs. Kennedy from the shoulders up, clad in a rose-colored dress, with a triple strand of pearls around her neck, gazing directly ahead wearing a hint of a smile. In the background: the White House, baby carriage on the portico.

The White House, as the cover suggested, would be Jacqueline Kennedy's domain. Hers, a reader could assume, would be a primarily domestic role. Although she claimed an acquired interest in politics, "instinctively" she shrank "from the hail-fellow habits of politicians" and took "no part in her husband's political planning." Given her elite education and clear intellectual acumen, her "displays" of "political naivete" led observers to wonder if she adopted a "dumb Dora masquerade," of the kind she reportedly had utilized as a young woman, fearful of "scaring her friends away by being both beautiful and bright." Her plans for the White House belied not only her native intelligence but a practiced savvy in communicating her views. Since her husband's election she had spent time "reading every available book on the White House," which were "giving her a connoisseur's knowledge of the place." While noting that she would change the White House "in subtle ways," Jackie Kennedy shared her view of what the home should be: "The White House is an 18th and 19th century house, and should be kept as a period house. Whatever one does, one does gradually, to make a house a more lived-in house with beautiful things of its period." Jacqueline Kennedy clearly had a plan in mind, even as she hinted only "subtle" changes to come. In downplaying potential plans, JBK revealed what she had learned of politics, how she had grown astute at gauging expectations and paving a way to do as she wished with minimum pushback. While her efforts may have been focused on the domestic space of the Kennedys' lives, the public nature of the White House meant she was subverting a purely domestic ideal.

In an article of notable revelations, perhaps most striking was Jacqueline Kennedy's statement defending her separation from her husband's trade: "Jack wouldn't—couldn't—have a wife who shared the spotlight with him." And yet it was Jacqueline Kennedy, not her husband, who graced the cover of *Time*'s inauguration issue. With the election won, fascination with Jacqueline Kennedy had not come to an end. That genie was out of the bottle. Throughout the Kennedy administration, Jackie Kennedy, independent of her husband, became an increasingly prominent public figure—and like her husband lived at a kind of intersection between politics and celebrity. In some ways embodying a domestic role, mother to her children, hostess of the White House, she likewise embodied a version of American womanhood that went far beyond expectations of domesticity, as when she cultivated a revived commitment to arts and culture in the nation's capital, traveled internationally (both with the president and on her own), and led her famed restoration of the

White House. In considering JBK's role "on the stump," *Time* relegated her role to one primarily of "décor." The visual appeal of Jacqueline Kennedy captivated American attention, and throughout her time as first lady, she was sure to emphasize her dedication to domestic and familial obligations. But even as she became something of an aesthetic model to which American women might aspire and that international populations might admire, media coverage of and public response to the first lady demonstrated the potential power and appeal of a public woman expertly expressing and defending distinct views on topics related to art, history, and cultural development and exchange.[2] In performing and promoting expected elements of femininity, Jacqueline Kennedy, with a growing understanding of media and image, and increasingly a celebrity figure in her own right, crafted the space to pursue projects of her own choosing and in her own manner, benefiting her husband's administration but in a distinctly personalized way. This balance of satisfying personal interests but in a fashion that served others contributed to a largely positive media framing of the first lady and a nuanced view of American womanhood as the 1960s began.

* * *

From November 8 through January 20, Jacqueline Kennedy's life changed dramatically. Her husband was elected president of the United States. She gave birth, weeks early, and faced the recovery of a Caesarean surgery. She traveled to Palm Beach to take part in the extended Kennedy family holiday and prepare herself for her new role. She began arrangements for a move from her Georgetown home to a new residence, the White House, where she would assume the role of first lady and face the established expectations of that non-office. All this, in roughly two months, at thirty-one years old.

Virtually no coverage considered the potentially overwhelming nature of this string of events in such a compressed timeline. Of course, JBK had a staff to help with it all—raising the children, preparing for the move, organizing a new home. But the expectation that she would accept this fate, happily, without complaint, seemed a given, revealing a broader expectation that American women were to shoulder their lot, whatever that lot might be. Such expectations pervaded American media and culture. Serving a family should bring a woman joy. If one looked to popular sitcoms of the era, one found women who "never complained, smiled a real lot, were constantly good-natured, and never expected anything from anyone."[3]

To some degree, Jacqueline Kennedy acquiesced to this picture. In one column, syndicated by UPI, JBK was quoted as "often [having] said that her life revolves around her husband's." Her priority in serving as first lady was "to make the presidency, which her husband John F. Kennedy has called the 'loneliest' job, not so lonely for him and her family." While her age, disposition, and artistic rather than political inclinations made her "wary of the White House," she resolutely committed herself, good wife that she was, to "taking a new look at the job and preparing herself to meet the tasks that lie ahead."[4]

But Jacqueline Kennedy also approached her impending change in position strategically, with "plans to set her own pace," and in so doing, created a template for future holders of the non-office as she navigated her path. Perhaps as a result of her "mixed feelings" about taking up residence in the White House, Mrs. Kennedy planned to assume her title as first lady with the support of "two secretaries and a public relations aide." Mamie Eisenhower's public relations had been handled by her social secretary or the presidential news secretary. Not even Mrs. Roosevelt had a press secretary. Jacqueline Kennedy pioneered this position.[5] The volume of correspondence and attention JBK had received during the 1960 campaign, combined with her understanding of the importance of image and image control but reticence to sacrifice privacy, necessitated an expanded first lady's staff. Ultimately, forty people worked to support JBK's public duties. Revealing something of the priority she placed on loyalty and efficiency, JBK selected women who had been "close to the Kennedy official family long before the presidential election." Mary Gallagher, her secretary during the 1960 campaign, Pamela Turnure, formerly of John Kennedy's press secretary Pierre Salinger's staff, and Letitia Baldrige, Mrs. Kennedy's friend from Miss

Porter's School, would assist Jacqueline Kennedy in her official and professional capacity. Their very hiring revealed something of JBK's view of this position as one of labor, which required organization and assistance to proceed as she desired.[6] As one pre-inauguration article reported of JBK, "Her secretaries say she is amazingly well organized for the new life which she begins next Friday."[7]

Never one to relish the pace, the attention, or the frenetic energy required of the campaign trail, Mrs. Kennedy likewise aimed to maintain a low profile upon her arrival in the White House. In a memo to her press secretary, Pamela Turnure, JBK directed, "My press releases will be minimum information given with maximum politeness."[8] After she had served a year in her non-office, *Newsweek* offered a summation of the Jacqueline Kennedy ethos: "(1) I shall be seen and not heard at least not heard much; (2) I shall discourage fashion stories in every way except by the clothes I wear; (3) I shall restore the White House, to the way it ought to have been; (4) I shall have distinguished artists in, as guests and performers; (5) I shall rear my children myself, in privacy; (6) I shall get involved only in projects I have time for, but I shall get very involved in those."[9] As John Kennedy's advisor Ted Sorensen recalled, JBK's distance from the press should not have come as a surprise. During and then following the 1960 campaign, JBK provided no indication that she intended to engage in any sort of partnership with media. In this respect, she was unlike her husband, who enjoyed cultivating relationships with journalists. What the two shared in their approach to media was a desire to wield some measure of control, which led them to provide good news or stories of their liking and shun efforts to cover topics that did not fit with the image they aimed to project. Mrs. Kennedy, in particular, endeavored to maintain a sharp division between her public and private life: she would provide information about her public activities, but she wished for her private life to be off limits. In her effort to manage her public image, biographer Barbara Perry argues, "Mrs. Kennedy preserved the value of her political currency and the symbolism she created around it and her husband."[10]

Even with her organization and attention to detail, even with her efforts to manage coverage, it is unlikely that Jacqueline Kennedy expected quite the public response that marked the early weeks of January 1961. Her physical appearance and personal style had been debated endlessly throughout the 1960 campaign, but in the aftermath of her husband's victory, what had once been campaign concerns became celebrated Jacqueline Kennedy hallmarks. Even with controversy over her spending, Mrs. Kennedy "by a 'landslide' vote topped the list of best dressed women in 1960."[11] Beyond merely admiring JBK's fashion, however, many women aspired to replicate the "Jackie Kennedy look," from hair to makeup to clothing to posture.[12] Plastic surgeons suggested that the Jacqueline Kennedy nose had become a popular request among patients.[13] Columnists humorously noted numerous women's proud insistence on reporting that "everyone says I look like Jackie Kennedy."[14]

Those who looked like Mrs. Kennedy naturally seemingly reaped the benefits of that resemblance. As Gay Pauley noted in her syndicated column on the proliferation of Mrs. Kennedy "Look-Alikes," "The Helena Rubenstein salon in Washington reported customer requests for Mrs. Kennedy's hair style began during the campaign when there was some controversy over whether it was becoming." Since JFK's election, adoption of JBK's style had increased. As one San Francisco hairdresser noted, "About 30 percent of our customers are asking for the Kennedy coiffure. We've had a big increase in the last 10 days." Businesses believed in the mass appeal of her style. As a representative from the Frances Gill agency noted, "We get calls for Kennedy types from publicity people, photographers, ad agencies, the magazines, the people putting on fashion shows."[15] Indeed, columnist Inez Robb reported, "It is impossible to open a newspaper and scan the ads for bargains at the January sales without encountering a reasonable likeness of Jacqueline smiling from every advertisement. Stores were lightning quick to order their ad artists to incorporate her bewitching type of good looks in the company layouts."[16] Steve Carano, president of a mannequin firm, went so far as to create mannequins resembling both the president and

Mrs. Kennedy. Claiming to have "informal clearance" from a "proper source," Carano rejected the idea that creating such models was inappropriate. He said, "We certainly made it in good taste. I don't know if it's any different from all the newspaper ads and every young girl in the street trying to look like her. Mrs. Kennedy is the biggest thing in fashion today. We tried to compliment her."[17]

As columnists noted, consideration of JBK's look had bordered on obsession during the 1960 campaign. But the obsession had been with whether or not her look was fitting for a first lady. She was fashionable, to be sure—but was she too chic? Too daring? These questions, it seemed, were answered by her husband's victory. When she was no longer campaigning on his behalf, no longer actively asking for approval—of him and of her, given the role she would adopt if he emerged victorious—questions about the appropriateness of her style were quieted. Once he (and she) had won office, Americans' concerns seemingly dissipated. Her hair was no longer like a mop but rather a stylish coiffure women hurried to copy. Her status changed, of course, and her look became fitting of a first lady *because* she would be first lady. But there is also something to be said about the shifting views of women when they are aspiring to a position as opposed to when they have achieved the position. Where during the campaign her judgment and authority were questioned, once Jacqueline Kennedy assumed the position of first lady, she and her husband and her family were accepted and understood as embodiments and representatives of American excellence and beauty and style.[18]

As she prepared to make her home in the White House, Jacqueline Kennedy continued to insist that fashion was the least of her concerns. While she may have blanched at the extent or obtrusiveness of reporting on her "look," the care with which she cultivated her personal style, with which she constructed a sophisticated image, clearly indicates that fashion was, in fact, a priority. But her concern over her image was very likely that—concern over the public image she presented, both on her own and alongside her newly elected husband. *Time*'s inaugural profile highlighted the visual appeal of Jacqueline Kennedy and suggested this might be her primary contribution to her husband's political career. With more attention given to her style than to possible points of interest as first lady, media coverage indicated that the first lady's fashion influence would be *the* influence of her position. But even that suggestion failed to take into account the actual scope and import of such power, what her look might suggest to and about women, both in the United States and abroad. Such limited expectations failed to consider the work JBK might undertake as first lady, and what the public nature of her actions and selected projects would suggest about the intersections of politics and culture and women's capability in navigating either or both of those worlds.

* * *

In preparation for her role as first lady and in anticipation of her White House look, while she was still in the hospital, recovering from childbirth, Jacqueline Kennedy invited designers to her hospital room to pitch their ideas for her look. When Oleg Cassini entered the room, he saw the sketches of his competitors and told Mrs. Kennedy he was uninterested in the position if it meant he would share the workload with other designers. He believed one designer should create one look for the first lady, something unique, distinct, and memorable. His vision for her was like those of a costume designer for a movie star. He proposed "a new look, a new concept, my interpretation of how Jacqueline Kennedy should appear in her role as First Lady." Rather than selecting from previous designs, he "created a concept for her." As he recalled, years later, he told her, "I want you to be the most elegant woman in the world. I think that you should start from scratch with a look . . . that will set trends and not follow them." In their discussion, he found her receptive to his ideas, and was impressed with her style, her attention to detail, and her understanding of what her wardrobe might communicate. Of their discussion, Cassini wrote, "We spoke of how fashion is a mirror of history; we discussed the message her clothes would send—simple, youthful, elegant—and how she would reinforce the image of her husband's administration through her presence."

Cassini's sense was that Jacqueline Kennedy, through her aesthetic choices, had the "opportunity for . . . an American Versailles." With her plans for the White House, still kernels at this moment, to serve as an American showpiece and a site for cultural celebration, Cassini's point of view struck exactly the right note.

In a December 13, 1960, letter, JBK followed up with Cassini. She shared logistics—providing him contacts for shoes and bags, discussing sketches she would like to review, and giving him some indication of what she would require of him moving forward. She also used the correspondence to make sure he was up to the task and to emphasize what she desired from their partnership. She revealed her astute awareness of the attention her wardrobe would receive and her need for him to guarantee that no detail was overlooked. She confessed the relief she felt to be working with Cassini and to have "some control over my fashion publicity," which, she wrote, had "gotten so vulgarly out of control," and her determination not to have her husband's administration "plagued by fashion stories of a sensationalist nature."[19] In communicating this point of view, JBK revealed the scope of her understanding of image making and its importance to the Kennedy presidency and her willingness to engage in the effort required of striking the right note.

Immediately, Cassini began work on JBK's look. In addition to crafting evening gowns for the inaugural galas she would attend, he paid particular attention to the event of the inauguration itself. John Kennedy, now elected, emphasized his vigor and his youth by going hatless, and Cassini likewise wished to illustrate Jacqueline Kennedy's break from the past. Conscious of "how she would look with other people," Cassini wanted her to stand out. His idea was a simple fawn wool coat with a sable collar and a restrained flare. To keep the focus on Mrs. Kennedy's face but to finish the look, Cassini chose what became known as one of JBK's signatures, the pill-box hat, and, indeed, fulfilled his promise that Jacqueline Kennedy would set rather than follow trends. As the *New York Times* reported, "Mrs. Kennedy has a reputation for wearing smart clothes smartly," and at the inauguration, "it was easy to see why."[20] Also prophetic was his claimed prediction about the contrast between Jacqueline Kennedy and the other women on the inaugural stage: "All the other ladies will be loaded down with furs like a bunch of bears, but dressed like this, you'll stand out. . . . Not only will you look even younger, but you'll make the President seem more up-to-date."[21]

The vibrancy that Cassini aspired to in his designs for JBK were also part of her aspiration for the feeling of the White House. Jackie Kennedy's style extended beyond clothing. Letitia Baldridge recalled that White House parties of previous administrations had been "stiff and glacial." JBK believed the "addition of warmth . . . did not exclude dignity and a sense of awe at being a guest in the President's home," and so endeavored to personalize White House parties.[22] During the first two years of the Kennedy administration, Mrs. Kennedy participated in a total of 136 events, with the president and Mrs. Kennedy entertaining seventy-four foreign leaders, almost of all them in the White House.[23] As Baldridge recalled from her years as Jackie Kennedy's social secretary, each state visit required "days and days of agonized planning." The work of entertaining was shared by the White House, the State Department, and the Washington embassy of the visiting nation, but as a biography of Jacqueline Kennedy published in 1962 noted, "It is the First Lady who receives credit for the successes, and the blame for the failures." Aware of that fact, Mrs. Kennedy approached parties with "conscious planning and attention to an endless number of details."[24]

A party concluded was not a party out of mind. After an event, JBK would write one of the long-hand memos for which she became well known in the White House, noting what had gone well and what might be improved. As press secretary Pierre Salinger noted, "Her attention to detail was legendary."[25] She saw these events as fundamental to the image and understanding of her husband's administration. This labor and attention to the most seemingly insignificant minutia in the name of entertaining might be dismissed as the expected domestic contribution of a wife to any upwardly mobile husband, but in the cases of White House entertainment, when the Kennedys imagined—rightly— that the nation appeared and was assessed on an international stage, the image of the nation, which John Kennedy integrated into the substance of his politics, was crucial.[26]

The Kennedys hosted their first White House party just ten days after JFK took the oath of office, and the difference in tone and style from previous administrations was, Mrs. Kennedy's personal secretary claimed, "precedent-shattering."[27] Future events followed in the same elegant, informal style. As the *New York Times* reported in April 1961, no longer did guests to the White House wait in a long receiving line to be greeted by the president and first lady. Rather, they mingled as the Kennedys circulated throughout the room. Instead of "sitting stiffly at the formal dining table," guests sat at circular tables of eight, where conversation need not be confined to the person either on one's right or left. Small centerpiece bouquets, candle light, and a "glowing" fireplace added ambiance. All this, along with animated conversation and dancing until 2:00 a.m., indicated that "Mrs. Kennedy had achieved success in transplanting the lived-in informality of her private home in Georgetown to the museumlike formal reception rooms of the White House." A priority for Mrs. Kennedy, the article suggested, was to make the White House into a "home," an endeavor, one imagines, many female readers, especially, assessed with some measure of empathy and regarded as holding some appeal.[28] As contemporary biographer Charlotte Curtis noted, for all the elegance of the Kennedy style, the style of entertainment "suggest[ed] the informally gracious ways of a wealthy, culturally aware and well-traveled family."[29] This move away from convention, from what many would call "stuffiness," reflected the cultural shift of the sixties.

But while Jacqueline Kennedy viewed these entertainments as representative of her husband's administration, she also believed, especially when entertaining international guests, that they reflected a view of the nation as a whole. Further, she seized upon White House events as a means of communicating her belief that Washington, DC, should be at the center of American cultural celebration and, more broadly, set "a tone for the arts which would encourage culture around the country." Those within the Kennedy White House recognized JBK as instigator of the cultural focus. As presidential historian Robert Dallek notes,

"Kennedy embraced the arts during his Presidency, partly in response to Jacqueline's affinity for high culture. While he genuinely shared his wife's regard for the life of the mind, Kennedy also understood that it was smart politics," especially in the context of the Cold War. After the October 1961 performance by the American Shakespeare Festival, Charlotte Curtis claimed, "The White House had replaced Carnegie Hall, the Metropolitan and the Palace as the goal of many performers."[30]

Pierre Salinger named as the high point of JBK's cultural activities the November 1961 concert by renowned cellist Pablo Casals at an event honoring Governor Luis Munoz-Marin of the Commonwealth of Puerto Rico. Having long committed to a self-imposed exile from nations recognizing Spanish dictator Francisco Franco, Casals was impressed by John Kennedy's efforts for peace and wished to honor the president. The concert was Casals's first official appearance in the United States since 1928, and, given these political undertones, as the *New York Times* suggested, the event "transcended mere music making," perhaps especially when the president introduced the performers and emphasized the arts as an "integral part of free society." Attending were the United States' top composers, one of whom noted of the invitation to the event, "It's the closest thing we've ever had to being honored by the head of our government."[31]

Recognizing commitment to the arts as "one aspect of the New Frontier," the *Times* suggested the hope of "many creative figures in America that the interest in the arts displayed by the White House cannot help but spark an awareness from the public about the importance of culture in the American scheme of things." The *New York Times'* review of the Casals concert appeared on the front page of the publication and was written by future Pulitzer Prize winner for criticism, Harold C. Schonberg. In Salinger's estimation, this fit with JBK's desire that drama at the White House be reviewed by drama critics, musical performances by music critics, and various cultural efforts by those with related expertise.[32]

Personally adorned in a style meant to communicate youth, elegance, and modernity, Mrs. Kennedy likewise cultivated these qualities in the entertainments she hosted at the White House. As JBK endeavored to bring attention to her public role rather than her private life, her fashion and the events over which she and her husband presided received sustained media attention. She was beautiful, and her parties were grand. Arthur Neale suggests that part of John Kennedy's appeal was that he simultaneously communicated that he was "one of us" and also the "best of us." One might suggest the same of Jacqueline Kennedy.[33] If, as first lady, she represented American women, then American women were stylish and cultured, modern and sophisticated. They were wives and mothers, managing households, but that was not the extent of their roles or capabilities. In his assessment of the Kennedys' "famous state dinners, elegant costumes, and skillful management of the media," Michael Hogan argues that John and Jacqueline Kennedy "represented themselves as idealized versions of president and first lady. They embodied in their performance all that was good in American life, and in the process, idealized the nation itself. They were young and vigorous, hopeful and optimistic, idealistic and pragmatic, beautiful and sophisticated, cosmopolitan and confident, rich and powerful."[34]

Jacqueline Kennedy, then, was wrapped up in the New Frontier symbolism of her husband's administration. The events hosted at the White House served to communicate that the president's home was a central location for American culture, a culture linked to excellence and modernity, democratic in nature, hallmarks of the New Frontier. Various historians have rejected the notion that John F. Kennedy was more style than substance, arguing that his style was part of his substance, and that separation of the two is a false dichotomy.[35] Jacqueline Kennedy was fundamental to the development and presentation of that style. Recognition of her role in the New Frontier imagery reveals the ways in which public and private life overlapped, not only in politics but in marriages of the time more broadly.[36]

On the international scene, an early trip to Canada in May 1961 suggested the potential global appeal of Jacqueline Kennedy. Cassini created a press kit, approved by Pamela Turnure, regarding Mrs. Kennedy's wardrobe. But as Cassini recalled, it "only seemed to fuel a

President John F. Kennedy and first lady Jacqueline Kennedy attend a performance of "Mr. President" at the National Theater, September 25, 1962. Young, beautiful, and stylish, they modeled an aspirational pairing for American citizens. Abbie Rowe, National Park Service/John F. Kennedy Presidential Library and Museum.

media frenzy and was not done again. There was concern that interest in Jackie's clothes would overshadow the issues and accomplishments of the administration."[37] JBK appeared in a Pierre Cardin wool suit in a vibrant shade of red, matching the uniforms of the Royal Canadian Mounted Police, and it is in this ensemble, with a member of the force, that Mrs. Kennedy appears on the cover of the May 21, 1961, issue of *Life* magazine. So charmed by JBK were the Canadian people that Senate speaker Mark Drouin claimed, "Before your election, Mr. President, many Canadians searched the civil registers to see if she was a Canadian. They found she was not, but we all took heart from

Jacqueline Kennedy leans in to converse with Robert Frost at the Nobel Prize Winner's Dinner, while her husband, John F. Kennedy, talks with Pearl Buck, April 29, 1962. Observers often noted how Mrs. Kennedy's body language communicated her interest in whatever it was her conversation partner was saying. Robert Knudsen, White House/John F. Kennedy Presidential Library and Museum.

the fact that she is of French ancestry. . . . Her charm, beauty, vivacity, and grace of mind have captured our hearts."[38] Before the trip, staffers had warned the president and first lady that the Canadians historically were a cool audience, but Mrs. Kennedy "won the hearts of the usually blasé Otawans."[39] Letitia Baldridge, who traveled with the Kennedys, recalled that "the noise of shouting, clapping, screaming, joyous people almost deafened me."[40] Both Cassini and Sorensen heralded Mrs. Kennedy as a political asset on her husband's international travels, with Cassini going so far as to call her "a powerful symbol for the United States."[41]

John Kennedy's desire that she accompany him on this trip, the response of Canadian officials and crowds, and her appearance on the nation's premiere photo essay publication all point to Jacqueline

Kennedy's power as a public figure. JFK's well-documented concern regarding global public opinion meant that he did not come lightly to this decision to include his wife in his travels.[42] As much as her husband, she projected an image of youth and vitality and culture, and in doing so as first lady of the United States, suggested that these were the broader hallmarks of the nation and its population. In representing a model of American womanhood, Jacqueline Kennedy suggested not only American women's rightful place in the world beyond the home but, in being publicly heralded, also revealed a cultural acceptance of this idea, at home and abroad.[43]

Several consecutive European state visits followed soon after the Kennedys' Canada trip. Perhaps the best-known anecdote in all of Jacqueline Kennedy's official travel as first lady came during the June 1961 trip to France, where she made such an "extraordinary impression" on the French population that the president remarked, "I do not think it altogether inappropriate to introduce myself to this audience. I am the man who accompanied Jacqueline Kennedy to Paris, and I have enjoyed it."[44] The president did not oversell her appeal, as *Life* titled coverage of the first lady "The President's Scene Stealer," and *Time* reported, "From the moment of her smiling arrival at Orly Airport, the radiant young first lady was the Kennedy who really mattered."[45] In France, Jacqueline Kennedy embraced her public role, touring various cultural sites and giving interviews (including one televised and in which she spoke "very commendable" French), and subsequently found herself heralded by compliments in French newspapers and, as *Life* suggested, went from "one triumph to another."[46] As the two engaged in talks regarding the future of Western Europe and the modern world, a visible generational divide existed between forty-four-year-old John Kennedy and seventy-year-old Charles de Gaulle. But the divide between old and new was perhaps better illustrated by images of the French leader clearly being charmed by the United States' first lady—and not only because of her beauty, accentuated as it was in American styles designed by Cassini and then French fashion by Givenchy, but also due to her knowledge of French history, culture, and language. French journalist

Andre de Coizart spoke directly to the first lady's possession of these attributes as he praised JBK's "beauty, facility with European manners and languages, and love of the arts."[47]

Jacqueline Kennedy's symbolic importance as a representative of a cultured, prosperous America was even more pronounced in Vienna, where President Kennedy engaged in talks with Soviet premiere Nikita Khrushchev. The tensions of the Cold War played out clearly in the nation abutting the Iron Curtain. As Letitia Baldridge recalled, when Soviet motorcades passed through the streets, crowds responded with a cold silence. When the Kennedys' motorcade arrived, however, Baldridge claimed that it "instigated near-riots of joyous, screaming Viennese," and people ran alongside trying to keep up with the Kennedys' car. This difference in reception was even more pronounced when a crowd of approximately three thousand gathered outside the Palais Pallavicini and began chanting "Jac-kie!," ignoring the fact that the first lady was with Nina Khrushchev. Mrs. Kennedy, Baldridge recalled, "handled the crisis with great diplomacy." She went to the balcony, waved to the crowd for a moment, and then returned with Mrs. Khrushchev, holding her hand aloft. The crowd, Baldridge claimed, "loved it," and amended their chant to one of "'Jac-kie!' 'Nin-a!'" Even the premiere could not resist her appeal, expressing his desire to shake her hand before her husband's. As they sat side by side during their meal, he regaled her with tales, in response to which she "feigned amazement" and "laughed heartily" as the moment necessitated.[48]

Jacqueline Kennedy's powers were distinctly feminine. She was beautiful, charming, amenable, and accommodating to notoriously difficult men as she engaged in one-on-one conversations. Mrs. Kennedy served in a kind of soft-power capacity, listening as much as she spoke, attracting rather than coercing, but admittedly, attracting through traditional feminine beauty and a willingness to play to the egos of powerful men. In the Cold War climate, however, her appearance and behaviors and public response to her appearance and behaviors suggested an American advantage. As the Spanish *La Nacion* suggested, "A new force has appeared in the political arsenal . . . a new 'secret weapon'—beauty."

President John F. Kennedy, French president Charles de Gaulle, and first lady Jacqueline Kennedy stand on the steps of the Elysee Palace, France, May 31, 1961. Mrs. Kennedy's youth was especially pronounced in her interactions with the French president, who was charmed by her linguistic skills and knowledge of French history. Everett Collection Inc./ Alamy Stock Photo.

Expanding from there, the publication claimed, "'To be pretty' presupposes a high grade of social progress, and requires investments in creams, perfumes, lotions, and clothing which no Communist country can now manage, nor will conditions for many years in the future allow it." In both individual encounters with world leaders and as witnessed and interpreted by international crowds, JBK was a powerful public diplomat.[49]

In her more active engagements in France and Austria, Jacqueline Kennedy was an engaged cultural observer, someone eager to learn more of the nations and their people. Coverage of and response to JBK, Carol B. Schwalbe argues, meant that "for millions of people around the globe, [Mrs. Kennedy] embodied the hopes and youthful promise of the New Frontier, indeed of America itself."[50] While JBK, with the help of Cassini, always took care with her styles abroad, she was not merely an adornment for her husband. She was by his side for official state functions, but she often was on her own as he engaged in traditional government-to-government diplomacy with other world leaders. Jacqueline Kennedy, even independent of her husband, still drew crowds, and thus, was still newsworthy.

International response to Mrs. Kennedy generated a sustained coverage of her comings and goings during these trips. There had been no question of coverage for her postwar first lady peers, Bess Truman or Mamie Eisenhower, because they never joined their husbands on such occasions. While coverage of Jacqueline Kennedy generally presented her as apolitical, Betty Houchin Winfield suggests that JBK participated in a kind of partnership to help JFK win the White House. In these international travels she reveals herself as an ongoing partner to her husband's political endeavors, even post-election.[51] Together, the Kennedys projected—on the world stage—an image of the United States as young and modern, cultured and cosmopolitan, confident and capable. As much as Jacqueline Kennedy claimed a traditional spousal role, the Kennedy union, in their domestic entertainments and international travels, suggested something of a modern partnership. And audiences at home, delighting in international fanfare for the first lady, accepted this model.[52]

Jacqueline Kennedy's public diplomacy, adjacent to her husband, indicated her value as a cultural ambassador of the nation. Through her style, she communicated a modern and elegant image of the United States, cultured and curious, a vision that played to the sense of the nation JFK wished to communicate at this pivotal moment in the Cold War contest.[53] Whether viewed as a decorative complement to her husband's work of hard politics or an embodiment of the vision of America he intended his administration to communicate, JBK drew attention independent of her husband, which suggested the appeal she held on her own. Such was this appeal that in March 1962, JFK's administration sent Jacqueline Kennedy, without her husband, as a goodwill ambassador on a "semi-official" tour of India and Pakistan. Accompanied by her sister Lee Radziwill, JBK left her husband and her two small children in Washington, DC, and distanced herself from any sort of domestic obligation. On this trip, Jacqueline Kennedy not only was the main draw but was the primary laboring party of the visit. The itinerary, without any sort of diplomatic negotiations or policy meetings, emphasized "sightseeing and a few highly selective looks at welfare activities for children." Details and instructions for exercises intended to improve relations with the United States totaled one hundred pages.[54]

A caravan of reporters accompanied the first lady on her travels, and in the *New York Times* she received daily coverage, sometimes appearing on the front page. When all was said and done, Jacqueline Kennedy had received four hundred thousand words of print coverage and over one thousand minutes on broadcast television.[55] Kennedy family friend Joan Braden, who had gone along on the trip, ostensibly to cover the first lady's travels for the *Saturday Evening Post*, noted that many of the reporters covering Mrs. Kennedy felt as though they were reporting on "a glorified fashion show," and were getting little in the way of copy. When they asked ambassador to India John Kenneth Galbraith, who handled press briefings during JBK's time overseas, how the first lady was liking India, they received responses along the lines of "Why, I don't know. She seems to love it." Braden admitted, "Nobody really knew what Jackie Kennedy was thinking or feeling. She was always smiling, always beautiful, always loved, but she seldom said anything."[56] On one of the rare occasions when Mrs. Kennedy did speak, before a host of microphones, she maintained her usual points of focus: art, history, and culture. After a day at the Shalimar Gardens in Pakistan, JBK, clad in a bright yellow coat, topped with a golden garland, said, "I must say, I'm profoundly impressed by the reverence which you in Pakistan have for your art and for your culture, and for the use which you make of it now. My own countrymen, too, have a pride in their traditions. So I think, as I stand in these gardens which were built long before my country was born, that that's one more thing that binds us together and which always will."[57]

As a goodwill representative of the United States, Jacqueline Kennedy succeeded enormously. As her assigned Secret Service agent, Clint Hill, recalled, "More than one hundred thousand people lined the roadway as we proceeded by motorcade into central New Delhi. . . . Snake charmers, men on the backs of camels, bullock carts and their drivers all lined the route waving and shouting, 'Jackie! Jackie! Welcome Mrs. Kennedy!' I had seen this kind of reception in Paris and South America, but on those trips she had been with the president. Here, all of these people had come out *just for her*."[58] When an estimated eight thousand Pakistanis waited to greet Mrs. Kennedy, another member of the first lady's Secret Service detail noted, "'It is *unbelievable*. Reminds me of the receptions we used to get for Ike, but I've never seen anything like this for a first lady.'"[59] Indeed, the government of India's Overseas Communication Service reported that the coverage of Mrs. Kennedy's visit was the second largest received by any visiting dignitary since India's independence in 1947 (President Eisenhower was first).[60]

The *New York Times* chronicled Jacqueline Kennedy's visits to historic sites and children's hospitals, with heads of state and young native artists, riding an elephant and a camel and expressing delight at skilled riders at a Pakistani horse and cattle show. As Paul Grimes, who reported on the trip, noted, "Mrs. Kennedy seems to be enjoying herself thoroughly. She appears to have adjusted to being the object of siege by cameramen, reporters and thousands upon thousands of smiling

Jacqueline Kennedy attends a horse and cattle show in Pakistan, March 22, 1962. Her enthusiasm for events such as this was met with great fanfare by the Pakistani population and made for excellent copy in reporting in the United States. Cecil Stoughton, White House/ John F. Kennedy Presidential Library and Museum.

Indians." In Udaipur, when Mrs. Kennedy stood up in an open car and "did the Namaste and waved," the crowd "roared." Schoolboys shouted, "'Jackie ki jai!' (Hail Jackie) and 'Jackie zindabad!' (Long live Jackie)."[61] In assessing the meaning of the first lady's visit, Grimes concluded, "No one seemed to believe in the wake of the visit by the United States President's wife to Pakistan and India that her presence would have any significant political impact. Nevertheless, there was a distinct feeling that the publicity it had invoked both in this area and in the United States would contribute to mutual understanding."[62]

In the immediate aftermath of Jacqueline Kennedy's visit, Walter McConaughy, ambassador to Pakistan, corresponded with Jay Gildner, assistant press secretary of the Kennedy administration, and affirmed Grimes's assessment. He wrote, "Now that Mrs. Kennedy's visit is over, it is increasingly clear that it was strikingly successful both in bringing to Pakistanis generally a new insight into the American character, and in presenting a vivid picture of Pakistan to the American public." Through her visit—and the resulting coverage, which included documentary films produced by the United States Information Agency (USIA), *Invitation to India* and *Invitation to Pakistan*, shown internationally—JBK fostered cross-cultural communication and goodwill.[63] Mrs. Kennedy's "personality and charm," McConaughy noted, had been essential in drawing response from the Pakistani people. "Returns," he noted, "continue to come in that show how successful the arrangements were and how pleasant an impression was made on both the American and Pakistani press."[64] In his letter to the president, the ambassador wrote, "She has won the confidence and even the affection of a large cross section of the Pakistani populace who feel that they know her and know that they like her. I believe benefits to our relations with Pakistan will be reflected for a long time in ways intangible as well as tangible."[65]

Before the trip, the USIA imagined that footage of Mrs. Kennedy might be effective, estimating, as diplomatic historian Nicholas Cull suggests, that JBK "was a propaganda weapon of the first order," but it fell short in imagining just *how* desirable that footage might be. In proposing documentaries of her trips to India and Pakistan, George

Stevens Jr., who became director of the USIA Motion Picture Service in February 1962, and fellow filmmaker Leslie Stevens wrote to USIA director Edward R. Murrow in November of 1961, noting that footage of Jacqueline Kennedy could demonstrate the "seriousness with which our country takes the Indo-Asian people and provide eyewitness proof of our true democratic spirit." Further, they would show the first lady's desire to "*learn* from Pakistan: who its people are, what they hope for, their wants and needs, their culture and their accomplishments." Still, Stevens tempered expectations when he confided to Murrow, "We will see how much we achieve."

Director Leo Seltzer, who had traveled to Southeast Asia a month before the first lady to acquire background shots, produced footage that "blended the fantastic settings, exotic clothing, and closeups of the indigenous people." While images of *Invitation to India* highlighted the traditional and the ancient, narration educated viewers about India's ability to combine its historic civilization with the "contemporary world of today." There is no mention of the Cold War, but India is celebrated as the world's largest democracy. It is JBK's voice that concludes the film, emphasizing a vision for the future shared by India and the United States. In *Invitation to Pakistan*, just as in the India film, Jacqueline Kennedy is shown interacting with the population, and "her genuine delight in the visit illustrates the simple pleasures that come from sharing one's culture, friendship, and a common desire for peace and security." In the final moments of the film, rather than emphasizing what Pakistan had to gain from a relationship with the United States, Mrs. Kennedy communicated her wish to learn more about Pakistan.[66] If listening and cultural diplomacy made up part of an emergent approach to international relations, Jacqueline Kennedy—both in person and on screen—was a skilled American representative.[67]

Even as senior officials at the USIA doubted the appeal of these films, Stevens's speculation about demand among international audiences was on point. Initially intending to distribute the films to India and Pakistan alone, the USIA eventually received so many requests for the films that the agency reported "extreme difficulty in handling all the requests for use of these subjects with the number of prints made." Ultimately, the USIA distributed *Invitation to India* in twenty-nine languages and *Invitation to Pakistan* in twenty-two languages throughout seventy-eight countries. Additionally, United Artists purchased the editing rights from USIA and created *Jacqueline Kennedy's Asian Journey*, which was shown with the 1962 release of *Taras Bulba* starring Yul Brynner and Tony Curtis.[68]

While South Asian newspapers praised the films, in the United States, some journalists and congressional representatives raised questions and critiques regarding the cost of the trip and JBK's distance from the average citizen of each nation visited.[69] Defending Mrs. Kennedy against critics who thought her self-presentation was too grand and critiqued the fact that she failed to "mix with the people," Alex Dreier of ABC commented on JBK's appeal and influence in shaping views of the United States:

> Mrs. Kennedy is doing a fine job of representing her country. She is no average American . . . and nobody ever thought she was. She is the president's wife . . . and she looks and dresses and acts the part. . . . If Jacqueline Kennedy were Mrs. Nixon . . . or Mrs. Anybody Else . . . we would be happy to see her making the trips she has made. In far too many places . . . we have the undeserved reputation of being a war-like nation. Sending a pretty, thoughtful young lady abroad is one of the best ways in the world to dispel that fiction.

Assessing her importance beyond her travels to India and Pakistan, Dreier speculated about the real motivation behind critiques of JBK: "What very well may be griping some columnists and commentators is that when 1964 rolls around . . . they not only are going to have to beat John Kennedy. They are also going to have to beat Jacqueline Kennedy. And it's going to be a tough daily double to beat . . . trips or no trips!"[70]

Mrs. Kennedy, then, increasingly was regarded as a political asset at home. Abroad, her appeal was unquestionable. In evaluating the value of the documentaries of Jacqueline Kennedy's travels, Schwalbe assesses the importance of the USIA films in their context: "At a time when the United States was trying to consolidate its influence over the free world and gain the support of diverse people in nonaligned nations, these non-political documentaries proved politically and culturally beneficial to the Kennedy administration."[71] Pierre Salinger reported that press coverage of the trip was "excellent." Beyond the political—tangible or intangible—the visuals of Jackie Kennedy on the trip are stunning. With Cassini, she had decided upon a wardrobe that alternated between vibrant colors and subdued ivories, intended for her to stand out either by her own ensemble or alongside the brightly colored saris adorning those by whom she was surrounded.[72] The delight she expressed in her experiences, as evidenced both in photographs of her trip and in the USIA film, marked her as an adventurer, a person comfortable among those unlike herself.

Perhaps most famous is the image of Mrs. Kennedy in front of the Taj Mahal. She stands before its majesty, confident and comfortable. She is a lady of the early 1960s with her signature white gloves and white handbag, but she is fashion forward in a bright blue and green sleeveless dress, whose pattern clearly was inspired by Indian prints. Undoubtedly, Jacqueline Kennedy operated from a position of privilege, and a trip of this nature was far easier when one traveled as JBK traveled, but the mother of two small children embarking on a globe-trotting adventure, visiting with heads of state in 1962 America was a noteworthy occurrence.[73] As the model of American womanhood, JBK reflected the expected feminine appearance and decorum, but she also represented independence and a cultured curiosity.

In a retrospective account immediately following the trip, however, JBK presented her travels neither as a turning point for herself or American women nor as an endeavor of particular political significance. As JBK told her friend Joan Braden, after Braden asked her for an exclusive, "I'm glad I went, but I'd never take a trip like this again without Jack. There were moments like that time in Lahore at the governor's house, when I sat at the window and looked at the fantastic lighted trees reflected in moonlight pools, and wondered what I was doing

Jacqueline Kennedy poses in front of the Taj Mahal during her goodwill trip to India, March 15, 1962. Cecil Stoughton, White House/John F. Kennedy Presidential Library and Museum.

so far away alone, without Jack or the children to see them." But even as she expressed an urge to return to the domestic side of life, she recounted how fascinated she had been to learn something of the history of the region, an undertaking she performed in advance of visiting any international location. Talking with Braden, she expressed particular interest in Emperor Akbar, who had ruled the Mogul Empire during the sixteenth century and whose rule was, as JBK declared, "as enlightened a rule as any I've ever heard of." In assessing the history of the region, however, Mrs. Kennedy segued to discuss the present. As she told Braden, "I'd never heard of [Akbar] until I started reading for this trip. That's why I think travel is so important and I'll always care so much about student exchanges. Not only does it teach you about the past but, once you've been among the people and gotten to know some of them, their problems are so much more real to you than they are from home, and you become more sympathetic."[74]

Braden wrote about Jacqueline Kennedy as though she were two people. On the one hand, she was a regal figure, almost like a queen, cheered by her adoring subjects. On the other, JBK was nearly childlike, gazing in astonishment at the grandeur of the Taj Mahal. In her interview with Braden, JBK likewise reflected a complexity. Painting herself as a supportive spouse and dedicated mother, she was hopeful that her trip would benefit her husband's administration but refrained from identifying herself as a political agent. She situated herself domestically by espousing her happiness to be returning to her family, but she likewise pontificated on the value of travel and cultural exchange. She celebrated the intimacies of private life but expanded upon the necessity of exploring beyond one's known environment. Jacqueline Kennedy's complexity was on full display as she played to expectations of American women but expanded what might be accepted of this population at a time when cultural changes were afoot.[75] As this was the case with Mrs. Kennedy's travel, so it was also the case with a project that had kept her closer to home.

* * *

Beyond her influence as a style icon, cultural ambassador (domestically or abroad), or public diplomat, Jacqueline Kennedy also embraced, as her interview with Joan Braden revealed, a decidedly domestic role. She often emphasized her commitment to motherhood. Even with the care provided by Maud Shaw, Caroline's and John's Irish nanny, JBK delighted in her children, and dedicated herself to maintaining for them as normal a life as possible given the circumstances of their upbringing. She responded to requests for articles about motherhood, as evidenced in an article she penned for *American Weekly*, in which she discussed her approach to childrearing: "The personality of the child seems to guide you. Maybe if you start with love, security and discipline and just work from there, being sensitive to your child's developing interests— the 'raising' would be more rewarding all around—and infinitely more fun."[76] In the article, Mrs. Kennedy championed children's imaginative and inquiring capacities, counseled patience, and celebrated sharing passions for art and literature and history. Her devotion to motherhood complemented her role as helpmate to her husband, with her dedication to benefiting or advancing his administration demonstrated through her travels or the events she planned and oversaw in the White House.

Mrs. Kennedy's sense of the domestic, however, extended beyond familial roles and responsibilities and very clearly included her plans for the structure in which they lived: the White House. In her restoration of the White House, JBK provided Americans with their most sustained view of the first lady, through print media coverage and then her famed 1962 television tour. And while the work she did toward the White House's rehabilitation took place in her temporary home, it simultaneously took place on a national stage, in a structure of national symbolic significance. Accordingly, many who followed her efforts and watched her White House tour evaluated Mrs. Kennedy as a public figure. Her self-presentation communicated the notion that here was no bored housewife, redecorating her home on a whim, and instead showed JBK as performing a kind of professional labor. Whereas in White House cultural events and in much of her travel, JBK was affiliated with her husband, and often intended to play a supporting role, in

Jacqueline Kennedy prioritized her maternal duties while in the White House. Here she takes her children for a sleigh ride in the snow on the White House grounds, February 13, 1962. Cecil Stoughton, White House/John F. Kennedy Presidential Library and Museum.

her White House restoration and tour, Jacqueline Kennedy was a more independent public figure in her own right.

Shortly after John Jr.'s birth and just before JBK traveled to Palm Beach for the Christmas holiday, Mamie Eisenhower hosted Jacqueline Kennedy for a tour of the White House. The two undertook a reportedly strained tour (Jackie Kennedy, barely two weeks postpartum, had asked for a wheelchair; Mrs. Eisenhower had one at the ready but never presented it), at the end of which Mrs. Kennedy requested White House chief usher J. B. West to send blueprints and photographs of the home to Palm Beach. Mamie Eisenhower never revealed to West her views about JBK or the tour, but the morning after the visit predicted to the usher, "She's planning to redo every room in this house. . . . You've got *quite* a project ahead of you." In what West called "the voice she reserved for disapproval," Mrs. Eisenhower continued, "There certainly are going to be some changes made around here!"[77]

Indeed, the tour of the White House solidified plans Mrs. Kennedy had for the foreseeable future. Horrified at the worn and dated furnishings and décor she encountered upon visiting the presidential residence, JBK determined to make a White House restoration her primary focus as first lady. Before leaving for Florida, Jacqueline Kennedy ordered books from the Library of Congress to begin her research for her planned restoration.[78] She believed the White House should pay tribute to the fascinating national history that might be told through material culture, and she immediately undertook the work necessary for such a project despite reservations of those in her husband's administration who feared her "tampering" with the presidential mansion would be met with public backlash at efforts to alter a beloved, highly symbolic structure.[79]

Almost immediately upon taking up residence at the White House, Mrs. Kennedy indicated that she had plans for the presidential residence. On February 3, Pamela Turnure informed the press that the first lady wished to share with the nation "some startling things she has learned historically about the White House."[80] Not quite three weeks later, as promised, after having finished decorating the family quarters and continuing a sustained conference with numerous experts, JBK revealed her intention to undertake "a major cultural project—furnishing the White House with authentic items of the time of its construction." Mrs. Kennedy allowed David E. Finley, chair of the Fine Arts Commission (FAC), to speak of the project's value. He asserted that the project was one the FAC had long been interested in, and referenced Mount Vernon and Monticello as historic homes that had been "preserved and furnished to carry out the historical theme throughout." The White House had no such theme, with furniture having been acquired in various administration changeovers and without attention to historic value or periodization. Finley suggested that he and the FAC had long hoped to follow the lead of other historic homes in the White House, "which belongs to all Americans, and we are, therefore, especially gratified that Mrs. Kennedy has seen fit to give leadership to this project."[81]

After the announcement of Mrs. Kennedy's plan, which included a laundry list of the art experts and collectors who now were part of the twelve-person committee who would raise funds and locate furnishings, her White House team provided a steady stream of press releases detailing donations, finds, and plans for the project. Over the course of JBK's first six months in the White House, Pam Turnure provided the press with information about the furniture and china contents of the White House at the beginning of the project; about the appointment of a curator, Lorraine Waxman Pearce; and about the acquisition of "furniture belonging to George Washington, Abraham Lincoln, James and Dolley Madison, James Monroe, Martin Van Buren, Nellie Custis, and Daniel Webster." Given Jacqueline Kennedy's known penchant for all things French, a July 4 release included the note, "Where non-American furnishings have been acquired, it is because they have some connection with American history, or are similar to furnishings used by Presidents in the White House in the past." Releases emphasized also that many of the acquisitions were donations and thus were not financed with taxpayer dollars.[82] The first lady took care to cross her t's and dot her i's from the first. For someone cast as apolitical, she had an acute grasp of the necessity of doing things the right way and in a manner most likely to limit potential critique.

It was in the September 1, 1961, issue of *Life*, which featured a cover story on Jacqueline Kennedy and her "absorbing project," that a broader American audience got their first taste of the exacting standards established by the first lady in her White House effort. She said, "Everything in the White House . . . must have a reason for being there. It would be sacrilege merely to 'redecorate it'—a word I hate. It must be *restored*—and that has nothing to do with decoration. That is a question of scholarship." Demonstrating a political savvy and sophisticated understanding of the past, Mrs. Kennedy spoke of the evolving nature of the executive office and the need to reflect the varying tastes of the men who had served as president. She had conducted her own research and relied on advice from the Smithsonian as she laid out her plans. This may have been a "pet" project, but she was hardly changing the home to meet her personal style or individual taste. She further revealed her understanding of the need to conduct business in such a manner as to limit dissent by noting that even before moving into the White House, she had recruited a team of experts, among them Finley, chairman of the National Commission of Fine Arts, and Henry Francis du Pont, one of the nation's foremost authorities on antiques.

Articulating her sharp understanding of the need to establish the validity of her project, Jacqueline Kennedy especially celebrated du Pont's joining of her committee. She said, "I didn't know or care what Mr. du Pont's politics were. . . . Without him on the committee I didn't think we would accomplish much—and with him I knew there would be no criticism. The day he agreed to be chairman was the biggest red letter day of all."[83] Beyond the legitimacy du Pont conveyed, he also brought with him a powerful network of antique dealers, collectors, and potential donors. While Mrs. Kennedy may have viewed politics as a preserve primarily for men, here she revealed a keen understanding of the way of the political world and the necessary steps one might take in navigating potentially choppy political waters. Even more, she revealed a sense of how to frame the project to communicate its validity and the seriousness with which she was undertaking it.[84]

Appreciation of the issues and concerns of those assisting with the restoration extended throughout the *Life* article. While much of the text depicted Jacqueline Kennedy as an investigator undergoing some kind of treasure hunt, there also was evidence of JBK's clear appreciation for the practicalities of her undertaking. In previous years, collectibles from within the White House had "disappear[ed]." As Mrs. Kennedy attempted to solicit donations from collectors, she had to assure them that such a disappearing act would not occur. To that end, after meeting with JBK, New Mexico senator Clinton Anderson, chair of the Senate Interior and Insular Affairs Committee, introduced a bill in 1961 "to establish the Executive Mansion as a national monument under the auspices of the National Park System." Additional legislation provided for the White House's ownership of donated artifacts and stipulated that, if moved from the White House, objects would go to the Smithsonian, where they would become part of the collection. Relatedly, it was Mrs. Kennedy who initiated the founding of the

White House Historical Association, dedicated to the preservation of the home and efforts to make it accessible to the public.[85]

In February 1962, nearly eighty million viewers saw the embodiment of Jacqueline Kennedy's labor and the satisfaction she took in her work as she toured her temporary home with CBS reporter Charles Collingwood, and further explained how she had gone about acquiring furnishings, artwork, wallpaper, and textiles in her effort to rehabilitate the sorely neglected home. In her explanation about how the White House restoration had been organized, how it was taking place, what her role was, and how she was administering her duties, Mrs. Kennedy provided a behind-the-scenes view of the labor she embarked upon as first lady. While *Life*'s audience had read about her undertaking, now they could see it on full display. An estimated forty-six million people chose to do so, 75 percent of the viewing public. She brought the White House home restoration into the homes of the American people. In so doing, she likewise made public a model not only of a woman of education and expertise but of a woman whose education and expertise were valued and respected by others and celebrated on a national stage.[86]

Collingwood conducted part of his interview with the first lady in the office space reserved for her White House business, where he inquired about the methods by which she selected items and determined how the White House might be restored. She began with a description of the process for renovation: "Since our work started we've received hundreds of letters every day. This is where we evaluate all the finds, see if we want to keep them, if they'll fit into our budget." When asked about her overall plan, she demonstrated a measure of flexibility and explained where motivation for the project had originated: "Well, I really don't have [a plan] because I think this house will always grow and should. It just seemed to me such a shame when we came here to find hardly anything of the past in the house, hardly anything before 1902. I know when we went to Colombia, the Presidential Palace there has all the history of that country in it. Where Simon Bolivar was, every piece of furniture in it has some link with the past. I thought the White

House should be like that." Throughout the program, Mrs. Kennedy provided a detailed history of the White House and its evolution over the years. As she and Collingwood moved through the house for the full tour, JBK's historical acumen revealed itself time and again as she described the past uses of various rooms, the evolution of style, and background information about the objects now inhabiting the space (and stroked donors' egos as she mentioned them by name). All this she did without cue cards or prompts. During her performance, just one retake was ordered—and only because a camera malfunctioned. In the aftermath of the filming, Collingwood noted, "Everyone from the lowliest porter to the director felt they had been involved in one of the landmarks of this infant [TV] business."[87]

In her description of the restoration process, Jacqueline Kennedy emerged as an expert, as someone capable of overseeing a team of highly skilled workers, someone adept at negotiating with and attracting donors, someone with a clear view of the larger significance of the work at hand. Again, she emphasized, this was not redecorating. Even if this was only a matter of semantics, her political savvy led her to make clear her distinction between the two words. Her tastes, she asserted, were a moot point. Rather than making decisions based upon her personal preferences, she emphasized that she relied upon a "committee which has museum experts, and government people and private citizens on it." Once the committee reached a decision, "everything we do," she said, "is subject to approval by the Fine Arts Committee." This was about the self-presentation of the nation and the display of material objects that communicated a rich national heritage. Mrs. Kennedy was an authoritative figure, confident in her ability to create a vision of the White House that communicated what the presidential residence ought to communicate. Clearly, this was work. In doing this work, JBK presented a model of professionalism at a time when this element of women's lives was not always made visible on a national stage. And though the number of working women was on the rise, very often employment took the form of a job rather than a career and occurred under the supervision of men.

Of Jacqueline Kennedy, Lady Bird Johnson remarked, "She was a worker, which I don't think was always quite recognized."[88] Her work and its value, however, were recognized very clearly by those writing to the White House after the tour. Telegrams and letters received in the days following the broadcast—sixty-three hundred in just three days—corroborated Mrs. Kennedy's press staff's assertion that the tour had been a success.[89] While it was not uncommon for writers to applaud the first lady's beauty and grace, focusing on appearance and demeanor, many praised JBK's hard work, ranging in description from congratulations for the "tremendously fruitful effort you have been engaged in" to recognition of the "exacting job you have undertaken" to praise for her "efforts in restoring the historical treasures of our American heritage." Betty Rockwell, a self-identified Republican from Phoenix, spoke directly to the work done by the first lady: "You and your committee deserve many accolades for a job that has long been overdue." Another Republican, Roy M. Frisby of Chicago, similarly commented upon Mrs. Kennedy's "restorative work" and deemed it a "magnificent contribution to the American people." Dr. and Mrs. Maxwell Fields of Los Angeles, California, described JBK as "informative and knowledgeable" in their congratulatory telegram. So impressed by her presentation of information was one couple that they went so far as to call her presentation "culturally and historically spellbinding."[90]

Responses to Jacqueline Kennedy's work linked the tour to a shared and often overlooked American history and heritage. Some writers equated the restoration of the White House with JBK's patriotism, as one writer from Chicago did when he praised JBK's "respectful look on our forefathers and American people." Harry Karrass of Brooklyn considered the contemporary political climate as he wrote, "What a wonderful alternative to the maniacal pseudo-patriotism of the Birchites, et al. A warm sensation of pride in our country, our White House, and our First Family. Thank you." Like Karrass, other writers, in praising Mrs. Kennedy's efforts, celebrated her contribution in her specific role as first lady. "Your highly gifted ability in selecting associates and assembling White House artifacts is your perfect gift to our nation," wrote one Los Angeles resident. An El Paso family echoed these views as they wrote, "Mrs. Kennedy congratulations on a job well done and in the manner it was presented to millions of TV viewers to preserve the historic events of a great country the United States of America is sincerely a great deed in itself. You deserve America's highest award for truly you have earned the title America's First Lady." In sum, many writers cheered JBK's presentation for what one person called her "fine background, culture, knowledge and individuality," all of which, the writer claimed, "left an overwhelming impression."[91] If, as first lady, Jacqueline Kennedy represented *the* model of American womanhood, then the complexity of the model was on full display.

American media echoed citizens' praise, as indicated by the *New York Daily News*'s evaluation that Mrs. Kennedy had given a "really professional, relaxed performance." Journalists addressed the public's assumed reservations about JBK's project and asserted that her performance should have allayed their fears. From the initial voiceover, wrote the *New York Herald Tribune*, Jacqueline Kennedy's "recounting the history of the White House, accompanied by appropriate old prints and photographs . . . should certainly have convinced skeptics that the youthful mistress of the Presidential Mansion is making her changes in its décor with a deep respect for the past." The *New York Daily News* emphasized the first lady's skillful labor in reporting, "The overall impression one gained from this TV expedition was of the energetic work of Jacqueline in attempting to turn the White House into an artistic and historic shrine for the American people. Through astute detective work many old pieces of furniture and paintings have been recovered and so placed as to reflect the periods during which they were created." The *Boston Globe* cheered Mrs. Kennedy, reporting, "Her performance, straightforward and unpretentious, revealed an artistic sensitivity, an antiquarian's acuteness, and a sureness of historical knowledge which established her beyond question as distinctly a person in her own right, as well as a charming woman." For those who might have missed the broadcast, the image cast by media was one of Jacqueline Kennedy's "efficiency and professionalism" across a variety of fields.[92]

While Mrs. Kennedy and Collingwood had been joined by the president at the end of the broadcast, the first lady was not outshone, nor was she assumed as merely her husband's helpmate. Instead, as noted by responses to her White House tour, the presentation established (or reinforced) a separate identity for the first lady, one marked by great poise, expertise, and intelligence, all of which she seemingly had no reservations in displaying for all the world to see. To be sure, the first lady was a model of expected midcentury upper-class femininity, wearing pearls, a slim red dress, and low heels, and many media outlets commented on her feminine, "breathy" voice. But Jacqueline Kennedy's traditionally "feminine" appearance, paired with what many saw as the service she had provided to the nation in her undertaking, proved women's ability to move beyond strictly domestic roles. And the widespread praise JBK received demonstrates the public's comfort with this model of womanhood.

Beyond the millions of Americans who viewed the program, people in 106 countries, including six behind the Iron Curtain, saw Mrs. Kennedy lead her White House tour. In addition to the footage of the tour shown in the United States, the first lady, linguist that she was, at the urging of USIA chief Edward R. Murrow, taped particular mentions of the White House as the "People's House" and special prologues in French and Spanish for her foreign-language audiences. As the United States engaged in a heated Cold War with the Soviet Union, and American government endlessly endeavored to demonstrate capitalism's and democracy's superiority to communism, such media served as an invaluable weapon in the conflict. When, in 1959, Vice President Richard Nixon debated Soviet premiere Nikita Khrushchev on the merits of the model American home versus the model Soviet dwelling at the American exhibition in Moscow, the two men also invoked the status of American and Soviet women in their claims of national superiority. In her televised tour of the White House, poised, graceful, knowledgeable, and surrounded by fine things, Jacqueline Kennedy, who already had won over de Gaulle and Khrushchev on the Kennedys' 1961 European trip, communicated a positive view of the United States to an international audience. Indeed, in Moscow, the American Embassy's cultural attaché showed the film to 150 invited guests. "Following the showing," read a memo received by John Kennedy's press secretary, Pierre Salinger, "the Attaché was besieged with requests for information materials on the US."[93]

The Kennedy White House, of course, would not have sent the film to so many international locations, nor would it have so closely monitored international response, had the president's team not anticipated positive feedback and intended to make use of it. The political and cultural capital of Mrs. Kennedy revealed itself in this effort. From needing to be convinced that Jacqueline Kennedy was an asset to her husband's campaign in 1960, the Kennedy administration recognized how valuable she was in this conflict that necessitated weapons of all kinds.[94] As evidenced by global response, this international effort hardly conveyed the notion that the standard model of midcentury American womanhood was one of mere domesticity or subordination. In London, the *Sunday Times* reported, "You don't often get a conducted tour of a stately home with a guide so charming and so obviously absorbed in the scholarship of her subject. Mrs. Kennedy didn't just learn that script off by heart for the occasion; her profound knowledge and sympathy shone through. A delightful person of unassuming dignity and naturalness, with a good, well-stocked mind, for whom one's respect is increased." From Sweden, the liberal *Expressen* was "ecstatic, saying that no one had ever done such an effective public relations job for the United States." In an advanced screening for fifteen journalists at the United States Information Service in Tel Aviv, "The writers commented very favorably on Mrs. Kennedy's cultured ways, her obvious deep love for American history and her understanding of artistic value." A memo shared with Pierre Salinger reported, "The resulting publicity led to a 'run' on the film which has been in great demand and is booked for several weeks in advance."[95] Across the globe, Jacqueline Kennedy not only generated interest in the United States but also served to enhance respect and appreciation for American leadership, American people (not just women), and American culture more broadly.

And yet, the performance was not without its critics. Norman Mailer penned a blistering critique for *Esquire*, in which he lambasted not only the tour but Jacqueline Kennedy's public persona, one he found devoid of authenticity. He mocked her voice. He mocked her self-presentation. What she offered in the tour, he charged, was not history but rather an infliction of the past upon viewers. They were "pummeled" and "depressed" with facts. From Mrs. Kennedy, he wrote, "One was not being offered education, but anxiety." Mailer's disdain for the White House tour was not the only grievance he wished to air. Beyond the tour, JBK's commitment to the arts was, in Mailer's estimation, superficial at best. The arts as she saw them failed to challenge the status quo the way he believed true artists (like himself) challenged (and elevated) public life. Another response to the tour, also mocking but far gentler in tone, was the segment "The Tour" featured on Vaughn Meader's *First Family* album, in which actors mimicking JBK and Charles Collingwood spoofed the program. Hapless camera men knocked over priceless antiques. Collingwood and JBK accidentally happened upon the president as he was singing in the shower. Not only Mrs. Kennedy's voice, but the name dropping and linguistic stylings repeated throughout her tour were fodder for the comic impersonator's Kennedy record, which sold six and a half million copies during its first six and a half weeks on the market. But even these responses reveal the extent of Jacqueline Kennedy's reach, the way she captivated and seemingly demanded response from those bearing witness to her public presence.[96]

* * *

In 1962, Jacqueline Kennedy is reported to have said, "People told me ninety-nine things that I had to do as First Lady, and I haven't done one of them."[97] While some might regard such a statement as evidence of JBK's dereliction of duty, as a petulant rejection of tradition and decorum, an alternate reading of Mrs. Kennedy's words speaks to her desire to have as much control over her life as possible. As an unofficial, unpaid position, the first ladyship came with expectations, but no actual requirements. Jacqueline Kennedy took advantage of the fluidity of the post and chose projects of her own interest in a decisive manner and set standards subsequent first ladies likewise adopted, such as the hiring of a press secretary. She set clear parameters and made sure that her staff enforced them and that her husband's staff was aware of them.

The volume of Jacqueline Kennedy coverage was staggering. Curiosity about the first lady knew no bounds. And while her approval ratings remained high, the controversy she had generated as a candidate's wife did not disappear upon her husband's taking the oath of office. Her parties were grand and sophisticated. They also were costly. JFK's press secretary, Pierre Salinger, found himself defending and defining expenses for events such as the July 1961 state dinner at George Washington's Mount Vernon, where the Kennedys hosted Muhammad Ayub, president of Pakistan. The public raised eyebrows at her habitual weekend retreats to hunt country in Virginia and private overseas adventures such as her summer 1962 Italy trip, where images of Caroline water skiing with JBK frightened citizens concerned for the girl's safety and images of Jackie Kennedy dancing in nightclubs scandalized those worried about national morals.[98] Even her celebrated White House tour had its critics, such as the *Washington Post*'s Maxine Cheshire, who published an eight-part series in September 1962, speculating about the influence of French designer Stephane Boudin and sharing behind-the-scenes details about unnecessary expenditures and the first lady's reportedly sometimes poor behavior.[99] Jacqueline Kennedy's independence and initiative were largely accepted when they suggested some kind of service to the president or the nation, but if her behavior seemed at all self-serving, media was quick to draw attention to a perceived impropriety.

A 1962 Gallup poll revealed something of Americans' views of the unconventional first lady. What people liked best about Jacqueline Kennedy was reflected in the words they used to express their approval, which included "attractive, pretty, good-looking; good personality; intelligent, educated; makes a good impression abroad; interested in culture; a good mother; friendly, warm; a good mixer; poised; sweet, nice."

When describing what they liked least about JBK, those polled suggested the following areas of disapproval: "travels too much, away from family; in the limelight too much; her hairdo; her taste in clothes; undignified; her voice, the way she talks; spends too much money, wastes money; pictures in the paper in a bathing suit; doesn't wear the right attire to church; too much social life, parties."[100] Even this cursory overview reveals the tightrope the first lady walked. What some people liked best about Mrs. Kennedy might well be mentioned by others as among the first lady's failings. And there was an irony to critiques that the notoriously private Jacqueline Kennedy was regarded as too often in the "limelight."

Jackie Kennedy both was and was not what Americans expected—either as first lady, or as a woman in her own right. In Betty Houchin Winfield's evaluation of JBK, she notes that she took the "accepted, if not expected route." The ways Mrs. Kennedy was unexpected often generated positive public reaction and, in turn, received positive framing in mainstream media. JBK embraced heterosexual marriage, motherhood, and a feminine appearance—albeit one marked by modern fashion and style—and adopted sophisticated cultural pursuits not uncommonly assumed by women of an elite class. These pursuits, however, she embraced unapologetically, with demonstrated intelligence and expertise, in a public and professional manner. And she did so on a national stage, as potentially the most often featured woman in American media. In a male-dominated news world, the first lady stood out especially as a relatively rare woman in media's coverage of party politics. If the first lady was the woman interpreted to represent "public perceptions of the part women should play in American life," then Jacqueline Kennedy reflected, to some degree, competing expectations of American women, but also something of an undercurrent of change underway.[101] The question of how to reconcile questions of independence and duty, autonomy and support would continue to shape coverage of American women and media framing of Jacqueline Kennedy in the years to come, and perhaps never more than in the sustained coverage she received following the life-changing events of November 1963.

WIDOW

Investigating the public response to the assassination of John F. Kennedy, social scientists suggested that 90 percent of Americans were aware of the event within an hour after it happened. Even those who had not seen television reports or heard radio broadcasts learned from friends, family, or coworkers who had either called or shared the news in person.[1] From approximately 12:30 p.m., Central Standard Time, on Friday, November 22, 1963, when bullets struck the president's neck and the back of his head, until Monday, November 25, when his body was laid to rest at Arlington National Cemetery, American media produced a steady stream of reporting on the assassination and its subsequent investigation, the plans for John Kennedy's lying in state and funeral procession, and the possible future of the badly shaken nation. The Associated Press and United Press International sent news of the assassination to more than one hundred nations.[2] Networks canceled regularly scheduled television programs, and newspapers removed advertisements to make room for more assassination-related copy. The president's death was the only news through Monday night, as the media attempted to offer the American public both information and consolation.[3]

At the center of the unfolding events was Jacqueline Kennedy, at her husband's side during his Texas trip, embracing her role as asset to her husband's administration and in anticipation of the 1964 campaign.[4] Her proximity to her husband—her sharing of the physical space in which his assassination occurred, her subsequent efforts to remain close to his body, and her position as his wife—meant that Jacqueline Kennedy was a key figure in American media's and the American public's efforts to

President John F. Kennedy and first lady Jacqueline Kennedy arrive in Dallas, November 22, 1963. Cecil Stoughton, White House/John F. Kennedy Presidential Library and Museum.

process the assassination and memorialize the nation's fallen leader. Just as she crafted an iconic vision of her husband in the days following his death, her orchestration of and participation in his lying in state, funeral, and burial made her, too, an iconic figure for a generation of Americans.[5] Across that long weekend in November, Jacqueline Kennedy was the primary woman in the American imagination, and popular understanding of her in this moment took place through a particularly gendered lens.

Seated next to him in the limousine making its way from Dallas's Love Field to the Trade Mart where JFK was scheduled to deliver a luncheon address, Jackie Kennedy waved to one side of the crowd as her husband concentrated his attention on the other side of the street. Photographs of John Kennedy, captured in the seconds following the shooting, then, necessarily include Jacqueline Kennedy. Photographs taken immediately following the assassination are the only truly candid images of Jacqueline Kennedy in the whole of the imagery related to her husband's death. She climbed on the back of the limousine, ostensibly to retrieve whatever pieces of his skull had been dislodged by the bullet's blast. Images of JBK, in her pink Chanel suit, being pushed into the back seat by her Secret Service agent, Clint Hill, were among the most widely circulated in afternoon editions of newspapers or front pages appearing the next day.[6]

The other widely reprinted image of Jacqueline Kennedy, on November 23, and then in the days and weeks to follow, was of her standing by the side of Lyndon Johnson as he took the oath of office aboard Air Force One. Her trademark pillbox hat removed, Mrs. Kennedy had just lived through a harrowing two-hour period during which she had witnessed her husband's murder and seen her life changed irrevocably. Her face suggests something of the trauma she had endured, but in the most famous version of this photograph, she is not crying. She might best be described as shaken but composed, or, as Frances Lewine, who had covered her since her arrival in the White House, wrote, "with the tragedy written in her face."[7] Johnson requested her presence to serve a symbolic function: the wife of the slain president, witnessing his successor's swearing in, suggested a seamless—if jarring—transition of power.

President Lyndon B. Johnson is sworn in aboard Air Force One, with Jacqueline Kennedy by his side, November 22, 1963. Mrs. Kennedy agreed with LBJ that her presence would communicate the legitimacy of his presidency and help Americans accept the transition to his administration. Cecil Stoughton, White House/John F. Kennedy Presidential Library and Museum.

The system would hold. Jacqueline Kennedy believed Johnson was right in having her present. "In the light of history," she said, "it would be better if I was there."[8] However difficult it may have been for her, it was the right thing to do. It was a sacrifice worth making.

These elements of the photograph with Johnson, of Jacqueline Kennedy, shaken but composed and willing to sacrifice in order to do the right thing, were not just evident in that moment but are key themes for evaluating the public understandings of Mrs. Kennedy from the afternoon of November 22, when she prepared to return to the capital with her husband's body, to the evening of November 25, when, in the White House, she received the many foreign dignitaries who had traveled to Washington, DC, to join the slain president's funeral procession. In harnessing her emotions, Jacqueline Kennedy largely received praise from media, her husband's political compatriots, and the American people. In assessing her oversight of the funeral, oversight she refused to cede, words like "dignity," "honor," "courage," and "majesty" were among those most often used by those who honored the former first lady as they memorialized her husband. Mrs. Kennedy, it seemed, put her own grief to the side as she proceeded in service to others—her husband's memory, her children, and the nation as a whole. Such self-sacrifice generated tremendous praise.

Memorialists and journalists likewise used the language of instinct to describe Jacqueline Kennedy's actions. They sensed that JBK had responded instinctively to this tragedy, and with a predisposition for good taste, arranged her husband's lying in state, the details of his funeral and the funeral procession, and his final resting place. To suggest that this detailed planning was the result of instinct denies the very conscious decision-making process in which Jacqueline Kennedy engaged. Aside from her immediate reaction to the fatal bullets that pierced her husband's body, the primary instincts Jacqueline Kennedy displayed were a commitment to protect her husband's legacy and a determination to cement his place in history. From there, she took very deliberate care in the crafting of a funeral procession, and some have argued, even a mythology, of John F. Kennedy. Whatever she had learned of politics, media, and image in the years since she had become a politician's wife was on full display in the days following John Kennedy's assassination. For a figure so routinely dismissed as apolitical (a truism reasserted in assassination coverage), Mrs. Kennedy revealed a keen sense of pageantry and its uses. As Maurine Beasely writes of JBK, she was intensely attuned to the "importance of ceremony and the consolation of rituals." Mark White, in his assessment of the cultural history of John F. Kennedy iconography, evaluates Jacqueline Kennedy in this way: "It is easy to think of Jackie as being cut from a different cloth to her in-laws; her restrained elegance and their hard competitiveness. But when it came to her late husband's image and legacy, her pugnacity exceeded even theirs."[9]

But that is not necessarily how she was framed by those bearing witness to the very public mourning of a notoriously private figure. Jacqueline Kennedy, while clearly tied to her husband, had flourished as Jacqueline Kennedy (or even just "Jackie") during her tenure as first lady. In the aftermath of the president's death, she was, in many ways, recast as Mrs. John F. Kennedy. In relationship to her husband's assassination and her labor to prepare a funeral befitting the man and his office, her role as a dutiful wife and mother defined her. Even beyond her service to her immediate family, her care of the nation in this time of sorrow was given a maternal tint. Media suggested she had crafted the funeral to reflect her husband's interests and what he would have wanted. And in her bearing, observers claimed, she revealed a strength of character that spoke to principles her husband had embodied: most notably, courage and public service. Her behavior, a credit to her, was also a credit or a testimony to him. As the public assessed Jacqueline Kennedy's behaviors and arrangements over the grim days of late November 1963, she appeared more tied to her husband, more his wife than an independent figure in her own right, than she had been during much of their shared time in the White House. In placing duty to him—and to the nation— above her own emotional needs, she was in many ways the perfect, self-sacrificing wife. In this capacity, the authority she exerted in overseeing the president's memorialization largely was recognized and accepted by the American public. Understanding of Jacqueline Kennedy as Mrs. John F. Kennedy, his wife, and then his widow, dutiful even after his death, would be the lens through which many would evaluate her not just for the year of her official mourning but for the remainder of her life.

* * *

John Kennedy left no funeral plan. Catholic practice required burial of the dead within three days of expiration. Jacqueline Kennedy, just hours after she found herself a thirty-four-year-old widow, turned to the obligations at hand.[10] Mrs. Kennedy began her plans for the funeral while headed for Andrews Air Force Base aboard Air Force One. But the funeral was only one part of the responsibility she undertook. In addition to her recognition of her symbolic importance alongside Lyndon Johnson, she likewise understood the symbolic significance of her appearance and that of her slain husband. JBK was careful to keep her husband's wounded body from the cameras, intending that people's last memory of him be as he was in life rather than in death.[11] Mrs. Kennedy chose to remain in the attire she was wearing when her husband was killed, and journalists, who had long focused on the first lady's appearance, repeatedly remarked on the pink suit that became such an iconic symbol of the assassination.[12] She refused to wash the blood from her person, famously stating, "Let them see what they've done."[13] Rather than bringing her husband's body directly to Washington, DC, to be processed at Gawler's Funeral Home, she demanded he be brought to Bethesda Naval Hospital for his autopsy and preparation.[14] From the motorcade to Parkland Hospital to Air Force One to the Naval Hospital to the White House, Jacqueline Kennedy remained in her "blood-splattered suit, stockings and stained shoes" and never left her husband's side, information repeatedly referenced in written coverage of the assassination and confirmed via photographs reprinted widely throughout the United States.[15]

The details of Jacqueline Kennedy's experience on November 22, 1963, made their way into newspapers around the country by November 23 and continued to appear in the weeks that followed. Beyond the routine who, what, where, when, and why of journalism, however, the tragic and emotional nature of John Kennedy's assassination prompted an element of editorializing in reporters' coverage of Jacqueline Kennedy following her husband's murder. Journalists dramatized JBK's experience and suggested emotions she might have been feeling, even as she shared none of this with reporters. They speculated about her thoughts in a manner that emphasized her role as a devoted wife and mother. The nation had lost its leader, but she had lost her husband, and her children, a father. The sharing of personal and familial details, accurate or not, about a family Americans believed they had come to know generated enormous empathy as Americans imagined how they would have endured such a tragedy.[16]

The rapid transformation of Jacqueline Kennedy's Dallas motorcade experience was one trope employed by writers to communicate the shock of the assassination. Pictures of the Kennedys at Love Field, Jackie Kennedy with an enormous bouquet of roses in her arms, were paired with images from the motorcade after the shooting. With irony, several articles reported that Nellie Connally, first lady of Texas, riding with her husband, Governor John Connally, on the seat in front of the Kennedys, had turned to the president just before he was shot and said, "You can't say Dallas isn't friendly today."[17] An article from the November 28 *Bangor (ME) Daily News* underscored the instantaneous nature of JBK's changed status: "One moment a happy married woman, the first lady of a great nation; the next a young widow and a former first lady—her beloved husband of only 10 years cruelly take from her by the assassin's gun."[18] Adding to the horror, of course, was the fact that she bore witness to her husband's murder. Descriptions of Jacqueline Kennedy "cradling" her husband's "body in her arms," and "strok[ing] his brow as they rushed to the hospital" provided readers with a graphic depiction of events, one that emphasized the Kennedys' marital bond and communicated the first lady's devotion to her husband.[19]

Jacqueline Kennedy's very presence in Dallas underscored her commitment to her husband and his political endeavors. Coverage emphasized her willingness to aid him in advance of the 1964 campaign, which was precisely the reason she had joined him in Texas. As an article from the front page of the *St. Paul Dispatch* noted, "Mrs. Kennedy decided only this month to go politicking with her husband because he 'needed' her. Campaigning has never been her cup of tea, but she told staffers on the Texas trip, 'get set; we're going to do a lot of campaigning.' She was thrilled with the crowds who had turned out to see them."[20] Discussion of Jacqueline Kennedy's reluctance to enter the political world reinforced interpretations of her as an apolitical figure, which had been prevalent during the 1960 campaign, and ignored her political significance during JFK's administration. Such framing held to a fairly traditional understanding of "politics" that was domestic and campaign oriented and a world of men in which women played a tangential role.[21] It also underscored JBK's willing devotion to her husband's career and interests, despite her alleged distaste for politics, and further affirmed views of her as a model wife.

In reporting on Jacqueline Kennedy's immediate response to her husband's death, countless articles referenced her insistence on remaining by her husband's body. UPI reported, "Mrs. Kennedy said good-by to her husband with a kiss on his lifeless lips and then slipped her ring on his finger. And from then on—from the emergency room in the Dallas hospital through the sad flight home, to the naval hospital where he was prepared for burial until she brought him home in death to the White House—she was at his side."[22] A North Carolina article that identified JBK as "An American Heroine" reported on her tenderness, sharing that "when the body came off the plane, she was with it, touching the casket lightly, as though reaching out for a hand, and she rode with it, in the ambulance, to the Naval Hospital."[23] Media framed Jacqueline Kennedy as a figure of duty and devotion, committed to her husband in life and death. Visually representing this tie was the *Lebanon (PA) Daily News*, which placed photographs of the Kennedys' 1953 wedding alongside pictures of Jacqueline Kennedy following her husband's coffin into the White House.[24] Critiqued for what some considered a show of too much independence during her husband's administration, at the tragic end to John Kennedy's life and its immediate aftermath, Jacqueline Kennedy was assessed as a model of wifely virtue.

Linking her even more to family and private life, discussion of Jacqueline Kennedy's maternal role also appeared in consideration of the former first lady. Preston McGraw's widely reprinted article shared via UPI Dallas suggested that JBK's "thought was to return to Washington to her children, Caroline, 6, and John Jr., who will be three next week."[25] Media speculated about how Jacqueline Kennedy would share the news with the Kennedy children, who would be waiting not only for her but also, as the *St. Paul Dispatch* dramatically reminded its readers, "for their father, President John F. Kennedy, who will not return."

The public had become familiar with the children since they first entered the White House, and their father's "deep affection for them," the same *Dispatch* article asserted, "captured the nation's imagination."[26] The two children, whose birthdays were just days apart, were meant to have celebrated, first at the White House and then at Cape Cod, just before the traditional Kennedy Thanksgiving gathering at Hyannis Port.[27] Beyond the tragedy of Dallas, coverage of Mrs. Kennedy often reminded readers of the heartbreak of the recent death of her infant son, Patrick Bouvier Kennedy, who had been born on August 7 and died on August 9. The *Long Beach (CA) Independent-Press-Telegram* presented a sympathetic portrait of the former first lady in noting, "Of Mrs. John Kennedy it must be said that with the death of a husband following close upon the death of a child, she had had more grief in a few short months than any woman should be required to bear."[28]

Coverage of the events of November 22 played to readers' emotions, even as the *St. Paul (MN) Dispatch* reported, "It was a harsh day and it left Mrs. Kennedy dazed and tearless, almost unable to show emotion."[29] Publicly, JBK presented a composed face; privately, she had begun methodically determining her husband's funeral preparations. Perhaps Jacqueline Kennedy's most immediate decision regarding the funeral was that it should share key elements with the funeral of Abraham Lincoln, a president who also had presided over a divided nation and likewise been assassinated. An article in the special Memorial Section of the *Chicago Sun-Times*, published on December 29, 1963, took readers behind the scenes of efforts to carry out the decisions Mrs. Kennedy made while headed for Andrews Air Force Base. Robert Kennedy shared Jacqueline Kennedy's message with Kennedy brother-in-law Sargent Shriver after the president was pronounced dead: "Mrs. Kennedy has asked that this be as distinguished a tribute as we can possibly make it." With help from JFK's special assistant on the fine arts, Richard Goodwin, and family friend artist William Walton, Shriver began the process of modeling the East Room as it had been when Abraham Lincoln's body had lain in repose, a task that entailed the acquisition and arranging of black curtains, yellow candlesticks, antique oil lights, a crucifix, and an honor guard to "receive the President's body with appropriate dignity and ceremony." When Jacqueline Kennedy finally returned to the White House at 4:30 a.m., she declared that "everything had been done exactly as she would have done it."[30] On Saturday, November 23, more than four thousand "friends, officials, congressmen, diplomats, staff members, and newsmen" offered demonstrations of respect and mourning for the slain president.[31]

Jacqueline Kennedy determined other elements of her husband's funeral and lying in state, all of which combined to communicate a very specific image of the slain president. The funeral would be held at St. Matthew's Cathedral, just blocks from the White House. JBK rejected the idea of holding the funeral mass at the Shrine of the Immaculate Conception on Catholic University's campus in part because she and her family had never attended mass there and in part because she desired greater intimacy than the large basilica would provide. The proximity of St. Matthew's would allow Mrs. Kennedy to walk behind the casket as the funeral procession moved from the Capitol to the Church.[32] She chose singers from their 1953 wedding to perform at the funeral. The Irish Guard John Kennedy had admired during a 1963 trip to Ireland were invited to appear at the president's burial, and bagpipers who had delighted the president and his family on November 13 when they had played at the White House were asked to march in the funeral procession.[33]

Jacqueline Kennedy was the deciding voice on all details of the funeral, and she was not swayed by concerns related to outside preference or security. She committed herself firmly and fully to a memorialization of John F. Kennedy that communicated what she believed people ought to know about him: his idealism, his faith in democracy, his love of country. She, who had so clearly understood the importance of image and pageantry while serving as first lady, showed just how masterful was her grasp of political theater. The performances on the combined stages of the White House, the Capitol, St. Matthew's, the streets of Washington, DC, filled with a mourning public, and, finally, Arlington National Cemetery, communicated the image of a beloved leader who had died in service to a nation he had loved and honored. The catafalque on which his coffin rested was the same that had held President Lincoln, linking him to that much admired leader. The simple caisson that carried JFK's coffin, the very same that had carried Franklin Roosevelt's body in 1945, passing a diverse crowd of more than a million mourners, was meant to suggest something of Kennedy's democratic leanings, his lack of ostentation, and his appeal to the masses. Rather than acquiescing to Kennedy family requests to lay JFK to rest at the family's plot in Brookline, Massachusetts, Jacqueline Kennedy held firm that he belonged not just to the Kennedys but to the nation, and thus should be buried in a site of national honor. Her decision to light an eternal flame at the Arlington burial site guaranteed her husband a memorial that would become part of the patriotic pilgrimages so many American citizens made to the nation's capital.[34]

As first lady, Jacqueline Kennedy had often made the White House a place of theater and pageantry, and her sense of image and drama informed the plans she made for her husband's funeral, procession, and burial. The penchant for detail that had become so well-known among the White House staff was on full display in her plans to honor the slain president. Funeral invitations and the Mass cards, floral arrangements, musical accompaniments, the horses that would pull John Kennedy's caisson: she had specific ideas for each component of the pageant aimed to memorialize her husband. Efforts to commemorate John Fitzgerald Kennedy had to be in perfect alignment. Jacqueline Kennedy intended that the funeral say something about John Kennedy, the man, as much as John Kennedy the president. Emphasizing his religion, his heritage, and his interests, JBK created a memorial rife with symbolism, tinged with emotion, and marked by personal touches.[35]

Jacqueline Kennedy's first public appearance after the assassination took place on Sunday, November 24, when she accompanied her husband's casket from the White House to the caisson that would deliver JFK's body to the Capitol to lie in state. Via limousine, she traveled with her children to the Capitol Rotunda, where the casket was made available for viewing by the American public. After eulogies from Chief Justice Earl Warren, Speaker of the House John McCormack, and Senate Majority Leader Mike Mansfield, President Johnson laid a wreath by the casket. Before leaving the Rotunda, Jacqueline Kennedy, with Caroline, knelt beside the coffin and kissed the flag draped atop it. When she left the Rotunda with both of her children, John Jr. having been returned by the Secret Service agents who had taken him when he had become antsy during the program, Jacqueline Kennedy was met by thousands of mourners preparing to pay their respects to John Kennedy.

Monday, November 25, was the funeral. After retrieving the coffin from the Capitol and bringing it before the North Portico of the White House, more than one hundred world leaders, led by Jacqueline Kennedy, walked behind the caisson carrying John Kennedy's body to St. Matthew's Cathedral. Flanked on one side by Bobby Kennedy and on the other by Teddy Kennedy, Jacqueline Kennedy, face shrouded behind a black veil, remained completely composed walking not only before the crowds gathered on either side of the street but also before audiences— domestic and international—watching as the procession was broadcast live. Following the requiem mass, JBK, along with Caroline and John, followed the casket out of the cathedral and down its front steps, at which point John Jr., on his third birthday, issued his iconic salute.[36]

Following the mass, mourners traveled to Arlington National Cemetery where, just below the Custis-Lee Mansion, and in direct line of vision of the Washington Monument, John Kennedy was to be buried. After a military tribute, including a flyover by fifty jet fighters, representing each state of the union, a twenty-one-gun salute, and a lone bugler playing taps, the eight-man honor guard (integrated, to communicate John Kennedy's commitment to civil rights) folded the flag that had draped the president's coffin and handed it to cemetery superintendent John Metzler, who, in turn, handed it to Mrs. Kennedy. Once JBK received the flag, she took a lighted torch from a military officer and moved forward to light the Eternal Flame she had chosen for her husband's gravesite. Jacqueline Kennedy exchanged several words with the commanding officer, General Philip C. Wehle, thanking him for his efforts to see through her requests regarding her husband's burial. She then joined hands with Bobby Kennedy and left Arlington. Following the burial, she returned to

Robert (Bobby) Kennedy, Jacqueline Kennedy, and Edward (Teddy) Kennedy lead those walking in President John F. Kennedy's funeral procession to St. Matthew's Cathedral, November 25, 1963. Security concerns failed to dissuade Mrs. Kennedy from her determination to walk behind her husband's horse-drawn casket. Abbie Rowe, National Park Service/ John F. Kennedy Presidential Library and Museum.

the White House and received the foreign dignitaries who had come to pay tribute to her husband.[37] Though she was no longer first lady, this seemed her official conclusion to her tenure in that role.

* * *

Historians have written extensively about the myth making of John Kennedy's person, presidency, and legacy that originated in the events following his assassination. A mythic image of Jacqueline Kennedy like-wise emerged.[38] She controlled the details of her husband's viewing, funeral, and burial, and she controlled her emotions, but it was the media that framed a vision of Jacqueline Kennedy that in many ways, like their framing of her husband, was larger than life. She became, as many employed the title of John Kennedy's 1957 Pulitzer Prize–winning volume, "a profile in courage," a representative of the values many had so admired in her husband, a model for women to follow, and a source of national succor. She succeeded in shouldering an inconceivable weight, and evaluations of her public presentation in the days following the assassination often ascribed tremendous power to the former first lady. The gravity of the circumstances in which she found herself gave enhanced magnitude to the class and style she had demonstrated during her husband's administration and made those elements of her person that much more admirable. But even with a clear record of orchestrating performances and imbuing them with grandeur during her time as first lady, evaluation of the nature of Jacqueline Kennedy's power reflected a tension between agency and instinct and whether her power and performance were expressions of her own volition or inspired by her fallen husband. There appeared a reluctance to accept and acknowledge Mrs. Kennedy's capacity for political theater, an unwillingness to admit her capacity to understand the political world more broadly, and a desire instead to characterize her behaviors and decisions as testimony to her fallen husband. She claimed an authority in overseeing the tributes to John Kennedy, but the extent to which the public accepted her authority varied.

With so much television coverage being devoted to the assassination and funeral, Jacqueline Kennedy's plans and her performance were witnessed and evaluated on a massive stage. UPI television critic Rich Du Brow evaluated the importance of Mrs. Kennedy's behavior in relation to the distribution of her image. Calling her "courageous and dignified," Du Brow insisted that JBK's conduct was essential to building the "public confidence" of the "millions watching on television." Republicans and Democrats alike, he argued "are indebted to her immeasurably." He wrote, "With her triumph of taste, breeding and inner strength, and by her full public participation, she somehow gave a stately and noble ending to an event that began in sordidness and seeming insanity." While the participation of visiting foreign dignitaries communicated the seriousness of the procession, Du Brow suggested it was Mrs. Kennedy who set the tone for her husband's funeral, and relatedly, the nation's response to his death. "If she had failed at being up to the challenge, the tone of the proceedings—not only Monday but throughout the tragedy—could have descended to an even deeper gloom, collapse of prestige, and sense of hopeless barbarism than prevailed." Such analysis gives prodigious weight to Jacqueline Kennedy's importance as a public figure, and she, great responsibility, and reflects the broader sense of television's power in the early 1960s. As Du Brow continued, he revealed as much: "For televiewers, the symbolism of her bearing and courage for representatives of our friends and foes, and for the watching world, was explicit. For a woman who prizes privacy, dearly, it was a personal sacrifice and a national gesture in the great sense." But Du Brow stopped short of recognizing Jacqueline Kennedy's planning and behavior as a political act, hailing her contribution as "the legacy of non-political national honor as expressed by his lady."[39] As public as her mourning was, as much as she performed before an international audience, such an assessment of JBK relegated her to a more private role, limiting her political agency or authority.

Even if he was reluctant to ascribe political agency to her, Du Brow's sentiments reflected the near-universal praise given Jacqueline Kennedy for her composure. In the days immediately following the assassination, media reflected on the broad consensus: "A recurring theme expressed by every one of the newsmen who brought us the terrible details of tragedy has been admiration for Jacqueline Kennedy."[40] Chronicling Mrs. Kennedy's behavior step by step, the *Stanly News & Press*, of Albemarle, North Carolina, offered this assessment of her bearing across the span of events following John Kennedy's assassination: "Mrs. Jacqueline Kennedy cradled the head of her dying husband en route to the hospital, rode with his body in the plane to Washington, remained near him all through the night, visited him in repose in the East Room of the White House, maintained dignity and stately composure in all her many appearances at the Capitol, the final rites, and the reception afterward at which the heads of state formally paid their respects to her." Her behavior, the paper proclaimed, marked her as "heroic, an example for American womanhood of all the years to come."[41] Ruth Lee, writing for the *Springfield (GA) Herald*, gestured to the influence JBK had enjoyed before the assassination and suggested how that influence might serve a new purpose in years to come as she wrote, "Many have tried to imitate her in the past in dress, etc.; they would do well to take a lesson from her grace, dignity, and sense of duty in trying times."[42] If popular wisdom held that women were the "weaker sex," Jacqueline Kennedy's controlled emotional response to the national tragedy that affected her so personally suggested a reserve of strength. While assessments of the former first lady's behavior suggested that other women might aspire to emulate JBK, an alternative reading of her public performance might indicate the underlying strength so many women demonstrated not only in moments of crisis but as a cornerstone of their character. This likely was no surprise to women who assessed their abilities as separate and separately valuable from men's and were often called upon to demonstrate strength in private life, but this public expression by Jacqueline Kennedy offered a powerful representation of women's fortitude.[43] A column in the *Delaware County (PA) Daily Times* speculated on this sentiment directly, noting that "composure under fire—strength and persistence of purpose in the face of incredible tragedy" has "always been a woman's lot."[44]

Related to Mrs. Kennedy's grace under pressure was an associated courage in bearing the load of personal sorrow and civic obligation following her husband's death. The *Lewiston (ME) Evening Journal* recognized the specificity of JBK's case in noting, "Jacqueline Kennedy had proved herself eminently worthy as First Lady. She had displayed the sort of courage that may be found in few people. . . . This tremendously brave young wife and mother has held her head high and carried through a multitude of obligations which do not confront the average woman following the death of a husband." Those who had criticized JBK "as too young, too frequently pictured water skiing, and too much inclined toward high fashion" had underestimated "as brave an American woman as any who have been written about in history."[45] The *Portland Oregonian* recognized the effort of her self-presentation, referring to Mrs. Kennedy's "disciplined courage," while the *Mount Olive (NC) Tribune* attributed her ability to bear the strain of tragedy to her upbringing: "One might say that all her life's training, stemming as it did from wealth, position, and the best education, was to develop just the kind of person who would always do, say, and be the right thing. One could say, not unkindly, that for this she was born, and she was not untrue to her birth."[46] One Pennsylvania editorial went so far as to insist—with positive intent—that JBK was "an Aristocrat," possessing a "quality of bearing . . . which can hardly be learned in a lifetime. It takes generations." Jacqueline Kennedy proved in "her personal attention. . . . to details" that she was "equal to the hour, and the way she handled those details and carried herself during the hour of sorrow left no doubt in the minds of those who saw her on television" of her aristocratic nature.[47] These evaluations celebrated JBK's ability to show control and summon strength, whether from some inner reserve or from a lifetime of lessons related to proper comportment.

Other appraisals of Mrs. Kennedy, while positive, drew different conclusions about the root of her public behavior and stopped short of attributing whatever power she had wielded to her own calculation. A North Carolina story, while referring to JBK as "An American Heroine," called hers "a performance of instinct, not conscious direction," effectively denying her agency and ignoring the very specific direction she had given regarding the memorialization of her slain husband.[48] A Massachusetts media voice praised Jacqueline Kennedy's "control [over] her feelings and emotions," which allowed "that her husband's funeral would be a period of national solemnity, rather than hysteria."[49] But another Massachusetts organ suggested that the "personal courage" she showed was "natural" and "unwitting," denying conscious effort or awareness of the importance of her self-presentation.[50]

Some evaluations of Jacqueline Kennedy suggested that the bravery she demonstrated was an embodiment or a representation of the courage they believed to have defined John Kennedy. The valor she demonstrated and the contribution she made to the nation stemmed from a final fulfillment of wifely duty. Part and parcel of her "steadfast devotion" to JFK, her behavior reflected "the same type of strength her husband had displayed so many times."[51] Many journalists made use of John Kennedy's particular interest in courage, as evidenced by *Profiles in Courage*, in their discussion of Jacqueline Kennedy's comportment. A widely reprinted article from the Washington AP advocated that the next edition of JFK's book should include "a new chapter—a chapter leading all the rest. This—the world would agree—should bear the simple title 'Jacqueline.'"[52] Frances Lewine's widely reprinted re-creation of JBK's "ordeal" noted that the former first lady was "spared little" in the seventy-five hours that passed from John Kennedy's death to his burial, but had resolutely shown "determination to carry on in her husband's tradition of personal courage."[53] Her behavior, the *Greensboro (NC) Times* insisted, was not only in the spirit of her fallen husband ("the same type of strength her husband had displayed so many times") but was inspired by the loss of him: "The steadfast devotion to her husband was not displaced in her mourning, but was magnified, and we are certain, had her husband been present for the occasion, he would have said, 'Well done, Jackie.'"[54]

Overall, coverage attributed tremendous power to both Jacqueline Kennedy and the position of first lady. Claims of JBK's fitness for the non-office suggested a reverence for the role even above what had been demonstrated during the 1960 campaign when critics had doubted her potential to fill the position sufficiently. But in the capacity of the assassination, JBK, as recent first lady, evaluators asserted, served as a representative of the nation, in this instance, in her slain husband's stead. She shouldered a weight that was not outlined, but that observers seemingly took for granted and seemed to believe only she could have endured in the graceful style she did. The American penchant for individualism was on full display, both in the suggestion of one person's value and heroism and in the belief in Jacqueline Kennedy's position as that one person. Like the exceptional women celebrated in midcentury periodicals, the women who possessed such particular skill and resolve to stand out among all other women, Mrs. Kennedy likewise possessed singular qualities that allowed her to deliver a particular kind of succor to a nation badly in need of comfort and reassurance.[55]

* * *

In the weeks following the assassination and funeral, Jacqueline Kennedy received sustained consideration. Supplementing the immediate coverage Americans had learned from television and their local newspapers, weekly news magazines, in their issues following JFK's death, reported on the series of events following his assassination with greater distance and consideration of their broader meaning. In a "Letter from the Publisher," *Life*'s C. D. Jackson praised the speed and breadth of coverage from other forms of media, and expressed his desire that *Life* not merely "reprise the hour-by-hour events" or "duplicate the newspapers' wealth of information." The publication, so well known for its photo essay, aimed "to bring memorable moments into sharp focus; to show with force and clarity the faces and hearts of people caught up in the news; to paint with swift, broad strokes a look and feel of the event that would stand for many years as a permanent record of the day; to make all who shared in it agree, this week or a decade from now, 'yes, that's how it was.'"[56] Of the news weeklies, *Life*, especially, had a massive reach; a 1954 study suggested the magazine reached 22.5 percent of the population. For coverage of the topic of Kennedy's death, its reach likely extended further.[57]

The image-heavy glossy weeklies printed variations of images many Americans already had seen, in many of which Jacqueline Kennedy was at the center. Perhaps because of the more compact nature of these periodicals, and the holistic presentation they provided of the assassination and events following, citizens were inclined to preserve them. Beyond the planned weekly issue, magazines like *Life* also produced a special John F. Kennedy Memorial Edition, which included compiled coverage along with selected quotations that best reflected the emerging mythic view of JFK. Americans rightly assessed the historic nature of this event even as it was happening. After reading the November 29 issue, Paul Jokelson of Scarsdale, New York, wrote *Life* to share that he would "keep it for myself and my children as a memento of our late President." Hans Sachs of New York City went further, calling the issue "an unforgettable document of our time, worthy of being preserved for our children and grandchildren." Others wrote to request a rerunning of issues that had sold out, revealing the national demand for commemoration of President Kennedy.[58] These periodicals shared with television and daily news coverage in constructing a lasting narrative of the assassination, its aftermath, and its meaning for the American nation and its people.

In their text, the weekly magazines' assessments of Jacqueline Kennedy mirrored much of what had been written in newspapers around the nation. Dora Jean Hamblin's essay in the December 6 issue of *Life* celebrated Jacqueline Kennedy's sense of "solemn pageantry." Hamblin praised JBK's attention to detail, and her commitment to arranging the memorializing of her husband with elements "that the President would have liked."[59] In an article considering all members of the extended Kennedy family, *Time* emphasized Jacqueline Kennedy's sense of responsibility and authority, her sense that she, among all those who had known him, knew how to orchestrate her husband's funeral: "Well aware that her family and friends might otherwise spare her painful decisions, she insisted that she meant to see to it 'that people will remember all the best things about him.'"[60] *Newsweek* rounded out this sentiment, in noting, "Her bearing through a three-day public ordeal gave poignant meaning to her husband's memory after the brutal pointlessness of his murder. A nation that ached to comfort a widow took heart itself from her courage and grace." In considering the excellence and emotion of JFK's funeral, the magazine gave Jacqueline Kennedy full credit: "The details that cut the day to the measure of John F. Kennedy reflected the wishes and the taste of Mrs. Kennedy. 'She wanted,' as one aide explained afterward, 'to make this *his*.'"[61] As his wife, she was uniquely tied to him and thus was uniquely qualified to craft the most fitting of memorials. She had orchestrated the funeral and endured the tragedy as she had as a testimony to him and in service not only of him but of the nation.

An advantage the magazines had, as Jackson suggested, was an opportunity to assess the various elements of the assassination and the
days following as a whole, considering their influence as a collective.
Hamblin's essay, for example, beyond repeating sentiments previously
expressed, evaluated Jacqueline Kennedy's significance in the larger
sequence of events. With particular consideration of the subsequent
events transpiring in Dallas, when Jack Ruby broke through police
lines to shoot and kill assassin Lee Harvey Oswald, an event broadcast
live on national television, Hamblin imagined the importance of the
contrast JBK provided to this scene. She wrote, "From this primitive
violence the watchers could turn to see Mrs. Kennedy, in a black suit
and black lace mantilla, walking out of the White House and up the 36
marble steps of the Capitol. There was no hand at her shoulder, no veil
to hide her face. With each gloved hand she held a small hand, and her
quiet eyes were fixed on the casket moving slowly up the steps ahead of
her." In a world seemingly descending into chaos, Hamblin suggested,
Jacqueline Kennedy provided an image of dignified composure. Instead
of the worst of what the nation offered, she suggested the best.[62] Adding to that sentiment was the *Saturday Evening Post*'s sharing of "other
remarkable, less-publicized things" Mrs. Kennedy did "in the first day
of her grief." The *Post* reported what Americans might not have known,
given attention to other elements of that November weekend: "She offered Mrs. Johnson all her help for their move into the White House.
Then she called in her brother-in-law, Attorney General Kennedy, and
asked him to phone the wife of Dallas detective J. D. Tippitt, who
had been killed by Lee Harvey Oswald, the principal suspect in the
assassination of her husband. 'What that poor woman must be going
through,' said Mrs. Kennedy."[63]

Greater detail about Jacqueline Kennedy's hand in directing John
Kennedy's funeral and previously unknown elements of her responses
to events in which she was inextricably bound enhanced both admiration and sympathy for the former first lady. A feminized maternal
calm contrasted greatly with male violence. Notions of Mrs. Kennedy's
nurturing sympathy, extended during her own time of grief, suggested

kindness and a giving nature, a penchant to put others before herself. Self-sacrifice in the name of others has long been an idealized attribute of womanhood, and JBK's willingness to put the nation's relief above her own made her the ultimate symbol of an esteemed feminine ideal. But those details came second hand, as news shared with journalists by those to whom Mrs. Kennedy had shared her thoughts, or as assessments made by those bearing witness to her behavior.

In the December 6 issue of *Life* readers received their first insight from Jacqueline Kennedy herself. The standout piece in the spate of issues coming in the weeks following the assassination, Theodore White's "Epilogue for President Kennedy" was an essay informed directly by White's visit with Jackie Kennedy at Hyannis Port just after the 1963 Thanksgiving holiday. She recalled to White what she remembered of November 22, the hot sun and the tremendous crowds. After her husband was shot, she remembered efforts to "separate him from her, to sedate her, and take care of her." But she would not allow it: "She wanted to be with him." She told White that when Patrick died, JFK had placed his St. Christopher medal in the baby's coffin. He had asked her to give him another on their tenth wedding anniversary. She had found that medal, given barely two months before, on his body after the assassination. In just a few paragraphs, Mrs. Kennedy effectively communicated her devotion to her husband, and his devotion to both his family and his faith. She made elements of their private life part of the public record in a manner that she, the far more private partner in their union, typically did not.

But her remarks to White were not merely meant to share an inside view on the day of the assassination or even the Kennedy family. Her aims were much further reaching. She endeavored to establish a legacy for her husband's presidency and the memory that would follow. She regretted not remembering one of "Jack's" usually "classical" quotes, establishing his intellect, and instead coming back, time and again, in the days since his assassination to "this line from a musical comedy . . . he loved to hear: *Don't let it be forgot, that once there was a spot, for one brief shining moment that was known as Camelot.*" She tied that line, and her husband's alleged love for it, directly to his administration, saying to White, "There'll be great Presidents again . . . but there'll never be another Camelot again." Her husband had countered her sense of history as "something that bitter old men wrote" with his "hero idea of history, the idealistic view," which, very clearly, was the way she wished people—and history—to remember her husband, as the man who had given the nation "one brief shining moment."

It is in Jacqueline Kennedy's discussion with White that any suggestion of her "instinctual" responses to the assassination again must be dismissed. JBK reveals—as she had during her years as first lady—that she understood very clearly the power of image and media. Beyond understanding the power of image and media in politics, Mrs. Kennedy likewise seemed aware of her own power. As the person imagined to be closest to John Kennedy, in an era still of assumed "togetherness" between husbands and wives, when there was meant to be a particular link and fulfillment found in matrimony, Jacqueline Kennedy claimed—and was granted—authority over the intimate details and thoughts of her husband's life. In this moment, one of the few times she would speak publicly of private recollections of her husband, she established a long-lasting view of President Kennedy. Following the funeral and memorialization she had orchestrated, her framing of her husband's administration as a kind of modern-day Camelot punctuated the vision she had crafted in the days immediately following the assassination. Such was the power of Jacqueline Kennedy's framing that White communicated it without challenge. When the first round of scholarship on John Kennedy's administration appeared—penned primarily by his intimates, like Arthur Schlesinger and Ted Sorensen— they balked at this framing, but failed to challenge it directly. With deference to Jacqueline Kennedy, they accepted this narrative of her husband as they accepted her authority over his legacy.[64]

In attempting to solidify her husband's place in American history and the public imagination, Jacqueline Kennedy's suggestion about the significance of JFK's administration played to a view of John Kennedy as a man of style rather than substance. His administration had not been one of universal successes, on fronts foreign or domestic. For Jacqueline Kennedy, though, her husband's importance was as much in what he represented as in what he accomplished. The feeling of his administration, the sense of youth and vitality and possibility, that she had helped cultivate, was an intangible that seemingly resonated with many Americans and especially after the tragic nature of his death, an intangible that Michael Hogan argues "had more to do with myth, magic, legend, saga, and story than with political theory or political science." Hogan posits that JBK constructed Camelot to avoid historical accounts that focused too much on "a narrative of presidential achievement and could not fully capture what her husband had meant to the nation."[65] Similarly, historian John Hellman suggests that Jacqueline Kennedy's interview with White demonstrated a kind of "grand intimacy" through which "she offered the public what she believed was the right way to understand the Kennedy administration, and thus the seeming absurdity of its abrupt end."[66]

Media coverage was not the only location where emotion and sentiment and feeling pervaded discussion of John Kennedy's death. In the weeks following the assassination, congressional representatives joined together to share memorial addresses and tributes in eulogy to the slain president. Jacqueline Kennedy's construction of her husband's administration as a kind of Camelot resonated among these elected officials, some of whom submitted White's essay along with their own remarks or included quotations from the article in their statements, as part of the official record.[67] Whether motivated by an effort to shore up political power or a demonstration of authentic emotion, acquiescence to Jacqueline Kennedy's construction of her husband's immediate legacy suggests that her vision struck a chord as members of the House and the Senate alike paid tribute to the "myth, magic, legend, saga, and story" of John Kennedy and thereby accepted the authority of his widow to frame his presidency.

Beyond the dedications to John Kennedy, representatives and senators shared their views on JBK's importance, views that often echoed those expressed and made popular by recent American media, views that contributed to a widespread popular imagining of Jacqueline Kennedy. Themes of duty and devotion, to both her husband and her nation, joined with celebrations of her courage and her position as a model for others to follow. Some politicians shared their own views, while others included sermons from religious figures or articles from local newspapers, or, like Warren G. Magnuson of Washington, inserted an address by former Washington congressman and United States senator Mr. Clarence C. Dill, which Dill had delivered on November 25, 1963, at the Spokane, Washington, courthouse: "In all the mythological tales of the love of gods and goddesses, in all the love stories of the kings and queens of history, in all of Shakespeare's creation of love scenes, you will not find such a beautiful, exquisitely fine demonstration of wifely love as Jacqueline Kennedy's act to symbolize her everlasting devotion."[68]

The sense of history, aided by the passage of several weeks since the assassination, also factored into assessments of Jacqueline Kennedy. She may have originated the myth making of her husband in her orchestration of the funeral and interview with Theodore White, but politicians building on post-assassination coverage contributed to a mythic view of Jacqueline Kennedy as a figure of particular historical significance. Congressman John E. Moss of California asserted, "A tribute to President Kennedy would not be complete without mention of the great courage of his widow. Her conduct from the moment tragedy struck should make every American more proud. Perhaps no woman in history was ever called upon to play a more difficult role under more brutal or tragic circumstances. No one could have done it better." Moss referenced the British assessment of Mrs. Kennedy's having given "the American people something they lacked . . . 'majesty.'" He continued, "We must recognize that the grief felt by each of us was only a small part of that felt by her. How many of us with our small part of the burden could have conducted ourselves with the grace, the courage, and the majesty of Jacqueline Kennedy?" Congressman Edward P. Boland of Massachusetts expressed a similar sentiment in stating, "At no time within the memory of man has such a burden of grief blanketed a wife and mother. And never has anyone stood so erect, so majestic in such anguished hours. She has set an example and inspiration that can never be surpassed."[69] The notion that Jacqueline Kennedy and only Jacqueline Kennedy was capable of bearing up under such pressures echoed the celebration of the individual presented in American media and made JBK a figure of particular national significance.

Other addresses likewise celebrated Jacqueline Kennedy in an individual capacity, but in a manner that suggested her actions had been fundamental to the nation's ability to go on in the wake of her husband's assassination. In assessing the importance of Kennedy's funeral and the successful transition of power, Senator James O. Eastland of Mississippi said, "The events that have transpired since the fatal moment on Friday afternoon, November 22, have again demonstrated the awesome majesty and dignity involved in maintaining the continuity of government in these United States. The beloved wife of the deceased President played a brave and courageous role in this solemn and heart-rending drama." Beyond the maintenance of American government, Minnesota congressman Joseph Karth declared that "the majesty of [Jacqueline Kennedy's] presence turned a Nation transfixed by the awful horror at Dallas to what in effect became a reconsecration of our democratic institutions." New York congressman Seymour Halpern saw Jacqueline Kennedy's comportment as more than a demonstration of "the utmost love for her husband." In his estimation, she had shown "a noble concern for the welfare of our country, and a touching courtesy toward all who came to mourn her husband's death." Representative Roman C. Pucinski shared a similar view in noting, "In the depth of her tragedy, Mrs. Kennedy, through her stature and her majestic behavior, has given all of us as Americans the strength we needed in our moment of greatest despair." Rather than merely inspiring women with her behavior, Jacqueline Kennedy had inspired the whole of American citizenry. California congressman Harlan Hagen said this directly: "In the grim days following the death of her husband . . . Jacqueline Kennedy demonstrated qualities of courage, devotion, and dignity which will live in the memory of us all. I am certain that her reactions under stress inspired millions of Americans to lead better lives in the service of our society."[70] In these assessments and those like them, politicians attributed tremendous power to Jacqueline Kennedy. And yet, even as identifying her position as one of power expanded the notion of who and what might be considered political, in tying JBK back to her husband, the eulogies situated her as much in the private realm as they did the public and political world.

Even more than offering thanks to Jacqueline Kennedy for what she had done, either as first lady or in the days of her most immediate widowhood, some political figures suggested the ongoing nature of Mrs. Kennedy's civic responsibility. In the address delivered by Joe Skubitz of Kansas, Skubitz said, "John Fitzgerald Kennedy is gone. But as surely as the night follows the day the spirit of John F. Kennedy will live on. His work is finished. The heavy burden now falls upon the shoulders of his wife, Mrs. Jacqueline B. Kennedy." Skubitz continued by celebrating "the courage, the fortitude, the majesty" of Mrs. Kennedy, and its effect on those watching her. His sense that she would shoulder a future burden indicates an expectation that she would continue to perform some kind of public role now that her husband's ability to do so had come to a conclusion. The Republican congressman imagined a continued link between Jacqueline Kennedy and John Kennedy, and his language indicated an expectation that she would become the public representative of her slain husband's legacy and ideals. Kentucky congressman John C. Watts assessed Jacqueline Kennedy at an even higher level. He declared that Mrs. Kennedy's "dignity, love, and courage . . . obliterated the evil of that moment in Dallas." In so doing, he asserted, "She has symbolized, for all the world to behold, the triumph of good over evil."[71] This is the public image she would have to live up to for years to come.

* * *

The Eternal Flame at Arlington became a kind of consecrated site, significant and symbolic of the promise tied to John Kennedy's rhetoric.[72] Due in part to the traumatic nature of Kennedy's assassination but also shaped by the response to his death, largely led by Jacqueline Kennedy, he "became sanctified, looming larger than life as a sacred symbol of tragedy and heroism in American life."[73] In death, John Kennedy became a symbol as much of what he might have been as of what he, in fact, had been. Those left in his wake, for the foreseeable future, inevitably would falter in comparison to a man who became, in the days and weeks following his death, shrouded in myth. Assessments of Jacqueline Kennedy cast the former first lady also in mythic terms. Congressmen Roland V. Libonati of Illinois, in eulogizing JFK, regarded JBK as "the true mother with her darlings at her side, statuesque in bearing, facing her grief with regal acceptance of tragedy, like the Madonna at the Crucifixion." She "stood in silent adoration of her love with a dignity that captured the hearts and emotions of millions throughout the world. No one can deny that as the late lamented President passed through the Portals of Oblivion, a deep sense of pride for her permeated his very soul."[74] A still-living madonna, having pleased a slain martyr, inevitably would find it difficult to live up to the standard even of herself.

The nation mourned John Fitzgerald Kennedy. But pockets of its citizenry viewed his death with ambivalence, if not delight. The Texas trip, and the visit to Dallas, in particular, had been regarded by the Kennedy staff with a sense of trepidation. They had anticipated a hostile response in the conservative hotbed. William Manchester, author of the official history of the assassination that would be published four years later, included a particularly hostile response to the first lady in an anecdote about an Oklahoma City physician whose reaction to the assassination was to grin and say, "Good, I hope they got Jackie."[75]

Such a hateful comment suggested a contingent who were unimpressed and unmoved by the venerated portrait of the former first lady that emerged in the early days and months following John Kennedy's death. While less cruel, responses collected from a study of college students responding to the assassination likewise diverged from positive feelings for JBK. As one of the college students, interviewed immediately following the assassination, said, "You know, she is still very young and attractive," but, he added, "she's finished, really as a woman. I really feel as though she's had it."[76] This same young man recalled, "An announcer said, 'Mrs. Kennedy is acting impeccably.' Those were his words. 'Impeccably,' I remember that one, and I didn't like it at all. I thought she's been acting impeccably for too long." When asked what this indicated to him, the man continued, "I thought if she had shown some emotion, I might have felt 'well maybe she really is a real person.' I don't know, I just . . . never did like her." Providing a minor defense of Mrs. Kennedy was another student who noted, "I don't think the camera could show it that well. From their description she was fairly red-eyed most of the time and that is evident. Now she didn't break down sobbing, or anything like that, but I think if you'd ever seen anybody do that in a funeral, it bothers you even more than a person who can compose himself, stay fairly well composed, and I think she did that and that's to her credit." Another student chimed in, "As long as I'm reassured that the emotion is there, I admire her for remaining composed. I had no desire for her to break down and cry and all."[77]

The notoriously private Jacqueline Kennedy mourned on a world stage, largely as a means of paying tribute to her fallen husband. In adopting such a public role, she subjected herself to assessment above and beyond even what she had known as first lady. While the majority of the coverage JBK received celebrated her decorum and composure, her dignity and sense of ceremony, she was not immune from critique. For the Oklahoma City doctor who hoped for her demise, she was almost surely an extension of her fallen husband, an embodiment of his politics so derided by an increasingly vehement right wing of the Republican Party. The interviewed college students, dissatisfied with the performance of her mourning, saw JBK as a figure they had a right to judge and who, it seemed, should have been cognizant of the obliga-tion she had—to them, to the nation—to behave as they imagined fit. In either case, she was not a person of her own volition. She belonged either to one man, or to an entire nation.

As first lady, Jacqueline Kennedy emerged as Jacqueline Kennedy, a figure in and of her own right. With her husband's murder, with her dedication to crafting the beginnings of his legacy, she underwent a reframing that, in many ways, cast her as Mrs. John F. Kennedy. Even

Jacqueline Kennedy departs the White House with her children, December 6, 1963. Cecil Stoughton, White House/John F. Kennedy Presidential Library and Museum.

in her position as a wife, or, more accurately, a widow, roles for women with which the broader American culture was comfortable and familiar, a public woman was afforded a fairly fine line. She should show emotion but not too much emotion. She should embody the political principles of her husband but in a manner that made clear that they came from him. In the case of Jacqueline Kennedy, responses to her in the aftermath of the assassination suggested that the public had full and legitimate right to assess her look, her public behaviors, and her private decisions. And so while the public granted JBK some measure of authority after her husband's death, there remained a contingent confident in their right to assess and critique the former first lady. The matter-of-factness with which such members of the public evaluated JBK suggests that this was the standard a public woman accepted if she wished to remain in the public eye.

Not two weeks after the assassination, in her famed interview with Theodore White, Jacqueline Kennedy expressed horror at speculation she might leave the United States to live abroad. To White, she said, "I'm *never* going to live in Europe. I'm not going to 'travel extensively abroad.' That's a desecration. I'm going to live in the places I lived with Jack. In Georgetown, and with the Kennedys at the Cape. They're my family."[78] At this point, she provided evidence of her dedication to her husband's memory, and the familial legacy to which her children—Kennedy children that they were—belonged. Her interview with White was part of that. In 1964, when she sat down with Arthur Schlesinger to record her reminiscences of her husband, she likewise dedicated herself to the building of John F. Kennedy's legacy. Following her husband's death, her plan was a year of mourning. In that year, she would find her position as a public figure intensified by the specter of her husband and what his memory came to mean to the nation. The nature of her fame, the inescapability of her husband's memory, and social and cultural changes underway—in that first year and then in the years beyond—would transform public reactions and responses to JBK, and the result would be a far more complicated range of understandings of the woman cast as martyred widow in late 1963.

[4]

SINGLE WOMAN

By the Monday following John F. Kennedy's death, Jacqueline Kennedy had received forty-five thousand condolence letters. Within seven weeks, she had received eight hundred thousand such messages. As late as 1965, she continued to receive fifteen hundred to two thousand letters each week, for a total that ultimately exceeded 1.5 million pieces of correspondence.[1] On January 14, 1964, she issued her first public statement since the assassination. On a nationally televised broadcast she thanked the American people for their outpouring of sympathy and support. "The knowledge of the affection in which my husband was held by all of you," she said, "has sustained me and the warmth of these tributes is something I shall never forget." Making clear her ongoing bereavement, she noted of the letters received, "Whenever I can bear to, I read them."

Jacqueline Kennedy intended to acknowledge every letter. She further intended that each should be saved and placed in a library paying tribute to her late husband. Delighted that she might one day share with her children this evidence of their father's effect on the world, she imagined a larger audience, one comprised of "future generations" who would one day learn "how much our country and people in other nations thought of him." To the American public watching her broadcast, she said, "I hope that in years to come many of you and your children will be able to visit the Kennedy Library. It will be, we hope, not only a memorial to President Kennedy, but a living center of study of the times in which he lived and a center for young people and for scholars from all over the world." Jacqueline Kennedy, whose decisions immediately following John Kennedy's death had created a specific and celebrated image of the man, revealed in this broadcast that her image-making efforts were far from complete.[2]

The letters Americans and citizens of the world sent to Jacqueline Kennedy, however, were hardly focused only on John F. Kennedy. The image making of the White House years and then those terrible November days had established, for many Americans, a particular vision not only of John Kennedy but of his wife as well. Many writers celebrated Jacqueline Kennedy's comportment in the aftermath of the assassination, and language employed in letters echoed mainstream American media's assessments of Mrs. Kennedy in the time following her husband's death. Dr. Robert Cates of Jackson, Mississippi, praised JBK's "absolute dignity, strength and grace," while Madge E. Asselta of Hyattsville, Maryland, celebrated JBK's "unselfishness" and wrote, "You are a great lady, Mrs. Kennedy, and you put us all to shame when you showed us what courage means."[3]

Some citizens hoped Mrs. Kennedy's public life would not come to an end. Some expressed the sentiment that, in their minds, Jacqueline Kennedy would forever be first lady.[4] In February 1964, Janeen Ostby of Pomona, California, imagined a range of possibilities for JBK's future: "When your official year of mourning is over, I hope that you will return to some facet of public life. You are qualified to enter so many fields—art, journalism, government, fashion, etc. You truly have become a symbol and a goal for American womanhood with your sense of beauty, dignity and grace." The sense of Mrs. Kennedy as a symbol of womanhood was one shared by Airman Third Class Kenneth R. Wiggs Jr. From Lowry Air Force Base, Wiggs identified JBK's symbolic importance and asserted that she meant as much to the nation as her husband had.[5] So great was her effect on the population that Philadelphians Mr. and Mrs. Hugh B. Robinson Jr. insisted to Jacqueline Kennedy, "You have set a standard that no woman could possibly equal."[6]

Beyond JBK's public life and meaning, condolence letters also addressed the future of her personal life and wished for her an eventual return to happiness. Moved by her television thank you, Mary F. Nies of Florence, South Carolina, wrote with feeling to Mrs. Kennedy and reflected the closeness many Americans had felt to the First Family: "Why shouldn't I say to you what I would say to a good friend: that I hope you will marry some day someone who will give you and the children love and companionship. There are many who care about you and want you to be happy." In the same spirit, Dora W. Wildesen of Gormonia, West Virginia, wrote, "I hope my dear you will fine [sic] some fine man who will make a good husband and father to your children. You are to [sic] young to live alone."[7] Mrs. Kennedy had achieved happiness, many writers believed, as a married woman. To achieve happiness again, then, would require another marriage.

Little more than two weeks following the assassination, Ethel M. Robinson of Norristown, Pennsylvania, wrote that she hoped JBK would now "enjoy a greater measure of privacy."[8] The extent of the correspondence Mrs. Kennedy had received to this point—and then would continue to receive—cast a dubious shadow on public acceptance of such an effort to retreat to a private existence. As the standard to which other women—and she, herself—would be measured, JBK failed to receive a reprieve from the public curiosity and media attention that had become ubiquitous during her White House years. In the early months following John Kennedy's death, representations of Jacqueline Kennedy focused primarily on her transition from wife to widow, on the tragedy that had befallen her, and on her efforts to soldier on for the sake of her children, her husband's memory, and a country in mourning.

As the 1960s progressed, the United States found itself a nation in flux. Just as the country changed, so too did Jacqueline Kennedy. Not content to serve indefinitely as national widow or shattered martyr, positions in which she had been granted a measure of authority and a right to a public voice, Jackie Kennedy continued to live, despite one letter writer's suggestion that "a part of you died when your husband died."[9] Part of JBK's life remained dedicated to her children and her husband's memory, but another part of her life appeared dedicated to reclaiming her sense of self. As much as well-wishers desired happiness for her, and eventually, a return to romance, the public had a sense of what that happiness should entail, how Jacqueline Kennedy should behave, and who the appropriate man for her might be. Rather than a mourning widow, by the mid-1960s, Jacqueline Kennedy appeared more like one of the independent single women increasingly visible in American culture. The autonomy she claimed raised questions not only about the ways she was conducting her private life and personal relationships but also about the means by which she endeavored to oversee the legacy of John F. Kennedy and her right in doing so. The authority she enjoyed as a widow was replaced by a media framing of a Jacqueline Kennedy in need of guidance, a woman who would do better to rely upon the voices and opinions of a concerned Kennedy family or of the American public more broadly. They, not she, knew what was best for her.[10] The transformation of public sentiment regarding Jacqueline Kennedy— which became increasingly critical as the 1960s progressed—revealed cultural anxiety about an independent woman dedicated to pursuits and interests beyond the familial or domestic, particularly as this style of womanhood became increasingly widespread and the woman touted as the "model" for American womanhood seemed to embody it.

* * *

In the year following John Kennedy's death, during which Jacqueline Kennedy committed herself to a year of mourning, public attention to and desire for information about the Kennedy family failed to wane.[11] At various points through 1964, the nation's glossy picture magazines, respectable, mainstream institutions of the media world, paid particular homage to John Kennedy, and by association, his widow. Mrs. Kennedy, who preferred to celebrate her fallen husband on his birthday, May 29, rather than his assassination anniversary, cooperated with *Life* magazine to create an issue featuring the former president's personal effects. These would be on display as part of a special exhibit opening in New York City and then traveling the nation to raise funds for the John F. Kennedy Presidential Library. Certain that people would want to see his famed desk and iconic rocking chair, Jacqueline Kennedy, with the help of Robert Kennedy, selected additional items that would reveal a "rather personal side of the President." "I have parted with some of our greatest treasures, the pictures, objects and books, which he always kept at home," she said. "These are the things I hope will show people how he really was."[12] Among the items featured in *Life* were the president's beloved scrimshaw, a painting he had completed during his convalescence from back surgery in 1955, and a childhood letter he had written, justifying his request for a raise in his allowance.[13]

Both the *Life* issue, published approximately six months after her husband's death, and the memorial issue of *Look*, published near the one-year anniversary of his assassination, emphasized the turmoil Jacqueline Kennedy had endured since she had accompanied her husband to Dallas in November 1963. *Life* suggested she had imposed "social exile . . . on herself." The library planning seemed her most public activity, but her appearances, the periodical noted, were "restricted geographically to the world in which she now lives—Washington, New York, Boston." While *Life* noted that JBK had crafted for herself and the children a routine, the paragraphs following the depiction of the exhibit's items suggested a pervasive grief that was "quiet and constant."[14] The omnipresence of her husband's memory, and her struggle to manage her anguish, were echoed in the *Look* memorial issue from November 1964. Kennedy intimate Laura Bergquist penned the article, which was accompanied by images of John Jr., Caroline, and Jacqueline Kennedy with the extended Kennedy family at the Hyannis Port compound. After her courageous public display at her husband's funeral and burial, Bergquist wrote, Jackie Kennedy encountered "abysses of despair when she thought she *couldn't* manage or go on; when she felt 'I am a living wound,' and wondered if she wasn't failing her children as a mother—perhaps it would be better for them to live with Uncle Bobby and his family. No, said her brother-in-law, she had to carry on. And so she did." While sometimes, Bergquist asserted, Mrs. Kennedy imagined, "'My life is over,'" she ultimately was buoyed by her responsibility to Caroline and John, her obligation "to get through one day after another until the children were grown and on their own."[15]

Jacqueline Kennedy cooperated with these publications, and so this depiction could be regarded as the result of emotions she was unable to conceal, a conscious crafting of image, or some combination of both. *Life* noted that in Jacqueline Kennedy's "small world," "Friends find her almost always in a reminiscent mood." Socializing with the Kennedy brothers, members of John Kennedy's ever-loyal inner circle, and friends they had shared, *Life* reported, "They all talk about the late President much of the time."[16] Bergquist's portrait of JBK a year after her husband's death suggests Jacqueline Kennedy's preoccupation not only with her husband's death but also with his image and his memory. Mrs. Kennedy aimed not to be "bitter," but seemed to reel at the injustice "that he who was so unvindictive toward his political opponents could inspire such hatred . . . that he who loved children so had to suffer the loss of Patrick. . . . that she couldn't have borne more children for him . . . that the world, while remembering him, tends to think of him as an 'atypical' President, as if an American politico could not be civilized and literate . . . that a man whose emotions ran so deep was stereotyped as 'cool and detached.'"[17]

While sympathetic to Jacqueline Kennedy, these portrayals suggested a woman struggling to come to grips with the world in which she now lived, without any real context or consideration of what that world entailed. In considering the exceptional nature of public response to John Kennedy's death, Ellen Fitzpatrick notes, "It is hard to recall today that the culture of self-revelation and public confession that is so much a part of contemporary America did not exist in that period. . . . The world of manners stressed propriety, decorum, and deference. Many considered rectitude, reserve, and reticence as virtues rather than regrettable vestiges of repression one sought to overcome."[18] Jacqueline Kennedy's ongoing sadness, her continued despair, perhaps especially in the wake of the tremendous composure she demonstrated following John Kennedy's death, warranted mention rather than being something taken for granted by readers. There is also the reality that Jacqueline Kennedy lived in a world where hundreds of tourists gathered outside her Georgetown home every day. Her husband's image appeared on any number of souvenir items throughout Washington, DC. Within months of his death, she had cultivated an exhibit of his most personal effects and begun oversight of the early stages of his presidential library. She continued to receive, at the time of Bergquist's article, "a tidal wave of some 800 letters a day."[19] While a year of mourning, especially given the circumstances of her husband's death and the resulting changed circumstances of her own life, seems reasonable, the sustained mourning, the alleged desire to reminisce all the time might not be a state of mind entirely of Jacqueline Kennedy's own volition but rather the result of expectations put upon her. The media had fixated on the image of a dedicated wife in the months since John Kennedy's death, and this distraught version of Jacqueline Kennedy was in keeping with this vision of the former first lady.

In *Look*'s memorial issue, Mrs. Kennedy shared her own vision of her husband, one aligned with the image she had begun crafting immediately following his death, while also communicating something of her struggle in living without him. Remembering him as "so full of love and life," JBK lamented that each day leading up to the anniversary of his death had presented her with the thought, "But this day last year was his last day to see that." Thinking of a year's passage since his death, she wrote, "It will find some of us different people than we were a year ago. Learning to accept what was unthinkable when he was alive, changes you." Plaintively, she continued, "I don't think there's any consolation. What was lost cannot be replaced." The vision of John Kennedy communicated by his wife was almost otherworldly: "Now I think that I should have known that he was magic all along. I did know it—but I should have guessed it could not last. I should have known that it was asking too much to dream that I might have grown old with him and see our children grow up together." Without any real admission or acknowledgment of her role in the creation of his mythic status, she noted, "So now he is a legend when he would have preferred to be a man."[20]

Laura Bergquist's profile of Jacqueline Kennedy, in calling her a "living legend," suggested that it was not only John Kennedy who had attained a fabled status. And while Bergquist imagined that facing such a condition in life rather than death must be "an impossible role," she contributed something to that vision as she recalled of JBK's November 1963 performance, "It was her toughness and discipline that carried a nation through the trauma with a transcendent dignity."[21] A February 1964 feature in *Ebony*, "The Lady in Black," likewise spoke to Mrs. Kennedy's magnificence as understood specifically by African Americans— following her husband's death but established during her tenure as first lady. In an issue that also posited that John Kennedy had surpassed Abraham Lincoln "with regard to personal attitudes toward their dark brothers," E. Fannie Granton wrote about the particular affection— one that "defie[d] analysis"—Black Americans had for Mrs. Kennedy. Referencing the symbolic significance of the integrated honor guard that had participated in JFK's funeral, Granton asserted that JBK's actions as first lady "expressed her racial conviction more eloquently than speeches could have done." Granton looked to Mrs. Kennedy's warm reception of African heads of state, her support for artists of color, and her general inclusion of Black Americans on official guest lists as evidence of the "extremely effective program of integration she brought to the White House." An optimistic reading of JBK's racial attitudes, Granton's article communicated a celebrated image of Mrs. Kennedy, based upon her style, her behaviors, and her ability "to hold her own next to a man as illustrious as JFK."[22] As the remaining partner in such a celebrated union, JBK faced the high expectations of a largely adoring and still extremely curious population.

* * *

The extent of public curiosity meant that a certain segment of the population would not be satiated by periodic memorial issues of mainstream publications. For that readership, there was a strand of American media that specialized in rumor and speculation. Jacqueline Kennedy had been fodder for fan magazines even during her years as first lady. Beyond "respectable" women's magazines such as *McCall's* and *Ladies' Home Journal*, she had regularly been featured in and on the cover of *Screenland*, *Motion Picture*, and *Movie TV Secrets*. Mrs. Kennedy's fashion was a popular story angle, but during her White House years, other themes, such as "The Modest but Envied First Lady" or "The Glamorous Political Figure Who Did Not Neglect Her Children" also emerged. Jackie Kennedy's name on a magazine cover enhanced sales, and readers especially coveted a behind-the-scenes exclusive, or a suggestion of insider information on a potentially scandalous topic, like *Photoplay*'s September 1961 headline "What Jack Kennedy Is Hiding from Jackie." The secret: back pain. Essentially, the story was a nonstory. The headline promised something that it failed to deliver, but the promise of delivery brought readers back time after time.[23]

In Irving Shulman's 1970 evaluation of fan magazines' coverage of Jacqueline Kennedy, he noted that during John Kennedy's presidency, hundreds of citizens wrote to the White House, angry at what they saw as the "the commercial use made of the First Family."[24] The White House staff replied to such letters by noting, "Mrs. Kennedy was a public figure; she had, therefore, no control over articles, photographs, and capriciously eccentric interpretations of events with which she had been associated, or would be associated in the future. The White House neither approved nor sanctioned the use and likeness of the first lady by publications of a sensational nature." The White House form letter was made public, but, essentially, fan magazines could do as they wished. And they did. Responding to a reader's letter complaining about Mrs. Kennedy's appearance on the cover of the May 1962 *Photoplay*, the periodical justified inclusion of the first lady in its pages: "Mrs. Kennedy symbolizes tastefulness and beauty. Even more, she is America's newest star. Stardom is not limited to Hollywood, it transcends professions, countries, races, and creeds. As newsworthy as she is charming, Mrs. Kennedy is in every sense a beautiful, glamorous, exciting star who deserves to be on the cover of *Photoplay*."[25] To some degree, fan magazines were ahead of the curve, recognizing—and admitting—the intertwined nature of politics and celebrity in modern America. With the ongoing coverage of Mrs. Kennedy, readers, Shulman speculated, "became increasingly convinced that the articles were knowledgeable pieces and that the First Family welcomed the attention." In subsequent years, this understanding would expand to include a sense that reporting on JBK occurred because she behaved in a manner justifying coverage.[26]

Jacqueline Kennedy's appeal only increased in the years following John Kennedy's assassination, and magazines alternately trotted out old information under nostalgic headlines or generated bolder tags teasing readers with alleged secrets to be revealed. Suggesting the private thoughts of Jacqueline Kennedy and those closest to her, as though such thoughts had been shared with fan magazine authors, the publications sometimes pushed the boundaries of good taste as they offered conjecture about JBK's innermost thoughts and future plans. Shulman, sympathetic to the former first lady, noted, "Speculation followed speculation to spin a story where none existed and—more significantly—to signal the intention of fan magazines to deny Mrs. Kennedy hope of relief from their unwelcome concentration."[27] In the 1960s, the audience for these magazines was on the rise.[28]

Keeping Jacqueline Kennedy tied to John Kennedy, the March 1964 issue of *Photoplay* reminisced about the pair's courtship. While the images accompanying the text portrayed them as something out of "the best fairy tale tradition"—sailing, walking along the beach, sitting alone on the porch of the Hyannis compound—the article referenced their "spasmodic courtship." JFK appeared a thoughtful if not ideal suitor: "Jack is considerate (he introduces her to all the assorted members of his large-large family); attentive (he sends her flowers and candy; he also sends her books on government, politics and history—and she *reads* them); persistent (he takes her everywhere—to movies, plays, bridge games, parties, dinners, friends' houses; he even shows her how to play Monopoly and to her amazement she discovers that she *likes* it); tender and considerate. But he doesn't say four words, 'Will you marry me?'"[29] The article humanized the two figures who had by 1964 become larger than life. In the recounting of their courtship, John and Jacqueline Kennedy fell into the time-worn gender tropes of the reluctant groom and the eager bride and were made that much more recognizable. And yet there was something idyllic about their pairing. Images of them, younger and untouched by the years to come, provided readers with a nostalgic view steeped in romance. In presenting the picture of a couple who had ironed out differences and clearly enjoyed the challenge each presented to the other, the article suggested that Jacqueline Kennedy, as she recalled "the wonderful days of her marriage" and endured "all the lonely, lonely nights of her widowhood," would be hard pressed to find another partner as well suited to her as John Kennedy.[30]

In sustained but also often sympathetic coverage of Jacqueline Kennedy, the emphasis on what she had lost was established through the ongoing sanctification of John Kennedy. Following through on the midcentury assumption that marriage was a woman's desired state, a theme that loomed large in celebrity magazines, articles suggested that Mrs. Kennedy's widowhood was especially painful because of the nature of her fallen husband.[31] An April 1964 article appearing in *TV Radio Mirror* shared with readers "What Jackie Prays for Now" and promised them "An Unforgettable Story." In considering her regular visits to JFK's gravesite, the article admitted, "The prayers of Jacqueline Kennedy—private utterances, heard only by God—can naturally only be guessed at." And yet, "knowing this courageous young woman as we have come to know her, loving her as we have all come to love her," author Ed DeBlasio felt comfortable speculating about Jacqueline Kennedy's inner world. With attention to her children, the article imagined a desire that they inherit "the moral courage and the spiritual strength [their father] bequeathed them." In offering prayers of thanks for those who had shown her kindness and shared their strength, for herself, DeBlasio speculated, Mrs. Kennedy issued up "prayers for strength . . . strength to keep her husband's memory alive when others begin to forget . . . strength to see his work through to completion."[32] Following John Kennedy's death, the magazine posited, his work became hers.

In her widowhood, *TV Radio Mirror* asserted, Jackie Kennedy remained a model wife, steadfast and dedicated to her husband's principles and purpose. An article in the March 1964 issue of the periodical—"How a Mother Hides Her Tears . . . Jackie's Struggle to Teach the Children Why Kennedys Don't Cry"—did much the same. Questioning why JBK brought the children to their father's funeral, why she pushed them back into a daily routine so soon after his death, the article asserted that she had done so because *"this is what Jack would have wanted her to do."* Revisiting the funeral, months later, with nothing new to add but more speculation, *TV Radio Mirror* asserted, "It was up to her—his widow, the mother of his children, and the first lady who had shared his deeds and dreams—to hold back her own overwhelming grief and to set an example for her children and the nation to follow." Sharing his "deeds and dreams" and, of course, the Kennedy name, she followed the family edict: "Kennedys bury their dead and then they go on and do the work that has to be done. But in public, at least, Kennedys don't cry."[33]

While she is tied to John Kennedy, and to the family name, Jacqueline Kennedy here is also granted remarkable power, much as she had been in immediate assessments of her behavior following the assassination. The rehashing of details in the fan magazines, motivated by the desire for readership guaranteed by a Kennedy cover image or storyline, also sustained the kind of "living legend" status articulated by Bergquist.[34] The *TV Radio Mirror* article recounted JBK's actions and went so far as to suggest that she maintained an orderly sense of her obligations immediately following her husband's assassination: move from the White House; buy a home in Georgetown; change their Virginia home's name to one JFK would have liked; work on the monument for JFK's gravesite; pursue the creation of a National Culture Center in Washington; and maintain her husband's memory. From this list, Jacqueline Kennedy emerged, as she had immediately following John Kennedy's death, as fully dedicated to her husband, selflessly prioritizing dedication to his legacy as more important than her own grief. If readers had any trouble assessing how they should feel about Mrs. Kennedy, its author made the intended meaning plain: "In his book, 'Profiles in Courage,' the late President had written: 'Courage is a diamond with many facets.' In future editions, one new chapter should be added (and we are sure John Fitzgerald Kennedy would approve). A chapter of one word. 'Jackie.'" For those who imagined JBK as the model woman, this selflessness, this dedication to home and family was part and parcel of what made her so exemplary.[35] But casting JBK in such a manner also ignored the ways she had been more than this, the ways she had challenged tradition and developed an image independent of her husband. It ignored, too, how she had been critiqued as first lady and thus contributed to unrealistic expectations of Mrs. Kennedy.

As the year anniversary of JFK's death approached, consideration of Jacqueline Kennedy shifted. Rather than celebrating primarily her strength, articles emphasized—as did those of the more respected periodicals—her ongoing heartache. Leslie Valentine, a frequent contributor to the fan magazines, penned articles for both *TV Radio Mirror* and *Photoplay* in September of 1964. "Jackie's Newest Heartbreak," appearing in *TV Radio Mirror*, suggested by its title new information, but the heartbreak seemed rooted unsurprisingly in John Kennedy's assassination, exacerbated by Jackie Kennedy's inability to escape his memory. Valentine quoted Robert Kennedy, who, when asked about JBK, said, "I think that maybe it gets worse for Jackie instead of better." When John Kennedy was killed, the nation mourned with Jacqueline Kennedy, but then, the nation went "about its business once again" while she continued to grieve. Georgetown, the place where they had lived together, brought little solace, in part because she had found her home overrun by tourists, desperate to catch a glimpse of Jacqueline Kennedy and her children.[36]

In the *Photoplay* feature "The Love Jackie Doesn't Want—But Needs!," Valentine, while arguing that the love of the nation "helps [Kennedy] carry on . . . *forces* her to carry on even though she may want to do otherwise," also noted the "heavy demands upon the one who receives" that love. In Mrs. Kennedy's commitment to her husband—and the nation—she had spent her year of mourning "not seeking blessed forgetfulness, but pouring over painful memories, recording her recollections, preparing meaningful memorials to which the nation and the world can turn for inspiration and dedication." And while she saw his likeness and heard his words all throughout Washington, DC, and saw that he was "indeed remembered," it then became necessary to ask, "Can she find in this remembrance honor for him, or respect for herself? Can she find assurance that, when her year of mourning ends, her husband's name will be safe with the American people, that she will be free at last to seek solitude and, perhaps, some measure of happiness?"[37] In speculating about JBK's ability to be her own person, separate from association with her husband, Valentine posed a question that was not specific just to this widow but was a question with which many women, expected to dedicate themselves fully to husband, home, and family, might relate.[38]

Even more than the memorial articles in *Life* or *Look*, Valentine's *Photoplay* article recognized the context in which Jacqueline Kennedy grieved and the demands she faced as John Kennedy's widow. While Valentine's penchant for melodrama was on full display, the author acknowledged that whatever grief JBK continued to process did not occur in a vacuum but was the result of the world in which she lived, where national expectations loomed large. Of Mrs. Kennedy, Valentine assessed, "It must seem to her today that the world prefers that she never smile again, that her countrymen expect her to remain forever frozen as the 'National Widow,' more a monument than a person." But then, as a writer contributing to widespread speculation about Jacqueline Kennedy, keeping an imagined version of her as a fixture in the news, Valentine asked, "If she prays to be saved from bitterness and despair, can any of us blame her? Isn't it partly our fault?" Such articles revealed a media world that might sympathize with JBK but was unwilling to stop talking about her.[39] And if Mrs. Kennedy refused to speak for herself, these publications would communicate on her behalf.

* * *

In the year following John Kennedy's death, public views of Jacqueline Kennedy situated her clearly as a widow. She faced widespread expectations that she would remain tied both to her slain husband and to the wider Kennedy family. But as her year of mourning came to a close—and even before its end—Jacqueline Kennedy's romantic life and matrimonial future emerged as topics of sustained interest. After 1964, when JBK was considered "The Bereaved Widow," Irving

Shulman posited, fan magazines' coverage moved steadily along to regarding Jacqueline Kennedy as "The Somebody Who Certainly Has to Get Married Again."[40] At a time of sustained consideration of what it meant to be a single woman, and the emergence of an increasingly visible singles culture, coverage of Jacqueline Kennedy endeavored to keep the former first lady connected to a man, be that JFK or the man she inevitably would wed. A sense of proper behavior and a belief that there was an appropriate man guided coverage. When JBK's actions and choices failed to comply, she found herself no longer a figure deserving of sympathy but rather one deserving of censure. Where the public had accepted the authority of Jacqueline Kennedy as she memorialized and mourned her husband, when those no longer seemed her greatest priorities, those evaluating her suggested her need for guidance and direction.

Interest in Jacqueline Kennedy's matrimonial future picked up pace at a moment when concepts of matrimony and its desirability were entering a state of flux. Any woman who might doubt the wisdom of early marriage and consider an alternative path could look to Helen Gurley Brown's 1962 text, *Sex and the Single Girl*, for affirmation of a lifestyle that did not (immediately) include marriage. Men remained central to Brown's conception of a woman's eventual fulfillment, but, with an eye especially toward those of an aspiring or working-class background, she advised young women to have a life beyond men and before marriage and to be sure they could support themselves. While reaffirming ideas about the importance of a woman's appearance and, especially, her sexual attractiveness, the book suggested the primacy of a woman's own desires and affirmed, in keeping with a broader culture shift to occur throughout the 1960s, that she might put her wants and needs before those of anyone else. Brown's single girl was without explicit political intent. Unlike the communally focused feminists of the later 1960s, who challenged institutions and pushed for legislation and hoped to achieve political and social equality, the single girl focused more on the day to day, more on the practicalities of her existence, more on herself. On her own, the single girl figured out ways to maneuver around a decidedly unequal system in which women were treated in a decid-edly unfair manner. From lemons, she made lemonade. And she had a good time in so doing. She worried not about a husband and not about children. She worried about money and, maybe, about her career in the long term. Most importantly, she took care of herself. Brown's vision for women submitted an alternative to the young married ideal of the 1950s, suggested that there existed a population that had actively selected this alternative, and indicated that the ideal, as it existed, was beset with limitations.[41]

In 1965, Brown became editor of *Cosmopolitan* and provided the fail-ing literary magazine with a full makeover. Brown created a monthly magazine designed for single career women—or "girls" as she con-tinued to call them. Unlike the women's magazines that highlighted women's roles as wives and mothers, the magazine presented women with an image of the single woman—the "Cosmo Girl"—as role model rather than cautionary tale, a shift that took place also in televised de-pictions of single women, such as *That Girl* (1966–1971) and, later, *The Mary Tyler Moore Show* (1970–1977). Media portrayals of the single woman often mediated the threat she posed to the social and economic order, but the enhanced visibility of this figure indicated the allure she held for an American audience living through a time of tremendous change.[42] The appeal of this type of womanhood even beyond actual single women in their twenties was revealed by the readership of *Cosmo-politan*. Only half of the magazine's readers were single, and fewer than half fell in the eighteen-to-thirty-four age group.[43] Youth, no longer a particular age, was an idea or frame of mind, a conception personified in many ways by Jacqueline Kennedy.[44]

Jacqueline Kennedy was a widow, and she turned thirty-five in 1964. Popular understandings of the "single girl" generally suggested that she was in her twenties or early thirties and had never been married. But the single woman of the mid-1960s took care with her appearance, paid attention to fashion, participated frequently in urban nightlife, and was known to be accompanied by a variety of male suitors. Portrayals of Jacqueline Kennedy in mainstream periodicals noted her propensity for all of these things. Her affluence meant she was not bogged down by the mundanities of housekeeping or childrearing and provided her with not only mobility but an ability to be mobile in style. While an appealing figure for many, the single woman, with her agency and autonomy, also posed a threat to the established order and, even as she was decidedly feminine in appearance, threatened to disrupt gender roles assumed to be natural and right. Ongoing public fascination with JBK meant that whatever perceived disruption she contributed would generate comment—and, relatedly, some measure of resistance.

In gossip magazines' endless chronicling of Jacqueline Kennedy, she sometimes appeared a woman who, when she had concluded her official year of mourning John Kennedy, had concluded mourning. Whereas evaluations of JBK suggested she had put her husband, her children, and the nation first in the immediate days and then the months following her husband's death, increasingly, coverage of the former first lady positioned her as a woman who put herself first. Articles questioned whether she was living up to the standard of her slain—and, throughout the 1960s, sanctified—husband. Travel to exotic destinations, an extravagant New York City lifestyle, and a steady rotation of male companions suggested self-indulgence rather than self-sacrifice. Even those articles that ultimately concluded that JBK had not violated some unwritten pact between herself and the American people, by repeating claims against her, justified the questioning of her behavior—and legitimated her place under a public microscope.

In January 1965, just after her year of mourning had concluded, *Photoplay* published an article entitled "The Indecent Attacks on Jackie." The article outlined the various accusations made against JBK in the year since her husband's death, ranging from speculation that "she mourned—and encouraged others to mourn—him excessively and for too long a period of time" to critiques that "she began dating again before the first anniversary of his death." Author Jim Hoffman censured other periodicals for misleading readers with misinformation about Jackie Kennedy's comings and goings. Leonard Lyons of the *New York Post* had reported on JBK's visit to the discotheque, Shepheard's, accompanied by Earl T. Smith. The *New York Journal-American* likewise reported on her visit with Smith, with whom she had "stayed and danced from 1:30 to 3:30." What each column failed to mention was the presence also of Mrs. Earl T. Smith. But in a publication genre that emphasized maternity and morality, even the mere discussion of JBK's late nights had the potential to leave readers shaking their heads at Mrs. Kennedy's having gone awry.[45]

Beyond addressing Jacqueline Kennedy's social life, the article repeated claims made by Shana Alexander and published in *Life* that JBK's appearance at the 1964 Democratic National Convention was that "of a reluctant doll going through the mechanical motions in which her heart was not involved." The article repeated claims about JBK's inconsistency in her proclaimed desire for privacy while simultaneously agreeing to campaign for Robert Kennedy in his bid for a New York Senate seat. A sense of Mrs. Kennedy as voicing a wish to be left alone but then living a life that garnered attention cast a negative shadow upon her. Speculation that JBK "encouraged a photographer to snap pictures of her rowing with the kids in Central Park" even as she articulated her dedication to "protect" them from such attention made her seem disingenuous, and led readers of the *New York Daily News*, which published these pictures, to write and express their disgust with her constant appearance in the press. While Hoffman defended JBK and noted that she had no control over the publicity she received, his article contributed to debate over the coverage to which she was subject.

Hoffman concluded his piece on a sanctimonious note, especially given the article's appearance in a publication dedicated to speculation about the private lives of public figures. He encouraged readers—whom he charged as responsible for the attacks on Jackie Kennedy—to accept a kind of golden rule mentality. All anyone could expect of JBK was that she "be herself." As for what his audience could do, Hoffman wrote, "We can attempt to put ourselves in her place for a few seconds. How would we like it if we were the victims of slurs and slanders, of half-truths and untruths, of indecent attacks? We'd wince, and feel hurt and cry. And we'd resolve that we'd never do unto others what was being done unto us. That's what we can do for Jackie. Now."[46]

And yet the very act of repeating accusations against JBK affirmed them. By noting the widespread press attention dedicated to Jacqueline Kennedy, and giving credence to claims, even when false, the article accepted as legitimate her place in the public eye and the public's authority to weigh in on her choices and action. In listing out the accusations and the alleged truths of JBK's life, Hoffman, despite claims that the public should accept Jackie Kennedy as she was, affirmed the acceptability of viewing her under a microscope. By writing an article that speculated about elements of what she surely would have argued were her private life and therefore not intended for public consumption, he contributed to continued conjecture about her motives and intentions. In defending her against charges of poor behavior, Hoffman indicated that JBK was in need of defense, that indeed, there were actions that could be regarded as illegitimate or unacceptable.

Hoffman, of course, worked in an industry whose primary focus was moving copy. Irving Shulman reported on an official of Macfadden-Bartell Corp., publishers of *Photoplay* and other fan magazines combining to total more than three million in circulation, who claimed, "We run Mrs. Kennedy frequently, and Mrs. Kennedy sells." Mrs. Kennedy sold so much, in fact, that an entire industry had emerged dedicated solely to coverage of her comings and goings. In his 1970 book, Shulman republished in its entirety a *Los Angeles Times* story that detailed the existence of "Jackie factories." Author John J. Goldman noted, "An assembly line of writers, editors, and researchers for a firm that publishes fan magazines toil here daily, turning out stories about Mrs. Jacqueline Kennedy. Old newspaper clippings are studied, latest biographies are read, pictures of Mrs. Kennedy are carefully chosen." To guarantee sales, magazines needed catchy cover lines, fragments that promised something readers did not know and would be excited to learn, lines often based on the kind of speculation critiqued by Hoffman.[47]

In considerations of JBK's private life, several strains of conjecture stand out: the lifestyle JBK should endeavor to follow, the ways in which she raised her children, speculation regarding how John Kennedy would assess his wife's current actions and behaviors, and possibilities related to her romantic future. With no comment from JBK, considerations of lifestyle choices and matrimonial prospects stemmed from photographers' tracking her travels and authors' efforts to obtain information wherever and from whomever they could. Determining the deceased John Kennedy's evaluation of his wife required reporters to revisit the past and demonstrate a willingness to engage in a particular kind of creative writing. Sometimes, indicating the presumed appeal these angles held for readers, these strands of consideration overlapped, as when authors considered how John Kennedy would regard Jacqueline Kennedy's assumed suitors.

The March 1965 issue of *TV Radio Mirror* included an article entitled "You're Going to Have a New Daddy." In contrast to the tease of the title, frequent Jackie Kennedy chronicler Leslie Valentine admitted that JBK's remarriage was not imminent. Nevertheless, the article began with the assertion, "The time is coming." Valentine recognized the selfless nature of JBK's year of mourning in noting her devotion "to her children—and her husband's memory," and suggested that if Mrs. Kennedy wanted to fulfill her maternal obligation, this devotion to Caroline and John should continue. While she might not be ready for remarriage, already "now is the time to begin to prepare the children, to begin to turn them away from the past toward a new life." Certainly, Valentine assessed, the children would have questions. In preparation for those questions, "Jackie must find a way to make sure that the answers she gives will be the right ones." Lest readers miss the import of this task, Valentine proclaimed, "Her children's future happiness depends on it."

Integrating the perspectives of psychological and religious "experts," Valentine revealed the tightrope a woman needed to walk if she were to perform her maternal duties to perfection. According to Dr. Tom Noyes, a New York family-relations counselor, remaining unmarried was an "unnatural situation," in which a mother too often was given to providing her children with too much of her "*exclusive* attention." A woman should remarry, but only if her feelings for her new husband were "genuine." If "she has unresolved doubts, if she is torn by inner conflict, [the children] will sense it, and nothing she says to them about making a good life with the new father will be effective." Father Fanning of St. Elizabeth's Church in Manhattan cosigned on the counselor's advising as he warned against the possibility of dedicating oneself too much to one's children, a practice certain to hurt them. Beyond that, Fanning asserted, "The death of a father really means a broken home."

Jacqueline Kennedy faced a narrow range of appropriate behaviors, amplified by the nature of her husband's fame and the tragic circumstances of his death. Noyes noted, "It is absolutely crucial . . . for the widow to keep herself from idolizing her dead husband! She must begin, long before the day she starts thinking about a second husband, to relegate her memories of the first to their proper place in the background of her life."[48] Six months later, however, Valentine wrote another article, again for *TV Radio Mirror*, that traded on those memories, justified by the arrival of what would have been John and Jacqueline Kennedy's twelfth wedding anniversary. Suggesting the alternate future JBK might be imagining had John Kennedy not been assassinated, Valentine painted a celebratory picture that was rife with memories of JFK's affection for the children, his love of reading, his favorite foods. But the reality for JBK, Valentine asserted, was that she "is not the fulfilled woman of her daydream, but a widow struggling, day after day, with her children's problems, her own basic needs, trying desperately to make the dream and the reality mesh wherever they can."

Valentine had ideas about how JBK's issues—her children's problems and her own basic needs—might best be solved. The "missing male figure in her children's lives" was the gravest concern. In imagining JBK's response to this need, Valentine conceived of JBK as attuned to public opinion: "The obvious answer—and she must know everyone is thinking it—is to give her children a stepfather." "A marriage of convenience," however, Valentine suggested, would help neither the children nor JBK. But in suggesting that the woman JBK saw when she looked in the mirror had "eyes . . . empty of hope, reflecting the heart within," Valentine wondered, "Is it possible to fill that heart with a second love?" As Valentine imagined JBK envisioning a domestic scene with a new man, the author concluded the reverie with a "shuddering" Jacqueline Kennedy. Ultimately, Valentine assessed, JBK "is not ready yet. Maybe someday—but not now. It is still too soon for a new love, a new marriage—and therefore, she must sorrowfully conclude, too soon for happiness, for the kind of perfect happiness she and the children had once known."[49]

This kind of happiness—for the widow and the children—would require not only effort on the part of Jacqueline Kennedy but also, as suggested by *Photoplay*, the oversight of Robert Kennedy. Employing a title that suggested more than it delivered, Jae Lyle's "The Man Bobby Protects Jackie from—and Why!" indicated Bobby Kennedy's effort to shield an unaware JBK from the "man who threaten[s] her present hard-won equilibrium and the prospect of future happiness." Already linked to a host of men—including writer John Gunther, producer Harold Clurman, actor Marlon Brando, esteemed liberal Adlai Stevenson, and shipping magnate Aristotle Onassis—Jackie Kennedy, as noted by Washington reporter Maxine Cheshire, fully was expected to "some day decide to build a new life for herself and her children.'"

Lyle asserted that Bobby Kennedy was unopposed to this and had no objection to a "stable, solid, secure and loving" man "who might make her a fine husband and be a good father to her children, who might indeed provide her with a new life." But other men, Lyle suggested, might prey upon JBK, and from these men, her brother-in-law endeavored to keep her. This "handsome, charming, cunning"—and in this article, despite its leading title, unnamed—man of the world, Lyle wrote, "already moves in many circles, important circles—but he feels he should have more. His objective—to latch on to a lonely—and preferably wealthy—widow; his goal—money and publicity. Jackie would be ideal for his purposes. She, more than any other woman—he feels— would make him the most important man in the world."[50] From this article, several points emerge: that Jacqueline Kennedy should have a future with another man, that she herself was not entirely capable of

discerning such a desirable man from a scoundrel, and that she continued to require the oversight of a Kennedy man. The capability she demonstrated in the White House and the independence for which she was
applauded in the days after John Kennedy's assassination are curtailed
as Lyle suggests her need not only for an honorable man with whom
to make a "new life" but also for someone to oversee her in the interim.

The necessity of a Kennedy man's approval likewise informed a September 1966 *Photoplay* offering from Leslie Valentine entitled, "How
Jackie Is Raising the Children: Would Jack Approve?" Valentine began
the article with a focus on JBK's "glamorous new way of life" and the
effect it "may be having on the children," a concern that allegedly had
emerged among "women, young and old, housewives and mothers,"
whose devotion to John Kennedy had been transferred to his widow.
Referencing the 1966 book published by the Kennedy's White House
nanny, Maud Shaw, Valentine recounted the alleged public surprise at
learning how much time Caroline and John Jr. had spent away from
their mother, especially given JBK's longtime emphasis on her maternal obligations. Valentine posited that JBK's reliance on Shaw was
legitimized by the demands of the White House and then the emotional upheaval following John Kennedy's death, but then asked—on
behalf of critical readers—why, at this stage, another nanny would
be necessary. In considering JBK's duties beyond child raising, Valentine wrote, "Surely, her own duties to the Kennedy Library could
be tended to between nine and three, her critics insist, and her office
staff handles her mail." Valentine, while claiming an air of objectivity, repeated alleged observations of those questioning JBK's approach
to motherhood: "These people who feel they have a right to criticize
Jackie point to her vacations without [the children] ('she took them
to Switzerland, but left them there when she went to Rome; she took
them to Argentina and left them behind when she went to Spain').
They read about how often she dined at fashionable restaurants ('does
nanny keep the children company at dinner?'), and how late she stayed
up at discotheques and private parties ('does she sleep through their
breakfast the next morning?')."

After John Kennedy's assassination, the public questioned JBK's commitment to motherhood, which she continued to prioritize as her primary obligation. Here, Jacqueline Kennedy and her children, Caroline and John Jr., sled in Switzerland, January 1966. Keystone
Press/Alamy Stock Photo.

Even with JBK's failings laid out, and, in effect, legitimated, Valentine asserted that John Kennedy would approve of his children's upbringing. Established as a figure of even and measured thought, John Kennedy, Valentine wrote, "believed that people should be themselves." JBK, Valentine asserted, "never pretended to be an Eleanor Roosevelt, devoted to good works, nor for that matter, to be a mother-next-door, whipping up brownies and wiping muddy footprints from the kitchen floor. She is a sophisticate, a big-city girl who was born to wealth." And her way of raising the Kennedy children reflected those qualities that John Kennedy had so admired in his wife. After an article establishing and validating critique after critique of JBK, Valentine concluded, "Would John F. Kennedy approve of the way in which his children are being raised? The answer is that no one can doubt that their mother's guidepost has been and still is the desire to make them into people of whom their father would be proud. He is gone and she must do it alone and in her own way."[51]

John Kennedy might approve of her lifestyle and parenting, but many readers were likely to reach a different conclusion, as evidenced by Irving Shulman's late 1960s effort to understand who bought fan magazines and what they thought about the coverage JBK received from these publications. Of the nearly two thousand people (primarily women) Shulman interviewed, "almost all women expressed indignation at the magazines for their intrusion on the former First Lady." But their outrage was accompanied by a variety of caveats, often revealing as much about their views of women and sense of meaning in their own lives as about what they might believe about Jacqueline Kennedy. Beyond speculation that JBK "liked the publicity," the women defended magazines' coverage of JBK by noting that she "should be more discriminating in her choice of friends and the places she visited," needed reminding "that she was a human being and no better than anyone else" and was not "above criticism," and benefited from coverage because the surveillance made her a "better mother." When it came to the world of romance, despite the ongoing speculation about JBK's relationship status undertaken by fan magazines, ostensibly to serve readers' interests, women interviewed by Shulman suggested that JBK "shouldn't be so concerned about getting married in a hurry."[52]

Despite that sentiment, articles suggested that in order for Jacqueline Kennedy to best fulfill her maternal obligation, remarriage was essential. Valentine revisited the theme that for John and Caroline "one crucial thing is still missing: a strong masculine figure in their lives."[53] In 1967, Jacqueline Kennedy's name was linked to a host of presumed suitors. An October 1967 *Photoplay* article quoted gossip columnist Walter Winchell as reporting, "Jacqueline Kennedy's intimates do not expect her to marry for at least three years, but they are gossiping about eligibles." Offering an opposition position was Kennedy's half-sister Janet Rutherford and her mother, Janet Auchincloss, who believed Jackie would never marry again "because anybody who married Jackie would be 'Mr. Kennedy' and we don't think any man would want to be that for the rest of his life." *Photoplay*, expert as it was on all things Jacqueline Kennedy, boldly proclaimed, "We don't agree" and offered up three potential husbands, "none of whom would ever have to take a back seat in the life of Jacqueline Bouvier Kennedy." While the list included a Honolulu hotelier and a Washington insider, the one of the three with whom JBK most often was linked was John Carl Warnecke, a man who, in this article and in more to come, was described as, in many ways, comparable to John Kennedy and thus was deemed a fitting replacement.[54]

The following month's issue of *TV Radio Mirror* highlighted Warnecke specifically. "He is her type of man," author George Carpozi Jr. wrote, "brilliant, distinguished, charming, outgoing, personable and completely compatible." John Kennedy had liked Warnecke and admired him for his participation in the 1940 Rose Bowl as part of the Stanford University football team. Warnecke had worked with JBK during her time in the White House, first in her 1962 efforts to preserve Lafayette Square and then as part of the White House Fine Arts Commission. After the assassination, he designed the memorial for John Kennedy's Arlington grave site and had assisted JBK in her initial plans for the John F. Kennedy Presidential Library in Boston. With his own career and reputation, Warnecke was the kind of man those close to

Mrs. Kennedy speculated she would need, someone "of some eminence and accomplishment in his own right who would not have to bask in Jackie's reflected glory or suffer by constant comparison with the public memory of her first husband."

Carpozi celebrated both Warnecke's physicality and his intellect, and on these counts compared him to JFK. A "mature man," as those close to Jacqueline Kennedy anticipated she would desire, Warnecke, at forty-eight, was "still young enough to possess the vigor and virility which so long distinguished JFK. He has never relaxed his hold on physical fitness." Carpozi noted similarities between JFK and Warnecke in the latter's commitment to his work and those who worked for him and in the fact that "his mind is always working at full tilt." Of Warnecke, Carpozi wrote, "He is the kind of man who should appeal most to a woman like Jackie," perhaps most of all because he "talks like a philosopher and poet. He is both strong and tender. He is an active businessman who still knows how to relax and enjoy life." But even then, "perhaps even Jackie herself has not yet realized how much they could mean to each other." Whether she was uncertain about Warnecke, or not yet ready to settle down, Carpozi believed it was about time and, in his estimation, Warnecke was as good a man as any. In concluding his article, Carpozi engaged in a kind of single-woman scare tactic as he noted that "no man . . . will wait forever for the answer he wants most to hear."[55]

Carpozi, who paid close enough attention to JBK's comings and goings to pen, in 1967, *The Hidden Side of Jacqueline Kennedy*, continued his coverage of the former first lady into 1968 when he speculated about another suitor, Lord Harlech, the former David Ormsby-Gore. His June *Photoplay* assessment was preceded by a February article that provided biographical information on Harlech, much of which linked him to John Kennedy. Harlech met JFK when he was a student at the London School of Economics, and the two became "intimate friend[s]," to the extent that when he became president, Kennedy called upon Harlech to serve as British ambassador to the United States. Harlech and his wife, Sylvia, had remained close to Jacqueline Kennedy following John Kennedy's assassination, and following Sylvia's 1966 death in a car crash,

JBK and Harlech had gravitated to one another. Author Kay Wendell suggested the sense this made. Beyond friendship with JFK, Harlech was "aristocratic, rich, grew up with money, is the same age as the late president would have been," all counts pointing to a likely compatibility with JBK.[56] Much as with Warnecke, Harlech was tied to JFK, and was a person JFK likely would have approved of as a suitable husband. Jacqueline Kennedy's selection of a potential mate, her endorsements of a man's suitability, was seemingly insufficient without also JFK's assumed sanction. The specter of her deceased husband loomed large.

And yet, for all the ways Harlech seemingly paired so well with JBK, for all the ways John Kennedy likely would have endorsed this union, Wendell outlined reasons why theirs would be a less than ideal match. On the one hand was a matter of public opinion. Speculating that the couple would live in the United Kingdom, Wendell suggested, "The thought of a martyred president's children living outside the United States might be too much for some." Privileging Jacqueline Kennedy's responsibility to her deceased husband, her children, and the American public over whatever her personal desires might be, and ignoring the likelihood of the continued and extensive time the Kennedy children would spend in the United States, Wendell added, "The feeling is very strongly felt that an American president's children should be raised American." Beyond the Kennedys' assumed expatriation, Wendell speculated that Jacqueline Kennedy's commitment to the Kennedy style could pose a problem. In noting the challenge posed by Harlech's children, the oldest of which were "all enthusiastically part of the hippie, far-out generation, London-style," Wendell opined, "It is hard to imagine Jackie putting up with this sort of thing." Highlighting her duty to her children and first husband, Wendell suggested that Jacqueline Kennedy's primary obligation was to them: "She is also aware of her responsibility as a Kennedy and of her duty to keep her husband's image strongly within the hearts of her children."[57]

Despite presenting drawbacks to the Kennedy-Harlech pairing, Wendell, claiming "insider" access, predicted that JBK would marry Harlech.[58] Carpozi's June assessment echoed this sentiment. Paying particular attention to the November 1967 trip to Cambodia Harlech and Jackie Kennedy had taken together, the author noted that rumors about their impending marriage escalated after the trip. Speculation likewise followed their February 1968 visit to the Greenwood, an antebellum plantation in Thomasville, Georgia. While the two arrived separately and attempted to keep their visit from the press, their time at the plantation became news for public consumption. Spending time riding, walking, and quail shooting, the two shared their "most important moment—a candlelit supper in the exquisite dining room on Sunday night." With information from an "informant," Carpozi described Harlech and JBK on a balcony "holding hands as they stood at the rail." He continued, "They spoke in whispers—but there was no doubt that the words they exchanged had an offspring of love." So certain was Carpozi that this was the night Harlech proposed and Jacqueline Kennedy accepted his offer of marriage, his article was accompanied by a mail-in survey asking *Photoplay* readers which style of wedding dress Mrs. Kennedy should wear. Assuring readers of Harlech's worthiness, Carpozi included this assessment, provided by one "confidant": "He's a charmer. He's witty, urbane, sexy, delicious, offers everything and could fit into any situation and scene."[59]

Carpozi, more than Wendell, seemed to sanction the possibility of a Kennedy-Harlech union. This might be related, in part, to the critique he had offered in his 1967 book regarding the former first lady's lifestyle. In discussing an incident in which Jackie Kennedy had balked at the sale of several letters she had written, Carpozi speculated that whatever anger she may have felt at her personal correspondence being put on the auction block failed "to dampen her penchant for action in New York's night life." Fall of 1965 was "Swingtime in New York," and JBK joined in full force, Carpozi asserted, reporting on a 1:00 a.m. nightclub request Mrs. Kennedy made for "the fastest music you've got" and her subsequent efforts to master hot moves: the Monkey and the Jerk. In responding to a Boston columnist's claim that Mrs. Kennedy, after her year of mourning, was making a return to society but that it "should not be construed as a springboard for her entrance into a full round of such events," Carpozi snidely opined, "Anyone who had been keeping an accurate tab on Jackie's participation in parties and other outings since her year of mourning had ended certainly would have known that Jackie had leaped from the springboard long before this." With her plan to go into seclusion when the second anniversary of her husband's assassination approached but then get out more in the social world, Carpozi pronounced that an increase in getting out might have produced a pace "humanly impossible to survive."[60]

As Jacqueline Kennedy had embraced New York's culture and night-life, as she had appeared at nightclubs and restaurants with an array of male escorts, in Carpozi's estimation, she no longer served as a model American woman, as many had posited immediately following John Kennedy's assassination. No longer did she appear to be sacrificing on behalf of her nation and family. She appeared to be doing what she wanted, whenever and with whomever she chose. Less like a widow and more like a single woman—independent and with means—Jackie Kennedy had changed at a time when the social and sexual culture for American women more broadly was in flux. The model of American womanhood failed to live up to the standard established by her own prior actions. Tied to a man, married once again, perhaps JBK could reclaim her status.

* * *

Beyond questions about Jacqueline Kennedy's decisions regarding her lifestyle, the Kennedy children's upbringing, and her ability to select the most suitable partner, her effort to exert ongoing authority over her husband's legacy, and specifically the chronicling of his assassination, attracted sustained attention in the second half of the 1960s. Where her attempts to honor him through his funeral, in the traveling exhibit of his possessions, in her attendance at memorials dedicated in his name, and in the construction of the presidential library were seen as legitimate expressions of her power, the public argument into which she entered with William Manchester, Harper & Row, and Cowles Communication's *Look* magazine over the publication of a chronicle of the day of and days immediately following John Kennedy's assassination cast a negative shadow on Jacqueline Kennedy's public image. In continuing to exert the authority she had claimed after JFK's death, she pushed the boundaries of what was seen as an acceptable assertion of power by a woman on her own. When recently widowed and perceived to be behaving in a manner dedicated to the national interest, JBK's authority was accepted and even applauded. When she seemed to have moved on and appeared to be curtailing national access to her husband's life and legacy, when her actions could be interpreted as self-serving, acceptance of her authority waned, as did popular support and sympathy for the former first lady.

In the early months of 1964, Pierre Salinger contacted historian Manchester about writing a "complete and undistorted account of [John Kennedy's] assassination" that would "avoid sensationalism and commercialism."[61] Selected by Jacqueline and Robert Kennedy, ostensibly due to his 1962 profile of John Kennedy, *Portrait of a President*, a book the *New York Times* described as "adoring," Manchester had in that case "volunteered" to the Kennedy administration "extraordinary controls" over his text, going so far as to send proofs of the book to the White House for review. Regarding the proposed book about Kennedy's death, the Kennedys promised Manchester that they would provide information and interviews only to him and no other authors. His account would be the official account of the assassination, a kind of "authorized history." Manchester, seemingly honored to tell this story, agreed that JBK and RFK could read the manuscript. In contract negotiations, it was Manchester who suggested his willingness to rewrite or delete material based upon RFK's or JBK's desires (and had suggested this be included in the contract; it was not). While Manchester's agent, Dan Congdon, attempted to secure financial remuneration for what he regarded as an "immense project," Manchester expressed a desire to "not bargain over a national tragedy." He would earn a nominal sum, including exclusive right to serialization funds, but the majority of profit generated by the book would go to the proposed John F. Kennedy Presidential Library.[62]

Manchester worked himself into a fervor over the book, eventually completing it during an eight-week stint that resulted in his hospitalization for exhaustion. When he finished the project in March of 1966 and offered the Kennedys a full draft, neither RFK nor JBK read the text but rather assigned representatives to do so. The book presented a heroic vision of John Kennedy, but the Kennedys' appointed readers balked at the level of personal detail included about the slain president and his wife, which they saw as invasive, and even more so at Manchester's treatment of Lyndon Johnson, which they believed could divide the Democratic Party and hamper Robert Kennedy's political future. A series of miscommunications allowed Manchester to believe, first, that RFK served as JBK's proxy, and then, that the Kennedys sanctioned the text when, in fact, internally there was no consensus. A telegram from RFK's secretary suggested to Manchester that the Kennedys had no objections to his moving forward with bidding over rights to serialize the text.[63] In *The Manchester Affair*, a quickly penned recounting of the drama that ultimately ensued, John Corry, who covered the conflict for the *New York Times*, chronicling exchanges among Manchester, his editors, the Kennedys, and the Kennedy representatives, revealed a spider web of assumptions, allegations, and suppositions among the key players, where miscommunication appeared the hallmark of the path to publication.[64]

Serialization was the one area where Manchester stood to make money from his labors. While interest in the text was expected, the winning bid to serialize Manchester's book, ultimately titled *The Death of a President*, came from *Look* magazine. The sum: an astounding $665,000. From here, miscommunication between the Kennedys and Manchester turned to contention. When, at the end of July 1966, Jackie Kennedy learned of Manchester's serialization deal, she balked at the designation of his as an "approved manuscript," when she felt that was not yet the case. Her concerns over the text also were personal: she did not wish herself or her children to be subject to the ongoing horror of seeing the assassination publicized over the originally planned seven issues, with her name used to promote the periodical. Moreover, the large sum drew heightened attention to the serialization and generated an even wider interest than initially anticipated. JBK chronicler George Carpozi, who wrote extensively about the conflict with Manchester in his 1967 tell-all about JBK, suggested, however, that Mrs. Kennedy was angrier about Manchester's hefty profit than anything else.[65] This, too, was the sense communicated by William Manchester.[66]

Beyond finances, there was a critical response to the notion of Jacqueline Kennedy's concerns about what information appeared in the text. Her secretary, Pamela Turnure, provided Manchester, in August 1966, a request for seventy-seven changes, dedicated primarily to "personal passages," with little if any concern for politics. In evaluating JBK's effort to exercise control over the publicizing of events surrounding her husband's murder and protect his legacy, despite her personal justifications, Carpozi wrote, "Jackie had suddenly taken it upon herself to be history's censor. She was going to manage what the public and the future generations of this country would know about the assassination. She had set herself up as judge and jury—and she would decide whether the people would or would not ever know about that day in Dallas." Jacqueline Kennedy went up against Harper & Row, *Look*, "and," Carpozi wrote, "as some of her more severe critics would say—against history itself." In a critique revealing his inability to imagine a woman both serious about her slain husband's legacy and an independent, modern figure in her own right, Carpozi skewered JBK for arriving at a meeting with *Look*'s lawyers wearing a mini skirt, an act he viewed as "a deliberate challenge to the world to accept her on her own terms." The sense of Jacqueline Kennedy as no longer the grieving widow in "isolation" was further communicated by Corry's inclusion of a description of JBK, offered by *Women's Wear Daily*, in which the publication called her one of the "REALGIRLS—honest, open, de-contrived, de-kooked, delicious, subtle, feminine, young, modern in love with life, knows how to have fun."[67] The seriousness and capability attributed to Mrs. Kennedy in the immediacy of her widowhood appeared no longer hallmarks of her persona. Someone labeled "delicious" and seemingly focused on "fun" had no business, it seemed, making decisions about what the public did or did not know about a seminal moment in their nation's history.

In an effort to resolve issues over the book, in September 1966, Manchester, accompanied by Kennedy representative Richard Goodwin, traveled to Cape Cod to meet with Jacqueline Kennedy directly. In Manchester's retelling of the meeting, his initial comment was about how "stunning" Mrs. Kennedy looked, suggesting, to some degree, her intention to disarm him with her beauty. After JBK—"at her most acrobatic"—waterskied while Manchester sat with John Kennedy Jr. aboard the boat pulling her, the two dove into the water and swam to shore. He recalled her use of flippers and his being provided with none, the ease with which she swam, and the struggle he faced. He claimed to have worried, "What if I drowned now? Would it end all the bickering about the book?" Manchester reported that even with JBK's promise of no "emotionalism," upon his raising the topic of the manuscript, its serialization and publication, it was clear that "nothing good" would come from the meeting. In later ruminations on the meeting, he wrote about the impossibility of "coherent discussion" with Mrs. Kennedy and her penchant for "tears, grimaces, and unhappy cries of *Jesus Christ!*" While Manchester later speculated that what JBK really wished was for no history to be written about John Kennedy's assassination, in this meeting, she suggested preference for a book only, to avoid "magazine hoopla and promotion." Manchester suggested that such a desire was reasonable, but simultaneously suggested that Jacqueline Kennedy behaved unreasonably. Her desire, he wrote, was that she and Manchester join forces to prevent *Look* from serializing the text, regardless of the contract into which Manchester had entered. In whatever legal battle ensued, Manchester would have Jacqueline Kennedy's full support. She believed *Look* would tread lightly, given her public standing. Manchester recounted her certainty that "anyone who is against me will look like a rat unless I run off with Eddie Fisher," a reference to the blowback Elizabeth Taylor received in 1958 upon entering into a relationship with Fisher, who was then married to American sweetheart Debbie Reynolds.[68] Anyone who imagined JBK as an imperious figure, desiring to do as she wished when she wished and imagining herself beyond censure, had their estimations confirmed by Manchester's tale. In his telling, he emerges as fully reasonable. Jacqueline Kennedy, on the other hand, is hysterical and beyond reason. *Esquire* magazine, which published an article from Corry, "The Manchester Papers," ridiculed JBK for her Fisher comment, printing the quotation on its June 1967 cover, along with an image of Jacqueline Kennedy sledding, arms around a figure (her son, John Kennedy Jr.) upon whose face Eddie Fisher's has been superimposed.[69]

Mrs. Kennedy underestimated Manchester's commitment to his text and overestimated both his deference to the Kennedys and the anxiety with which publishers would enter into a more public conflict with her. In a November 28, 1966, letter to William Manchester, Jacqueline Kennedy asked the author to remove information from twenty-five locations in the book and ten in the serialization, all of which she identified as of a "personal nature" whose confidentiality was "absolutely necessary to me and my children." In concluding the letter, she appealed to Manchester, "I cannot believe that you will not do this much." Manchester changed some but not all of the passages, and when his editors reviewed the changes, they found them to be minimal. When pushed to further edit, Manchester declared he was done. In a December 2 letter to publisher Mike Cowles, JBK claimed that she had spoken "too freely" to Manchester, and had relied too much on "his good taste and good faith." In this same letter, she expressed her reluctance to bring a suit to halt the book's publication. As late as December 10, the *Chicago Daily News* reported that Kennedy would not sue. And yet, on December 16, Mrs. Kennedy instructed her lawyer to file suit against Harper & Row, Cowles Communication, and William Manchester to prevent publication of *The Death of a President*.[70] From JBK's office came a statement penned by Ted Sorenson, in which he described Manchester's text as "tasteless and distorted" and suggested that the "private grief, personal thoughts, and painful reactions" of Jacqueline Kennedy and her children were not "essential to any current historical record." From JBK herself, there was no comment. In John Corry's retelling, as the suit was decided, Mrs. Kennedy "managed to remain almost supernaturally aloof."[71]

In the rehashings and retellings of the encounter between Manchester and the Kennedys—coming from the likes of Carpozi, Corry, and Manchester himself, offering a retrospective of his experience years later that was both defensive and derisive—the figure targeted for being the most unreasonable, for creating a scene where there need have been none, was definitively not Robert Kennedy. The difficult person in the Kennedy mix was Jacqueline Kennedy, attempting to exert an imperial and, in the eyes of her critics, unjustified authority and behaving in a manner that was selfish, irrational, and manipulative. It was she, the authors suggested, who required RFK to voice concerns he did not have and inject himself when he would rather not have done so. When Robert Kennedy sent an August 10, 1966, letter to Harper & Row publisher Evan Thomas, indicating his desire that *The Death of a President* be neither "published nor serialized," Corry argued that Robert Kennedy risked bad press and, not being an obtuse man, did so knowingly. He interjected himself in the publication process only "because Jackie Kennedy was raising hell."[72]

Jacqueline Kennedy, those chronicling her argued, had provided Manchester, in two grueling five-hour interview sessions conducted in May of 1964, with the information he had included in the text. If these were things she did not want revealed, Corry asked directly, "Why did she tell him those things?" This question, he concluded, without much effort to suppose what might have motivated her or what release she might have found in purging memories of a horror that had occurred just six months before, "does not lend itself to an easy answer."[73] In speculating about her disregard for the suit's capacity to hurt her brother-in-law's political ambitions, she no longer appeared a woman dedicated to family and country.[74] Combined with Manchester's recounting of his September meeting with her, the suit made her appear demanding and irrational, a woman determined to have her way regardless of the cost to others.

Those writing about Jacqueline Kennedy in relation to her conflict with William Manchester offered up a particular view of the public attention and consideration she had endured since John Kennedy's death. Corry noted, "Possibly as much nonsense has been written about Jackie Kennedy as anyone else in America. She is one of America's great commodities, and she sells newspapers and magazines and books. Robert

Kennedy does, too, and they both know it, and like most people, they would prefer that only nice things be written about them."[75] If it were a question only of "nice things" being said, Manchester's book would have posed little problem. The irony of the conflict over *The Death of a President* is that Manchester wrote primarily nice things about Jacqueline Kennedy. In the text, she appears fully dedicated to JFK, and Manchester makes multiple references to her unwillingness to leave her husband's body, a commitment he regards as fueled by a combination of wifely devotion and a sophisticated understanding of how such an act would be interpreted by media, how it would appear and what it would mean to the American public. In his text, Jacqueline Kennedy is savvy and smart and capable.[76] Beyond what she sees as her perceived duty or obligation to her husband's memory and legacy, evidenced through careful orchestration of her self-presentation and of the steps she takes in President Kennedy's immediate memorialization, JBK also appears fully aware of and attuned to the needs of those around her, from the secretarial staff to the Secret Service agents to John Kennedy's loyal companions and devastated compatriots.[77] Manchester also pays attention to the way Jacqueline Kennedy became larger than life in the aftermath of her husband's death.[78] His text, had it been published without conflict, likely would have contributed to that vision of her.

The *New York Times* offered regular updates about the progress and outcome of negotiations. The newspaper, on December 15, 1966, printed in full the statements offered by Jacqueline Kennedy, *Look*, and Harper & Row on the reasons for and responses to the suit. On December 17, again in full, the *Times* printed the affidavits of Jacqueline Kennedy and Robert Kennedy, the complaint filed by Jacqueline Kennedy, a March 9, 1964, letter from Manchester to Robert Kennedy, and a Memorandum of Understanding laying out the parameters for Manchester's authorial undertaking. Finally, in full once again, the January 17, 1967, issue of the *Times* offered statements in response to the settlement from Jacqueline Kennedy, Harper & Row, and William Manchester.[79] In intervening months, the paper offered up a variety of views on JBK, casting her both as a jet-setting fashion plate and as "Mrs. John F. Kennedy," a "formidable woman, with a great sense of privacy, and more important, a clear idea of exactly how this privacy can be invaded."[80] Columnist Tom Wicker viewed Mrs. Kennedy with a critical eye, noting that she had "chosen to cast public doubt from her position of immense prestige, on a book she and her brother-in-law commissioned but have not read and on an author they chose and gave preference." To question the integrity of both Manchester and his book, especially without having read the text, was, Wicker declared, "personally if not legally audacious."[81]

While the months leading up to the suit were drama filled, and the suit and its progress receiving sustained coverage, the actual resolution came about fairly quickly and with relatively little animus. In regard to the magazine serialization, of the sixty thousand words planned to appear in *Look*, JBK asked that sixteen hundred be removed. This caused little inconvenience with respect to publication, and both Manchester and publisher Cowles acquiesced. Mrs. Kennedy offered less opposition to the book, believing book readers to be "more understanding, more discerning." Of the 340,000 words, or 710 pages, the amendments she requested changed the book by seven pages, or approximately 1 percent of the text. Manchester agreed never to write of the assassination again, and he was allowed to mention only his wife in his acknowledgments for the book. On January 16, 1967, without courtroom action, the suit was settled.[82]

William Manchester, *Look*, and Harper & Row benefited from the controversy as a curious public eagerly anticipated the text that had generated so much controversy (and, surely contrary to Jacqueline Kennedy's wishes, learned much of what she had objected to as the conflict generated ongoing coverage).[83] Corry suggested that the inevitable outcome of JBK's protests was the enhanced appeal of the text: people wanted to know to what she objected so vehemently. Hours after *Look*'s first installment appeared, four thousand copies were sold just in Times Square. United Airlines purchased eighteen hundred copies for its flights, and passengers stole them from the in-flight binders. Gallup reported that seventy million Americans read one excerpt while fifty-four million read all four. Four hundred thousand advance copies of *Death of a*

President were ordered before publication; by the summer of 1967, it had sold a million copies. Corry offered further consideration of not only a public desire to know about JBK but the sense of an assumed claim to information: "There was some solemn talk about the public's right to know these things, as well as some sanctimonious chanting from columnists and magazine writers who insisted that other publications, never their own, were being indecent in exposing Mrs. Kennedy's secrets and private griefs. Still, it was inevitable that they would be exposed, and that Mrs. Kennedy would be wounded. America has made Mrs. Kennedy its public property."[84] In this capacity, those desiring full access to the "authorized history" of John Kennedy's murder were not so removed from those desiring full access to the private details of his widow's life.

While the dispute boosted the popularity of Manchester's text, the same was not true for Jacqueline Kennedy. Despite being at the top of a Gallup poll reporting the most admired women in the world, Mrs. Kennedy found herself subject to public critique after the "Manchester Affair." In a poll conducted by Louis Harris, "One in three Americans said he 'thinks less' of her as a result of the controversy." Most critical was the "growing body of affluent Americans, who were more prepared to think that the Kennedys were trying to dictate the writing of history. This group most rejected the claim that Jackie's privacy was being violated."[85] John Corry had opined about the nature of coverage of Jacqueline Kennedy in the years before the conflict over *The Death of a President*. He wrote, "There is a convention that goes with most things that are written about Jackie Kennedy: It is acceptable to say nearly anything if the story somewhere, somehow, declares or implies love, respect, and honest concern for her well-being."[86] In the aftermath of JBK's dispute with Manchester and his publishers, the necessity of couching Kennedy evaluations in a suggestion of goodwill (an optimistic assessment even then) seemed no longer a requisite.

* * *

Leslie Valentine, again assuming expertise on all matters Jacqueline Kennedy, for the April 1968 issue of *Photoplay* wrote that the nation, after John Kennedy's assassination "gave its heart irrevocably to his brave and beautiful widow Jacqueline. Jackie Kennedy could do no wrong. She was, in the best sense, America's queen. It grieves us to report that this is no longer the case." Having dedicated herself to fashion, her critics believed, rather than to the causes espoused by her late husband, JBK had "ignored the vast power bestowed upon her." While a desire to "shut out the world" immediately following the assassination was understandable, in the years since, Mrs. Kennedy had failed to "find the courage, or perhaps the desire" to weigh in on any of the "great issues of our time—Vietnam, civil rights, poverty, disease, rising crime and drugs."[87] In November 1963, JBK was touted for her public display of courage, despite widespread recognition of her penchant for privacy and her alleged political reticence, which journalists had repeated time and again since the earliest reporting on her. Not five years later, however, understanding of Jacqueline Kennedy's predispositions were disregarded. She, who "belonged to the public," would be judged according to their desires rather than her own.[88]

Asking if JBK was wasting her life, Valentine outlined the ways Mrs. Kennedy spent her time: "taking her children to the ballet; dancing at discotheques; vacationing in the tropics; riding to the hounds; lunching in fashionable restaurants . . . ; choosing clothes in New York and Paris; exercising in gymnasiums . . . ; attending art gallery openings." All of these things, to some degree, were fine, and to be expected among the routine of the affluent. But Jacqueline Kennedy occupied a special position, Valentine argued, related to her former position as first lady and due to the heroics she had demonstrated in the aftermath of John Kennedy's assassination. In Valentine's assessment, JBK also remained tied to conceptions of her late husband. Mrs. Kennedy's lifestyle and the activities occupying her time, Valentine wrote, "represent a sharp break with the kind of life that President Kennedy deemed worthwhile."

Valentine reprinted the musings offered in an article from the *Miami Herald*, which asked, "Why Must We Idolize Jackie When She Doesn't DO Anything?" Author Mary McGrath wrote, "For heaven's sake, what does Jacqueline Kennedy DO? It is becoming an embarrassment to read, continually, the chronicles of her days without ever stumbling across what might be considered a significant achievement . . . It does seem that in her 'busy' schedule she could find time for some expression of the social conscience her husband called on the country to display." Beyond the sustained link to JFK, McGrath's critique of Jacqueline Kennedy was related to sustained coverage of the former first lady, something beyond her control. Regardless, this point of view resonated with readers of the *Herald*, whose letters to the periodical supported her assessment at a rate of five to one.

Some of those defending JBK likewise tied her back to her late husband. This population claimed that her "life was justified because 'she gave her husband.'" In such an estimation, her suffering had paid for a lifestyle of her choosing. Time, however, had dulled the power of this argument, as evidenced by a suburban housewife's response: "She didn't give him. He was taken. She had no choice in the matter, so why give her credit for it, as if it were some calculated sacrifice on her part? President Kennedy's death was senseless tragedy, not his wife's accomplishment." Her actions in the aftermath of the assassination, the succor she had offered the nation, no longer seemed a contribution worthy of consideration, a dramatic turnabout from the vast majority of public opinion expressed in 1963. Time, the sense of a media world saturated by coverage of JBK, and critical interpretations of JBK's lifestyle choices in the intervening years had altered public views.

Jacqueline Kennedy offered little in the way of justification. Raising her two children as an unmarried woman of means, she came and went as she desired; she did as she pleased. In 1968, even with an image of the "single girl" well established, and a revitalized feminist movement emerging, it is not surprising that the former "model" of American womanhood living a life according to her own predilections caused pushback and concern. That model had been entrenched in a devotion to domesticity and familial responsibility. By 1968, even while still occupying a maternal role, Mrs. Kennedy seemed a decidedly undomestic figure. Despite efforts to link her to a man, she retained her independence and confirmed no romantic union. While this may have unnerved some portion of the American public, for others, it may have contributed to Jackie Kennedy's ongoing appeal. Valentine included sentiments from a woman identified only as a "secretary," who was posited as "speaking perhaps for most single women." This woman evaluated JBK in this way: "Jackie deserves none of the criticism. She is not wasting her life, she is merely going through a period of search— searching for something she has lost—a man to love. She has the money to search with elegance and style, at the best places around the world. I wish I could do it, too. Mrs. Kennedy is not a monument, she's a woman. She should be treated and pitied as one."

Valentine concluded the article by asking a series of questions: "Should such a beloved woman now be the target of a part of the public that seemingly demands more and more of its favorite heroes and heroines? Should Jackie now turn aside from the private, personal kind of life she leads, to become the kind of woman she basically is not and never was? And if she did, would this not be the greater sham? The bigger waste?" Even with Jacqueline Kennedy's commitment to keeping her private life private, however, she remained the subject of ongoing public consideration. When it came to the kind of life JBK should lead, *Photoplay* privileged the authority of its readers over that of Mrs. Kennedy herself, as it asked and then invited readers, "What do you think? Is Jackie wasting her life? We'd like to know. Send us your reply on the tear-out coupon on page 66."[89] In this capacity, it seemed, the public's sense of what a woman should be and do held greater weight than whatever her own desires might be. But Jacqueline Kennedy failed to feel compelled by those assessments. Moving into the future, she would continue to do as she pleased, with no explanation and seemingly little concern for public opinion.

[5]

FALLEN QUEEN

By the end of the 1960s, Jacqueline Kennedy indisputably was the most famous woman in the world. Communicating the level of her fame, the *Saturday Evening Post*, in a cover feature about JBK, invited readers into their publication by promising to share details regarding "The National Sport of Watching Jackie Kennedy." Alan Levy, who penned the story, remarked of her, "A public monument at 37, she is spied upon, hounded and sometimes bullied by a demanding press and curious public." "Harassing Jacqueline Kennedy," he noted, pushing beyond the magazine's indication that this was a uniquely American phenomenon, "has become a year-round international sport." While writing in a critical tone about those outlets making an ordinary existence impossible for JBK, Levy joined them for a week to make a point about the ways in which the public might gain access to Jacqueline Kennedy's private life. "*Women's Wear Daily*," he wrote, "never lets Jackie or her family out of its sight. In part, merely by charting Mrs. Kennedy's habits in *Women's Wear Daily*, a zealous New Yorker can virtually schedule his or her own encounters with the Kennedy family when they're in town. I did so recently—and saw one or more of them four times in two weeks." Levy spotted JBK twice at Central Park, once at Cordier & Ekstrom Art Gallery, and finally at Kennedy Airport, where she and her family were "greeted by an impatient throng of 7 reporters and 17 photographers."[1]

While Levy was seemingly in sympathy with JBK, and writing about her with admiration, his article publicized ways to find Jacqueline Kennedy, and in effect, repeated the behavior of the invasive reporters who hampered her freedom. More aggressively, the article included an illustrated map of

Manhattan that highlighted frequent destinations. The map detailed thirty locations—accompanied by specific addresses—where one often could find JBK, including her office, churches she regularly attended, and favorite cultural locations, restaurants, and shops. More troublingly, the article also included the addresses of her residence, John's and Caroline's schools, and the homes of various Kennedy relatives. Fred Sparks, who published a book on the first year of Jacqueline Kennedy's second marriage, reported on her particular ire at this article. "Why a map?" she allegedly complained. "And a detailed diagram showing just where the children are at various times of the day? Why is it important to give our addresses, or the name of the children's schools and times of classes? Why?"[2] For all the ways Levy may have intended to cast aspersions on publications like *Women's Wear Daily*, in the style of reporting he embraced for his article on Jacqueline Kennedy, he put the *Saturday Evening Post* in quite the same category.

Since moving to New York City, Jacqueline Kennedy and her children had dealt with overeager reporters and endured harassing letters, phone calls, and threats against their safety, including a bomb threat to their Fifth Avenue apartment in 1965, which an article in *TV Radio Mirror* suggested had shattered Mrs. Kennedy's sense of refuge in the city. "Jackie's island of safety has proved an illusion," the article read. "Jackie's feeling of well-being, her sense of hope and possibility, have again been engulfed by memories and moods from the past." Beyond the city, crowds gathered wherever JBK appeared. Curious spectators stormed her half-sister Janet Auchincloss's 1966 wedding in Newport in what *Photoplay* described as "a fiasco . . . a disorderly, howling mob scene" that necessitated the bride receive police assistance to make her way to the church. The same article that detailed the disruption to Janet's wedding and imagined JBK asking herself, "Oh God, How Much Longer Must I Hurt the People I Love?," imagined also the trial her fame brought to John and Caroline. "The only time they could enjoy ordinary activities, the healthy spontaneous behavior of childhood, came when they escape recognition," the article read, "which was, of course, when Jackie wasn't with them. It sometimes seemed as though the kindest thing she could do for her own son and daughter was not be seen with them." Caroline and John continued to receive Secret Service protection, but JBK, not unreasonably, worried not only about her children's safety but about their—and her own—emotional health.[3]

In June 1968, her concerns about safety escalated when Robert Kennedy, campaigning for the Democratic presidential nomination, was gunned down following his California primary win. Less than five years after her own husband was assassinated by her side, his brother, the Kennedy to whom JBK was closest and on whom she had relied in the years since JFK's death, met the same fate as his older brother. Those close to JBK worried about her state of mind after RFK's death.[4] When, four months later, she wed Aristotle Onassis, a desire to escape the United States, to take refuge from relentless publicity and potential danger, seemed perhaps the most plausible explanation. *Time*, in covering the union, quoted one Kennedyite: "Perhaps she feels she has not been very well treated by America."[5] But her behavior following the marriage, and the nature of her union with Onassis, as communicated by American media, contributed to a variety of other theories regarding what many saw as a strange, unnatural, and, most of all, disappointing pairing.

Into the late 1960s and the 1970s, Jacqueline Kennedy Onassis not only endured intensified attention from tabloid-style media but also sustained coverage from mainstream, allegedly reputable journalistic sources, indicating how much supposedly tabloid topics and styles had bled into the world of hard news, and how fundamentally notions of what news reporting should communicate and what it should accomplish had begun to shift.[6] Many of those speculating about the motivation behind JBK's union with Aristotle Onassis posited that she had wed the billionaire because of the respite from sustained publicity he might provide. But in marrying Onassis, JBK seemingly intensified media's—and the public's—interest in her private life. Because she refused to explain, or as many would have liked, justify, her decision to wed Onassis, various media forms attempted to explain her likely rationale, sometimes with empathy and a modicum of kindness, and sometimes from a position of judgment and censure. The competing views about Jacqueline Kennedy Onassis—known from her wedding forward as Jackie O—reflected the divided nature of coverage received by women featured prominently in American public life and mass media. When women were imagined to be seeking safety or protection for themselves and their children—and especially protection as provided by a man—media framed their actions as justified. When women were assumed to be following a purely personal animus, one that resulted in individual gain, financial or otherwise, their behavior was suspect and subject to critique. Such frames reflected an endeavor to make sense of JKO's actions, and very clearly did so according to recognizable understandings of women and their roles at that time. While some coverage considered JKO as a woman who, at midlife, had shouldered a tremendous burden and sought deserved reprieve, other sources chastised JKO for turning her back on her nation and her slain husband's family, disappointed to find the woman who had once given the nation the majesty it lacked was nothing more than a hedonistic gold digger.[7]

* * *

Fan magazines and tabloids long had directed attention to Jacqueline Kennedy's relationship to her slain husband's brother, Robert Kennedy. JBK, reticent as ever when it came to politics, willingly joined in campaign efforts when RFK ran for a New York Senate seat in 1964. Bobby Kennedy provided his brother's children with a father figure, and offered an ongoing shoulder to JBK as she struggled through the early years following the assassination. The most common frame journalists applied to their relationship was one in which Bobby offered Jackie support and protection, with articles implicitly suggesting that his commitment to his brother's family took time and attention he might have provided to his own. As a July 1965 article in *Photoplay* noted, "From the moment of Jackie's assassination, Bobby's main purpose in life—though his own heart lay dead in the bier with his brother—seemed to be to guide and care for his brother's stricken widow." At one point reportedly telling RFK, "I am a living wound," JBK was alleged to have expressed her fear that she was "failing her children" and wondered if they might live with his family. Jae Lyle, author of "The Man Bobby Protects Jackie

From—And Why!," speculated that RFK's recovery from the trauma of his brother's death was in some way related to JBK's reliance on him, the way in which she gave him "a sense of purpose." With confidence, Lyle provided an overview of RFK's perspective regarding his brother's widow and his role in her life: "The nature of her need was obvious— reassurance (he provided this), firmness (he told her that she must bring up the children herself), sympathy and understanding (in this he never wavered), and an image of male companionship and manly strength for Caroline and John-John ('She wants to keep an image of a man around for the children,' Bobby said at the time—and he gladly volunteered for that role)." RFK knew, Lyle asserted, that "he had to gently lead Jackie back from obsession with death to concern for life."[8]

Eve Pollard, in her 1969 biography, *Jackie*, suggested that JBK had never been close to Ted Kennedy in the same way as she was to RFK, needing as she did "the experience, the knowledge and security of older men," ignoring the fact that RFK was not quite four years older than his sister-in-law.[9] Such a description matched with other discussions of JBK as a "man's woman," with a penchant for "borrowing" husbands "the way other women borrow a cup of sugar" or particularly enjoying the company of men years her senior.[10] And reliance on Bobby—or, as would eventually happen, Ted—reflected the broader sense that it was the men of the Kennedy family with whom JBK had the strongest ties, that she and the Kennedy sisters were not cut from the same cloth.[11] Even before her husband's assassination, Jacqueline Kennedy, in an assessment of each Kennedy family member's particular attribute, had told biographer Mary Van Rensselaer Thayer that Bobby was "the one I would put my hand in the fire for."[12] A *Photoplay* article set to print in advance of RFK's June 6, 1968, assassination but appearing ghoulishly the month after his death by its title, "Why Ethel Wants Her to Wed—and Bobby Doesn't!," hinted at animosity extending beyond the Kennedy sisters and to Ethel Kennedy, RFK's wife. But while the article began with an anecdote about someone mistaking Ethel for Jackie and speculation about Ethel's preference for standing alongside RFK alone rather than sharing the spotlight with her sister-in-law, the piece ended with suggestion of a kinder motivation for

Ethel Kennedy's alleged desire to see JBK wed: that "Ethel, as one of the few women who really understands and appreciates Jackie, certainly understands her need for a husband, a home and a life of her own." Such a frame communicated something fundamental not only about JBK's relationship to her sister-in-law but also about prevailing views that a woman's happiness was directly linked to marriage.

The nature of Bobby Kennedy's influence on JBK invariably affected the possibility of a second marriage for his brother's widow. With his March 1968 decision to enter the Democratic presidential primary, RFK allegedly calculated JBK's potential impact on his campaign, with even *Photoplay* contributing its assessment of her political import: "Jackie, unmarried . . . would be an enormous political asset to Bobby."[13] But speculation that JBK would—and should—wed increased in frequency with each year following the end to her official year of mourning. In 1967, *Photoplay* advanced that Jacqueline Kennedy might marry architect John Warnecke; Hawaii hotelier John Spierling; or Beltway insider Michael Forrestal. With confidence, author Fred O'Brien noted, "Of course, the decision as to just whom Jackie will marry will be made by her and her alone. But whoever she does choose, we know she will choose wisely and well. And as she moves into her new life, it will be with the courage and grace that has justly earned her the blessing of all the world."[14] Here, JBK is granted tremendous license as a woman whose authority over her private life and decisions will be not only accepted but also respected by observers. By 1968, most gossip circuits speculated on either longtime Kennedy family friend Lord Harlech, formerly David Ormsby-Gore, or Roswell Gilpatric, the former deputy director of defense in John Kennedy's administration, as JBK's future partner.[15] If the partner were up for debate, however, what seemed certain was that Jacqueline Kennedy would remarry, demonstrating that even in the midst of an emergent singles culture, marriage remained central to framings of a woman's happiness.

When JBK determined that she would once again wed, it was to none of the figures most frequently mentioned in tabloid coverage of her love life. Instead, after a May 1968 Mediterranean cruise aboard the *Christina*, Jacqueline Kennedy returned to the United States and informed the extended Kennedy family that she intended to marry Greek shipping tycoon Aristotle Onassis. An early chapter in journalist Fred Sparks's 1970 tell-all, *The $20,000,000 Honeymoon: Jackie and Ari's First Year*, detailed the alleged exchange between JBK and her in-laws as she shared her news. Sparks described the meeting as a "solemn gathering . . . not unlike an emergency joint meeting of the House and Senate." Her announcement, it seemed, prompted a concerted Kennedy family defense. Sparks wrote, "The immediate reaction was: What will this do to the Kennedy image? No one for the moment thought about Jackie." Assuming insight into JBK's psyche, Sparks confidently asserted, "This she will *never* forget." Robert Kennedy allegedly asked her to delay the union, at least until the presidential election had been decided. Sparks indicated that RFK likewise worried about the Kennedy image, but beyond that, hoped that JBK would change her mind about Onassis between May and the election in November. Ethel Kennedy and Ted Kennedy's wife, Joan, reportedly were less passive in their resistance, employing what Sparks referred to as a "patriotic" tack, telling their sister-in-law, "Jackie, if you hurt our men by marrying *this* man, you will hurt the America they have been raised to serve."[16]

Both Sparks and biographer Eve Pollard painted sympathetic portraits of JBK as they imagined this setting. Sparks saw the Kennedys placing the family image and the political future of Robert Kennedy above the personal happiness of JBK. This, he suggested, was an ongoing theme in JBK's relationship with her deceased husband's family. "Once again," he wrote, "the only person not being given a thought was Jackie Kennedy." Her place in their larger family pattern, Sparks suggested, was adjacent at best. Pollard commiserated with what she saw as JBK's desire to escape the Kennedys and her role within that family and its mythology. In Pollard's estimation, JBK was ready to "change out of the Kennedy costume, which by now had become a shroud."[17] Marriage to Onassis would free her of the demands of—and financial reliance on—the Kennedy family.[18]

The press had paid minimal attention to Jacqueline Kennedy's relationship to Onassis as it had developed. In fact, the two had enjoyed a long friendship, largely facilitated by JBK's sister, Lee Radziwill, who sources speculated had once had her own romantic relationship with AO.[19] After the death of baby Patrick in August 1963, JBK had taken AO up on the offer to find escape and some measure of solace aboard the *Christina*, although JFK had been reluctant to have her go.[20] When she arrived at the yacht and Onassis prepared to leave the vessel, she insisted he stay. Even then, however, he informed his staff, "Mrs. Kennedy is the Captain."[21] JBK's enjoyment of the extravagant Onassis lifestyle did not escape notice, as Helen Thomas, reflecting on JBK's cruise in her 1975 memoir, noted of JBK, "She did not give the impression of being a lady in mourning."[22]

Jacqueline Kennedy's and Onassis's friendship continued after her cruise. AO called on her after JFK's assassination and even spent a night in a guest room in the White House before JFK's funeral.[23] After she left the White House, AO had visited her and the children in their Georgetown home, and Sparks posited that AO had been fundamental in encouraging JBK to leave Washington and resettle in New York City. It was Onassis, Sparks claimed, who encouraged JBK not to succumb to her grief, to remember that she still had a life to lead.[24] Pollard, who participated fully in the international speculation about the nature of JBK's motives in marrying AO, highlighted a letter JBK had sent to John Kennedy while aboard Onassis's yacht in 1963. Jacqueline Kennedy reveled in what she described as an "absence of tension," something she never felt in the White House. Pollard suggested this was Onassis's appeal: "This is what [he] gave to her, after all her trials and tribulations and the terrible memories America had for her."[25]

Shot by Sirhan Sirhan on June 5, 1968, Robert Kennedy died on June 6. Beyond the horror of Kennedy's assassination, his death meant that JBK no longer had an immediate political contest to concern her. The Kennedys would remain dedicated to preserving the overall family image, but JBK's marriage to AO no longer would bear influence on an election. A wait no longer was imperative. In fact, what seemed to become imperative was the marriage itself. After RFK's assassination, Ros Gilpatric described JBK as "alarmingly distraught." In an interview with JBK biographer Sarah Bradford, former RFK political aide William vanden Heuvel noted of JBK, "I think the violence of America in 1968, the Martin Luther King assassination and then Bobby's assassination two months later, the street riots, all of that, it was that kind of violent year and I think she was very anxious to protect the children."[26] After RFK's assassination, especially, Pollard speculated about Jacqueline Kennedy, "She must escape, but she must also feel safe."[27] The seeming prevalence of violence in American society and the anxiety vanden Heuvel suggested it caused JBK directly affected her desire to wed Onassis, in vanden Heuvel's viewing: "Onassis was a powerful figure in the sense of a man with enormous wealth, who could give what almost no government could give, which was privacy. Whether it was a yacht or an island, it was privacy—and also out of the United States." And so, JBK negotiated a prenuptial agreement with Onassis (albeit not without Kennedy approval and assistance), and the two planned the logistics of a wedding certain to attract attention on a global scale.[28]

At 3:30 p.m., on October 17, 1968, Jacqueline Kennedy's personal secretary, Nancy Tuckerman, presented to the press an announcement from Mrs. Kennedy's mother, Janet Auchincloss. Reflecting an ongoing commitment to the manners, mores, and practices of the elite class to which they belonged, the announcement read, "Mrs. Hugh D. Auchincloss has asked me to tell you that her daughter, Mrs. John F. Kennedy, is planning to marry Mr. Aristotle Onassis sometime next week." Likely prompted to make the announcement official by the previous day's prediction appearing in the *Boston Herald Traveler*, which suggested that Mrs. Kennedy would wed Onassis before month's end, Tuckerman was willing to divulge little in the way of details, noting that "no place or date has been set for the moment." Tuckerman communicated something of the secrecy of the intended union as she insisted to reporters gathered, "I didn't even know until a half-hour ago."[29]

With little in the way of detail from either Jacqueline Kennedy or Aristotle Onassis, the *New York Times*, the publication many regarded as the gold standard in American journalism, pieced together what information it could uncover on its own and, to some degree, replicated the kind of coverage common in gossip and fan magazines. Journalist Marilyn Bender, who would become well known for her years of business and style reporting at the *Times*, reflected on the nature of coverage received by Jacqueline Kennedy as she referred to "years of speculation and gossip and a day of intense rumor and reports." Bender noted that reports of a potential romance between JBK and AO "had been circulating in recent weeks," but they were joined by the simultaneous suspicion of a relationship between JBK and Lord Harlech, spurred on by a recent theater outing. With certainty, the *Times* reported that Jacqueline Kennedy and her entourage boarded a Boeing 747 belonging to Olympic Airways, a move necessitating the removal of ninety passengers to another plane. The plane held JBK and her children, her mother and stepfather, Janet and Hugh Auchincloss, and Kennedy sisters Patricia Lawford and Jean Smith. There was some indication of the possible religious pushback Mrs. Kennedy would face in marrying a divorced man, reference to Onassis's longtime relationship with opera star Maria Callas, and an accounting of time recently shared between JBK and AO. But such time was seemingly so difficult to account for that it was a picture of AO and his former flame Callas that accompanied the article rather than a joint picture of the soon-to-be newlyweds.[30]

Even with knowledge of JBK's intended marriage to Onassis in its nascent stages, reporting suggested immediate public dissatisfaction with her plans, a central frame for reporting on the marriage, given Onassis's ability to limit firsthand coverage of the wedding and the limited information provided by its participants. Those who watched Mrs. Kennedy leave her Fifth Avenue apartment with her children as they headed for Kennedy airport, Bender reported, "rejoiced and lamented" Mrs. Kennedy's decision "to marry a man more than 23 years her senior."[31] As for the Kennedys, Ted Kennedy's press aide spoke on his behalf, releasing a brief statement that read, "I talked with Jackie several days ago, and she told me of her plans. I gave her my very best wishes for their happiness," a response *Time* magazine described as "chilling in its formality and its brevity." Rose Kennedy and Ethel Kennedy, in refusing to comment on the union, seemingly suggested to a public predisposed to reject the pairing that the Kennedys were displeased with JBK's choice of second husband.[32]

Women's Wear Daily (*WWD*), the fashion-trade journal dedicated not only to fashion but also to the social side of designers and those they dressed, had covered JBK voraciously since her time as a candidate's wife. The periodical, which had earned her particular ire for claims about the extent of her spending and during her single years in New York City referred to JBK as "her elegance," reported on her engagement and impending marriage to Aristotle Onassis as if with bated breath.[33] Before delving into the minutia of the elegance of Onassis's *Christina*, the publication introduced speculation about the dissonance the union likely yielded on either side of JBK's family. *WWD* suggested, "This represents Jackie's final break with the Kennedy Clan" and further posited that "some people believe certain family members 'must be disappointed she's not playing the beautiful forlorn widow anymore.'" The paper also resuscitated the idea that some had believed that Lee Radziwill one day might marry Onassis, but with the October 17 announcement of her sister's engagement to the shipping tycoon, she was left "only the kid sister," a play on the rivalry theme that media often applied to assessments of the sisters' relationship.[34]

In reporting on the wedding, *WWD* continued its speculation about Lee's response to the marriage. According to "the informed Socials," the publication reported, Jackie Kennedy had once—not long ago—dissuaded Lee from divorcing her husband, Stanisław "Stash" Radziwiłł, to marry Onassis. "A Senator's wife," *WWD* continued, indicated that "Lee 'took to her bed for 10 days when she first heard the news.' Baby Lee was in Tunisia about 10 days ago and people who observed her there said she 'appeared very thoughtful.'" The same unnamed source asserted that JBK and Lee constantly competed, one trying to top the other. As to securing a marriage to Onassis, *WWD* relied upon the tried-and-true trope of women competing over a man at the expense of their own relationship, as it reported, "Jackie seems to have topped her sister again."

If JBK was the winner, and her sister the "good loser," as *WWD* suggested, the contest very clearly was related to having secured a husband with wealth the magnitude of Onassis's. The extravagance of the celebration was made evident in the reporting of the steps made to prepare for the wedding and reception. "Through the morning the *Christina* moved back and forth from Skorpios to Lefkas [the last point on the Greek mainland before Onassis's private island] picking up supplies," reported *WWD*, "like the red carpet, sprays of yellow and maroon orchids, special small bouquets of mimosa, four cases of Nicola—a Greek vermouth." The "lit up" *Christina* was the site of the reception, where "the swimming pool sprayed green and pink water . . . and pink champagne flowed like water."[35]

Relying on reports from unnamed sources, reading into official statements, observing from afar behaviors and body language of wedding participants, *Women's Wear Daily's* coverage of the wedding employed a tone of speculation, not surprising given the nature of the publication and its propensity to share gossip as observed and reported by informants known only as "The Eye." In this style of reporting about the wedding and the marriage, the periodical was hardly alone and hardly joined only by publications of a similar nature. The *New York Times*, *Life*, *Time*, and various esteemed publications also culled whatever details they could to create stories about the union that enticed readers not only with the promise of informing them but seemingly intending also to titillate them with an insider perspective. *Time*, the original American weekly news magazine, in its reporting reflected the ways in which news reporting was beginning to shift. Sharing the who (AO and JBK), what (a Greek Orthodox wedding ceremony), where (Skorpios, in a recently renovated chapel), and when (October 20, 5:47 p.m.) of the Kennedy-Onassis pairing, the publication, without a direct "why" from either participant, filled in the gaps with conjecture and possibilities as to the nature of the romantic pairing that the periodical claimed the world was "unable to comprehend or accept."[36]

Just a year before, *Photoplay* had asserted Jacqueline Kennedy's capability in choosing a second husband and had indicated the likelihood of public support whatever her choice might be. A more accurate prediction might have been about the public's sense of empowerment or

Jacqueline Kennedy and Aristotle Onassis are married in Skorpios, Greece, on October 20, 1968. The marriage shocked the public, which could not imagine the heroic and beloved Mrs. Kennedy choosing the older shipping magnate as her husband. UPI/Alamy Stock Photo.

legitimacy in responding to her choice. Mrs. Kennedy was not a film star, was not a politician, was not a figure who lobbied for celebrity or a public life at all. She had been, of course, first lady, but her time in that role had been brief and had concluded years earlier. Maybe it was not for the world to comprehend or accept choices she made relative to her public life and relationships. *Time*, in covering JBK's union with Onassis, ruminated on the nature of her celebrity and concluded as much: "Is it anyone's business? Of course not. The speculation, the gossip, the judgment of new motives may well be seen as rude and a little absurd. They are either too solemn or too shallow." And yet, the publication claimed for the public interest a kind of legitimacy in asserting that "Jackie Kennedy simply is not a private person who may escape such scrutiny," largely as a result of the "concern, sympathy and affection" a grateful public had extended to her as she bravely led the nation in mourning her slain husband's death. Further, *Time* posited, while JBK "seemed to detest the world's devouring and often cruel interest in her . . . she might well have avoided the public gaze, had she wished, by adopting a different style of life."[37] In marrying a figure as fantastic and ostentatious as Onassis, she had fueled the fire of public interest. About Mrs. Kennedy's choices, "The world had, it felt," biographer Eve Pollard wrote, "a right to question why."[38] This sense of ownership over JBK's life permeated news coverage across the spectrum of news outlets. So often, Jacqueline Kennedy's actions had been linked—or even attributed—to her first husband or her beloved brother-in-law. But here, when Mrs. Kennedy acted in a manner generating public disapproval, media granted her notable power on an individual scale—the ability to control the whole of a media world committed to knowing not only her whereabouts but her most private proclivities.

Even before Richard Nixon's Watergate scandal enhanced the public's sense of the value of investigative reporting, of the need to know the inner character and thought process motivating public figures, a quest to know and, ideally, understand Jacqueline Kennedy's private life prompted a barrage of reporters to cover her engagement to Aristotle Onassis and then follow her entourage to Greece, where journalists hoped to provide readers with whatever details they could. The marriage of a former first lady, ostensibly soft news, was covered as breaking news, appearing on front pages of publications certainly regarding themselves as respectable, cutting-edge, hard-news leaders. In 1978, sociologist Gaye Tuchman differentiated between hard news and soft news in this way: "Hard news concerns important matters and soft news, interesting matters." But Tuchman then followed up by noting the possibility of overlap between the two and the difficulty in determining which was which. That challenge was a direct result of the blend among styles of reporting, topics covered, and the fact that what might be considered "news" at all had shifted. In many ways, this matched cultural shifts of the 1960s that established private life as an increasingly public topic, where critics and commentators had greater leverage when it came to topics that no longer were regarded as taboo.[39]

The career of *Washington Post* reporter Maxine Cheshire speaks to the blending of hard and soft news underway during the late 1960s and reveals something of the ongoing spell under which JBK seemingly held the American public captive. Cheshire, who described her relationship with Jacqueline Kennedy as "never one of even strained civility," in her 1978 memoir, wrote bitterly of covering JBK's tenure as first lady when, Cheshire argued, she "thought we reporters were peasants, and thus too coarse to write about an aristocrat." Cheshire had begun her career with the *Washington Times-Herald* and when the *Post* absorbed that publication, she had joined that paper's society page. But Cheshire, in her memoir, was sure to make clear that her experience was not typical of a society-page reporter. Marie Sauer, the women's editor, "prided herself on putting hard news into her society pages." With the Kennedys' arrival in the White House, many women reporters had seen their beat expanded to include the White House, resulting from public fascination with the First Family—and Jacqueline Kennedy, especially—and journalistic possibilities during John Kennedy's tenure and beyond opened up.[40]

Cheshire recalled that managing editor of the *Post*, Russ Wiggins, praised her for her professionalism in covering Mrs. Kennedy: "It is the greatest tribute to your objectivity as a reporter that none of your true feelings about Jackie ever showed up in your copy." And yet, Cheshire, in her memoir, felt no such compunction to veil these "true feelings." Whether a function of the shift in genre or evidence of how times—journalistic or otherwise—had changed, Cheshire seemed to relish sharing her views on the person she clearly believed to be the "real Jackie" and also communicating her indignation at celebrations of JBK and the special privileges she so often seemed to be afforded.[41]

Cheshire's accounting of the Kennedy-Onassis marriage and the circumstances by which the public learned of it highlights the magnitude of interest in this story. Cheshire, again, from the vantage point of 1978, claimed, despite "never [having] printed anything about Jackie ever seeing Onassis, even on a platonic basis," that she had a premonition that JBK would marry Onassis and attempted to confirm with sources "all over the world." Cheshire lobbied Sauer and Ben Bradlee, then *Post* editor-in-chief, to allow her some leeway in putting forward her speculation. With "bits and pieces of information, but not enough to justify [her] hunch," Cheshire provided "a small item in my column that would, in a sense, prepare the public for the big news to come." When Truman Capote called Bradlee to confirm Cheshire's hunch, Cheshire wrote that Bradlee "dummied up an eleven-inch story for page one." Reflecting the tension still existing between hard and soft news, while also presenting a picture of herself as a person valuing the paper's reputation over her own, Cheshire noted, "I wasn't sure one was the best place for the story, though. I'd had this same kind of polite disagreement with Bradlee, and his predecessors, before. Was it better for a story broken by a member of the women's section to appear along with all the rest of the hard news on page one, or would it be more effective in our section of the paper? If we ran it in the women's section and the prediction wasn't accurate, then, as I told Bradlee, it would be my fault."[42] In the end, the story ran neither on the front page nor in the women's section. As Bradlee, reflecting the views of many of the *Post* staff and beyond, told a surprised Cheshire, "I lost my nerve. I really don't believe it. I don't believe she's going to do it."[43]

Cheshire was charged with traveling to Greece to cover the wedding.[44] She raged at Onassis's act of having the Greek government ground all planes in Athens the day of the wedding. Irate that he could "shut the country down" for JBK, Cheshire refused to accept the couple's efforts to block the press from the wedding. While no reporters were allowed access to the wedding, there was a suite at the Grande Bretagne Hotel where the "two hundred strong press contingent" would receive a daily pool report. Cheshire framed the privacy AO and JBK desired for their wedding as an act of censorship. Reporters received only the "government's account of the event it had prevented them from covering."[45]

Cheshire rebelled. After "shrieking like a madwoman" at the representatives from Olympic Airlines, Cheshire "stomped off to the ladies' room," only to find she had been locked in. Eventually picking the lock with a nail file, Cheshire escaped, hopped in a cab, and instructed the driver to take her to Skorpios, having no sense of the distance or time the journey would take. Cheshire arrived in Lefkas, where she found the Greek Navy patrolling the waters to keep journalists from Skorpios and approximately "two hundred reporters and photographers already there, and they were the most dejected group of journalists I have ever seen. . . . It was as if we had all gone to great trouble and expense to get to the dance, only to find the ballroom door locked." Bribing passage beyond the blockade, Cheshire was welcomed aboard an American yacht being sailed by Los Angeles Republicans who had interrupted their cruise of the Greek isles to drop in on the celebration. Cheshire may have enjoyed "marvelous snacks and dry, ice cold martinis," but she could neither see nor hear what took place as Jacqueline Kennedy wed Aristotle Onassis. Adding insult to injury, as she headed for a plane bound for Athens to receive the official report of the wedding, Cheshire fell and broke her foot.[46]

As if Cheshire's tall tale is not fantastic enough to this point, it continues. The doctor who set her broken foot possessed an eighteenth-century French desk set that Cheshire admired. He shared the name of the antique store from where it had come, and Cheshire visited the shop. In an exchange of small talk with the proprietor, he claimed to be "Aristotle Onassis' best friend in Athens." His proof: the *New York Daily News* cover photo of the wedding, in which he appeared alongside the bride and groom. He insisted on taking Cheshire to lunch, where he could share details of the celebration, culled from his self-described "photographic memory." From him, Cheshire received a firsthand point of view that communicated the "excitement of the wedding" and allowed her to write with unmatched detail and specificity. She wrote, clearly satisfied with herself, "There was no comparison between the rich account I was given and what the other reporters were able to glean from their own sources to add to the vacuities of the pool report."[47]

Cheshire's account of her reporting of the Kennedy-Onassis wedding veers to the absurd, certainly, but it also speaks to the level of public interest in the wedding, the appeal Cheshire knew the story held, and the *Washington Post*'s shared sense of the news value of this story.

In Cheshire's article, syndicated nationwide, she emphasized two points: Aristotle Onassis's wealth and Jacqueline Onassis's happiness. Cheshire opened her article not with a retelling of the wedding in the Skorpios chapel but with Jacqueline Onassis's appearance at her wedding reception aboard the *Christina*, where she allegedly entered the room "walking like a queen" and wearing "like a czarina" jewels of such magnitude that they "caused every person in the room to gasp." She wore a heart-shaped ruby ring surrounded by "dozens of diamonds, each of which could make up the engagement ring of any wealthy New York woman," so large that an observer noted, "You couldn't dial a telephone wearing it." The ring was accompanied by identical heart-shaped ruby earrings surrounded by "Ali Baba 'open sesame' kinds of diamonds." While adults were "almost dumbstruck with silence," Caroline Kennedy exclaimed over the jewels, and JKO gave her the ring "to try on her own hands and play with like a bauble." JKO was not the only one to receive gifts. Onassis, in what Cheshire reported to be a signature "style of hospitality," provided all guests with gifts of jewels and other assorted treasures.

As to the emotion of the celebration, Cheshire, again basing her report on AO's self-proclaimed best friend, quoted "one guest" who remarked on AO playing with the children before joining the adults for a wedding feast. "What a father he makes for Caroline and John," said this source. And then: "Every paper in the world should have a picture of the look of love that Jacqueline gave as she watched." The emotion continued during the feast, attended by nineteen, only three of whom were not related to the bride or groom. Jacqueline Onassis is said to have wept during the toasts, one of which came from Jean Kennedy Smith, who gave her blessing to her "dear sister," and another from Janet Auchincloss, who Cheshire claimed to have said, "My daughter is going to find peace now and happiness with you." The newlyweds sat side by side during the feast and then after, as others danced, they continued to sit near one another, holding hands. Cheshire concluded, "They never kissed, but Jacqueline Onassis looked so radiant that one person afterwards said, 'There was adoration in her eyes. . . . She turned her head like a swan to look at him. . . . Anyone in America who thinks she does not love him is a fool.'"[48]

Life, with no comment from either of the wedding participants and without Cheshire's access to Aristotle Onassis's alleged intimate, communicated a different point of view to readers of its November 1 issue: "No slightest hint of the warmth and companionship . . . was evidenced by the 39-year-old bride and 62-(or was it 68?) year-old groom when they were married last week. Jackie looked drawn and concerned as she went through the half-hour Greek Orthodox ceremony in the tiny, bougainvillea-covered chapel—almost oblivious of Onassis in his blue suit, white shirt and bright red tie." Rather than Onassis's hand, it was Caroline's that she "clutched" as they departed the chapel.[49] The image of AO and the former Mrs. Kennedy was reprinted across the globe, often with emphasis on their difference in age and appearance. Evaluations insisted on theirs as an odd coupling. What could have compelled either party to enter into such a marriage? This question was as much and perhaps more so the focus of immediate coverage of the union, given the limited details of the actual event. With information limited as it was, this rumination allowed journalists a means of feeding hungry readers' interest in the story.

Eve Pollard, in laying out potential motivations for JBK's link to Onassis, noted, "No one has mentioned the word love."[50] And yet coverage of the couple seemed in many ways preoccupied with the question of love. Upon first reporting of the Onassis-Kennedy union, *Time* had speculated, "'What does she see in him?' and 'Is it love?' will remain major topics of conversation even among worldlier citizens for some time."[51] And these questions did, in fact, persist. A 1969 *Photoplay* article suggested that observers found the notion of love distasteful: "The thought that seemed to upset most critics of the Jackie-Ari match was the possibility that theirs was a romantic marriage. While they could have disapproved of Jackie marrying for money, they could at least have understood that. But it is more than likely that there are quite tender and sincere feelings between Jackie and her second husband."[52] Paul O'Neill of *Life* assessed the marriage far more cynically. In his eyes, it would have been foolish to look at the Kennedy-Onassis wedding and "anticipate a teen-age rapture. Theirs was a merger from which both parties could expect to enjoy something far more invigorating—a heady stimulation of the ego." Leveling with the readers of *Life*, he wrote,

> Ladies . . . ladies . . . you've had a week to be scandalized, but now we must insist that you cease sputtering and be serious—those of you over 30, at any rate, who know husbands are to be endured. And gentleman . . . we're all carnivores here although you need not say so aloud. Are there any of us who really suspect that Jackie is not capable of an enormous satisfaction at a union so rich in drama, creature comfort, power, sudden independence of social constraint—and the sweet knowledge of breast-heaving by a million indignant and defeated females—or that Onassis is not bursting with pride at his bauble of baubles?[53]

But while O'Neil may have urged readers to get real and recognize the transactional nature of all marriages, the long-standing expectation of American unions was that they were based on romantic love. Other motivations were base, if not immoral, and certainly below a person like Jacqueline Kennedy. But the public seemingly could not imagine Jacqueline Kennedy having loved John Kennedy—and there existed a certainty that she had, built up over years of nostalgic reconsiderations of the couple's much photographed courtship, early marriage, and time presiding over the American Camelot—and then loving a figure like Onassis. With love an impossibility, other justifications had to exist. This opened JKO to judgment and a public who believed in the righteousness of their right to evaluate and the conclusions to which they came.

Time, in a section titled "Plausible Freudians," provided readers with a kind of armchair psychoanalysis of JKO and her reasons for aligning with what so many saw as a jarring figure. Some speculated that her selection of Onassis represented the former Mrs. Kennedy's desire for a father figure. Describing her father, John ("Black Jack") Bouvier III, as a "swarthy, swashbuckling stockbroker," *Time* noted that his daughter, upon his death, had "wistfully" described him as "a most devastating figure." Onassis, the periodical speculated, was of a similar kind: "Onassis is a man of considerable magnetism. Some of his friends profess to see him as part Alexander the Great (for whom he probably named his son), part a Hellenic Great Gatsby. He is iron-willed, infinitely considerate of his women, vain of his limitless ability to charm, entertain and protect those whom he likes or loves."[54] AO, then, seemed a man capable of taking care of a woman looking for care. JKO, drawn more to men than to women, as Eve Pollard speculated, was precisely that kind of woman, who "needed men, for kindness and care and companionship." And maybe, Pollard further posited, that was particularly true when the prospect of "life into middle age without a husband was probably a depressing thought."[55] Jacqueline Onassis, for all her fame and distinction, in such an assessment, is just another woman who cannot fathom the prospect of life without a husband to care for her.

The charisma Aristotle Onassis was alleged to hold, combined with the power his wealth afforded him, *Time* speculated, made him among the few men Jacqueline Kennedy *could* have married, one of the few who could hold his own in light of her unparalleled level of fame. Undoubtedly being measured against John Kennedy, what man, *Time* asked, could possibly stand up to that task? And then: "What man could possibly marry her, many wondered, and not end up as Mr. Jackie Kennedy?" The answer: "Aristotle Onassis, for one. While she will never be known simply as his wife, he will never be known simply as her husband."[56] Suggesting that the American public had insisted on envisioning Jacqueline Kennedy as a "queen," *Life* indicated that unofficial coronation had potentially contributed to the Onassis-Kennedy match: "Queens deprived of court and clout need kings or must make do with half measures. There have been very few rich, ruthless, unrestricted, old-fashioned, to-hell-with-you-Jack kings around of late—particularly unmarried ones." Aristotle Onassis, the publication asserted, was "one of very few."[57] The question of marital brinksmanship, considered by numerous sources, speaks to the scope of JKO's fame, assumptions of American marriage, and the broader category of masculinity. What man could endure being second to his wife, and what man could possibly compete with the intensity of JKO's celebrity? The notion that any man would feel fine with such a power differential and intend not to compete but complement or support JKO seems, in journalistic framings of the Kennedy-Onassis marriage, an impossibility.

Months following the wedding, *Photoplay* spoke directly to the masculine appeal of Onassis as the publication assessed him as possessing an "erotic temperament" and engaged in widespread speculation as to whether or not AO and JKO would have a child together. At the speculation's base was the publication's assertion that "Jackie and Ari bill and coo just like lovers everywhere!" About Aristotle Onassis's status as a man and sense of sexual prowess, author Angela Wilson wrote, "He has no doubts about his masculinity and will most likely be able to remain sexually active into his very late years. The age difference is not important because sexual attractiveness is not only physiological, it is also psychological and sexual powers depend on mental attitude." Continuing to play to traditional notions of gender, Wilson considered JKO: "Jackie has pronounced feminine traits like being somewhat shy and self-effacing. She is not aggressive." Side by side, Wilson concluded, "These strong masculine traits in Onassis and feminine traits in Jackie compliment [*sic*] each other."[58]

The scope of Onassis's wealth also, unsurprisingly, drew sustained analysis. Before their wedding, JBK was estimated to be worth nearly $20 million, but that money was of the Kennedy family and came with some measure of their oversight.[59] And while the average American certainly would ask about $20 million, "Wasn't that enough for Jackie?," *Photoplay* noted that for her to enjoy a lifestyle of true "opulence," she would need "much more" than the four hundred thousand dollars a year her own fortune allowed. "Is it possible," the publication asked, "that she had begun to believe what Americans were calling her—a queen?" With Onassis's wealth, and with him as "king" of Greece, that certainly seemed likely.[60]

Remarking on both JKO's fame and her penchant for expensive taste, gossip columnist Suzy Knickerbocker, quoted in *Time*, noted, "She could never marry a nice doctor and settle down in Connecticut to ride horses!"[61] *Life* also deferred to Knickerbocker's wisdom as she noted that Onassis would "supply trappings of wealth in the royal sense, put a navy and an airline at her disposal." Going further, Knickerbocker called into question Jacqueline Kennedy's alleged desire for privacy, suggesting that the appeal of Onassis was that "he will keep her in the newspapers—her way. 'Jackie has this love-hate thing about publicity. . . . If she had really wanted privacy, the way she says, she could've gotten it. But publicity is like dope and she's got to have that front-page fix.'" Beyond the goods Onassis's riches could provide his new bride, there was also the measure of power and protection his money allowed. Through marriage to Onassis, Paul O'Neil told *Life* readers, Jacqueline Kennedy Onassis could achieve "absolute control of her own environment, the power to impose her own tastes and wishes on those around her."[62]

Onassis's wealth and extravagant lifestyle and their contribution to the pairing—and the compatibility of that pairing—would be hallmarks of coverage dedicated to Jackie O and "Daddy O" (as *WWD* insisted on calling him) for the duration of their marriage. Shaping the nature of that coverage was the response the union elicited from the American public (and beyond). Celebrity and nightclub owner Sybil Burton Christopher "said the highlight of her Friday was listening to the Schrafft's Set mumbling over their early morning coffee—'How could she marry that old man?' The consensus along the counter was, according to Sybil, that Jackie is definitely off her pedestal."[63] From the pages of *Life*, Paul O'Neil reported, "Cab drivers have volunteered their opinion by the thousands: 'She don't need the money . . . she must be nuts!' So has the great American housewife. 'I feel almost as badly,' said a helpmeet in Atlanta, 'as when Jack was assassinated.' 'German women saw a halo around her head,' said an editor of Hamburg's illustrated weekly, *Stern*, 'but now it is gone with the wind.'"[64]

Time likewise spoke directly to the very tangible benefits Jacqueline Kennedy would enjoy as Mrs. Aristotle Onassis, but also considered the price she would pay for her newly acquired riches:

> Indeed, there is no doubt that on Skorpios, Jacqueline Kennedy will be queen of far more than she can survey: mistress of a private empire sustained by 200 servants and employees, wafted wherever she desires in her choice of two amphibians, a helicopter, the entire Olympic Airways system, or the *Christina*. Beyond this island and its pleasure domes there is the whole domain of international life and amusements, which she patently enjoys. Having stepped down from an uncomfortable American pedestal, she may find precisely the sort of life she has long sought.[65]

This language of "pedestal" and a suggestion of having fallen from it marked coverage of the Kennedy-Onassis union. Months after the marriage, *Photoplay* went further than to suggest a fall from grace and questioned whether the former Mrs. Kennedy might have been masquerading as a great lady when she had been so admired by the American people: "Was she after all as regal as a queen, or had the public been fooled into worshipping a well-rehearsed pretender to the throne?"[66]

In the January 1969 issue of *TV Radio Mirror*, the publication wondered outright about JKO, "Has she lost a nation's love?"[67] It certainly seemed that way. Beyond headlines and articles sharing people's personal expressions of indignation, some saw fit to write to JKO directly, much as they had following John Kennedy's assassination. A special "collector's edition" publication—*The New Jackie*—dedicated to the life and times of Jacqueline Kennedy Onassis noted in 1970, "Though many remained faithful to her and wished her only happiness, Jackie began to receive probably for the first time in her life, letters which could best be described as hate mail." David Reilly of Norfolk, Virginia, wrote to JKO regarding her marriage to Onassis, and *The New Jackie* shared his letter in full:

I was truly sorry about the death of your husband, but I am now sorrier still to have learned of your marriage to Aristotle Onassis. Your marriage has added insult to injury and rubbed salt in the wounds of an entire nation. Mr. Onassis is a long step down from President Kennedy and I'm sure if your late husband knew of this marriage he would turn in his grave. I admired you when you were in the White House and at your late husband's funeral, but I can no longer respect you since you live with Onassis in Greece.[68]

The day after the Kennedy-Onassis wedding, *Women's Wear Daily* wrote, "The wedding is over . . . but the talk goes on." The publication suggested a kind of national disbelief: "Most people find it hard to believe. Even Jackie. When a reporter addressed her as 'Mrs. Onassis' Sunday night she just looked stunned."[69] As Jacqueline Kennedy Onassis biographer Sarah Bradford notes, "Public reaction was uniformly hostile worldwide, from top to bottom of the social spectrum. Everyone felt that Jackie had betrayed her husband's memory, demeaning herself by marrying a vulgar, foreign tycoon"[70]—or, as Maxine Cheshire alleged Ben Bradlee had called Onassis, "that goddamn greasy Greek gangster."[71] Ideas about Onassis being beneath his new wife abounded, as did sentiments about how he was also beneath her fallen husband. Bradford suggests that the Kennedy family believed "she should have stayed the widow of JFK" forever.[72] In real time, biographer Eve Pollard assessed, "America and the Kennedys were reluctant to let her go." While the broader American public seemed to have been more flexible in imagining her future and ostensibly wished her the best in finding happiness in a second marriage, Onassis was not the figure they had had in mind. As Pollard wrote, Americans "were determined she was not to make a morganatic marriage. She must marry someone equal both to her high status and to her dead husband." Instead, however, with Onassis, they had the sense that "their princess had been left with the frog instead of the Prince."[73]

Fred Sparks, in considering the couple's first year of marriage together, saw the challenge Jacqueline Kennedy faced as a single widow in this way: "The press, and the curious nation, were truly schizophrenic about Jackie's private life. While on the one hand they were bursting to see their idol romantically involved, on the other hand they were shattered by the thought of John Kennedy's widow as the lifetime companion of another man. For them, there was no substitute for Camelot."[74] Her tie to John Kennedy, public memory of whom served as a kind of national memory, seemed to position Jacqueline Kennedy as a figure over whom Americans believed they had a kind of ownership. To betray her first husband's memory and the things he stood for in the public mind, as people believed she had done in uniting with Onassis, was to betray the nation and its citizens, leaving them, as Pollard suggested, "deserted" and "bereft."[75] *TV Radio Mirror* repeated the criticism JKO faced after her marriage: "she shouldn't have married a 'foreigner,' she shouldn't have married a man who is 'so old' and who doesn't 'look like' her first husband, and she shouldn't have 'deserted' her church—'certainly not' for a man with Onassis's 'questionable' business background in dealings with her own country—etc., etc." But like Sparks, the publication also admitted to the tension existing in expectations of and hopes for JBK: "Every single one of us has been wishing Jackie would one day find a man she could love, a man she could marry, a man she could settle down with in a new and happy life. Now she has. Should she lose a nation's love for that? Or doesn't she deserve that much, after all she's been through?"[76]

As Sarah Bradford assessed Jacqueline Kennedy Onassis once married to Aristotle Onassis, "The Queen had abdicated."[77] Following John Kennedy's assassination and the funeral that offered the first round of memorialization, the British responded to Jacqueline Kennedy's behavior by asserting that she had given the American people the majesty they had always lacked. An astute assessment of public views of Kennedy appeared in the January 1969 issue of *TV Radio Mirror*: "The love affair the nation had with Jackie was always something larger than life-size. She was adored as the vivacious and beautiful first lady of our most exciting President. She was revered as the tragic young queen, widowed by an assassin's bullets, who became the staunchest guardian of her husband's memory."[78] In death, JFK's memory, at this point, remained sanctified. But following her masterful performance at her husband's funeral, Jacqueline Kennedy had to keep living. In marrying Onassis, and then proceeding as she pleased, that is what she did. Pollard sensed Jacqueline Kennedy Onassis's media savvy and sense of image awareness. She entered into "a marriage she knew the world would hate," but chose to fulfill her own desires, having, as Pollard claimed, "looked after the world long enough."[79] Alice Kaplan, of Cedar Rapids, Iowa, wrote to the former first lady after her marriage to AO and expressed a sensitive understanding of JKO's predicament: "Although many terrible things have been said about you since your marriage to Aristotle Onassis, I want you to know that I understand your position and still respect you. I don't understand why people expect you to live out your life as an ever-grieving widow, but I, for one, do not. I know you are right and that your late husband would have understood."[80]

Kaplan's view, however, among those expressed publicly and recorded for posterity, is very much in the minority. In 1968, public expectations of women were that they looked out for others rather than themselves. In disregarding public sentiment, and more particularly the sentiment of a public who had held her in such esteem, Jacqueline Kennedy Onassis, it seemed, was biting the hand that fed her. Pollard offered a critical view of the public that had put JKO in such a position: "America had forgotten to look at the real Jackie. They had looked only at the myth. For a woman who loves balls, parties and fun, Jackie could not have nestled in the tragic mould America had devised for her for the rest of her life."[81] But the majority of media coverage of the newly minted Jackie O failed to look internally or assess critically the how and the why of the attention and assessment the former first lady received. From the outset, and then, in an even more pronounced manner, for the duration of her marriage to AO, in much of the reporting on Jackie O, she emerged as a selfish woman, out for herself, and this at a time when a reemergent women's right movement was claiming a woman's right to individual autonomy and self-fulfillment. Criticism of JKO's alleged selfishness could stand in as a critique of women's assertion to a right to put themselves before the many other populations that might vie for their time and attention.

Speculation as to JBK's motives came from innumerable sources. But publicly, she remained silent about her motivation. In 2017, however, the discovery of a series of letters she had sent to Lord Harlech in the days following her union with Onassis revealed JKO's innermost feelings. In a letter dated November 13, 1968, she reflected on the relationship she had shared with Harlech and explained why she had rejected his marriage proposal: "You are like my beloved brother—and mentor—and the only original spirit I know—as you were to Jack." Harlech, like so many others, had been shocked by JKO's decision to marry Onassis. JKO acknowledged the astonishment with which her marriage to Onassis had been met, as she wrote, "I know it comes as a surprise to so many people. But they see things for me that I never wanted for myself." By way of explanation, JKO wrote that "if ever I can find some healing and some comfort—it has to be with somebody who is not part of all my world of past and pain." She continued, "I can find that now—if the world will let us." Reflecting a desire for some measure of autonomy and a desire for control in a world that very likely seemed out of control, JKO reflected on Onassis's desire to end their respective loneliness by being together. Whether or not he could "protect [her] from being lonely," JKO wrote, "only I can decide if he can, and I decided."[82]

Longtime White House correspondent Helen Thomas, in her 1975 memoir, *Dateline: White House*, assessed Jacqueline Kennedy in such a way: "Many wanted her to continue to live the legend of the grieving widow forever. But Jackie was more realistic. I was not surprised when she married Onassis. Before the big event, a friend cautioned her: 'But Jackie, you're going to fall off your pedestal.'" While Thomas's overall evaluation of JBK during her years in the White House is overwhelmingly critical, she recognized JBK's humanity and intelligence as she reported her alleged rejoinder: "Her response was searing, logical, and pure Jacquelinian. 'That's better than freezing there,' she said."[83]

JET SETTER

With the approach of Jacqueline Onassis's fortieth birthday, not quite a year into her marriage to Aristotle Onassis, *Women's Wear Daily* published an assessment of the former first lady "at 40." In evaluating JKO's look, the magazine suggested a unanimous agreement: "Everyone agrees Jackie today looks better than ever. She's slimmer, her posture is better, and she radiates an assurance that even as first lady she lacked. Jackie has grown up. She's a real woman. No longer afraid of expressing herself." Erasing the modernity and trendsetting of JKO's White House look, *WWD* proclaimed that JKO had moved beyond the pillbox hat, pearls, and sleeveless shifts and had "broken out . . . with a dozen different looks." Age and maturity potentially had something to do with this transformation but so too did an altered cultural landscape and an enhanced personal freedom that came with the move beyond the constraints of marriage to a man in political office. As socialite and philanthropist Betsy Bloomingdale put it, "Her White House image has been transformed to a jet set way of life."[1]

But while agreeing that JKO looked good, those asked to assess the former first lady in 1969 disagreed about her cultural significance. One interviewee declared that "her influence has waned dramatically," another that "she's just as influential as she chooses to be." In the midst of the debate over the nature of JKO's import—as related to style or otherwise—there emerged ruminations also on her fame. Designer Victor Joris asserted that she was "the most famous woman in the world, probably the most photographed woman in the world." Mala Rubenstein of Helena Rubenstein maintained that even with a lessened influence, JKO was "very much watched by everyone," a point touched upon in Revlon's Bill Mandel's question, "Why can't the press just leave her alone and let her live the kind of life she chooses?"[2]

But leaving Jackie O alone was not what the press intended. *Women's Wear Daily* might print that suggestion, but the publication had no intention of following Mandel's advice. Indeed, *WWD*'s survey of popular perception of JKO was the second such state of the field published in the paper in eighteen months. In January 1968, before her marriage to Aristotle Onassis, the periodical asked not designers and socialites their views on the former first lady but average citizens, who likewise presented a range of views. From those who found her "magnificent" and "one of the top women in the world" to those who believed she was "horribly overrated," *WWD* suggested that there were few who had no opinion about then Jackie Kennedy. Some sympathized with the public nature of her life, but others indicated disdain for what they saw as her courting coverage. A Boston secretary stated that JBK "pushed the publicity too much" while the wife of a Harvard faculty member declared, "Frankly, I'm getting tired of reading about her." Many of those questioned suggested that she should marry again, with one Chicago police office proclaiming, "She should stay out of the limelight and find a husband and relax."[3]

And of course, JKO did find a husband. As for the relaxing and staying out of the limelight? Not exactly. In the 1969 public opinion survey about the almost forty-year-old Mrs. Onassis, those who continued to hold up the mythic Camelot of JKO's own creation were "disillusioned that Jackie married an older man after the storybook romance with John Kennedy." Others believed the former first lady had become too self-serving. "Some feel she's become simply a clothes horse and the goddess of the tabloids," *WWD* claimed, ignoring the fact that JKO had no control over the kind of attention or coverage she received by publications exactly like *WWD*. The 1969 compilation suggested that people did not want JKO to go away, but rather to do "something meaningful with her life a la Ethel Kennedy." After John Kennedy's death, journalist Susan Sheehan posited, the public had expected for his widow to become "an ambassador, a senator, a political kingmaker, or a do-gooder (like Florence Nightingale)—i.e., a serious person, a public figure in her own right." As JBK turned instead to private life, a decision interpreted as evidence of her disinterest in the pubic good, Sheehan suggested, "public disenchantment with Jackie set in."[4] Public desire, then, was for Jacqueline Onassis to maintain a public life, but one receiving not too much coverage and one dedicated to the service of others rather than what might be regarded as selfish interests or pursuits.[5] Essentially, she should serve the interests of others and, if necessary, at the expense of her own desires.

By 1969, the media world had changed dramatically since JKO had entered the White House as first lady, as had her status as a subject reported on in that world. In a landscape increasingly marked by more investigative coverage and sharing of intimate and personal details, JKO's private life was subject to more and greater speculation in the years following her marriage to Onassis. JKO's desire to be a person who enjoyed the world, but also desired privacy, seemed a tension that was difficult for audiences to comprehend. Indeed, Mrs. Onassis's court battle against paparazzo Ron Galella called into question whether, as a public figure, she had a right to privacy. Journalist Fred Sparks reflected this view when he wrote, "If the Onassises were really shattered every time they were made a fuss of in public—while cameras snapped—it would be easy for them, with all their resources, to live well off the urban mainstream as absolute recluses."[6] Neither relentlessly pursued public figure nor "recluse" offered a particularly desirable option. Surely there had to be some sort of existence in between those alleged choices. Furthermore, even if AO and JKO determined to live off the grid and out of the limelight, and even if tabloids and mainstream media abandoned contemporary coverage of the couple, there was nothing to guarantee that the growing array of tell-alls about either or both of them penned by Kennedy or Onassis intimates would cease publication. As it was, the Onassises continued to live public lives and continued to receive copious coverage. These assessments, focused as they often were on the excess of Onassis's wealth and JKO's spending, the nature of their marital life, and Jackie O's alleged poor behavior, contributed to *WWD*'s assertion that when it came to JKO's public image, "There are definitely cracks in the pedestal."

* * *

A frenzied interest in the Onassis union spanned its duration. Journalists reported on Jackie O as voraciously as they ever had, relying on observation, "inside sources" who alleged if not closeness at least proximity to JKO, and, as had become increasingly common, unapologetic conjecture. In Fred Sparks's preface to his text about the Onassises' first year together, he shared his methodology with readers, claiming not only to have read everything written about the couple but to have "talked to chambermaids, hairdressers, and interior decorators who have served Mrs. Onassis. I have also picked the memories of some of Jackie's intimate friends—and intimate enemies."[7] Christian Cafarakis, a former steward aboard the *Christina*, while having left his position before Jacqueline Onassis's arrival, claimed to share the private views of those who served under her direction. While JKO may have wed Onassis, in part, for the privacy he could provide, the relationship seemed only to enhance JKO's appeal as a public figure and embolden those who endeavored to cover her. Beyond book-length chronicles of the couple's excess, a lucrative market existed for "special edition" magazine-like treatments and visual evidence of that excess, and tabloids reported that Jackie content continued to increase an issue's circulation, all of which emboldened those who chronicled JKO through a variety of mediums.[8]

Sparks steeped his assessment of the Onassis marriage in the excess of their spending and asserted that the two spent "more money than any other couple on this earth."[9] As reported by Sparks, even this rate of spending did little to affect AO's tremendous fortune. For the average person, Sparks assumed, the notion of spending such an astronomical sum in just one year might seem an almost insurmountable task. And so he dedicated a not insubstantial portion of his text to outlining just how one might go about accomplishing such a feat, crafting an image of the Onassis pair, and JKO in particular, as almost compulsively hedonistic. Onassis had 202 servants on payroll, many of whom were dedicated to the maintenance of his residences in Monte Carlo, Paris, Montevideo, Glyfada (an Athens suburb), New York City, and on Skorpios, his private island; permanent hotel suites in New York's Pierre Hotel and the Claridge in London; and, of course, his yacht, the *Christina*.[10] In a full accounting of "WHERE DID ALL THE MONEY GO?," Sparks included, beyond homes and servants' pay, categories such as jewelry ($5 million); travel ($178,000); entertaining at home and dining out (just under $200,000); and the allowances for the children (just over $200,000).[11]

JKO chronicler Eve Pollard ruminated on the off-putting nature of Onassis's wealth, with the sense that Americans found the flaunting of such fortune unattractive. His "exhibitionism" and "ruthless pursuit of pleasure" were at odds with what the author assessed as the American way of wealth, whereby the economic elite "devote their money to founding charitable institutions, backing political parties and generally revealing a rather Puritan attitude to their money, guilt."[12] By all accounts JKO demonstrated very little in the way of guilt at her newly enhanced wealth, but if ever anyone had imagined her harboring such a sentiment, her relationship with Onassis disabused observers of the notion that she did not enjoy the privileges money allowed. In the late 1960s, when social movements for racial justice, free speech, an end to the Vietnam War, and, increasingly, women's rights disrupted the domestic scene and ushered in reconsiderations of national values and visions, Jackie O seemed concerned only with herself.

Reporting on Jacqueline Onassis indicated that she gloried in the excess her second husband's wealth allowed. In his overview of their first-year spending, Sparks listed one category as "Jackie's personal expenses," described as encompassing "dresses, furs, cosmetics and cosmetic care, 'minor' jewelry, her gifts to others," which was estimated at $1,250,000 for the year.[13] *Women's Wear Daily* delighted in chronicling the where and the what of JKO's spending. And the spending started immediately. An October 21, 1968, article read, "Jackie's been buying all over town. When Valentino was in town she ordered 'practically a whole new winter wardrobe' including the three outfits sketched in *WWD*, Oct. 7. She's also been having a field day at Adolfo—five pairs of harem pants that Jackie says 'make me feel naughty'; four vests; five pairs of Turkish (Ari was born in Turkey) slippers to match the harem pants; black Racine jersey pants; a silk crepe shirt; two black skirts—one in felt, one in velvet; three hats."[14] Reports on JKO's spending and style choices, often accompanied by pictures or illustrations of JKO, were *WWD* staples across the early 1970s.

JKO's reveling in her second husband's fortune served to divorce her further from the legacy of her first husband. John Kennedy, born to wealth, was not particularly demonstrative with his fortune. Notoriously short of cash, the millionaire often had friends—and even those who worked for him—pick up breakfast or lunch tabs. Before Jacqueline Kennedy, his personal style was mismatched and unpolished. As framed by American media, stories about and pictures of the extended Kennedy family playing sports on the massive front lawn of their Hyannis Port home or frolicking in the surf that came up to their property had a wholesome quality that suggested that the wealth that made possible their privileged environment was incidental rather than fundamental to who they were. Despite John Kennedy's family's enormous wealth, he projected a familiar quality to which many Americans could relate. Jacqueline Kennedy, whose spending had long caused JFK consternation, and whose pedigree often set her apart, may not have been familiar in the same way, but her continued devotion to the Kennedy family had generated public admiration. Media coverage had fostered a public sense of proximity to, of knowing, both John and Jacqueline Kennedy. In her new position as Jackie O, the former first lady seemed an altered figure from the one the American people had "known." While people close to the former first lady might not have been surprised by her decision to wed Onassis and her attraction to the jet-set life he afforded, Jeane Dixon, author of *Kennedy Confidential: The Complete Unbiased Story*, noted, "The public felt that perhaps it had been fooled all along by that sweet little girl image Jackie tried to create when her husband was seeking office and after, when she was

First Lady. Americans hate a phony."[15] That alleged duplicity stung all the more coming from a woman, and a woman so many had anointed first lady forever.

The tell-all penned by Christian Cafarakis, formerly of the *Christina* crew, confirmed an image of Jacqueline Onassis directly at odds with her image as caretaker of John Kennedy's Camelot legacy. Cafarakis, who in 1968 was able to surrender his position as Onassis employee due to what he claimed to be a fortuitous inheritance, assured readers that everyone who had spoken to him had done so freely, without entice-ment of payment. As far as he was concerned, his newfound wealth came not a moment too soon, as he emphatically declared, "I consider myself very lucky not to be in service of Jacq Onassis." "As you'll shortly see," he wrote, "she's not exactly easy to please." Indeed, he proclaimed, "Virtually everyone I know who's ever been in the service of Jacqueline Kennedy Onassis agrees that she's the most difficult and demanding mistress they ever worked for."[16] A staff seemingly accustomed to Ar-istotle Onassis's benevolent paternalism found that the behaviors and expectations of his new wife failed to live up to the master's alleged magnanimity.

Mrs. Onassis, according to Cafarakis, failed to adapt to the style and rhythm of Aristotle Onassis's life and staff. Instead, she maintained her own behaviors and expectations, all of which Cafarakis deemed excessive and unreasonable. Cafarakis wrote with particular sympathy for Helene, Onassis's Paris housekeeper, whom JKO "made to feel like an outsider." With no regard for the work she created for others, JKO typically "completely changed her clothes four times a day, and before each change she tried on dozens of dresses with different combinations of stockings and underwear. She casually dropped these garments on the floor wherever she happened to be. Helene had to follow her step by step to put everything away again, since she always became furious if she found anything out of place. Every time she took a bath, she used no less than a dozen towels, which somehow still didn't prevent her from dripping a little water wherever she went."[17] When traveling, she required "no less than twenty suitcases," which should not surprise anyone given Cafarakis's claim that she took more than three hours getting ready to go out, "trying on at least ten outfits before making a final decision." So particular was JKO that "before the discarded clothes can be put back in the closet, they all have to be sent to the cleaner to be pressed again. . . . Jackie is so finicky that she even has her stockings pressed, while every suit or dress that is sent to the cleaner is insured for several hundred dollars, even if it only has to be ironed."[18] Casting JKO in this light, Cafarakis succeeded in communicating a kind of oblivious cruelty as well as a picture of unreasonable, wasteful excess. Jacqueline Kennedy Onassis's look, so long celebrated, here is revealed as built on the demeaning labor of those she treated poorly. Equal parts spoiled, vain, and obtusely cruel, JKO, who had so disappointed the American public in her marriage to AO, is revealed as disappointing on a host of other levels. This telling corresponded directly with reports featured in Sparks's text, where the author quoted "an old-line society matron," a person from her life *before* Aristotle Onassis, who referred to JKO as "condescending" and possessing "an air of superiority that makes her look down on other women."[19]

As damning as were the claims of the exacting nature to which Mrs. Onassis subjected members of the Onassis staff, perhaps more incriminating was Cafarakis's revelation of the calculation that both Aristotle Onassis and Jacqueline Kennedy brought to their marriage. Although "not at liberty" to disclose his source, Cafarakis claimed to have details about the particulars of a marriage contract Kennedy and Onassis had signed in advance of their 1968 wedding. Cafarakis's detailing of the contract's various clauses demonstrated just how deliberate the two were about the means by which their not-quite-joint resources would be allocated. To communicate just how disparate their claims to said resources were, Cafarakis noted that then Mrs. Kennedy's property and income took up half a page, while Onassis's required twenty-seven pages to chronicle. Such a difference lent credence to the speculation that JKO's entry into her second marriage was materially motivated. Onassis took on many of his bride's expenses, ranging from upkeep and taxation of her New York apartment to expenses associated with her children to a monthly budget of ten thousand dollars for new clothes. Onassis likewise agreed to the demand that should his wife have need to travel via craft other than Onassis's Olympic airlines or via one of his private planes, "she's entitled to purchase six first class tickets, since she insists on the following arrangements: the seat beside her, plus the seats directly in front and in back of her, must always be empty; the two seats across the aisle to her right must always be occupied by the two detectives." From New York to Athens, this would run upwards of seven thousand dollars. By Cafarakis's estimation, it cost Onassis $450,000 annually to provide for JKO and her children, not to mention, the author opined, Onassis's frequent gifts and "the incredible expense of their daily life, whether they happen to be in Greece, Paris or New York."[20]

Contributing to JKO's reputation as disingenuous gold digger was the existence of contractual stipulations for what should happen were the couple to divorce. For people possessing the resources of Onassis or Jacqueline Kennedy, a prenuptial agreement was not uncommon. Those bringing such a range and volume of assets to a union would wish to protect their holdings. But for an American audience who had wished for Mrs. Kennedy a different kind of husband and a different kind of marriage, one befitting a once beloved first lady, the seemingly mercenary, coldly calculated nature of the agreement cast a shadow on the hallowed image of Jacqueline Kennedy. Cafarakis claimed, "If Onassis dies while Jackie's still his wife, she'll inherit $100,000,000 outright, while the rest of his fortune—which must be at least six times that—will go to his children Christina and Alexandre."[21] Beyond the possibility of death, however, the contract also made provisions for the potential of separation. If a divorce were initiated by Onassis, he would give JKO $9.6 million for every year of their marriage; if she initiated the separation within the first five years of their union, she would receive $18 million. If she initiated at some point after the five-year mark, she would receive an additional $18 million, paid out as an alimony over a span of ten years.[22] Viewed less as a means of protection for JKO, the divorce outline suggested for some observers a guarantee of payment for time served, hardly in keeping with the ongoing cultural expectation of marriage based on romantic love.

Just as Fred Sparks had concluded that the Onassis union was not a marriage marked by the 1950s America togetherness ideal, Jackie O and Ari having been together only 225 days of their first married year, other clauses of the contract indicated some measure of exchange in the relationship that had little to do with traditional expectations of love and matrimony. Clause 7 detailed that JKO "agreed to spend only Catholic holidays and summer vacations with her new husband. For the rest of the year, she reserved the right to travel alone and to visit her friends and family without asking her husband's permission." As grown people at middle age, long accustomed to doing as they pleased, and with a host of roles and responsibilities competing for their attention beyond their marriage, these measures guaranteed that each party would retain an element of autonomy even in their partnership. For people of their wealth, extended separations were hardly uncommon.

And yet for all the ways coverage of the Onassis/Kennedy pairing reminded readers that the super-rich proceeded in ways foreign to the average person, reporting on the couple continued to express disbelief that a couple could live at such a remove from one another and maintain a healthy, happy relationship. Armchair psychology, often accompanied by widely accepted truisms about men, women, and romance, peppered speculative assessments of the Onassis arrangement. For example, a 1970 *TV Radio Mirror* article invited readers to consider "Jackie's Lonely Nights in Her Bedroom." The text suggested that "a time comes when the souls of human beings—women, even more than men—begin to faint for lack of the atmosphere of affection they were born to breathe." This, the article mused, may well have been the driving force in JKO's decision to remarry. The union with Onassis, "even in its seeming sparsity of connubial commitment—affords a measurable enrichment beyond the utter desolation of unattended widowhood." Beyond communicating a sense of expertise in the world of marital pairings, the article likewise reflected broader cultural assumptions about the loneliness or desperation of widowhood, even for an active, affluent woman, as Jacqueline Kennedy had been prior to her marriage to Onassis. Marriage, the article advocated, was woman's natural state. And even if Onassis's visits to JKO were infrequent, JKO could "count on Ari to interrupt her loneliness on occasion—even if no one can foretell just when those occasions might be."[23]

Questions of the couple's intimacy, its frequency and ardor, pervaded contemplation about the Onassis union. Not surprisingly, it was clause 19, which provided that the two would have separate bedrooms, that drew particular attention.[24] Onassis himself framed their relationship in such a way: "Jackie is a little bird that needs its freedom as well as its security, and she gets them both from me. She can do exactly as she pleases, visit international fashion shows and travel and go out with friends to the theater or any place. And I, of course, will do exactly as I please. I never question her and she never questions me." "Little bird" aside, Onassis's statement privileged independence as a key element of a successful marriage. But for an American public with particular ideas about romantic love, and perhaps, even more, a still very romanticized vision of the Kennedy marriage, the businesslike nature of this contract cast the former Mrs. Kennedy in an avaricious light.

Indeed, in detailing Cafarakis's claims, Sarah Jones reported that *Photoplay* had taken the contract to a marriage counselor who responded strongly to its contents. He said,

> A woman who draws up such a document could not be in love with the man she was marrying. . . . She must have thought of this marriage as a business deal in which she sold a very small amount of herself at a very high price. . . . The saddest thing is her apparent need to have everything she wanted spelled out in black and white, legally protected—as if she didn't trust herself to get what she wanted from her husband by love. . . . This would indicate a surprisingly low opinion of herself.

Beyond the assertion that only a particularly damaged woman would desire such an arrangement, the counselor wondered, too, about the man who would accept such a proposal. What could a husband in this type of union possibly hope for? At the very least, a link to "a very cold woman who seems to be saying, 'I insist on your giving me complete security and at the same time complete freedom to do whatever I want, whenever I want, without having to give any consideration to you and your feelings.'" Ideas about the potential desire women might have for independence even within their marital unions was a nonstarter for this expert. The article, published as it was in 1972, when the women's rights movement was changing the very fabric of American public life and private relationships, seemed as much concerned with the broader landscape of marital shifts as it did with the Onassis agreement. At a moment when feminists were revealing the constructed and malleable nature of sex and gender roles, *Photoplay* was publishing alleged expert testimony that read a woman's exertion of personal authority as equal parts greedy and cold, with a skewed sense of intimacy and love. The alleged evaluation very clearly assumed Jacqueline Onassis as the instigator of the contract's provisions. Aristotle Onassis's motives were assessed as both pure and hopeful. Presumably readers were expected to admire someone willing to risk it all in hopes of an eventual "change of heart," yielding "a real wife, a warm and giving woman."[25]

Over the course of their marriage, coverage of the union ran the gamut. Some reports exclaimed over their public displays of affection.[26] Others speculated about their prolonged separations and Onassis's continued relationship with Maria Callas.[27] Private letters JKO had penned to Roswell Gilpatric were made public, one of which, warm in content and tone, she had sent during her honeymoon with AO.[28] Their regular and prolonged separations generated sustained speculation of plans to divorce.[29] In addition to coverage of the pair, magazines continued their ongoing evaluation of Jacqueline Onassis in her own right. Some reports raised questions (as they had before the marriage) about how she was choosing to raise her children.[30] And, of course, her body and the ways she chose to adorn it received constant evaluation.[31] In much of the reporting on Jackie O, she was cast as a selfish woman, putting her own desires above all else, and this at a time when American women, more broadly and some much more vocally, were claim-

Fashionably attired and wearing her signature sunglasses, Jacqueline Kennedy Onassis draws attention from those around her as she descends a staircase in Athens, August 8, 1970. Keystone Press/Alamy Stock Photo.

ing a woman's right to do so. While she stood apart from the women's liberation movement and the broader efforts of second-wave feminism, criticism of JKO's alleged selfishness could stand in as a critique of women's assertion to a right to put themselves before the many other populations that might vie for their time and attention.

In her 1970 assessment of JKO and the public's sustained and complex relationship to her, Susan Sheehan wrote about the propensity of media outlets to feature Jacqueline Onassis in their publications and on their covers. Sheehan noted, "A recent survey shows that whenever a piece about her appears in a magazine, that magazine's circulation goes up 5 per cent." On the flip side, in continuing coverage of JKO, "The magazines that publish these Jackie-pieces also note an increase of 5 per cent in letters-to-the-editor beginning, 'Don't you think it's about time to stop publicizing and propagandizing our Jackie?'" Anecdotally, Sheehan shared, "My only answer to a tiresome question I have been asked a lot lately—'Why are you writing a piece about Jackie?'—is 'Why are you reading this?'" As a whole, she assessed, "There seems to be no accounting for our obsession with Jackie and our concomitant embarrassment with that obsession."[32]

* * *

Much of the reporting that took place in the late 1960s and early 1970s relied on healthy doses of speculation. As demonstrated, sources claiming either proximity to Onassis, or a relationship to someone with whom AO or JKO interacted, often unnamed and unverified, contributed to whatever "news" there was to share of the couple, individually or as independent actors. Photographs of JKO, assessments of her body language, guesses about why she was where she was when she was there all informed the content readers continued to devour. She did little to confirm or deny allegations or expectations. Readers of reports on the former first lady could have their own views affirmed or challenged; the interpretation of JKO content was up to them.

Some assessments of JKO suggested that with a new marriage and name came a new identity. In chronicling JKO's fashion choices, a 1969

Photoplay article asserted that "with [a] new title comes a new personality."[33] Jeane Dixon reported that "one woman journalist said, 'I think it's time everyone stopped thinking of Jackie as a Kennedy, and started thinking of her as an Onassis—it's clearly Jackie's own wish.'"[34] But the notion that this was a "new Jackie" faced challenges from reports that rather than a change in behavior, her shift to Jackie O was more accurately an uncovering of who she always had been.

One such source came from JKO's former secretary, Mary Barelli Gallagher, who provided her own evaluation of JKO in a 1969 text, *My Life with Jacqueline Kennedy*. This source offered something distinct: an actual presentation of Jacqueline Kennedy Onassis (when she had been Mrs. John F. Kennedy) by someone with whom she had shared a sustained, intimate relationship, one that Ray Gallagher, the author's husband, claimed allowed her to see "all sides of Jackie . . . the tantrums, the sweetness when she was inconsiderate and when she was considerate—which wasn't often."[35] Gallagher's text fit with views of JKO as materialistic, selfish, and temperamental. Anyone imagining that Jackie O was a manifestation of a changed Jacqueline Kennedy, after finishing Gallagher's book, would conclude not that a new version of JKO had emerged but, rather, that they were seeing the real person for the first time. Beyond the tabloids, the end of the 1960s and start of the 1970s were marked by an emergent world of tell-all nonfiction books dedicated to the chronicling of her life, both past and present, and oftentimes intending to reveal the "real" Jackie.

JKO appeared in retrospectives on her first husband's administration, and often received fairly gentle treatment as a side figure in those texts. Early Kennedy histories penned by Kennedy intimates such as Evelyn Lincoln (1965), Arthur Schlesinger (1965), Ted Sorensen (1965), and Pierre Salinger (1966) contributed to the notion of JKO as a figure along for her husband's presidential ride, an astute if somewhat begrudging participant.[36] And John Kennedy, in these texts, emerged a man larger than life, sanctified beyond even Jacqueline Kennedy's own Camelot crafting. Had she maintained a perfect public image, JKO would have been hard pressed to live up to the widowhood deserving of the manifestation of John Kennedy's memory to this point. Even Maud Shaw's memoir of her time as nurse to the Kennedy children, while regarded as a betrayal by Jacqueline Kennedy, put the former first lady in a positive light.[37] The kindness of these retrospectives and representations of Jacqueline Kennedy stands in stark contrast, then, to the image crafted by Mary Barelli Gallagher, whose text instead confirmed the worst of what people were beginning to believe and expect of JKO in her new life as Jackie O.

Gallagher had worked for John Kennedy since his first term in the Senate before transitioning to a secretarial position for Mrs. Kennedy's mother, Janet Auchincloss, and then eventually working exclusively for Jacqueline Kennedy during the 1960 presidential campaign.[38] For Gallagher, President Kennedy was a hero, serious and committed to a life of public service, kind and warm and devoted to the nation and its citizens.[39] While senator, Gallagher recalled, John Kennedy would eat breakfast and read the morning papers downstairs. Upon his departure for his office, he would yell a farewell up the stairs. As Gallagher watched him go, she "used to wish that Jackie would eat breakfast downstairs with the Senator, or at least come down to see him off at the door."[40] But Jacqueline Kennedy, as described by Gallagher, was alternately aloof, demanding, and unpredictable in her moods. Unlike John Kennedy's mother and sisters, Jackie was, as described by Gallagher, "a reluctant campaigner" in 1960. When asked to engage with Kennedy's campaign, JBK, in contrast with the candidate's immediate family, approached requested appearances "with the attitude of being inconvenienced, rather than wholeheartedly, considering the ultimate goal that she could help reach." Imagining herself in JBK's position, and ostensibly communicating to the reader her superior approach to wifehood, Gallagher mused, "How thrilled I would be if it were my husband running for president." Unlike both JFK and, apparently, Gallagher, JBK "did not get a thrill . . . in hearing a crowd outside [the] window cheering." When Gallagher called Mrs. Kennedy's attention to the sight of her newly elected husband greeting adoring crowds outside their Georgetown home, rather than sharing Gallagher's delight, "she simply sighed, 'Oh, Mary . . .' and she continued with her own business."[41]

What, exactly, Jacqueline Kennedy's business was seemed to confound Gallagher. She entertained, but beyond that, Gallagher assessed Mrs. Kennedy's primary labor as "constantly fixing up one room or another." At her base, JBK was unlike the "average American housewife and mother," primarily, Gallagher asserted, because "she was born and groomed to a queenly role." Any of the typical labor required of running a household was completed by staff. She supervised rather than completing tasks herself.[42] Gallagher seemed intent on highlighting Mrs. Kennedy as a duplicitous figure as she emphasized her former employer's actual domestic obligations versus the ideal shared with and then communicated by the media. In particular, Gallagher drew attention to a feature published by *Life* magazine in 1960. In an article comparing the potential first ladies, Gallagher, at this time JBK's personal secretary, was mentioned not at all. The article indicated that JBK received and responded to all the correspondence she received on her own. Neither did Maud Shaw, Caroline Kennedy's nurse, appear in the text. A picture of Mrs. Kennedy tucking Caroline in for an afternoon nap was accompanied by the claim that Jackie raised the child "without a nurse." "If this was politics, I thought," Gallagher penned, "I might as well get used to it."[43] But rather than imagining this as a strategy employed by John Kennedy's campaign team, Gallagher's telling and tone suggested that this was an intentional misrepresentation of and by Jacqueline Kennedy, one embarked upon with a disregard for fairness or recognition of those who allowed her household to operate as it did.

In addition to critiquing what she regarded as JBK's lackluster enthusiasm for her husband's politicking, Gallagher highlighted how Jackie Kennedy felt no compunction to do anything that she did not wish to do—even when first lady. In Gallagher's telling, JBK was spoiled and demanding, as in one case early on in the White House when JBK spoke in "sharp and impatient tones" as she looked for a misplaced address book. But while the first lady apologized and blamed her sharpness "on the tensions of this first week here," Gallagher noted that "Jackie became more queenly in her demands, more used to issuing orders." As time went on, Gallagher wrote, "I could never tell which of Jackie's moods to expect next."[44] According to the former secretary's text, JFK went to great lengths to please his wife; this was not a behavior she reciprocated. Gallagher recounted a visit to Florida where JBK wanted to skip church. When JFK pushed her to attend, she wore a sundress, sandals, and kerchief. "The press was on hand, as usual, and didn't fail to mention that the outfit hardly seemed appropriate."[45] Here, Gallagher cast JBK as spoiled and petulant, showing little regard for her husband's image or office, or the price of her alleged poor behavior on either.

Gallagher's text did nothing to dislodge notions of Jackie Kennedy as an inveterate spender, dedicated to and desiring a life of luxury and leisure. Dating back to 1957, Gallagher claimed, JFK had been "irked" by JBK's spending and required Gallagher to provide him with "a complete list of checks written and exactly what they're for." But where Gallagher depicted Mrs. Kennedy's requests as demanding and mercurial, a request from JFK was "stern," and even if "angry," was often cast as implicitly justified. Gallagher claimed, "Jackie's finances would haunt my nights and days from then on, all through the White House years and even after."[46] There was JBK's obsession with her look and constant attention to "clothes, clothes, clothes." When, in 1962, JFK was "on the financial warpath" and Gallagher suggested that a way to save money was to cut back on wardrobe expenditures, JBK shifted instead to White House entertaining, proposing that a limit be placed on the number of cocktails enjoyed by guests—or even that half-drunk glasses might be refilled and recirculated.[47]

While making her way around the interview circuit, Gallagher insisted that she bore JKO no ill will. Her proclaimed motivations for writing the text were to "help the public understand Jackie and why she married Onassis" and to allow them to know Mrs. Onassis "as a woman . . . not a goddess."[48] And while her husband spoke directly of "the loot" he anticipated upon widespread release of the book, he emphasized the desire "to set the record straight."[49] For all those claims, the book is intentionally critical, or, as suggested by *Women's Wear Daily*, "gossipy and frequently bitchy."[50] The managing editor of the *Ladies' Home Journal*, the publication that serialized the book, leaned into the catfight trope, allegedly claiming, "Never underestimate the power of a woman writing about another woman."[51] There is little in the way of Gallagher imagining why JBK might have behaved in the manner she did, little effort to imagine JBK's motivations. Gallagher wrote, "Jackie saw herself as someone remote from the common herd, and did not want the public to think there had ever been any hardship in her life." In particular, JBK wished to keep private the details of her reproductive life—and the struggles she faced in that capacity. In a time when marriage and motherhood were widely regarded as the pinnacle of a woman's experience, and pregnancy not a topic discussed particularly publicly, facing struggle in this realm seems a very reasonable justification for one desiring a modicum of privacy. But Mrs. Kennedy was often in the news, and, as relayed by Gallagher, concerned with her image and the image of her husband. According to Gallagher, JBK scanned media coverage each morning and "took a good hard look at everything written about her or the Kennedys."[52] Gallagher assessed this behavior as a vain and inconsistent preoccupation of someone "allegedly" desiring privacy and failed to account for what very well may have been a desire to cultivate and maintain an image that satisfied this private person and allowed for some measure of control or equilibrium in a public life and public role not of her choosing, not to mention an awareness of her husband's keen attention to his presidential image.

As a whole, the Gallagher text is critical of JBK for failing to wholeheartedly embrace John Kennedy's desires—a very public life lived on a very public stage. By Gallagher's evaluation, JBK failed to dedicate herself sufficiently to her husband, her children, or her nation. By privileging at all her own desires, she automatically lost the ability to be an ideal wife and mother, that is, a person who served others above herself. This assessment paralleled critiques of Jackie O as she was evaluated over the course of her second marriage. And yet Gallagher concluded the book saying, "Jackie Kennedy was like a sister to me. . . . I wish her happiness and all good things." Gallagher invoked JBK's legacy making when she wrote, "I cannot express how much she enriched my life by letting me put one foot in Camelot."[53] For all her alleged devotion to John F. Kennedy and his presidency, however, Gallagher felt no compunction to hold up the myth of Camelot that Jacqueline Kennedy had worked to cultivate, at least as it pertained to the first lady, nor did she acknowledge the labor and devotion required of such legacy making. Instead, she shared a view of the former first lady as selfish and unreasonable, wanting things the way she wanted them, and then behaving poorly when her expectations were unfilled.

* * *

Alongside book-length tell-alls and the ongoing coverage by periodicals covering a host of topics and intended for an array of audiences, there existed, too, the question of Jacqueline Onassis's fame. Why was she famous? What did she do to deserve the attention she received? Should her daily comings and goings be considered newsworthy? Ruminations and questions of this kind had existed since the start of JKO's public life, but they increased in the late 1960s and persisted into the 1970s as the distance from her time in the White House increased and this once "most admired" American woman became a figure seemingly undeserving of public admiration or renown. Adjacent to these questions were considerations about the boundaries of public and private life. *Women's Wear Daily* shared Mary Barelli Gallagher's sense of Mrs. Kennedy's White House years: "Whenever she's questioned about her use of private information as a personal secretary to Mrs. Kennedy, she quickly replies—'Jackie was **not** a private person, she was a public person.'"[54] But what about the years since?

Jacqueline Onassis advocated on behalf of her—and her children's—right to privacy, and at a moment when questions about whether that was a right were very much under active legal consideration. While various sources posited JKO's delight with fame, she is very clearly on the record as desiring protection against unwanted coverage. And this is a topic on which JKO used her voice very forthrightly. While she may have offered little in the way of response to claims about her poor behavior or speculations about the life she lived or had lived, she was vocal in her defense of her right to a private life for herself and her children. Rather than following suggestions that she go off grid, JKO actively advocated on behalf of her right to be a private person navigating a public world. She was particularly direct in naming that desire in her public battle against celebrity photographer Ron Galella. In their 1972 trial, JKO argued for her right to move unencumbered in public spaces, without threat or fear from the sustained harassment she and her children had experienced at the hands of Galella for years. This right was not automatic. She, the pursued subject, had to prove the harassment and the resulting fear and unease it generated for her and her family. While Galella staked his ground on the basis of free speech and a free press, his language and behaviors, before, during, and even after the trial revealed a broader sense of ownership over the public sphere and access to the women who inhabited it.

In the fall of 1970, self-proclaimed "paparazzo" Galella had sued JKO and three Secret Service agents for "alleged false arrest and malicious prosecution." He claimed that Mrs. Onassis interfered with his ability to conduct his business in her attempts to dodge his picture taking and the agents, by obstructing his photographic efforts. In response, in March 1971, JKO countersued, "seeking compensatory and punitive damages of $1.5 million and injunctive relief, based on claimed violations of her common law, statutory and constitutional rights of privacy and intentional infliction of emotional distress, assault, harassment and malicious prosecution." The US government likewise became engaged in the trial, aiming to prohibit Galella from engaging with the Secret Service agents assigned to the Kennedy children. Heard between February 16 and March 23, 1972, the ultimate trial record included 4,714 pages and the testimony of twenty-five witnesses, supplemented by hundreds of exhibits. Predictably, the case drew sustained attention and sustained coverage from a range of outlets, many of which treated the trial like a spectacle, or as Lesley Oelsner of the *New York Times* posited, "a bit of healthy fun," as much as (and often more than) they did an effort by Jacqueline Kennedy Onassis to create boundaries that might allow her and her family to enjoy a modicum of ease beyond Galella's relentless pursuit.[55]

In the trial, Mrs. Onassis and her children itemized Galella's efforts to photograph them in a range of locations, situations, and pursuits. Galella aimed to chronicle the family entering or exiting their home, while attending/performing in a school play, on vacation in New Jersey, while riding bikes or taking tennis lessons at Central Park, while dining out and/or attending the theater in New York City or beyond. As noted by Judge Irving Ben Cooper, "He was like a shadow: everywhere she went he followed her and engaged in offensive conduct; nothing was sacred to him whether defendant went to church, funeral services, theatre, school, restaurant, or aboard a yacht in a foreign land." Bernadette Carrozza, editor of *Photoplay*, testified to Galella's proclaimed intimate knowledge of JKO's comings and goings, the "exits and entrances and stairways she used." In December 1971, he told her, "Nobody else knows what time Mrs. Onassis walks her dog. Nobody else knows what time she goes to Central Park. Only I know."[56]

Beyond episodes detailed at length in the trial (an exchange with Caroline Kennedy at the Central Park tennis club house, his intrusions at John Kennedy's school, and an altercation on the Central Park bike path), the decision included a range of disturbances caused by Galella, including instances where the Kennedy children "were caused to bang into glass doors, school parents were bumped, passage was blocked, flashbulbs affected vision, telephoto lenses were used to spy, the children were imperiled in the water . . . Plaintiff trailed defendant through the City hour after hour, plaintiff chased defendant by automobile, plaintiff and his assistants surrounded defendant and orbited while shouting." Judge Cooper noted witnesses' uses of the following language to describe Galella's "unnerving and often frightening" behavior: "'jumping,' 'lunging,' 'leaping,' 'rushing out,' 'snaking in and out,' 'dashing at me,' 'touching,' 'bumping,' 'scuffling,' 'blocking,' 'thrusting' his camera and circling (sometimes with assistants) in close orbit about defendant and her children." Galella was familiar with JKO, too, using direct address in his efforts to capture her attention—and, by extension, her image. As she described one exchange when she left her home, Galella "jumped out at me under the awning. . . . He was grunting, and he said, 'Glad to see me back, aren't you, Jackie?' And then he took his camera strap and he flicked me on both sides of my shoulders as I was walking to the car. He came so close." As she described getting in her car and Galella's continued pursuit, she concluded that it was "one of the most aggressive ways he has ever come at me."[57]

The persistence of Galella's paparazzi attack brought this testimony from Jacqueline Onassis: "It caused me anguish. It caused me fear for my safety, for the safety of my children. At times it caused me terror, distress, no peace, no peace of mind, fear for what was going to happen to them and to me when we would encounter him again; also being under surveyance [sic], imprisoned in your house, all that deportment over all this time has caused an enormous strain and unhappiness, and all of that on me, for myself and for my children." JKO's children, John, age eleven, and Caroline, age fourteen, weighed in in affidavits for the trial. John said, "I feel threatened when he is present. I very much wish to avoid him. I think anyone would fear someone who follows you everywhere." Caroline added, "Unfortunately, I am one of his favorite targets . . . have been subjected to numerous unpleasant and often dangerous incidents with him . . . I don't feel safe when he is near and will go to great lengths to avoid him. He never lets me alone. He scares me."[58]

Even with the detailed extremes of his behavior, Galella and his attorney dismissed the ideas that he presented a real threat or generated fear or anxiety from his efforts. And yet in her testimony, JKO used language that included "terrified," "frightened," "stunned," "startled," "afraid," "anguished," and "humiliated." Galella's lawyer, Alfred S. Julien, made a point to hold up pictures his client had taken of JKO, and ask if she had been afraid at the moment the image was captured. His claim: that she "grossly exaggerated" her sense of fear when pursued by Galella. The inability or unwillingness of Galella and his counsel to imagine the fear and anxiety he generated in JKO or her children, and

Jacqueline Kennedy Onassis arrives at New York's federal court on March 3, 1972. She was in a legal dispute with paparazzi Ron Galella, seeking an injunction prohibiting him from coming within one hundred yards of her. Everett Collection Historical/Alamy Stock Photo.

the onus put upon Mrs. Onassis to sufficiently present and perform her fear, reflects a historic propensity to doubt women, to silence them, to make them feel that the public world is less theirs than it is the men's with whom they must share that space. JKO and her children shared a particular history. More than once their lives had been upended by a stranger committing a violent act on a loved one. They possessed, surely, a particular understanding of potential threats to them and their family from persons beyond their control. About her physical response to Galella, JKO shared the following while on the stand: "I always try to keep smiling when Galella is there. I know he wants to catch me looking terrified . . . When Mr. Galella is photographing me I tried to keep a smile, keep my head up, act as normal as possible because I believe he wants to provoke an unusual response or gesture, a frightened look or shielding one's face or something, so I try to keep my head up and keep smiling."[59] While an average woman might not share the experience of being tracked by an aggressive photographer, one can imagine other women employing such a strategy when catcalled or approached by a strange man in a public space. JKO's visage was not about an absence of fear but a mechanism for masking it.

Jacqueline Kennedy Onassis's testimony is of particular value because her voice and her views are at the heart of the transcript. There is no need for speculation or guesswork. She was telling the judge—and the broader public—what she wanted. And she was a force. In the decision, Judge Cooper called her "candid and careful, frequently searching for the proper word in order to be precise; she was not given to exaggeration." This demeanor she maintained during a cross-examination the New York Times reported on as "bitter, repetitious, prolonged and rasping." During the early years of her marriage to a public figure, she had become attuned to the importance of image crafting. In her testimony, JKO was measured and even. She was respectful of the court and the rule of law. That courtroom presentation, certainly, was adjacent to her desired public image more broadly. In the courtroom, with time and space to speak, she was able to communicate something of the image she desired to have on public record.[60]

The court engaged in ruminations about privacy, about the right to free speech and a free press, about what constituted newsworthiness. It considered the effect of Galella's antics on JKO's and her children's peace of mind and sense of safety navigating the public world—and ultimately determined that was a right people had, and one that outweighed the right to free speech or freedom of the press of the kind Galella claimed at the heart of his defense of his actions. Cooper's decision condemned Galella for his behavior at trial (not to mention censured his counsel). Cooper's final decision exposed Galella as an inveterate liar: "The record is studded with instance after instance where plaintiff's testimony was clearly perjurious. Often his own testimony exposed the perjury and at other times his very testimony compelled its rejection; on occasion he was forced to acknowledge the falsity of his testimony."[61] The judge was deliberate in highlighting the bizarreness and invasiveness of Galella's behavior. In the case decision, he added, "We were simply aghast at trial, and continue to be, at the unlimited effrontery with which plaintiff initiated, attempted to sustain and failed miserably to establish, his spurious assertions. Indeed, brazen is the word for Galella."[62] From this assessment, Galella's behavior—at trial and in the world as a whole—emerged as fully unacceptable.

As Cooper wrote, "The proposition that the First Amendment gives the press wide liberty to engage in any sort of conduct, no matter how offensive, in gathering news has been flatly rejected." In a section of the decision entitled "Balancing the Right of Privacy against the Impingement on 'Speech,'" Cooper considered just how much JKO should have to endure. What "sacrifice" should be required of her "in order that some portion of the public may learn what she wore while walking on the public streets, or her appearance at the theater and public functions, or her department store purchases, or what she ate in restaurants? Does the Constitution insist on that too? Surely, such a contention belittles the great wisdom that is the hallmark of the Constitution." He continued in his consideration about the need to balance the protection of an individual's right to privacy and extension of constitutional rights more broadly, writing, "Clearly, the First Amendment protects freedom of expression with respect to public affairs matters relevant to the self-government of the nation. . . . Mrs. Onassis is a public figure, whose life has included events of great public concern. But it cannot be said that information about her comings and goings, her tastes in ballet, the food that she eats, and other minutiae which are the sole product of Galella's three years of pursuit, bear significantly upon public questions. . . . It merely satisfies curiosity." In sum, Cooper concluded, "We see no constitutional violence done by permitting defendant to prevent intrusion on her life which serves no useful purpose."[63]

When all was said and done, Galella and anyone in his employ received parameters for what were sure to be his continued pursuits. He (and they) could not approach within one hundred yards of JKO's home or the children's schools, and he was to stay seventy-five yards from John and Caroline and fifty from JKO. He was prohibited "from performing surveillance of defendant or her children; from commercially appropriating defendant's photograph for advertising or trade purposes without defendant's consent; from communicating or attempting to communicate with defendant or her children."[64]

Cooper stopped short, however, of acknowledging JKO's full claim to a private life in public space. "We do not agree with plaintiff's trial attorney who contended at trial that whenever defendant is on public property, she regards it as her private domain." Mrs. Onassis outlined her views in this way: "I consider it private when I am walking on a public street . . . I consider private errands private." For her, walking through Central Park was a private act conducted in a public place. The court upheld her status as a public figure—but with parameters on what, exactly, constituted "newsworthy" behavior. As Lesley Oelsner shared in the *New York Times*, "Much of the legal theory on which [JKO] relies has not yet been firmly established." At the very least, however, Judge Cooper determined, "There is no general constitutional right to assault, harass, or unceasingly shadow or distress public figures."[65]

Judge Cooper found the evidence of the case compelling enough to use language such as "assault," "harass," and "distress." But those covering the case were seemingly less convinced of the actual threat Galella presented or unwilling to read as legitimate the fear he caused JKO and the Kennedy children. In March 1972, *Esquire*'s cover story was a Ron Galella profile, with what presumably was intended as a clever title, "Why Won't Jackie Onassis Leave Ron Galella Alone?" Author Bruce Jay Friedman detailed what he regarded as Ron Galella's cultivation of a particular kind of "specialization." Friedman reported that Galella had obtained nearly four thousand images of JKO in "'frightened deer'–type poses" and, successfully avoiding efforts to deter him, "the tall paunchy shutterbug has relentlessly tracked his prey to at least two of the four corners of the earth, nailing her in Capri, Naples, Scorpios, Peapack, New Jersey, Brooklyn Heights, the bowels of Chinatown and midtown Manhattan bicycle paths." The "shutterbug" terminology suggested an unthreatening vision of Galella, although the idea that he regarded JKO as his "prey," and Friedman's willingness to trade unproblematically in that kind of terminology, indicated an almost implicit acceptance of both Galella's mission and his methods.

Friedman recounted an exchange between Aristotle Onassis and Galella, in which Galella claimed that AO asked why he continued to pursue JKO with such ardor. Galella said, "I'm not a sadist, giving her pain. . . . If not for me, people would kill themselves with curiosity about her and the kids. There is a big void for an American paparazzo with courage and I am filling it.'" Friedman wrote with admiration about Galella's "perverse gentleness" in his renderings of JKO. In Galella's images, Friedman assessed, there was not one bad shot of JKO. If Galella was such a skilled technician, why resist him? Why not agree to a formal shooting? Friedman shared Galella's ready response: "'Too smart,' he said. 'If she stopped ducking me, she knows the market on her would dry up.'" In Galella's telling, JKO's desire for privacy was a ruse. In his estimation, she was a willing participant in his pursuit of her (and her children, a pursuit that receives limited engagement in this article). In an alleged exchange where JKO addressed Galella directly, noting that he had been "hunting" her for three months, he assessed the interaction in this way: "She seemed fascinated," said Galella. "And why not. We have a lot in common. I'm persistent. I get what I want.

So does she. She wants to dominate, to do things when *she* wants. I say no, I'm Italian. It's got to be when *I* want."[66] Friedman offered nothing in the way of critical assessment, suggesting there was nothing particularly unusual or unproblematic about Galella's claimed access to JKO.

Much as Galella's counsel had dismissed JKO's actual concerns, other media coverage did much the same. As *Life* shared, "Seldom has a court of law been put to such a glamorous but trivial test."[67] Rather than engaging in actual reporting about the parameters of the case, or taking seriously the questions about the boundaries between public and private life, the coverage was incapable of moving beyond what seemingly had become the tried and true frames for writing about JKO. Her appearance merited mention: she "looks terrific. . . . All else seems irrelevant and immaterial." The article asked what presumably were meant to be a series of pertinent questions: "Is he a pest, or worse, a menace? Has he frightened her? Has she interfered with his livelihood? Did she have him flung into a snowbank?" A final question posed, and posed in a magazine issue in which this was the cover story: "Does anybody care?"[68] The article suggested that the case, motivated by "staggering pettiness," still raised "a serious issue: the unfettered pursuit of a bona fide story vs. an individual's privacy," but ultimately suggested that it was "doubtful" that Mrs. Onassis could "ever hope to enjoy real anonymity."[69]

Galella was hardly chastened by the experience. Indeed, he and Mrs. Onassis would return to trial in the 1980s. He was undeterred, and he was buoyed by compatriots who saw nothing *really* wrong in his pursuit of JKO. Despite the court's decision—and a denial of a subsequent appeal—he continued with his tracking of JKO and the Kennedy children. He maintained his emphasis on his right to free speech, dedicating his 1974 book, *Jacqueline*, "to a spirit of a free press whose purpose is to inform the public through pictures and words—photojournalism."[70]

In recounting the incident when he pursued Caroline during a tennis lesson in Central Park, when JKO ran away from him, Galella wrote, "What made Jackie run? She had never done that to me before." In the years he had pursued her, this was a first. But rather than interpreting this as an effort to escape him, Galella pondered, "Why does she want me to chase her?"[71] For him, theirs was a relationship, a game. And for him, his point of view was the only interpretation that mattered. He made that even more explicit when he wrote about his perceived right of access to JKO: "As long as she stays in the apartment, Jackie is in another world as far as I'm concerned, because I would never sneak into the apartment to take a picture of her. That's private. But as soon as she walks out the front door of the building, she's in my world. That's public."[72] In this assessment, the world was his more than hers. This reading very directly communicated that each time Mrs. Onassis stepped into the world, she handed over a kind of access or ownership to her person. In her trial, JKO rejected that entirely—and yet, even after the trial, here was this book, with *her* name on it, published—by a trade press—by the man hell bent on maintaining a hold on her. With all of JKO's power and privilege and resources, the book represented the rejection of women's claim to public space on their own terms. But Jacqueline Onassis would continue to stake that claim for the rest of her life.

* * *

In his 1972 text, Christian Cafarakis confidently asserted that there was "no doubt that by 1970, Onassis had decided to get a divorce." Spurred, in part, by AO's declaration that their marriage was over, Cafarakis claims, however, that JKO "realized she was deeply in love" with him and made a concerted "effort to be an obedient and docile wife at all times." At the time of his book's publication, Cafarakis assured readers that things were looking up for the Onassis pairing.[73]

Whatever obedience Cafarakis imagined for JKO did not extend to her decision to take Ron Galella to court. According to biographer Sarah Bradford, Aristotle Onassis had "been furious" about the choice, believing it only further publicized the photographer. On December 22, 1973, the *New York Times* reported, when Paul, Weiss, Rifkind & Garrison failed to receive payment for legal services provided Mrs. Onassis in her case against Galella, they sued Mr. Onassis. Six days later, the

Times published an article reporting that Jacqueline Kennedy Onassis would pay the bill because, as Mr. Onassis said, "I had nothing to do with the damned thing."[74] Their $20 million honeymoon, by all accounts, was over.

In January 1973, AO's son, Alexander, died in a plane crash. Onassis was bereft, and reports suggest he "went through a long depression." Whatever reconciliation Alexander's death fomented between Aristotle and Jacqueline Onassis was fairly short lived.[75] Increasingly, Onassis was a very sick man, diagnosed in 1974 with myasthenia gravis, a neurological disorder that caused a weakening of muscles, and particularly the muscles controlling the upper eyelids. The related weakness and fatigue debilitated AO. He could neither conduct business nor even his daily (or night) life in the manner or at the pace he had long maintained. He and JKO often were apart. Hospitalized at the American Hospital in Paris in February, Aristotle Onassis died on March 15, 1975.[76]

Jacqueline Kennedy Onassis was not present for her husband's death. When she arrived and was met by the usual mob of photographers, she flashed a smile that seemed hardly the look of a grieving widow. In a July 1975 issue of *Photoplay*, alleging to provide details about "the Merry Widow," the periodical shared a quotation from Apostolos Zavitsianos, the priest who oversaw AO's funeral procession and claimed to be "shocked" by JKO's smile throughout the proceedings: "In all the funeral services I've conducted," he said, "this smile was a new experience for me." Disturbed, too, were Onassis's sisters and daughter, Christina, who, *Photoplay* reported, halfway through the funeral procession, jumped out of the car with her stepmother to escape JKO's "frivolous attitude."[77] The laudations JKO received for her public display following her first husband's assassination would not be repeated upon the death of her second husband. Indeed, coverage of JKO in the aftermath of her second husband's death fit the frame media increasingly had used to assess her over the course of their not-quite-seven-year marriage.

Following Aristotle Onassis's death, JKO and Christina Onassis engaged in sustained negotiations over AO's will, which provided his widow around $3 million, "a bequest far less than published reports

John Kennedy Jr., Jacqueline Kennedy Onassis, Caroline Kennedy, and Senator Edward Kennedy attend funeral services for Aristotle Onassis in Skorpios, Greece, on March 18, 1975. Onassis died in Paris on March 15. UPI/Alamy Stock Photo.

indicated she would receive," which some accounts projected as high as $200 million.[78] Various sources indicated that AO had been in the process of filing for divorce before the worst of his illness took over. In the final year of his life, he succeeded in having Greek law changed from the standard practice of allotting widows one-quarter of their husband's total holdings. He had penned an alternative will early in 1974 and had had JKO sign an amendment to their original marriage contract, which, rather than providing additional security as JKO seemed to have imagined, limited her right to his estate. Jacqueline Onassis and Christina Onassis engaged in a contest over the distribution of AO's fortune that lasted until October 1977, when JKO received $20 million "in return for abandoning all further claims to his estate." The notion that JKO contested the document or aimed to get more than she deserved solidified ideas of her as a gold digger, as greedy and duplicitous, as having wed Onassis for base purposes.[79]

Reporting on AO's death and JKO's response was in keeping with the kind of speculative assessment that had marked their marriage. In this case, however, JKO spoke. Of Onassis, she said, "Aristotle Onassis rescued me at a moment when my life was engulfed with shadows. He meant a lot to me. He brought me into a world where one could find both happiness and love. We lived through many beautiful experiences together which cannot be forgotten and for which I will be eternally grateful."[80] She offered no critique of him or explanation of their time together—or apart. When she used her voice, she did so deliberately. As important as what she said is what she left unsaid. As she moved on to a second round of widowhood, that penchant to speak with discernment when she so desired and to leave some things unsaid would become a hallmark of her public persona and a strategy that would result in another round of interpretation of her public image.

*   *   *   *   *

      *   *   [7]   *   *

*   *   *   *   *

PROFESSIONAL

In 1979, *Ms.* magazine, the publication born of the women's liberation movement, dedicated its March issue to women who worked. Appearing on the cover was Jacqueline Onassis. Just a few years before, such an appearance for such a topic would have been improbable if not impossible (indeed, some readers blanched at the selection of JKO for the cover, taking her feature as a sign that hell had frozen over). Beyond Mrs. Onassis's engagement with the question "Why does this woman work?," readers were met with Gloria Steinem's ruminations about JKO, the trajectory of her adult life, and the ways in which she had been assessed publicly. Reminiscing about her own coverage of Jacqueline Kennedy following John Kennedy's assassination, Steinem recalled asking numerous observers what they believed the former first lady should do next. Mrs. Kennedy did not share her plans, but suggestions from outside sources abounded. In thinking about her article from 1964, Steinem wrote, "No one even mentioned the idea that she might simply lead her own life. With feminist hindsight, it's clear that neither I nor anyone I interviewed was paying her the honor of considering her as the separate human being she was and would have been, whether or not she had become the wife of a President." She was, in the eyes of many, tied to John Kennedy and the Kennedy family, and their identity—public, political—was hers. For Steinem, that explained the jarring feeling observers experienced when Jacqueline Kennedy married Aristotle Onassis. "Her second marriage choice and her supposed transformation," Steinem wrote, "just didn't make sense; a problem understood by any woman who has had the experience of being treated

* 227 *

like a totally different person, though the only change is the identity of the man standing next to her."[1]

After the death of Aristotle Onassis, Steinem noted, "The speculation about her future plans seemed only to have split in two. Would she become a Kennedy again (that is more politically influential and serious) or remain an Onassis (more supposedly social and simply rich)?" Even in widowhood, JKO was tied to and was anticipated to follow the path of one of the men with whom she had shared distinct years of her life. The notion that Mrs. Onassis might have plans or interests of her own, separate from either John Kennedy or Aristotle Onassis, seemed wholly unanticipated. At forty-six years old, her teenage children largely self-sufficient, Mrs. Onassis did what many women of the 1970s did: she took a job. "No one was predicting she might go back to work in the publishing world she had entered briefly after college," Steinem wrote, "and to the kind of job she could have had years ago, completely on her own."[2]

Steinem's view of JKO was nuanced and sensitive, empathetic and attuned to the world of unique and unparalleled celebrity JKO inhabited (which very likely explains JKO's willingness to participate in and contribute to this particular issue of *Ms.*). Steinem admitted her own desires for how Mrs. Onassis might have used her platform, wishing "that she would use her clout to work publicly for the issues of women and powerless groups in general." "But," Steinem noted, "wanting her to use that power may be unfairly close to wanting to use her, however life-saving the cause." And Steinem acknowledged how routinely JKO was used, both with her knowledge and in ways and by those of whom she might be unaware. For example, in a little restaurant near Steinem's office, there was "a current, blown-up newspaper photo of Jackie in its window. She's just sitting alone at the counter obviously unaware of any camera—but not only was the photograph taken and published without permission, it's now being used by the restaurant's owners to sell hamburgers." Her fame was inescapable, and even if JKO managed it, there was no way for her to ever fully control it. Steinem saw that, and in acknowledging how, for Jackie Kennedy Onassis, "everything is fair game, even a cup of coffee," Steinem made sense of "the appeal of a Greek Island and a strong friend—especially in those post-Kennedy years when crowds waited daily outside her apartment door." Thinking about JKO after Onassis and thinking about her decision to take a job at midlife, Steinem marveled at "the resolve it must take to enter the ordinary work world each day; something she has been doing for more than four years now."[3]

Gloria Steinem granted Jacqueline Kennedy Onassis recognition as a whole person, propelled of her own volition. She saw and named, too, the landscape JKO navigated as she endeavored to follow a path of her own choosing. "Not only are there professional Jackie-watchers lurking around many corners," she wrote. There was also "speculation of her past marital life, unauthorized books, sensationalized headlines, and thinly disguised movies to be survived."[4] Such was the media world Jacqueline Kennedy Onassis inhabited during the second half of the 1970s. Fan magazines and celebrity tabloids continued to craft an image of the former first lady, but the field had expanded in a world where expectations and understandings of what constituted hard and soft news had become ever more intertwined and behind-the-scenes tell-alls by alleged insiders who claimed to share previously unknown secrets flooded the market. In addition to navigating the world in real time, JKO, if she engaged with contemporary media, was confronted over and over again by speculation about and unveilings of her past.

Steinem's sensitivity to JKO was fairly unique. Ruminations of "Who Is Jacqueline Kennedy Onassis?" continued across a range of publications and outlets, although, had chroniclers been willing to take her words and deeds at face value, those queries fairly easily could have been laid to rest. Jacqueline Kennedy Onassis had long articulated and acted upon her interests: history, arts, culture. She had talked about these things before the White House and then had made them priorities as first lady. In her second widowhood, these again were locations of particular emphasis and engagement for her, both in her publishing work and in her social life and locations where she lent her name and her fame. But coverage of JKO even as a woman independent of any man was not necessarily about JKO as an individual. As Mrs. Onassis navigated midlife, and largely in a way that seemed of her choosing and dedicated to her interests, she remained linked to the men, as Steinem noted, with whom she had spent the earlier parts of her life. Those chronicling JKO, determined to make sense of her, seemed unable to do so without framing her as someone's wife. This was true especially of John Kennedy, who, in a more cynical world of post-Watergate political journalism, was the subject of a host of retrospectives and tell-all revelations that tarnished the Camelot mystique to which JKO had dedicated so much of her legacy making. But for all the claims about JFK—and the associated claims about Jacqueline Kennedy and the nature of their union—JKO maintained a commitment to discretion, to keeping what had been a life lived on a public stage still a place deserving of some privacy. She maintained, too, her commitment to her first husband's legacy with the work she continued in the establishment and opening of the John F. Kennedy Presidential Library. In a world where people increasingly shared their innermost thoughts and feelings and private reminiscences, JKO was unique for her decision not to follow that path. And where she had stood out in the earlier part of the decade for reasons that drew censure, this distinction reestablished, for many, JKO's public stature.

* * *

Shortly before she became a widow for a second time, Jacqueline Kennedy Onassis, reluctant focus of ongoing media attention, volunteered her voice for a cause close to her heart: the campaign to Save Grand Central Station. On January 21, 1975, New York State Supreme Court justice Irving H. Saypol invalidated the building's designation as a landmark for preservation, ruling that building owner Penn Central could proceed with a plan to build a fifty-nine-story office tower above the station. Making reference to Grand Central's "long-neglected faded beauty," Saypol was clear in his opinion: "Esthetics is not for decision here."[5] Many New Yorkers disagreed, including Jacqueline Kennedy Onassis. Building on a documented love for history and a lived devotion to New York City, JKO joined the Committee to Save Grand Central for an opening press conference in the Oyster Bar on January 30, 1975. While she did not deliver the central address, which highlighted the architectural and cultural significance of the station, and spoke only briefly, her appearance at the event made it that much more worthy of news coverage. "If we don't care about our past we can't have very much hope for our future," she said. "We've all heard that it's too late, or that it has to happen, that it's inevitable. But I don't think that's true. Because I think if there is a great effort, even if it's the eleventh hour, then you can succeed, and I know that's what we'll do."[6]

Within a year after joining the Committee to Save Grand Central, Mrs. Onassis was on the Municipal Art Society's (MAS) board of directors. If her every move was chronicled by those dedicated to reporting her comings and goings, the Grand Central effort was a location where JKO put her stardom to use. And if the former first lady tended not to offer any justification for her decisions or behaviors, the preservation effort was a location where she willingly shared her point of view. Laurie Beckelman, who had been on the MAS staff since 1973, assessed JKO's influence on the effort in this way: "Because of *her*, people popularized preservation. Every magazine in America and Europe knew about Jackie and Grand Central."[7]

Jacqueline Kennedy Onassis was unafraid to use whatever muscle her name afforded her on behalf of the celebrated venue. New York City mayor Abraham Beame had been advised by counsel not to challenge Saypol's ruling. If the city appealed, Penn Central would ask for $60 million. New York City, verging on bankruptcy, could not afford it. JKO nudged the mayor, sending him a letter at the end of February 1975 on her personal stationery, in her elegant long hand. "Is it not cruel to let our city die by degrees, stripped of all her proud moments, until there is nothing left of her history and beauty to inspire our children?" she asked. "If they are not inspired by the past of our city, where will they find the strength to fight for her future?" Framing the effort as part of the national story and a potential location for national celebration, she added, "Maybe, with our bicentennial approaching, this is the moment to take a stand, to reverse the tide, so that we won't all end up in a uniform world of steel and glass boxes."[8] The language JKO employed to encourage the mayor was consistent with the language she used not only across the Grand Central campaign but also across her ongoing and long-standing efforts to preserve the past as part of a national legacy and as a gift to future generations of citizens, to which not only her children but all American children belonged.

JKO revealed in her letter to Beame, too, that she had lost nothing when it came to her image-crafting chops. She deftly invoked the memory of John Kennedy, continuing her legacy work and tying Beame to the president in offering a similar experience the men had shared. "I think of the time President Kennedy was faced with the destruction of Lafayette Square, opposite the White House . . . about to be demolished to make way for a huge Eisenhower-approved Government Office Building. All contracts had been signed. At the last minute he cancelled them—and as he did so, he said, 'This is the act I may be most remembered for.'" That kind of remembrance, JKO suggested, was possible for Beame, too. "Your life has been devoted to this city," she reminded him. "Now you serve her in the highest capacity. You are her people's last hope—all their last hopes lie with you." This was a moment for both service and courage. "It would be so noble if you were to go down in history as the man who was brave enough to stem the tide, brave enough to stand up against the greed that would devour New York bit by bit," she wrote. "People now, and people not yet born will be grateful to you and honor your name."[9]

The campaign continued until the various appeals against the 1975 ruling made their way to the Supreme Court. On the day the court was to hear arguments on the case, JKO and hundreds of other Grand Central activists rode from New York City to Washington, DC, aboard the Landmark Express. In explaining the group's mission, Mrs. Onassis said, "If Grand Central Station goes, all of the landmarks in this country will go as well. If that happens, we'll live in a world of steel and glass."[10] Frederick Papert, who led the Save Grand Central campaign and had been part of Robert Kennedy's 1968 presidential bid, remarked

Jacqueline Onassis stands in train doorway as she prepares to ride the Landmark Express. UPI/Alamy Stock Photo.

about the train's arrival in Washington, DC, "People came out on that day to see Jackie. Mrs. Mondale, Senator Moynihan were two powerful Washington presences, but they loomed in the background once she appeared. But it didn't matter because in coming to see her, people came in droves, they saw, they heard, we won!"[11] The court ultimately sided with preservationist efforts and ruled that New York City could prevent construction on Grand Central. By this time, Ed Koch had taken over as mayor. In response to the ruling, which he could not resist labeling as a "landmark decision," he said, "This fight waged by the City of New York in support of preserving those parts of our architectural heritage worthy of preservation was important not only for New York but other cities throughout the country."[12]

If JKO's fame was inescapable, and seemed unlikely to abate any time soon, at this stage in her life, she regarded it as somewhat "unremarkable." By the late 1970s, biographer William Kuhn suggests, "she neither loved the attention she attracted nor hated it. It was just there."[13] But it appeared, too, that she found a certain usefulness for it: she would trade on her fame for causes in which she believed and within networks where she was afforded some measure of space and respect.[14] JKO's refrains in her efforts to aid the Grand Central undertaking were about the value of the past and the world of the nation's children's future. Her points were clear and dignified and high minded. And whatever critiques she had drawn since her marriage to Aristotle Onassis, she had remained a person whose sense of what was valuable was unmatched. As noted by urbanist Roberta Grandes Gratz, "Jackie, the great arbiter of good taste in fashion, food, and architecture, raised the consciousness of the nation to the importance of historic preservation."[15]

Grand Central was but one location for JKO's sponsorship. Her words and actions in the name of salvaging evidence of the nation's past buoyed the efforts of those looking to preserve urban structures and neighborhoods as an act of civic virtue and commitment to the greater good. She lent her name and her fame as well to the Metropolitan Museum of Art, the American Ballet Theater, the Center of Photography in

New York, and a range of other artistic or cultural causes. Her appearance at various benefits and events meant increased coverage. Sometimes she would make a comment or two, but perhaps even more, her attendance at these kinds of events communicated something of how she preferred to spend her time and what it was that brought her particular joy. Indeed, those things were the very things she had claimed to love for as long as anyone had asked her what it was that interested her most.[16]

* * *

JKO was able to dedicate herself to preservation and the arts in a more sustained fashion during the 1970s since she increasingly spent most of her time in New York City, both because she was no longer part of an intercontinental relationship and because she, like many other women of the decade, embarked upon a career. Her longtime friend and one-time social secretary, Tish Baldridge, recalled urging JKO to enter the workforce after Aristotle Onassis's death. Baldridge told the *New York Times*, "I really felt she needed something to get out in the world and meet people doing interesting things, use that energy and that good brain of hers." Baldridge had connections at Viking, and urged JKO to contact Thomas Guinzburg, who had known the Auchincloss family for years. And so, in September 1975—a year of major transition for JKO—she began work at Viking Press, hired as a consulting editor. Guinzburg rightly predicted JKO's discerning eye and her range "of not-quite-ordinary contacts," some of whom, ideally, she might persuade to pick up a pen. Meeting with the press on her first day, Guinzburg stated, "She has taste and energy and a broad background in the fine arts."[17] To begin, her primary job would be "to acquire books." Then, Guinzburg shared, "as she became more familiar with publishing procedures, she could work on the books and with the writers to whatever extent appealed to her. She could create books and so on."[18] This is what Jacqueline Kennedy Onassis did. And she brought intensity and integrity to her work, first at Viking and later at Doubleday, where she would work for the rest of her life.

Starting in the fall of 1975, JKO had a routine, and a more recognizable or even potentially relatable routine than she had had for years. She worked part-time and kept to a fairly standard schedule. She stayed at home a lot. She attended events and openings around the city. She spent weekends with her horses in New Jersey. She summered in Hyannis Port and, later, Martha's Vineyard. Jacqueline Kennedy Onassis's life, as she shifted from her mid- to late forties was, as she put it, "very dull."[19] And she made sure to highlight that message whenever she was given the chance. From the perceived glamor of the jet-set lifestyle that marked the late 1960s and early 1970s, coverage of JKO in her second widowhood communicated a more staid vision of the still most famous woman in the world.

Some observers poked fun at JKO's endeavors. Syndicated columnist Art Buchwald suggested the challenge Viking would face in affording the office décor JKO inevitably would demand. In imagining titles upon which she might work, he offered, "Europe on $15,000 a Day." He suggested the rude awakening JKO would find in dealing with writers, who, unlike everyone else, might dodge her calls as she followed up on a manuscript's progress. His column refused to take seriously JKO's potential as editor and communicated that Viking had hired her as a stunt.[20] Trading on a sense of JKO as privileged and entitled, these observers (usually men) missed the mark. By all accounts, those working at Viking found Mrs. Onassis the consummate professional, eager to learn the trade and more than willing to engage in the mundane requirements of office work. She made her own copies. She got her own coffee. She answered her own phone. She was Jacqueline Kennedy Onassis, but she was also a member of the Viking team, "integrated into the fabric," as another Viking editor recalled.[21]

William Kuhn's *Reading Jackie* posits that while sharing little about herself with contemporary media, JKO shared much of herself in the books she chose to edit and the topics she included as part of a list that by career's end numbered nearly one hundred titles. Early on, while at Viking, the interests JKO was making clear in her commitment to history and preservation and culture were clear also in her early projects. A book about United States women's history, *Remember the Ladies: Women in America, 1750–1815*, was JKO's first undertaking. At a time when women's history was coming into its own, this text, corresponding with the upcoming bicentennial, was adjacent to an exhibition planned in Plymouth, Massachusetts, and detailed the role of women in the colonial, revolutionary, and early national period. The book blended text and images—of artwork, textiles, clothing, and other material culture. According to Mabel H. "Muffie" Brandon, who had been on the committee linked to the original exhibition and encouraged the creation of an accompanying text, JKO engaged in discussions about the necessity of representing women across various populations, insisted upon inclusion of home medical texts' reference to abortifacients, and delighted in Martha Washington's reference to Georgetown as "a dirty hole." JKO joined the authors in an editing session, "crawling around the floor, arranging picture layouts" and asked for explanation of editing terms that were new to her and would inform her work moving forward.[22]

Also significant was JKO's work on *In the Russian Style*, just one of two books bearing her name as editor. Attracted to the project by her interest in Russian culture and history, JKO also was motivated to embark upon the project due to the relationship she shared with former *Vogue* editor Diana Vreeland, who had joined the Metropolitan Museum as a consultant to the Costume Institute and had planned an exhibit dedicated to Imperial Russian material culture. JKO worked to create a companion volume to the exhibit, doing whatever research she could stateside and eventually joining Met director Thomas Hoving on a trip to the Soviet Union.[23]

In his memoir, Hoving shared a host of observations of JKO, from the astounding level of her celebrity to her commitment to the work of the book to the reception she received and the respect she commanded in the USSR. As he recalled the process of leaving Paris for Moscow, he noted, "I was flabbergasted at the crowds of photojournalists and reporters and television crews who hounded us as we departed Paris. All the mundane details of checking in at Charles de Gaulle, having our luggage weighed, trudging up the long, flat, black-rubber moving belts to the passport station were recorded step by step." His recollection shared something, too, of the ways in which JKO "graciously" managed the attention she received and also the assumptions made by those tracking her: "Jackie pasted a smile on her face and toughed it out. . . . By the time we had been in the Soviet Union, I had been characterized 'the new mystery lover' in the tabloids."[24]

In assessing her work, Hoving wrote, "I have never met anyone who . . . was so driven to learn. On the long flight from Paris to Moscow she asked for a full briefing on everything I knew about Russia— every detail. What she knew about the costumes impressed me. Her homework had been prodigious. She was punctilious when it came to giving credit to every person who had helped her and cited every book." JKO, Hoving recalled, had a particular desire for a green lap robe she knew Princess Elisabeth had worn on sleigh rides. Soviet representatives insisted the piece had disappeared, nowhere to be found in the archives. But then, after traveling to Leningrad and the Hermitage, their hosts took Hoving and Mrs. Onassis Kennedy, as they insisted on calling her, to a part of the museum where Hoving had never been. In the center of the room was a sled and JKO's desired green robe. Grandly, Hoving recalled, Viktor Suslov declared, "The robe of Princess Elisabeth you wanted, Mrs. Onassis Kennedy—and the original sleigh. We found it—for you." At JKO's request, the sleigh and robe were approved for the exhibit in New York. Hoving concluded his reminiscences by noting, "The visit helped the catalog—and the show—immeasurably. Both managed to achieve a balance of scholarship and allure which became the benchmark for all future Costume Institute exhibitions and made it easier for us to plan other exchanges with the Soviet Union."[25]

JKO did her due diligence in promoting *In the Russian Style*. She lunched with reporters and Viking head Guinzburg, who reminded those present "that the subject of the meeting was the Russian book and the Russian book only." His defense of his celebrity editor is evident in the *New York Times* coverage of the lunch: "Jackie wouldn't have allowed her name to go on the book if she hadn't been the prime mover behind it," he said. If anyone doubted how much work she actually did, he aimed to put those kinds of questions to rest. Adamantly, he rejected the notion of her as "a Hollywood type of star, with a double doing the hard part of the job." Joyce Maynard, reporting for the *Times*, seemed convinced of JKO's relationship to the book, noting, "Mrs. Onassis displayed considerable knowledge of Russian history as she spoke, but when the questioning turned to other areas, she was less expansive." And at this event, very clearly about her professional life, reporters begged for some kind of private revelation. Asked how her children viewed the text, she quipped, "Rapidly." She rejected the idea that "the kind of treatment she herself received in newspapers and magazines" was reflected in some way by the book's and exhibit's investigation into the lives of elite Russians of the czarist past. Maynard noted that JKO's "smile stiffened faintly" before she responded, "There's a difference between what is history and what's going on now." Keeping the conversation as focused as possible on her professional life, JKO shared, "'I always wanted to be some kind of writer or newspaper reporter. . . . But after college . . .' her voice drifted, 'I did other things.'"[26]

This notion of doing "other things," and more, having done those other things as part of the landscape in which she had come of age, was a theme JKO ruminated upon in the conversation she had with Gloria Steinem about her relationship to work. She reminded those reading *Ms.* that before her first marriage she had held a job at a newspaper. While her title at the *Washington Herald* in the mid-1950s had been the diminutive "Inquiring Camera Girl," this was not what she shared or how she framed the work she did then. "Being a journalist seemed the ideal way of both having a job and experiencing the world, especially for anyone with a sense of adventure." Journalism would not be her path now, but that seemed largely related to the fact that she had found such fulfillment in her editing work, noting that while journalism offered "variety," it did not "allow you to enter different worlds in depth, as book publishing does." Once married, JKO shifted gears, largely, she indicated, due to prevailing expectations of her time and station. "What has been sad for many women of my generation is that they weren't supposed to work if they had families," she shared.

PROFESSIONAL

"There they were, with the highest education, and what were they to do when their children were grown—watch the raindrops come down the windowpane? Leave their fine minds unexercised?"[27] JKO, in her position of privilege, provided both by her substantial wealth and also by the discretion afforded her during her time as first lady, hardly had to leave her fine mind unexercised. But her acknowledgment of that as a prevailing—and limiting—point of view suggests an evolution in her viewpoint since 1961, when she told *Life* magazine that part of her motivation for her White House restoration effort was that "every boy who comes here should see things that develop his sense of history. For the girls, the house should look beautiful and lived in. They should see what a fire in the fireplace and pretty flowers can do for a house."[28]

Some *Ms.* readers rejected JKO as a representative of working women. Her wealth and privilege and lack of public support for bona fide feminist causes made her less than desirable for those preparing to take women's liberation into the 1980s. But she offered echoes of Betty Friedan's *Feminine Mystique* (albeit sixteen years after its publication) when she said, "Of course women should work if they want to. You have to be doing something you enjoy. That is a definition of happiness: 'complete use of one's faculties along lines leading to excellence in a life affording them hope.' It applies to women as well as to men." From her telling, the publishing world brought JKO both great happiness and a sense of purpose. "What I like about being an editor is that it expands your knowledge and heightens your discrimination," she told Steinem. "Each book takes you down another path. Hopefully, some of them move people and some of them do some good."[29]

One can imagine, then, how JKO might have felt when a text took readers down a path that resulted in pain rather than joy. For two years, work at Viking proceeded smoothly. Early in 1977, the press acquired a manuscript by British author Jeffrey Archer, *Shall We Tell the President?*, the plot of which centered on a planned assassination of an American president based on Ted Kennedy. JKO did not work on the book at all. But when it was reviewed by *New York Times* book critic John Leonard, he made a particular dig at Mrs. Onassis. The book, he wrote, "is trash." He continued, "Anybody associated with its publication should be ashamed of herself."[30] When asked if this was a direct reference to JKO, Leonard said, "Of course I was partially referring to her. She should have objected. . . . She could have stopped publication if she wanted to."[31] In 1966, when JKO had attempted to put limits upon distribution of and information included as part of William Manchester's *Death of a President*, observers balked at what they saw as her efforts to censor history. And yet, here, a decade later, she received criticism for failing to employ her power to limit the publication of a text.

The book, which outraged the Kennedy family, who seemingly directed at least some of their ire at JKO, ultimately caused her to resign from Viking.[32] In a statement released by her spokeswoman, Nancy Tuckerman, JKO indicated that when she had first learned of the book, she had attempted to "separate my lives as a Viking employee and a Kennedy relative." After publication, however, when outside parties suggested she had been involved in the acquisition of the text and that she was unaffected by its eventual publication, "I felt I had to resign."[33] According to Deirdre Carmody's reporting in the *New York Times*, Tom Guinzberg's statement to the *Boston Globe* contributed to JKO's decision. He was quoted as saying that JKO "didn't indicate any distress or anger when I told her we bought the book in England several months ago." Tuckerman countered this telling with a claim that JKO had, indeed, been disturbed by the acquisition "but did not feel she should interfere with its publication." Guinzberg, Tuckerman indicated, had advised JKO not to read the book as it might upset her.

JKO's only eventually offering objections to the book and never having read it suggested to gossip columnist Liz Smith that "the lessons of the past are still largely lost on this lady." In Smith's assessment, JKO's resignation was a "self-generated controversy" certain to keep the spotlight on Archer's book rather than limit public interest. Smith referred back to JKO's objection to Manchester's book and assessed her response to *Shall We Tell the President?* as the "same exact thing." With no consideration of the outside influences or familial pressures affecting JKO's decisions, Smith concluded that if JKO had really objected to the text, "she could have resigned some months back on some other pretext."[34] This alternative path still ended with Jacqueline Onassis's resignation. Her life and her ability to move forward remained tied to a marriage that had ended more than a decade prior. However JKO chose to respond to the Archer book, it seemed, someone would find some reason why her action was the wrong action.

In 1977, however, beyond the usual suspects sharing what they believed to be JKO's shortcomings, there was a growing cadre of feminist voices weighing in on the world, among them columnist Ellen Goodman. And Goodman regarded JKO as a person navigating a complex range of expectations and obligations. Would she "stay up nights worrying about Jackie"? No. But, in regarding JKO's resignation from Viking, Goodman was "struck by the way in which her life is still inexorably ruled by a marriage that has been over longer than it lasted." The idea of *Shall We Tell the President?* seemed to shock Goodman not at all. "If there's a national fear to sell, someone will sell it," she wrote. "If there's a mass emotional button to push, someone will push it." The Archer novel, Goodman noted, was just the latest in what was nearly a fourteen-year stretch of JKO's saga as John Kennedy's widow. Surely, "to survive," JKO had "had to stop caring, to lower her threshold of outrage." Goodman was sympathetic to JKO's resignation statement, that she attempted a kind of compartmentalization—her life at Viking and her life linked to the Kennedy family. In thinking about JKO as a Viking employee, two years in, Goodman asked, "Should she have protested?" and then concluded, "Her obligation, even her right to protest seems a bit fuzzy."[35]

The publication of the book hardly was JKO's responsibility, Goodman determined. But what was she to do? Her compartmentalization was for naught. She remained Kennedy bound. "She was called to account in print." And then what? JKO had embarked upon a working world when she need not have. Goodman saw it this way: "She had finally tried to make a life rather than marry one." But her first marriage, long over, continued to exercise a hold on her. And while Goodman was hardly awash in sympathy for the former first lady, she saw something in her relatable to many women, single, advancing toward middle age, children no longer needing them as they once did: "What do you do with the rest of your life?"[36]

Fortunately for JKO, she was a desirable hire and soon made her way to the publishing powerhouse of Doubleday. As she told Gloria Steinem, part of the appeal of this house was its size, offering a place for "almost every subject and kind of book."[37] Moving on from her departure from Viking, JKO used what she had learned in her first years as an editor and built upon those skills as she continued with her editing work for the rest of her life. In talking with Steinem about her professional life in 1979, JKO represented herself as an excellent editor and a powerful advocate for her authors. She referred to the joys of her career and what about it she loved, but the heart of her conversation was the titles she had shepherded through publication, from a biography of Chicago mayor Richard Daley to a historical fiction centering American women's lives to a how-to guide for urban preservation. JKO emerged as a person of varied interests, innate curiosity, and intellectual openness as she noted that that was "part of an editor's job. You keep asking everyone—friends, authors, agents, experts; anyone with access to a particular work—if they know of a person who should be published or a subject that should be treated."[38] She provided readers with what she wanted them to know about her work and what she was willing to share about herself—and that was a public, professional version of Jacqueline Kennedy Onassis as an independent figure in her own right. In *Ms.*, she was allowed some agency in contributing to her own frame. Other treatments and considerations, however, refused to release her from the men to whom she had once been wed.

* * *

While JKO had been subject to critical coverage during her marriage to Aristotle Onassis, John Kennedy's legacy had remained intact. Ongoing veneration of the slain president contributed to the horrified responses to JKO's second marriage. The cultural turn of the late 1960s and early 1970s, however, yielded a media landscape more willing to challenge authority, to question government agencies and political leaders, and to air whatever missteps or misdeeds public figures had committed along the way. This applied both to assessments of leaders in real time and to reconsiderations of those from the past. By the end of the 1970s, revelations about the late John Kennedy unveiled a seamier side to JKO's constructed Camelot. As a result, her first husband's conduct and the nature of her first marriage became fodder for those looking to expose the "real" John Kennedy.

When John Kennedy was elected president in 1960, the prevailing notion among the press was that a president's private life was his private business. The many personal accounts from and historical treatments of John Kennedy's years in the White House have revealed just how much staffers, aides, reporters, and even Jacqueline Kennedy knew about the president's extramarital sexual relationships.[39] In the late 1970s, however, claims about JFK's sexual proclivities were news to the broader public. A particularly revealing case of JFK's infidelity came to light as a result of the 1975 Church Committee, a Senate select committee dedicated to uncovering the abuses of power that had occurred within various government agencies dating back to Dwight Eisenhower's administration. Inspired by the Nixon White House's disregard for the rule of law and the investigative reporting that had revealed the Central Intelligence Agency's practice of spying on antiwar activists, the committee aimed to provide citizens some measure of transparency about internal government operations. In the course of the committee's hearings, in discussing potential assassination plots against Fidel Castro developed by the CIA, the committee discussed a mutual "friend" John Kennedy shared with Mafia leaders Sam Giancana and John Rosselli. The friend, the public learned from the *Washington Post* in November 1975, was a woman: Judith Campbell Exner. And she and Kennedy had been more than friends. The concern: What information had she shared and with whom? In assessing the role Giancana and Rosselli had played in aiding the CIA, the Church Committee ultimately concluded that President Kennedy had not been aware of assassination plots under consideration. The link to Exner seemed a curious one, though, and once revealed, became the subject of deeper investigation.[40]

Exner, who claimed to be horrified by the attention resulting from the committee (and traumatized by FBI surveillance), vowed to share her side of the story. In 1977, her recounting was published as a book-length tell-all detailing the exact nature of her love affair with John Kennedy, from the 1960 campaign and continuing into his presidential administration. Exner was precise in her recounting of events, naming a February 7, 1960, dinner in Las Vegas as the first time she met John Kennedy. Within days of meeting the politician, Exner claimed an intense reaction to him: "I knew something was going on inside me that I could not fully comprehend. I was becoming restless, anxious in ways I could not satisfy. I saw myself as a rudderless ship in a storm, being tossed in all directions, without the slightest bearing on where I was headed." The feeling, her text suggests, was mutual. The two exchanged numbers, and Exner recalled, "There was no question that this was the beginning of what would be a long and intimate relationship."[41] On February 12, she wrote, Kennedy sent her a dozen red roses and called her from the campaign trail. He was delighted they had met, she said, and was eager to see her again. "From that moment on," Exner claimed, "the phone calls never stopped."[42]

Beyond phone calls, the two arranged to meet. So committed was Kennedy to seeing Exner that he proposed a New York meeting on March 7, 1960, the night before the all-important New Hampshire primary. "What a man," Exner recalled, "to find time" to see her at such a pivotal moment in the campaign. Meeting in a room at the Plaza, Exner initially balked at the prospect of intercourse. When a disappointed John Kennedy prepared to leave the room, she called him back. In her remembrance, they kissed, and he said, "I have so looked forward to being close to you, to making love to you, and then to just lie in bed and talk the way two people can talk after making love." Convinced by the sincerity of his words and spurred on by the ardor of her own desires, Exner acquiesced, and as she put it, the two "made love."[43]

Exner was detailed in her evaluation of Kennedy's love making. While she described herself as "very emotional and very demonstrative" in bed, JFK "was there to be serviced." Maybe this was a function of his bad back, Exner allowed, or, also possible is that he was accustomed to being "spoiled by women." And yet, that first evening at the Plaza, Exner gushed, "He couldn't have been more loving, more concerned about my feelings, more considerate, more gentle." After sex, they talked at length, sharing stories of themselves, and he confided his feelings about the campaign. Exner felt certain Kennedy cared for her, but she claimed a sense of unease not only because of his marriage but also due to the prospect of his presidency. Whatever reservations those realities brought forth, however, were not strong enough to stop the affair from moving forward.

And move forward it did. Kennedy stayed in contact as he continued with his campaign. Whenever possible, he aimed to see Exner, including, she claimed, at the Georgetown home he shared with his wife and child. Exner claimed that being in "Jackie's house to see her husband" put her in turmoil, but her "interest in Jack, my need to be with him, was stronger than my conscience." Hers was not the only conscience to consider. In recounting her visit to the home, Exner took aim at members of the Kennedy staff who claimed no knowledge of her or her relationship to John Kennedy. She recounted a call to Evelyn Lincoln, Kennedy's secretary, to arrange the meeting. Lincoln, she wrote, "was extremely cordial as always, and told me how happy Jack would be that I was in Washington." She shared numbers at which she had telephoned both Lincoln and Kennedy and addresses she knew they both had kept. Her presence seemed unremarkable either to the household staff or to the lobbyist who was meeting JFK while she was there.[44]

Beyond their physical relationship, Exner claimed that the two talked of love, with Kennedy asking her if she would ever feel such emotion for him. At that stage, she was sure she could. After intercourse, as the two engaged in "pillow talk," in what Exner identified as a rare departure from his customary confidence, Kennedy raised the possibility that he might not win the nomination. Should that happen, he proposed the two go "off and sit on a deserted beach somewhere for a whole month, maybe longer, just the two of us. We're going to hide from the world." At a subsequent meeting in Florida, Exner claimed that Kennedy told her, "There will be some changes in my life if I don't get the nomination." She did not press the matter, but her sense was that Jackie would instigate a separation if the campaign did not yield a successful conclusion. Exner and Kennedy, however, did not delve into particulars about his marriage beyond his indication that his "marriage was not a happy one." As Exner wrote, "I didn't want to discuss his wife and from all indications the feeling was mutual."[45] Of course, John Kennedy became the Democratic nominee and went on to win the presidency, so neither the island reprieve nor a change in marital status ever came to pass.

Kennedy invited Exner to the inauguration, but ultimately she decided not to attend. To give credence to her claims, she included in her book telegrams from the Inaugural Committee and tickets to the Inaugural Ball. Once established in the White House, Kennedy had her come and stay the night. Exner claimed that Kennedy communicated that he wished she could always be in Washington. "Wouldn't you like to come to White House functions?" he asked, seemingly oblivious to the very obvious conflict of interest in her attendance.[46] Their relationship suffered due, at least in Exner's estimation, to the demands of the office, which left JFK feeling constricted. When he talked to her about where they would go and what they would do if able, it was someplace they could be alone, without the demands or requirements of other parties.[47] Ultimately, Exner believed Kennedy became imperious as a result of his office, and his behavior took a turn. Their schedules made meetings more difficult. If Exner failed to prioritize a meeting, she claimed, the president became petulant. She began avoiding his calls, and then, the calls stopped coming—but not, she asserted, as a result of a directive or unveiling of suspicions from a meeting with J. Edgar Hoover, as claimed by the Church Commission. Rather, the love affair ended for reasons one might have predicted even at its very beginning.[48]

Exner was but one of a host of women linked to John Kennedy. Other tell-alls recounted the tall tales of Kennedy's sexual escapades from youth through the presidency, with staffers and starlets, overlooked and not infrequently facilitated by members of his inside circle.[49] Exner's text is unique for both its length and its detail, and the fact that its origin was a senatorial investigation and so was corroborated, at least in part, by external evidence. Even though Exner alleged that major publishing houses rejected her account and media largely refused to engage with her text, for Jacqueline Kennedy Onassis, it would be difficult to disregard the account as mere hearsay.[50] What did she think and what had she known? The world was dying to know. As she skied with her family in Salt Lake City at the end of 1975, even before the full extent of Exner's relationship with JFK had been shared, reporters descended on JKO, as she described it, "like an army advancing." When asked about John Kennedy's relationship to Exner, White House staffers, and other women, she offered no comment.[51] Not in December 1975 and not ever.

There are a range of ways to imagine the motivation behind JKO's silence. Where she very clearly had put the nation before herself in her masterful memorialization of John Kennedy, in holding back on whatever married life to the man had been and instead focusing on what he and his administration had represented, she may have committed once again to shouldering an internal burden so that a greater national good could prevail. Or, stemming from a more direct personal motivation: this was her children's father. Their having already lost him, in so violent a fashion and at so young an age, one can image JKO, dedicated as she was to their upbringing, wishing to shield them from the added loss of his celebrated image. In a time when so many public heroes had fallen, felled either by a bullet or by their own misdeeds, to continue to provide an esteemed vision of a man so many had loved might be regarded as an act of service. It is also fully possible that the many reports of JFK's various sexual indiscretions may have been too mortifying to engage with, and JKO may have been putting on a master class of compartmentalization. There is a long history—both before and after John Kennedy—of political wives standing by political husbands in the face of their misbehavior, whether publicly broadcast or not. This may have seemed a path of least resistance.

Whether this was a service undertaken primarily for her children's memory of their father or for the nation more broadly is immaterial. Various parties benefited from JKO's decision to let this particular past lie. What would she have gained from engaging in retrospective considerations of her first husband's infidelities? Not enough, apparently, to weigh in. For a person so relentlessly chronicled and considered, for whom, as Gloria Steinem noted, even a hamburger could never just be a hamburger, to keep something for herself was an act of personal agency in a world that offered her very little in the way of control. In saying nothing, she said a mouthful. Who was the real Jacqueline Kennedy Onassis? Someone uninterested in dredging up the past, recounting sordid details, or telling anyone anything she did not want them to know.

Beyond her link to John Kennedy, JKO, even after settling the terms of his will, could not escape her connection to Aristotle Onassis. JKO had offered the public very little in the way of information about her experience with Onassis. For years, books and magazines had offered alleged insider information, and even after AO's death, there seemed to be a market for content about the couple. Or so imagined Universal Pictures in 1978 as the studio offered audiences *The Greek Tycoon*, a film starring Anthony Quinn and Jacqueline Bisset as characters based very clearly, despite studio claims otherwise, on Aristotle and Jacqueline Kennedy Onassis. Taking liberty with timing and personal details, the film imagined, with limited success, the motivations behind the still seemingly incomprehensible pairing and, more successfully, re-created the opulent lifestyle the two enjoyed.

Theo Tomasis, the title (and main) character, is a rich and powerful and charismatic shipping magnate. Elizabeth (Lizzie) Cassidy, when she first meets Tomasis, is married to Massachusetts senator James Cassidy, who has his sights set on the presidency. Theo and Lizzie, despite their obvious differences, enjoy one another's company and feel a mutual pull. The film indicates a friendly relationship before any sort of romantic connection between the two, just as JKO and AO shared

Actors Jacqueline Bisset as Lizzie Cassidy and Anthony Quinn as Theo Tomasis in *The Greek Tycoon*, 1978. colaimages/Alamy Stock Photo.

long before they wed. Tomasis is married to the mother of his son, Simi (who begs him for a divorce), and paired with a long-time lover, Sophia Matalas (based on Maria Callas, AO's real-life love). Cassidy, by all accounts, enjoys a loving relationship with her husband.

Following the loss of a baby, Cassidy joins Tomasis on his yacht for some much-needed time away from the pressures of her life as now first lady to President James Cassidy. Suspicious of Tomasis and his intentions, James balks at Lizzie's desire to travel to Greece, proclaiming, "Tomasis is a dangerous man. I don't want you involved with him." Attuned to the potential media coverage the first lady's presence would generate—especially were she to attend unescorted—the president is explicit in reminding her that people watch and read into every move they make. And yet, Lizzie gets her way and joins the Tomasis party. Their friendship this time holds an undercurrent of sexual tension, of a more menacing mutual attraction. They swim and dine and dance with an idyllic Greek landscape as their setting. Tomasis tells Lizzie,

"You make me feel so alive." When she insists that she must return to America, she says she can never return to his yacht, the underlying message being that their attraction is too much and the temptation of being with Tomasis is too great.

Fate, however, intervenes. While strolling on the beach, James Cassidy is assassinated, his wife by his side. Tomasis offers Lizzie his sympathy and his counsel—and an escape from the pressures of public widowhood. Tomasis encourages Lizzie to join him in Greece. After a year, he urges, it is time for her to live and to do something for herself. But even after her husband's death, Lizzie is tied to the Cassidy family. Her brother-in-law, John, who had served as her husband's attorney general, now plans to run for the presidency, and Lizzie's support is considered essential. When she tells John she intends to go to Greece, he is anguished, imagining her with "that Greek" and imploring her to put the Cassidy family and the United States above her own interests. "If you hurt the family," he proclaims, "you hurt the country." Here, the film puts words into Lizzie Cassidy's mouth that, over time, had been imagined as motivations behind the decisions Jacqueline Kennedy had made in 1968. She tells John that she is "tired of Cassidy politics and having to share my loss with all of you." She is ready to be done serving as a "public shrine." In this fictional telling, the childless Cassidy has within a year processed her loss. She tells her brother-in-law, "Yes I am a widow; but the pain's not that sharp, not now. The dead are dead. I don't weep . . . anymore. I choose not to."

The timeline of events is condensed. Rather than the nearly five years between JFK's assassination, RFK's run for the presidential nomination, and the Onassis marriage, Cassidy and Tomasis pair off in just over a year. It is a film set in real time, and so the aesthetic is very 1970s. When Lizzie Cassidy travels to Greece, every possible desire she has is met by Tomasis's army of servants. In a scene where she lounges poolside on the Tomasis yacht, she has only to ask for a lunch of Greek delicacies and the steward is eager to oblige. Bisset's expression in playing the role is one of both self-satisfaction and an easing in to being accustomed to such service. Who, the film asks, would turn down this kind of luxury?

While in Greece, Tomasis, recently divorced, pushes Cassidy toward marriage. As the film imagines this scene, it is very clearly Cassidy who requires the convincing. "To be married again, if I was to do it, to be controlled again by any man," she assures Tomasis, "it would be you. But I just don't want it." He insists he can give her whatever kind of union she wants. And what is more, he can give her whatever she wants. And she wants it all: "To be allowed anything . . . to be permitted anything. To come and go. To have no restrictions. To have anything." She is not interested in settling. "I want everything," she tells him. The film inserts the Onassis marriage contract here, and points to the groom as its creator. Everything, Tomasis says, can be in writing. He sees nothing unromantic about it. Indeed, to him, "a marriage contract is the way it should be." He makes explicit reference to time; at the very least, he must have ten nights together each month. He likewise is deliberate in naming funds. He promises fifty thousand dollars a month for whatever Cassidy desires. If she travels, she can have another thousand dollars a day. She will have access to charge accounts. She will want for nothing. If the marriage fails, she will receive $10 million for every year they were wed. If they are still married at Tomasis's death, she'll receive $100 million.

Tomasis's financial promises apparently excise Cassidy's reservations about another marriage. The two wed. It is a marriage marked by tumult and passion and jealousy and aggression. Tomasis's son, Nikko, is suspicious of Cassidy and assumes this is just his father once again collecting people, wanting to stake a claim to the "most famous woman in the world." On their wedding night, she expresses similar suspicions, asking (maybe a beat too late) why he had wanted to marry her. "There's no other woman like you in the world," he proclaims, following up with, "You make me feel fantastic." This, after he had just taken a phone call from Matalas, promising to visit her the next day. Cassidy kicks him out of their marriage bed. This would not be one of his ten nights. When Tomasis embarrasses Cassidy in front of guests, she charges that he is a "boar," an "animal," and a "miserable son of a bitch" as she attempts to strike him over and over again, which only feeds his ardor. As he subdues her, he begs, "Let's go to bed." As a whole, there is little internal exploration of the couple's romantic motivations. They seem largely compilations of caricatures established over the previous decade. As one would get from a rehash of tabloid speculation, they are motivated—in various turns—by a desire to own, to control, to be adored, to be spoiled.[52]

The film includes the death of a beloved son, financial and legal troubles, and a chronic illness that we learn toward the film's end will cut short Tomasis's life. For all the links to the realities of the Onassis pairing, however, some parts of the story are amended, presumably to streamline the retelling and provide feeble credence to the notion that this is a fictionalized tale about any Greek tycoon, not necessarily Aristotle Onassis. There are no Cassidy children to consider. There is no daughter aggrieved by a beautiful young stepmother. There is no indication that the two are on the verge of divorce when Tomasis learns that he is very, very ill. The film skims the surface of the Onassis relationship and offers more in the way of a visual panoply of material excess.

Critics widely panned the film. When reviewers offered a point of praise, it was for the film's opulent settings. Filmgoers desiring a behind-the-scenes view of the lifestyles of the rich and famous might delight in the voyeurism provided by the film, but those hoping for a better understanding of the Onassis pairing would, as film critic Roger Ebert noted, find themselves "witnessing a multimillion-dollar cinematic edition of the *National Enquirer*" rather than learning anything substantive about the couple. Was there love in this union? Maybe. Was there money? Definitely. Ultimately, what viewers were left with is what most people suspected all along, although, as Ebert posited, "Isn't the movie a little callous in suggesting that the President's widow was also essentially a cash purchase by the tycoon—and saw herself as such? Or did she?" He could not be sure. "The movie never really deals with her feelings."[53]

* * *

As the 1970s concluded, new publications like *People* further mainstreamed the kind of gossip that had long marked fan magazines. For years, there had been a market for paperback speculations. In the late

1970s, that market opened up to allow for a world of hardcover unauthorized biographies, perhaps best reflected by Kitty Kelley's *Jackie Oh!* Published in 1978, the book, Kelley claimed, offered information never before shared, a result of the more than three hundred interviews she conducted and supplemented with copious research on her subject. Revelations about John Kennedy's sexual appetite, his limits as a lover, and psychiatric and shock therapy treatments Jacqueline Kennedy received during her first marriage are among the particular details Kelley trotted out. The overall communication of JKO is one of a selfish woman, given to casual cruelty and possessing a penchant for projecting an image of Jacqueline Kennedy Onassis rather than sharing an authentic version of that person, whoever she might be.

In his syndicated review of *Jackie Oh!*, Mel Watkins of the *New York Times* savaged the book. In theory, he suggested, a book of this kind could be a legitimate endeavor and could share with readers something beyond the satisfaction of a nosy curiosity, if the author "exercise[d] some discrimination" and organized material "in a sensible manner." That, in his estimation, was neither a priority nor evidenced in the result of Kelley's undertaking. For him, *Jackie Oh!* "rarely emerges from the muck with which it is pasted together." As a whole, it was a "rambling, repetitive, loosely structured series of sketches" of Jacqueline Kennedy Onassis since her marriage to John Kennedy. People knew Mrs. Onassis, at least to some degree, Watkins asserted. For a book like *Jackie Oh!* to be justified, it needed to offer "deeper insight into the personality of a woman who, despite the publicity, has remained enigmatic. The author's groping notwithstanding, no such characterization emerges here; what we get is innuendo, amateurish psychology and airy speculation." Beyond a critique of Kelley's evidence and analysis, Watkins had choice words for the tone of the book. It was, he wrote, "irritating; niggling and rancorous throughout, it hinders the book's credibility."[54] Watkins found the book more telling of Kelley than of its intended subject. The desired conclusion seems to have driven the narrative. Kelley's intention was "to portray Mrs. Onassis as a cold, pretentious plotting woman whose chief virtue is her occasional devotion to her children." Reading what might be considered silences of the text, Watkins concluded with a sympathetic view of JKO. Rather than fitting into the mold Kelley aimed to construct, JKO "instead . . . emerges as a private person, admittedly prodigal, who still resists the unwanted public role into which she was thrust. In short, she remains opaque." In conclusion, he wrote, "Only Miss Kelley's intentions become transparent."[55]

Whatever its flaws might have been, as with the *Greek Tycoon*, *Jackie Oh!* found an audience. As noted by Rudy Maxa, the press run on the hardcover was 150,000, and the book debuted on the *New York Times* bestseller list. Paperback rights were alleged to have sold for five hundred thousand dollars.[56] For decades, Jacqueline Kennedy Onassis had been a presence, a person with whom the public felt a sense of familiarity and connection. In the two decades since Americans had developed that relationship with her, the culture had changed to one in which people both asked for and expected more from their idols. But while the culture of expectation may have changed, JKO had not. Those intent on digging up alleged truths of her previous marriages or inner motivations would do so with or without her consent or comment. Their actions were beyond her control. Her own words and actions, however, were another story.

Jacqueline Kennedy Onassis maintained a commitment to public duty and familial obligation, to issues and causes of her choosing. To that end, in October 1979, Mrs. Onassis, accompanied by her children and surrounded by Kennedy family members and public figures of national renown, attended the opening of the John F. Kennedy Presidential Library. While the dedication occurred many years later than those invested in its creation would have imagined, the structure was a triumph. Designed by I. M. Pei and ultimately figuring at a cost of $12 million, the "white concrete and glass library," located on Columbia Point, offered an appropriately nautical view of "white sailboats dart[ing] across the blue bay."

Jacqueline Kennedy Onassis, "cool and composed," sat on the platform next to her children. While she welcomed President Jimmy Carter "warmly," the *Times* noted that "she seemed to stiffen" when he took

Jacqueline Onassis at the opening of the John F. Kennedy Presidential Library, Boston, Massachusetts, October 20, 1979. Ilene Perlman/Alamy Stock Photo.

the liberty of kissing her cheek, a stiffening later confirmed by Arthur Schlesinger's recollections of the day. That is essentially the whole of the coverage of JKO offered by the *New York Times* as related to the library dedication. For a woman so endlessly chronicled, in this instance, media cast her as a supporting figure. For all the work she put into the library, for all the work she had done to build her husband's legacy, the reporting on the event centralized the rivalry and impending potential Democratic primary contest between Carter and Ted Kennedy, each of whom used the event to lay their own "claim to the legacy of President Kennedy."[57] Before approximately seven thousand guests, they offered glowing tribute to the thirty-fifth president. About John Kennedy, President Carter said, he reflected "the ideals of a generation as few public figures have ever done in the history of the earth." Senator Ted Kennedy, the youngest of the Kennedy siblings, offered a message of uplift: "In dedicating this library to Jack we can recall those years of grace, that time of hope. The spark still glows. The journey never ends. The dream shall never die."[58] The Camelot imagery created by Jacqueline Kennedy in 1963 continued to wield tremendous influence.

Jacqueline Kennedy Onassis did not speak at the opening of her first husband's presidential library. She attended in support of his memory, of her children, of the Kennedy family. She listened as those who had followed or wished to follow his path to the presidency extolled the virtues of his service in the executive office. Whatever she thought of the framing of his legacy years after she had contributed her own ideas about what that might be, as with so many things, she kept to herself. Even without comment from her, however, in evaluating the dedication of this space, it seems both a curious and a telling thing that a media world so often so committed to offering guesses about the "real Jackie" would leave this moment unexcavated. Perhaps a desire to centralize John Kennedy on this day and in this space contributed to that over-sight. But, again, how telling that centralizing John Kennedy could happen with so little regard for Jacqueline, when she, ever since his assassination, had continued to be evaluated by the relationship she had shared with him. This remained true even as she navigated the final months of her life and in the days and years following her death.

[8]

ICON

Those who questioned Jacqueline Kennedy Onassis's fame, who wondered why she received the attention she did, were met with an abundance of explanations following her death on May 19, 1994. In the days and weeks that followed, journalists, politicians, and friends contributed to a national outpouring of memorialization that offered ruminations on JKO's significance to the nation, in real time and as it had once been, and to its citizenry. Immediate coverage shared that she had returned home on May 18 after her doctors indicated her cancer had moved beyond treatment. John Kennedy Jr. spoke to reporters outside her Fifth Avenue apartment on May 20, 1994: "Last night, at around ten-fifteen, my mother passed on . . . surrounded by her friends and her family and her books and the people and the things she loved. And she did it in her own way and in her own terms, and we all feel lucky for that, and now she's in God's hands." Articles outlined the details of her funeral and burial. Regular and guest columnists, some of whom had shared a relationship with JKO or had some particular link to her, attempted to make sense of who she had been, and even more, what she had meant and to whom.[1]

New York Times columnist Frank Rich shared his views a week after Mrs. Onassis died. He offered readers a kind of transparency in how he had assessed his response to JKO's passing and how it had revealed something of himself he had not expected. In this way, he claimed, he was not alone. "In my own informal poll," he wrote, "everyone old enough to remember her husband's Presidency had the same response to the death of Jacqueline Kennedy Onassis, conveyed in almost identical words: 'I never expected to be as upset as I was.' And my own was no different: After the announcement was dropped . . . my tears caught me by surprise."[2] A week after her death, his grief persisted.

Reporting on the coverage dedicated to JKO, Rich picked up on the following themes: "grace, dignity, style, class." These qualities marked memorialists' tributes, but for Rich, they reflected a "public image" more than they offered insight into the actual person, Jacqueline Kennedy Onassis. In imagining what this script revealed, Rich asked, "Could this be one outpouring of grief that says more about the mourners than the mourned?"[3] In a word: absolutely. In surveying the world of public mourning of celebrities at the end of the twentieth century, media historian Carolyn Kitch identifies "death as an unstable public moment in which people feel compelled to assess their identities and beliefs."[4] Such was the case upon the death of Jacqueline Kennedy Onassis.

The idea of JKO being used as a barometer for viewpoints and values of a broader public, as a stand-in or representative for notions of American women, culture, or history was the story not only of her death, however, but also of her public life. Since 1960, JKO had most often served as a symbolic representation of American women, as an illustration of behaviors either correct and exemplary or entirely inappropriate. When she died, what she represented expanded to suggest a view of the nation and its people, a figure whose passing allowed for ruminations about a lost past and a present that failed to measure up. Some retrospectives engaged in JKO's union with Aristotle Onassis, but those that included him as a chapter of her life did so relatively quickly, noting the disappointment of the pairing or identifying a momentary fall from grace. More often, JKO was transported back to the early 1960s, first as a symbol of the New Frontier and then as living embodiment of the Camelot ideal she had initiated following her first husband's brutal death. In bringing her up to date, celebrations of her cultural contributions, career success, and exemplary performance of motherhood merited mention but not as much or as consistently as her commitment to personal privacy, a trait heralded by many admirers.

Rich ticked off the versions of womanhood for which JKO might serve as a stand-in, from feminine archetype to ideal mother to "a closet feminist," which was language *Feminine Mystique* author Betty Friedan had applied to her. He asked, "Was she the last gilded American princess, frozen in time in that bloodied pink suit?" The truth is that Jacqueline Kennedy Onassis was all of these things on their own or in some combination. Beyond textual offerings of these versions of JKO, mourners were offered visual panoplies of JKO over the course of her public life, from young wife and new mother to first lady to Kennedy widow to sunglasses-clad Jackie O of the 1970s jet set to 1980s New York elite. The public who so insistently had assessed her public life could put whatever spin on her they chose. Because she had guarded her privacy so relentlessly, mourners' versions or visions of her could stand untested by her own definition of her meaning or intentions. And that commitment to privacy, which had stymied so many for so many years, became a badge of honor, a quality deserving of the utmost praise.

In death, Rich posited, it seemed JKO had become "a neutral figure on whom any American could therapeutically project anything whatsoever." Such projection had long occurred, and the claim of neutrality before or even after death seems misplaced. Memorialization of JKO offered a master class in both remembering and forgetting. For years, JKO had been attached to the men to whom she had once been wed, and subject to conjecture of various kinds. In death, however, "even the seamier details of both her marriages, long a national obsession, were abruptly stricken from the record." Many of those looking back on Mrs. Onassis's life had been children when she was in the White House, and were only just coming of age when John Kennedy met his brutal end. For these mourners there seemed a particular attachment to JKO as a symbol of a lost innocence, for the nation and for these individual memorialists. She was tied to a man but also to a moment. "Perhaps the reverential grief for Mrs. Onassis gave expression to an unacknowledged national yearning—even a ravenous need—for a higher common purpose during this bitterly partisan time," wrote Rich, hinting at a more civil political past than existed in a 1990s increasingly marked by partisan culture wars. "Because every Jackie mourner, finally, agrees on one point: she represented something larger and better than most of us." Mourning the death of what JKO represented as much as he mourned her actual death, Rich suggested that tributes to and considerations of JKO's import had succeeded in "resurrecting a shared memory of the national idealism thought to have been buried forever in the cynical decades since Dallas."[5]

In death, as she had in life, JKO continued to be a person of intense public interest. Tributes acknowledged the public's long fascination with her and attempted to name what she had meant to the nation and its people. Those memorializing JKO, beyond talking about her, also contemplated the image and meaning making that had marked her public life. Many memorialists were transparent in their discussions of her, acknowledging how they were framing JKO as more than a single person in identifying her symbolic importance, even as they were not necessarily in agreement about what it was she symbolized. This diversity of claims staked on JKO offers testimony to just how powerful she was as a symbol, able to stand in for a host of viewpoints and values. People could put whatever meaning they desired onto her. In attempting to make meaning of her life, those offering their two cents revealed as much about themselves and the world in which they lived as they did about the life and person of Jacqueline Kennedy Onassis.

* * *

Throughout the 1980s and into the early 1990s, Jacqueline Kennedy Onassis seemingly found some measure of peace. New York remained her home base, and she continued with her regular respites in New Jersey and Martha's Vineyard. She continued her work at Doubleday. Her children, who avoided the scandals that plagued a host of Kennedy cousins, were nearby, and Caroline's marriage to Edward Schlossberg brought three grandchildren into JKO's life. She had her friends. She enjoyed a long-standing relationship with Maurice Tempelsman. Maybe because she was older, maybe because her life was as "dull" as she claimed, efforts to track her abated somewhat, and as many of her friends recalled, she had become adept at managing her celebrity so that it was incidental rather than all-consuming. Biographer Edward Klein suggests that in her sixties, Mrs. Onassis was at "the height of personal contentment and professional fulfillment."[6]

In November of 1993, as she often did, JKO joined a fox hunt in Virginia. She received care after being thrown from her horse and knocked unconscious. A doctor's visit revealed swelling in her groin, and she was prescribed antibiotics. To celebrate the new year, she and Tempelsman sailed to the Caribbean, but a persistent cough and more swelling led them to cut the trip short. After another doctor's visit and a series of tests, JKO received a diagnosis. She had non-Hodgkin's lymphoma.[7]

Mrs. Onassis began chemotherapy, and this she undertook without public knowledge for the first several weeks of 1994. She continued with her work and usual routine. On February 11, 1994, the *New York Times* shared a statement about JKO's diagnosis provided by Nancy Tuckerman. Motivated by "speculation and rumors" about JKO's health, Tuckerman revealed, "She is undergoing a course of treatment and there is every expectation that it will be successful. . . . There is an excellent prognosis. You can never be absolutely sure, but the doctors are very, very optimistic."[8] Even those close to her were surprised. Arthur Schlesinger read about her diagnosis in *Time*. When the two subsequently spoke on the phone, he recalled her saying, "It's a real case of hubris. I have been so proud of being so fit. I have been doing my push-ups every day; I walk every day; I never smoke; I take excellent care of myself; I have been so pleased with my good health—and now this has happened—hubris." Even then, she concluded, "But it is not too bad."[9]

JKO proceeded as though she expected a full recovery, which was fitting given the American Cancer Society's indication that patients diagnosed with non-Hodgkin's lymphoma had a 52 percent chance of living at least another five years. Scott Moyers, who worked with her at Doubleday, recalled that after Christmas, she had invited him to her office and shared her diagnosis, saying that "she felt great, and there was a good chance she was going to beat it." Friends recalled letters they received in which she talked about resuming their "festive lunches" or indicating that "there was nothing to worry about, that spring had finally arrived, and everything was now well."[10] She agreed to serve as chairwoman for the American Ballet Theater's spring gala, scheduled for May 9.[11] Tuckerman continued to share statements indicating that JKO was in fine shape. In late April, she told Arthur Schlesinger, "You know, Arthur, during this whole business she has not once complained."[12] But optimistic outlooks and language masked the reality that JKO's treatments failed to contain the cancer.

The cancer extended to her spinal cord and brain. Even more aggressive treatment failed to curtail its spread to her liver. In the week before her death, Tuckerman had played down the severity of JKO's condition. "She's fine," she had said. "She goes in for routine visits, routine treatment. That's what this is." When an anonymous health worker from New York Hospital–Cornell Medical Center spoke to the *New York Times*, motivated, they said, by an alleged fear that Tuckerman's statements might lead to a "mistaken impression of the care" JKO received, Tuckerman acknowledged her understatement of her friend's condition. She admitted to an effort to keep things "low-key" because, in keeping with the way in which JKO had lived her life, "we really feel her medical situation is private and we did not feel we have to reveal everything to reporters."[13]

With no hope that further treatment would change her prognosis, Jacqueline Kennedy Onassis returned home. She received visitors. Tuckerman shared, "She was alert some of the time. She could hear." As comfortable as she could be and surrounded, as her son indicated, by people and things she loved in a place she loved, Jacqueline Kennedy Onassis died. She was sixty-four years old. Tuckerman told the press, "It was very peaceful."[14] Outside her apartment, "hundreds of spectators lined the avenue . . . continuing a vigil" that lasted for days. The doorway to her apartment building was "flanked by dozens of reporters, photographers and television and radio crews." Tour buses stopped. Mourners left flowers or tokens of tribute. The *New York Times* reported that those gathered to pay tribute to JKO "were a model of decorum compared to the press, which stampeded and stumbled over barricades in frantic chases to videotape or photograph celebrities or shout questions that were ignored."[15] Eileen Stukane, a fellow New Yorker, left a bouquet of long-stemmed red roses. She noted that the beautiful spring day called to mind the "many times she had spotted Kennedy Onassis and her companion, Maurice Tempelsman, walking through Central Park." In explaining her feelings about JKO's passing, she said, "I will miss her as part of the landscape, not only American, but right here in New York City."[16] Joseph Rokacz, a lawyer who lived on the other side of Central Park, joined the vigil, seemingly unsure why. "I feel like an idiot," he said. "But I saw it on television and I couldn't sleep. She's a woman that I grew up with my whole life . . . There's nobody to replace her. . . . There's nobody out there that has her kind of magic."[17] Said Eleanor Walker of Newark, "I feel like she was a part of me and I'm a part of her. . . . She was a wonderful woman."[18]

The public was not granted access to Jacqueline Kennedy Onassis's funeral, held at St. Ignatius Loyola Church in New York City, the same church where she had been baptized in 1929. Television cameras recorded the comings and goings of those who attended, and those who were inclined could watch her coffin carried by pallbearers in and out of the church before it was flown to Arlington National Cemetery, where she would be buried next to her first husband. Her family released details about the poems and verses read, and the tribute of her brother-in-law, Senator Edward Kennedy, was shared in full. Caroline Kennedy read Edna St. Vincent Millay's poem "Memory of Cape Cod," included in a book presented to Jacqueline Bouvier in June 1946, acknowledging her receipt of Miss Porter's School's Marie McKinney Memorial Award in Literature. Maurice Tempelsman shared one of JKO's favorite poems, "Ithaka" by C. P. Cavafy. John Kennedy Jr. offered a passage from the Book of Isaiah, sharing that while "we struggled to find [readings] that captured my mother's essence," ultimately, they had selected readings focused on her "love of words, the bonds of home and family, and her spirit of adventure."[19]

In Ted Kennedy's remarks about JKO, he began with a story from the previous summer, in which his sister-in-law had encouraged him to greet Bill, Hillary, and Chelsea Clinton, all of whom had just arrived to join them for an afternoon at Martha's Vineyard. The senator and JKO were on the upper deck of Tempelsman's boat. When Kennedy noted that Maurice was already in place to welcome them, JKO replied, "Teddy, you do it. Maurice isn't running for reelection." With this anecdote, Senator Kennedy revealed just how much the "apolitical" Jacqueline Kennedy Onassis understood about politics, media, and image. He indicated, too, what she offered to those she loved, noting, "She was always there, for all our family, in her special way."[20]

For Ted Kennedy, JKO was singular. His proximity to her, the closeness of an actual relationship spanning decades, meant that it carried particular meaning when he said, "No one else looked like her, spoke like her, wrote like her, or was so original in the way she did things. No one we knew ever had a better sense of self." But he understood, too, that he and his family shared her with a larger community. "She was a blessing to us and to the Nation," he said, "and a lesson to the world on how to do things right, how to be a mother, how to appreciate history, how to be courageous." The intimacy of having been part of the same family for forty years permeated Kennedy's remarks, which touched on his brother's presidency and assassination and JKO's fundamental role in both but also celebrated hallmarks of her character and the affection she showered on those she loved. He tied Mrs. Onassis to his slain brother: "I often think of what she said about Jack in December after he died: 'They made him a legend, when he would have preferred to be a man.' Jackie would have preferred to be just herself, but the world insisted that she be a legend, too." Kennedy concluded in a way that speaks to the tension between public and private that so marked Jacqueline Kennedy Onassis's life as he said, "She graced our history. And for those of us who knew and loved her, she graced our lives."[21]

Those who knew her, who had had a personal relationship with JKO, placed the emphasis on her, privileging what was particular to her. Their tributes were marked with hallmarks of her words and behaviors and habits and personality. They noted the ways in which, for them, she was a distinct and unique person even as they acknowledged the public claims that had been made on her private life. Public memorialization coming from those who had covered her, or who had grown up with images of her over the span of her public life, often tied her to others, naming her significance in what she gave to those beyond herself, be that her family, her husbands, or her nation and its citizens. The difference between JKO the person and JKO the symbol was put into sharp relief. This distinction or this disconnect was always part of her public life. She had lived a life with actual relationships as an actual person but had also endured a life of public assumption in which she had been subject to symbolic importance put upon her from those denied any real access to her, who imagined and generated a sense of her from whatever information, accurate or otherwise, was made available and subsequently pieced together. As noted by Arthur Schlesinger, who had known JKO a long time but had seen her less in recent years, "One felt she was always here, and now one feels that a great light has gone out of our lives."[22]

* * *

The extinguished light identified by Schlesinger had shone beyond those in JKO's immediate orbit and extended to a public that had long tracked her movements and thus endeavored to make sense of her passing. In writing about celebrity death and memorialization, Carolyn Kitch asserts, "A celebrity's death is a moment for public discussion of shared ideals and identities."[23] Those who had been famous in life come to symbolize even more in death. Jacqueline Kennedy Onassis, as she was memorialized, was tied to notions of nation and history and generation. As mourners made sense of her death, they tied her to the country and to themselves. "When they cover celebrity deaths, journalists seem to stand on this fault line; they speak to, and on behalf of, the public, while openly sharing their own reactions," writes Kitch.[24] Beyond the reminiscences and meaning making that took place in American media, the United State Congress on May 23, 1994, opened the floor to tributes from its members. There, senators and representatives likewise engaged in efforts to make sense of JKO's life and her importance to the nation and often in a strikingly similar fashion to those sharing their thoughts on the pages of American newspapers and magazines. In tributes printed on those pages or shared by those elected by the nation's citizens, a common theme emerged: Jacqueline Kennedy Onassis "was 'one of us' while also representing our greatest hopes." Her death might be "tragic," but it also provided the opportunity to take stock of the nation as it was and pay tribute to "societal ideals that temporarily had been forgotten."[25]

Various elements of JKO's life appeared in mourners' tributes as they celebrated her contributions to the American nation and its people and honored what had been her particular gifts and achievements. Some mourners highlighted her cultural efforts during her White House years and beyond and identified her role in securing federal funding for the arts. Others, like longtime New York senator Daniel Patrick Moynihan, emphasized her contributions as she drew attention to the nation's rich heritage and lent her support to preserving its historic structures. Her years as an editor, the joy that work gave her and the skill with which she approached her trade, likewise bore mention. These elements of her life, however, were referenced in varying degrees and combinations. Sometimes they were there, sometimes not. These individual threads of JKO's life struck individual chords depending on the author penning the tribute. These components of JKO's life, likely fundamental to knowing her as a person or individual, were not necessarily the image of JKO that immediately came to mind among those who had largely followed her life as reported by American media.

Joshua Meyrowitz writes about the concept of the "media friend," a figure with whom members of the population believe they have "intimate knowledge and empathetic connection." Jacqueline Kennedy Onassis, in the public eye for nearly four decades, was a media friend for many people, a figure whose life they had chronicled, and alongside whom many had grown up or grown old. As Meyrowitz writes, "We follow celebrities through various phases of their personal lives and public activities, and their life stages often become some of the key signposts we use to mark and recall the different periods of our own lives." Having played such a key role in the aftermath of John Kennedy's assassination, a core memory for so many Americans who remembered precisely where they were when the president was shot, Jacqueline Kennedy Onassis had the power to remind people of a very particular time and place, both for the nation and for themselves.[26]

That power of time and place played out in the version of JKO most consistently invoked in memorialization efforts. Most people had known JKO only through media, through image rather than interaction. That media remained available. With JKO, mourners could choose from a massive array of images spanning nearly four decades. As one could fixate on a particular image, so, too, could one choose to exclude those images or iterations that failed to fit with the desired narrative. Using particular moments from JKO's life allowed mourners to make her whatever they desired her to be, and she could thus symbolize whatever qualities they wanted to attribute to or share with her. As a result, the versions of JKO most often invoked were those related to John Kennedy's assassination and his subsequent memorialization. Images and footage of her from November 1963 were frozen in real time, had lived on during her life, and continued to live on after her death. Those images had been reproduced, reprinted, and republished over the course of JKO's life. Even people who were not alive for that moment had seen representations of it and knew, at least superficially, JKO as she had been then. In their memorials, mourners, whether they bore witness to those days or not, fixated on what that rendition of her meant. That version—tied to nation, husband, children, and an idealized sense of the past—was imagined as the best version of JKO. The conduct of the newly widowed Jacqueline Kennedy paired with the style of American womanhood widely considered the best vision of womanhood, even more than thirty year later, one marked by self-sacrifice and devotion to the needs of others rather than the needs of self.[27]

Michael Oleskar of the *Baltimore Sun* devoted considerable consideration to the assassination and its aftermath, noting that it "was the last time we got a clear fix on Jackie, and we found the image so compelling we spent the rest of her life recycling it in our heads, no matter what else happened to her."[28] If, for many mourners, the November 1963 image of JKO was the defining image of her life, it was accompanied by a very clear desire that they could excise the "Onassis" from any reference to JKO. With thirty-one years having passed, those writing had been young—or at least younger—in 1963, and they took pains to marvel at JKO's youth and the composure she summoned at such a young age and on such a public stage. Much as the myth making and lore attached to John Kennedy froze him in time at the moment of his death, writers expressed a desire to do the same to JKO, regardless of the fact that she had to go on living. Oleskar followed up on his previous observation: "And there she is, suspended forever in our collective consciousness: teaching us all how to grieve, showing us how a civilized people can conduct themselves and making us see ourselves in her image."[29]

Former Ronald Reagan speech writer Peggy Noonan shared similar ideas in her paean to the former first lady, appearing in the pages of *Time*. Noonan looked back to JKO as a representative of a specific time and place and lamented the passing of that time and place and its people. What had come after, it seemed, had proven to be a disappointment. The disappointment, or the fact that Jacqueline Kennedy Onassis *had* disappointed, was not explicitly addressed, but Noonan hinted at it when she wrote of the value and meaning and significance of the former first lady's public display in November 1963: "A lot of us thought that anything good or bad she did for the rest of her life, from that day on, didn't matter, for she'd earned her way, she deserved a free pass, she'd earned our thanks forever." In Noonan's assessment, what had come after was immaterial. JKO's post-assassination life, in Noonan's telling, served only to tie her back to the era in which she had initially become known to the American people. In her adept and poignant memorialization of her fallen husband, Noonan asserted, Jacqueline Kennedy peaked. The remainder of her life mattered not. She would live in that long weekend in late November. Her performance in those days would define her, to use Oleskar's and Noonan's language, "forever."[30]

Except that for whatever collective consciousness Oleskar and Noonan referred to, the reality is that JKO did not continue in a suspended reality. She continued to live her life, one her friend writer Pete Hamill, in his tribute to her, called "brave and difficult."[31] Because she continued to live, she often failed to live up to expectations that emerged as part of her post-assassination performance. That failure, however, and the resulting disappointment loudly expressed by the public were largely erased, or, at the very least, sanitized in most tributes. Representative Benjamin Gilman of New York declared that JKO's "conduct throughout the remainder of the 1960s set an example which all of us in the future should use as an appropriate role model," a view those observing her social calendar in the mid-1960s, weighing in on her dispute with William Manchester in 1966, and then, finally, responding to her marriage to Aristotle Onassis in 1968 had not shared. Congresswoman Corrine Brown of Florida posited that JKO remained "an object of public admiration until her death," with no indication of the ebbs and flows of that admiration.[32]

In offering what he framed as a shared assessment of JKO, the *Baltimore Sun*'s Oleskar reflected the propensity to limit Aristotle Onassis's role in the JKO narrative—or, at the very least, cast him as incidental rather than fundamental. Oleskar wrote, "Over time, we pushed aside the business with Onassis. It was an aberration in her life, and in our embrace of her, and we wanted to pretend it hadn't happened." In suggesting that the Onassis marriage was an "aberration" to be "pushed aside," Oleskar indicated a willingness to forgive JKO for behavior that deviated from her norm, or from the standard to which the American people held her. But Jacqueline Kennedy Onassis indicated not at all that this was an aberration. She never saw the need to explain or excuse her relationship with Aristotle Onassis. She never appealed for forgiveness. In his assessment, however, Oleskar was hardly alone. In so much coverage of JKO, AO appeared not at all. He was not mentioned at her funeral. He did not fit in the image of JKO that was of greatest use to a broader American public. "What we sought from her for the last three decades," wrote Oleskar "was a retrieval of her White

House life, and the weekend in Dallas, where we'd lost what felt like innocence."[33]

JKO's legacy, Peggy Noonan submitted, was a link to a better, nobler past: "She was a connection to a time, to an old America that was more dignified, more private, an America in which standards were higher and clearer and elegance meant something, a time when elegance was a kind of statement, a way of dressing up the world, and so a generous act." Suggesting a world gone wrong, Noonan reported the melancholy views of a Jacqueline Kennedy Onassis intimate: "She didn't grow up in front of the TV set, but reading the classics and thinking about them and having thoughts about history. Oh . . . we're losing her kind." Communicating an image of beauty and class and intellect, Noonan painted a portrait of JKO in keeping with the best of the image the Kennedys had endeavored to construct during the years they had resided in the White House while ignoring the conscious construction of that image and a political media world that already rewarded if not required it.[34] Noonan admitted to an awareness of how mourning for Jacqueline Kennedy Onassis was about more than mourning for Jacqueline Kennedy Onassis: "Few people get to symbolize a world," she wrote, "but she did, and that world is receding, and we know it and mourn that too."[35]

In writing about the importance and legacy of Jacqueline Kennedy, Noonan joined those who zeroed in on the assassination of John Fitzgerald Kennedy and the days that followed his death. During those days, Jacqueline Kennedy had buoyed a nation and redeemed a people who felt a great shame at what had happened to the president. "She took away the shame by how she acted," Noonan wrote. She continued:

> She was young, only 34, and only a few days before she'd been covered in her husband's blood—but she came home to Washington and walked down those broad avenues dressed in black, her pale face cleansed and washed clean by trauma. She walked head up, back straight and proud, in a flowing black veil. There was the moment in the Capitol Rotunda, when she knelt with her daughter Caroline. It was the last moment of public farewell, and

ICON

* 271 *

to say it she bent and kissed the flag that draped the coffin that contained her husband—and a whole nation, a whole world, was made silent at the sight of patriotism made tender. Her Irish husband had admired class. That weekend she showed it in abundance. What a parting gift.

Noonan's effort to communicate a sense of majesty and nation inter-mingled with familial relationships and personal loss fits with a nostalgic view of the Kennedys and the related Camelot of JKO's constructing, with which American patriots, history lovers, and those well versed in Kennedy mythology are so familiar.[36]

When Wisconsin senator Russell D. Feingold spoke of JKO, he likewise cast her in a particular and celebrated historical light. Beyond the fact that JKO had been "such an important part of the history of the last five decades," he attributed to her a link to what he regarded as a more certain time in the nation's past. "We grieved for Mrs. Onassis because she reminded us of a time when we were more sure of ourselves and of our place in the world," he said. When she and her husband had resided in the White House, "it seemed as though people had more faith, not just in themselves, but also in their Federal Government." In Feingold's estimation, whatever sense of optimism Americans had shared prior to the Vietnam War and Watergate scandal had been lost. By her very presence, he believed, JKO had "remind[ed] us of how we were before this change and because of the power of nostalgia, her death makes that time seem further away than before."[37] Essentially, Feingold regarded JKO as a living vestige of a better time in American life. He was not alone. Representative after representative noted how JKO—in her tie to John Kennedy and his New Frontier ideals—had reflected an idealism that, for many, had inspired their love of country and commitment to public service. Alabama senator Howell Heflin made this point directly when he said, "She was our last link to Camelot and all that it symbolized, a living symbol of an all-too-brief slice of the past during which anything seemed possible."[38]

Longtime White House reporter Hugh Sidey anticipated those who might scoff at this line of commemoration. In offering his take on JKO,

Sidey insisted on the legitimacy of feeling shared by those who had been there and borne witness to the Kennedy White House. "Let the skeptics snort about Camelot," he wrote, "but there was something during the Kennedy years that was magic. Jackie was more of that than anyone admitted for a long while. She smoothed the rough Kennedy edges. As much as anyone in those heady days, she grasped the epic dimensions of the adventure. No small portion of the glamour of the Kennedy stewardship that lives on today came from her standards of public propriety and majesty."[39] Sidey's interpretation of Jacqueline Kennedy Onassis elevates her. She was fundamental to whatever the Kennedy administration meant to the American people. Then Senator Joe Biden identified the Kennedy pairing as part of the administration's appeal. "The couple in the White House looked like a promise, like the embodiment of hope as well as style." But Biden, like Sidey, also paid particular tribute to JKO as he insisted, "She represented part of what was best in us, part of what we aspired to be."[40] As a whole, the memory the Kennedy White House years communicated was one of possibility and opportunity and faith in the future.

Like Feingold, *Boston Herald* writer Joe Fitzgerald relied on a comparison between the "good" sixties of optimism and possibility and the "bad" sixties at which point all of that seeming promise came undone as the nation descended into chaos and disunion. A self-identified Republican, Fitzgerald admitted to a grudging admiration for Jacqueline Kennedy during her White House years, when he claimed it had been "so hard to find fault with her reign as First Lady." In his cross-aisle appreciation for her and all she represented, Fitzgerald indicated a kind of political civility, which so many lamented as sorely lacking in 1994. Even with the horror of the assassination, and the immediate pain shared by the nation and its people, Fitzgerald suggested, the assassination was just the beginning of a greater decline: "We didn't know how much we'd miss those days until we lived through the ones that followed, through Vietnam and Birmingham, through a convention in Chicago, from a motel balcony in Memphis to a hotel kitchen in L.A., places that now conjure up devastating memories and will forever more."[41]

It is worth a pause to consider who had access to the alleged innocence or possibility of the early 1960s, before the pioneering civil rights activism and legislation that worked to dismantle the long reach of Jim Crow, before an invigorated feminist movement challenged the second-class citizenship applied to American women by the nation's systems and institutions and culture, and before a cultural turn challenged an often stultifying conformity that silenced many citizens who wished to share views that pushed beyond an alleged American consensus.[42] Likewise, it is worth consideration as to what these figures gained in invoking the alleged innocence of that time. For many of the Baby Boomers born in the years just as John Kennedy was beginning his political ascendency, his assassination marked an end to their personal innocence as much as it did the nation's alleged innocence. If JFK's assassination had been a core memory, and one they linked to the end of their youth, the death of the woman then known as Mrs. Kennedy may very well have caused that sense of loss to resurface. The final vestige of their youth was now dead, and there was a kind of finality that came with that. That sense of loss extended beyond the loss of Jacqueline Kennedy Onassis. As much as this was an individual feeling by a particular subset of individuals, those mourning with a public platform invoked JKO in this symbolic way, both for the nation and for themselves. As political leaders staked a claim to the symbolic power of Jacqueline Kennedy Onassis, as they linked her to an idealized time in the American past, they invited others with no memory of that past to join them in their mourning for both JKO the person and the time period they claimed she represented. It was fully possible for individuals to stake these claims for conservative purposes as they lamented an alleged national consensus that existed before the revolutions of the late 1960s ruined everything, or as part of a liberal tradition linked to John Kennedy, his New Frontier, and an optimistic sense of the nation's future.[43]

In covering JKO's burial at Arlington National Cemetery, the *Colorado Springs Gazette Telegraph*, sharing coverage from the *Chicago Tribune*, proclaimed, "John and Jackie are together again." That reunion, the article suggested, was natural and right. Order had been restored.

"It was as though the 31 years since John F. Kennedy's death had vanished, as though her controversial second marriage to Greek tycoon Aristotle Onassis and her subsequent life as a super-rich New York socialite had never been." And even though she had retained the name Onassis even after her second husband's death, her decision in so doing was not infrequently invalidated. "She went to her grave, surrounded by Kennedys, as Jackie Kennedy."[44] David Shribman, writing for the *Boston Globe*, likewise insisted, "She will forever be Jackie Kennedy," although rather than freezing her at her husband's funeral, he chose as her eternal moment "Love Field in a pink dress with gold buttons and a blue collar."[45] Such was the resolve in linking her to her first husband and his family and a time more than thirty years prior.

In celebrating her life in the years since her first husband's death, when she had shown such self-control and exemplary behavior, a recurring theme among tributes was a celebration of the tenacity with which she guarded her privacy. This propensity writers tied also to a kind of mythic past before the onset of "an age when seemingly everyone wants to broadcast their inner secrets on TV talk shows." With admiration, Representative Carolyn Maloney of New York said of JKO, "She gave a great deal of herself, but she never gave herself away." And unlike those who had fallen victim to what Christopher Lasch famously identified as the Age of Narcissism, Jacqueline Kennedy Onassis "realized that there were stories worth telling other than her own."[46] The dignity or privacy ascribed to JKO were suggested as hallmarks of an earlier time and thus contributed to situating her in a more dignified moment in the nation's past, ignoring, in many ways, the fact that she had come to public life at a moment when political celebrity was on the rise and American media, when denied content from her, created content about her.

Even the ways in which she guarded her privacy, which, ostensibly, one might imagine as an act motivated by a sense of self, or an act of self-protection, became a kind of aspirational behavior, almost like a model she provided for the nation and its people. A catharsis or oversharing would have been selfish. To remain quiet, to keep from Americans her pain or disappointment, had, in fact, been a kind of sacrifice, another act of service. She had not revealed knowledge of or heartache born from her first husband's infidelities. She had not marred the image of Camelot that had been so much of her creation. As Pete Hamill recalled, "In the last decade, when every sleazy rumor about Jack Kennedy was treated like fact, she maintained her silence. And silence, of course, is communication."[47] Beyond her first husband, she had not soiled her own reputation by critiquing her second husband's temper or brutishness or insensitivity. For those pining for a lost innocence, JKO had been fundamental to keeping the notion of that innocence intact. But celebrations of a commitment to privacy had not been the case when JKO spoke out against William Manchester or Ron Galella. Then, her efforts at privacy had resulted in raised eyebrows or claims about a desire to censor. In 1994, however, her privacy was a virtue.

Boston Globe columnist Ellen Goodman offered her critique of the world of unauthorized biographies and public confessionals and ascribed to that culture a demand for the public's "right to know . . . the worst." Tell-all culture had not elevated American life. To the contrary. "In the 1990s," she lamented, "even politicians are expected to reveal their childhood traumas to talk show hosts. Wives are called upon to do confessional interviews about their inner feelings about everything, including their marriages. Everyday people line up for the chance to discuss dysfunctional families and 12-step horror stories in the name of 'sharing.'" Jacqueline Kennedy Onassis, Goodman noted, "didn't 'share.'" Noonan expressed similar views, as she posited that JKO "was a living reminder in the age of Oprah that personal dignity is always, still, an option, a choice that is open to you."[48] Echoing this theme was R. W. Apple Jr. of the *New York Times*, who wrote, "In a vulgar era when celebrity is something to be cashed in on, she seemed to many to symbolize a more refined and more ordered way of life."[49] It was her friend Pete Hamill who took stock of the cost of this privacy. "She did not retail herself, of course, did not work the talk show circuit or give interviews or issue press releases. The absence of information was filled with gossip, rumor, the endless human capacity for malice. She was able to immunize herself from most of this with irony and detachment, laughing at the more overblown printed fevers. She understood that she was the stuff that tabloid dreams are made of, combining in one person the themes of sex, death, and money. But she could be wounded, too."[50]

The sense that a public now mourning Jacqueline Kennedy Onassis had contributed to her pain was a truth too difficult for some to face. As Senator Howell Heflin of Alabama paid tribute to JKO, he not only celebrated her desire for and efforts to protect her privacy but went further in suggesting that the "public, for the most part, respected her privacy, admiring her from afar."[51] In this telling, not only JKO is deserving of praise but so also is an American people who allegedly followed her lead in minding their own business. Such a fiction obscures the relentless pursuit Mrs. Onassis endured, one often documented by those close to her who found themselves caught off guard at the magnitude of her fame and the insistence of strangers to know her thoughts and track her movement. On the flip side of Heflin's interpretation is Ellen Goodman's more forthright analysis. "We thought we knew her. We thought she belonged to us. . . . We followed her every move. But it was a compliment she didn't return, an intrusion she lived with but didn't welcome."[52] In death, that attention continued, unabated.

* * *

Jacqueline Kennedy Onassis had taken an active interest in the 1992 presidential candidacy and eventual presidency of William Jefferson Clinton. Hillary Rodham Clinton (HRC) indicated that JKO and John Kennedy Jr. were among the first contributors to her husband's campaign. The much-circulated picture of a young Bill Clinton in the Rose Garden meeting President Kennedy, combined with his articulated admiration for and efforts to link himself to JKO's first husband, very likely contributed to JKO's interest.[53] Mrs. Clinton visited JKO's apartment in June 1992 and recalled, "When I met her in that marvelous apartment with books everywhere, she made me feel like we were old friends." They talked about Mrs. Onassis's work and potential projects for the future and, convinced Bill Clinton would win, JKO gave HRC advice about life in the White House. As Ted Kennedy remarked in his eulogy, the Kennedys and the Clinton family had spent time together on Martha's Vineyard, celebrating Bill's birthday. When Mrs. Clinton recalled that day, she said, "We had a great night just talking about everything, and laughing, and it went late into the night."[54]

Both President Bill Clinton and first lady Hillary Rodham Clinton offered public statements when they learned of JKO's death. Bill Clinton's sentiments were similar to those offered by other public officials, especially those who had come of age with the Kennedy White House as a model. When JKO had been first lady, President Clinton highlighted her "uncommon appreciation of the culture that awakened us to all the beauty of our own heritage." Together, she and President Kennedy represented "such vitality, such optimism, such pride in our Nation, they inspired an entire generation of young Americans to see the nobility of helping others and to get involved in public service." Like others, he made mention of the assassination, noting how "in the face of impossible tragedy, she carried the grief of her family and our entire Nation with a calm power that somehow reassured all the rest of us." In the friendship that began with his candidacy, he expressed gratitude for the kindness she had shown him, Hillary, and their daughter, Chelsea, and the counsel she had offered about raising a family in the White House. Clinton's statement is a fine if not particularly unique tribute. He is deliberate in talking about "our" nation and "our" heritage, casting himself firmly with the citizenry of the United States and speaking with certainty about JKO's "extraordinary contribution" to the country and its people.[55]

The first lady, speaking in her own voice and expressing her own sentiments, revealed the ongoing evolution of the unofficial role extended to the president's spouse, a role that had grown and acquired additional expectations since JKO had lived in the White House. Mrs. Clinton, like so many others, spoke of JKO's "grace and style and dignity and heroism." But HRC dedicated more time in her statement to JKO's approach to motherhood, noting that she had been "selflessly devoted to her children." Like her husband, Hillary Clinton recalled the counsel JKO offered her about the "challenges and opportunities" of a White

House life and how she had carved out "the space and privacy that children need to grow into what they have a right to become." In other statements recalling meetings she had had with JKO, Hillary Clinton often referenced their conversations about family and motherhood and the challenges of the first ladyhood. HRC recalled JKO's insistence, "You've got to do things that are right for you. Don't model yourself on anybody else."[56]

While Hillary Clinton had her fans, who celebrated an accomplished professional and working mother during the 1992 campaign and then as first lady, she also faced detractors. Bill Clinton famously promoted his 1992 candidacy as a "buy one, get one free" situation. Voters would get two professionals in the White House. But in the unofficial, unpaid, undesignated role of first lady, the power allowed HRC and the clearly feminist model she represented and outlook she espoused had not appealed to the whole of the electorate as Bill Clinton had hoped. In her tribute to Jacqueline Kennedy Onassis, Mrs. Clinton tied herself to the model created by JKO and highlighted their shared role. Even if their experiences of motherhood had differed, motherhood was their bond. But beyond motherhood, Mrs. Clinton emphasized what she claimed as an essential lesson JKO modeled for the country. "If she taught us anything, it was to know the meaning of responsibility—to one's family and to one's community."[57] Though Hillary Clinton did not cast this quality as one particular to women, and even as it might well be attributed to anyone in public service, service to others—and before service to one's self—historically had been expected and celebrated among women. Reception of Jacqueline Kennedy Onassis over the course of her public life demonstrated that celebration, much as other reception reflected the consequences for appearing to put one's self before others. Hillary Clinton, learning more about life in the public eye every day, was astute in emphasizing—and, to some degree, tying herself to—this element of JKO's legacy. This was the hallmark of JKO's public life that Mrs. Clinton chose as a final tribute. In so doing, she not only communicated a truth about Mrs. Onassis but revealed a sense of what she saw as the expectation a person encountered in fulfilling the role of first lady, and perhaps even more, the expectation applied even still to women in public life.

In so many retrospectives on her life, Jacqueline Kennedy Onassis is more a symbol than a woman of flesh and blood. Whoever Mrs. Onassis was, whatever her intentions might have been, however she may have viewed herself had no real place in public remembering efforts. In the majority of considerations of JKO's life and meaning, the reality of her historical trajectory is largely erased, and there is little to suggest the complexity of the evolving cultural and political contexts during which her public life took place. Her importance is linked primarily to her first husband and children, his extended family, and the time during which he governed. Despite claims from South Dakota senator Larry Pressler that "no one thinks of Jackie as just 'President Kennedy's wife,'" in many memorial efforts, that role was fundamental to the articulated remembrance of her. Jacqueline Kennedy Onassis, beyond her connection to the staunchly Democratic Kennedy family, regularly was described as apolitical, but in public tributes she was deeply politicized, cast in symbolic significance of a better, nobler past, a powerful weapon in the culture wars of the 1990s. The obituaries and tributes paid to JKO tell us as much and maybe more about particular cultural and political predilections of the moment at which they were penned than they do about Jacqueline Kennedy Onassis and the world in which she lived. This penchant to evaluate JKO as a symbolic figure, to have her stand in as a representative for ideas about American women, culture, and public life was true for her at any given moment of her life as a public figure—and remained and *has* remained true in the days and years following her death. And in using her this way, those mourning her continued to privilege a version of Jacqueline Kennedy Onassis in which she served others and their needs rather than Jacqueline Kennedy Onassis herself.

CONCLUSION

In 1964, Jacqueline Kennedy sat down with Arthur Schlesinger for a series of interviews about her recently deceased husband. Portions of those conversations appear in chapters of this book. Her conversations with Schlesinger largely focused on John Kennedy, and that is fitting given that the intent of the effort was the cultivation of a repository of memories from those who had known JFK or been part of his administration, to be housed in the presidential library that would hold his papers.

This book highlights representations of and responses to Jacqueline Kennedy Onassis. But the oral histories feature her voice rather than providing an interpretation of her. Even when she is telling us about John Kennedy, she is revealing things also about herself. In her conversations with Schlesinger, she provides the frame.

As I revisited JKO's oral histories, I was struck by Caroline Kennedy's (CK) remembrances, included as the foreword to the published collection of these interviews, nearly as much as I was by JKO's recollections. CK's voice is not Jacqueline Kennedy Onassis's, but as a person who knew JKO, who had loved and been loved by her, who had been by her side through the chronicling assessed in this book, she offers a unique insight into her mother's thinking—and continues the effort to maintain a distinction between her mother's public and private lives. Notably, even as she is talking about her parents, Caroline Kennedy puts Jacqueline Kennedy Onassis at the center of her consideration, as a person in her own right. She is fundamental if we want a full understanding of John F. Kennedy. He is tied to her as much as she is tied to him.

In sharing her mother's materials, Caroline Kennedy is explicit in identifying the dilemma she faced in the years since JKO's death: "When does someone no longer belong to you, but belong to history?" That tension between the individual and something larger was a pressing concern for her mother, too, at any number of points during her life. CK shares her thinking in balancing her mother's penchant for privacy with her role as a public figure. Caroline Kennedy's effort is to "pay proper respect to both."[1] Guided by a sense of her mother's desires, and confident in her own judgment, she notes, "As the years pass, it has become less painful to share her with the world, and in fact, it is a privilege." But there was a strangeness, too, she noted, in knowing that people identified with and had their own sense of JKO, "but they don't really know her at all."[2] What CK would have them know were "her intellectual curiosity, her sense of the ridiculous, her sense of adventure, [and] her unerring sense of what was right."[3]

Caroline Kennedy, it is clear, knew her mother. And her strategy for sharing the oral histories JKO recorded with Schlesinger seems largely in keeping with JKO's sense of her private rights as a public figure. CK draws a line similar to that articulated by JKO in her court battle against Ron Galella. When fielding requests for access to her mother's thoughts and writings, she aimed to accommodate those related to JFK's career, the White House years, historic preservation efforts, or events of historical import. But JKO's "writings as a private citizen" were not for public consumption. In JKO's will, she requested that Caroline and John "make every effort to prevent publication of her personal papers, letters, and writings."[4] To CK, the Schlesinger interviews were about JKO's life as a public figure, and about her husband, for whom public service had been his life's work. The interviews had been conducted with the intention that they would one day be accessible to the public, an access Caroline Kennedy identifies as "an important American value."

Anyone reading Caroline Kennedy's foreword, or looking to the interviews for insight on the "real" Jackie, will be confronted by what Jacqueline Kennedy Onassis long articulated as her interests. Art. Culture.

CONCLUSION

Travel. History. Historic preservation. Faith in the nation and her first husband's vision of and for that nation. What Caroline Kennedy adds: an assertion of her mother's significance to her father's presidency in a manner beyond what JKO ever publicly articulated. She wants JKO's voice on the record because "it seemed a disservice to let her perspective remain absent from the public and scholarly debate."[5]

With limited editing of the text, Caroline Kennedy lets her mother's words stand. Highlighting that these interviews were conducted "only four months after she had lost her husband, her home, and her sense of purpose," CK imagines that there are things her mother would have changed or wished she had not said. Her views in 1964 did not remain static. She evolved. When CK asked her children to read the transcripts, they, like her, found elements of the conversations dated but also fascinating. And they wished Schlesinger "had asked more questions about *her*."[6]

Yes. Absolutely. I would like more questions about her, too. That said, JKO's answers to Schlesinger's questions about John Kennedy tell us something about her. For example, Schlesinger began a line of questioning about the White House restoration with an inquiry as to John Kennedy's response. Eventually, Schlesinger centers Jacqueline Kennedy, asking about criticism she might have received at the time. She highlights the positive response of both JFK and the public, and then she goes further in discussing not only public response to her but also the kind of framing she received from media. "I was never any different once I was in the White House than I was before, but the press made you different. Suddenly, everything that'd been a liability before—your hair, that you spoke French, that you didn't just adore to campaign, and you didn't bake bread with flour up your arms—you know everyone thought I was a snob and hated politics." John Kennedy, she claims, never made her feel a liability, although she was sure she was. At least during the campaign. There was a switch, however, once her husband became president, and she puts a point on it. "When we got to the White House all the things that I'd always done suddenly became wonderful because anything the First Lady does that's different, everyone seizes on it."[7]

She celebrates John Kennedy as "the most unself-conscious person I've ever seen." She rejects the idea that he or they were obsessed with image (even as many sources used for this book suggest otherwise). Again, she expresses her certainty that she "was always a liability to him until we got to the White House," but "he never asked me to change." And even when she was first lady, advisors had blanched at the prospect of the White House restoration and JBK's proposal of a guidebook. But she had seen both through, with her husband's blessing, and to great acclaim. "He knew," she said, "I was just being myself."[8]

Jacqueline Kennedy Onassis here demonstrates an astute analysis of American media and culture. She sees the power the press had to frame an individual to opposite ends, even when the individual in question had changed not at all, even when what had changed was the individual's circumstances or the world in which that person lived. In 1964, Jacqueline Kennedy had been in the public eye for just over a decade. She lived another thirty years, during which time she applied the lessons she learned early on. As public figure, not necessarily of her own choosing, at a time when politics and celebrity intersected, when hard and soft news became more obviously overlapping, she navigated an evolving American media landscape in a way that both stymied observers and drew admiration. She often followed a path of her own choosing, enduring the ebbs and flows of assessments about her much as she did the transition from campaign wife to first lady and then beyond. Response to her may have reflected broader ideas about American womanhood. But she was just being herself.

ACKNOWLEDGMENTS

I have been presenting on Jacqueline Kennedy Onassis for more than a decade and at a wide range of locations, among them the 1950s Media, Politics, Culture Conference at Texas Christian University; the First Ladies Symposium hosted by the Lucy Webb Hayes Heritage Center in Chillicothe, Ohio; the undergraduate Women's & Gender Studies Symposium held at King's College in Wilkes-Barre, Pennsylvania; the Biography Again conference at the State University of New York at Fredonia; and multiple meetings of the Popular Culture Association and the Berkshire Conference of the History of Women. I have loved talking to different kinds of audiences whose understandings of and familiarity with JKO have run the gamut. Copanelists, panel chairs, and audience members have offered feedback, asked questions, and shared thoughts on JKO that have pushed me to improve upon my ideas and better situate her in the worlds in which she lived. This book is better thanks to the communities with whom I have shared my research. My thanks also to the First Ladies National Historic Site for inviting me to give the Legacy Lecture in 2021 and for the enthusiasm and encouragement offered by members of the site's staff, especially Michelle Gullion.

Many thanks to archivists and librarians at the Browne Popular Culture Library at Bowling Green State University, the University of Dayton, the Ohio State University, and Kent State University for their help in making available sources and databases that were fundamental to this research. Archivists and librarians at the John F. Kennedy Presidential Library (JFKPL) made my visits both wonderful and useful.

Afterward, they continued to be in touch with me and offer assistance even after my trips had concluded. And in the world of online access to digitized sources, the JFKPL is top notch and was fundamental to my ability to keep working on this project during those peak pandemic years. Thanks, especially, to James Hill, who was so kind and so helpful to me in securing permissions for many of the beautiful images that appear in this book.

Librarians and staff at my home institution, Muskingum University, have been instrumental to this project in their efforts to keep up with my never-ending interlibrary loan requests. My thanks to Nainsi Houston, Karen Nelson, Josh Springer, and—in years past—Nicole Arnold, Linda Hatfield, and Alaine Kay for their kindness and assistance.

Thanks to Muskingum University for Faculty Development Grant Funds and funding provided by the Arthur G. and Eloise Cole Chair in American History, which allowed me to purchase materials and travel to a variety of locations to conduct necessary research for this project. Thanks to my colleagues in the Department of History at Muskingum: Alistair Hattingh, Laura Hilton, Bil Kerrigan, and Tom McGrath. Our community's unwavering commitment to scholarship, pedagogy, and service to our students and institution is unmatched, and I am proud to be part of our team. And to the many, many Muskies who have been with me in History and Gender Studies classes since 2010: thank you for letting me try out ideas about this book and many other things, and thanks for making it so often so much fun.

Many thanks to professors, colleagues, and friends who have offered feedback, support, and advice over the years: Amanda Adams, Lynn Bartholome, Deborah Cohen, Mike Foley, Tanisha Ford, Wendy Gamber, Amanda Littauer, Michael McGerr, Larry Normansell, Kara Dixon Vuic, and Molly Wertheimer. Thanks, especially, to Kathryn Cramer Brownell, Katherine Jellison, and Barbara Perry for their excellent feedback on the manuscript.

At New York University Press, I was delighted once again to work with Clara Platter and Alexia Traganas, and to work for the first time with Brianna Jean. Clara assured me she would move things forward and keep them moving, and did she ever! Her confidence in this project has been tremendous, and I am grateful for the enthusiasm, attention, and effort she has dedicated to it and to me.

Much love to my VNC pod—Gary Atkins, Iris Varley Atkins, Jim Dooley, Alistair Hattingh, Jane Varley, and Tanner Yurko. Our good times and celebrations have been sustaining to me and mine, and I am thankful for our little walking distance crew. A particular note of appreciation to Alistair, who has run literally thousands of miles with me and has listened to the book-on-tape version of this project and any number of other things history, teaching, and news related.

In the world of this Village, I must thank all of the many varied parties who have helped my husband and me raise up our daughter: our pod; generations of babysitters; the staff of the Muskingum University Center for Child Care and Development; everyone at the East Muskingum School District; her crafty godmother, Sarah Gotschall; the librarians at the Muskingum County New Concord branch; Mary Beth Caudill and the volunteers of the inspired programs she has created for the New Concord Area Arts and Recreation District; Meredith Brown and Girl Scout Troop 8210; and everyone who has contributed to the whirlwind of soccer and basketball and gymnastics and dance and theater and reading and games and fun that have filled her first ten years.

There is no greater band of friends and supporters than my Bloomington Woman Party buds. Brooke Aloe, Jennifer Cavalli, Bonnie Laughlin-Schultz, Shannon Smith, and I have been cheering each other on and yucking it up for years. Even now, when we have lived apart longer than we ever all lived in Bloomington, they are essential to me. We are rare birds of a feather, and we flock together.

The same goes for another real one, Carly Keeny, who has been thinking and talking and writing and non–poker facing about media and politics and all other things with me for decades. She is never surprised when good news comes my way, and she is never not in the front row, wearing her fandom on her sleeve. Why are we like this? I'm so glad we are.

Thanks to my in-laws, Joyce and Ron Eberly, who have helped many times when my husband or I—or both of us—have traveled for conferences or research or time on our own. I am grateful for their kindness and support. Much love to friends and family—the Dunaks, the Coynes, and the Pauls—whose warm welcome on New Jersey homecomings reminds me how lucky I am to have grown up as I did.

My daughter, Eve Dunak Eberly, has been along for the entirety of this ride. My first trip to the John F. Kennedy Presidential Library happened the year before she was born, and I was VERY PREGNANT during my first trip to the Browne Popular Culture Library. When she came to understand that I was writing this book, she often would ask about it and would cheer me on when I shared updates. There is so much joy in being her mom, in watching her grow and learn and share and shine her light. There is no system of measurement to communicate my love for her.

As with any project that takes a long time, I wavered on this one. Would I finish? What was I even doing? Eve does not imagine there are things I cannot do. The model for her belief is her dad and my husband, Keith Eberly. His confidence buoys me. He is calm and even and encouraging, and without the ways we share the labor of work and home and family, this book would not exist. My love and my thanks to him.

NOTES

PROLOGUE

1 Barbara A. Perry, *Jacqueline Kennedy: First Lady of the New Frontier* (Lawrence: University Press of Kansas, 2004), 30.

2 Carl Sferrazza Anthony, *Camera Girl: The Coming of Age of Jackie Bouvier Kennedy* (New York: Gallery Books, 2023), 129. Other speculation provided in John H. Davis, *Jacqueline Bouvier* (New York: Wiley, 1996), 151–52; and Perry, *Jacqueline Kennedy*, 31.

3 Davis, *Jacqueline Bouvier*, 150–51.

4 Anthony, *Camera Girl*, 44–56, 71–77; Sarah Bradford, *America's Queen: The Life of Jacqueline Kennedy Onassis* (New York: Penguin, 2000), 28–29; and Alice Kaplan, *Dreaming in French: The Paris Years of Jacqueline Bouvier Kennedy, Susan Sontag, and Angela Davis* (Chicago: University of Chicago Press, 2012), 16–46.

5 Bradford, *America's Queen*, 60–61; Davis, *Jacqueline Bouvier*, 152, 159; Perry, *Jacqueline Kennedy*, 31–36; and Mary Van Rensselaer Thayer, *Jacqueline Bouvier Kennedy* (New York: Doubleday, 1961), 87, 97.

6 Bradford suggests that the Kennedys were the force behind the delayed engagement notice while Kennedy biographer Thayer presents the delay as a lighthearted agreement between Bouvier and Kennedy. Bradford, *America's Queen*, 65–69; Perry, *Jacqueline Kennedy*, 37; Thayer, *Jacqueline Bouvier Kennedy*, 92; and "Senator Kennedy to Marry in Fall: Son of Former Envoy Is Fiancé of Miss Jacqueline Bouvier, Newport Society Girl," *New York Times*, June 25, 1953, 31.

7 The oldest Kennedy child, Joseph Jr., died in service during World War II.

8 Bradford, *America's Queen*, 68–69. Rose Kennedy and the Kennedy sisters had been active participants in all of JFK's campaigns. See Fredrik Logevall, *JFK: Coming of Age in the American Century, 1917–1956* (New York: Random House, 2020), 425, 521.

9 Patti Simmons, "New Chapter in Capital Romance," *Kenosha (WI) Evening News*, September 5, 1953, 6.

10 Babette Faehmel, *College Women in the Nuclear Age: Cultural Literacy and Female Identity, 1940–1960* (New Brunswick, NJ: Rutgers University Press, 2012), 32, 36, 74. Joanne Meyerowitz argues that an ongoing tension between domestic roles and public achievement marked mass-circulation magazine culture at this time, but the expectation of a woman's desire to fulfill a domestic role remained fairly fixed. Joanne Meyerowitz, "Introduction. Women and Gender in Postwar America, 1945–1960," in *Not June Cleaver: Women and Gender in Postwar America, 1945–1965*,

ed. Joanne Meyerowitz (Philadelphia: Temple University Press, 1994), 231–37, 242. See also Jessica Weiss, *To Have and to Hold: Marriage, the Baby Boom, and Social Change* (Chicago: University of Chicago Press, 2000).

11 Stephanie Coontz, *A Strange Stirring: "The Feminine Mystique" and American Women at the Dawn of the 1960s* (New York: Basic Books, 2012), 62; Barbara Ehrenreich, *The Hearts of Men: American Dreams and the Flight from Commitment* (New York: Anchor Books, 1983), 2–3, 8–9; and Faehmel, *College Women in the Nuclear Age*, 52–53. Bouvier's cousin John Davis speculates as much in his memoir about Bouvier's youth. See Davis, *Jacqueline Bouvier*, 172–73.

12 Anthony, *Camera Girl*, 288.

13 "*Life* Goes Courting with a U.S. Senator: John Kennedy and His Fiancée Enjoy an Outing on Cape Cod," *Life*, July 20, 1953, 96; and Anthony, *Camera Girl*, 277.

14 "Second Kennedy Wedding to Be 'Small Family Affair,'" *Lowell Sunday Sun*, June 28, 1953, 16. Jon Goodman, *The Kennedy Mystique: Creating Camelot* (Washington, DC: National Geographic, 2006), 9; Logevall, *JFK*, 101, 561–65; and David Nasaw, *The Patriarch: The Remarkable Life and Turbulent Times of Joseph P. Kennedy* (New York: Penguin Press, 2012), 665.

15 "Notables Attend Senator's Wedding: Senator Kennedy Weds in Newport," *New York Times*, September 13, 1953, 1, 25. Pictures of a "startled" Jacqueline appeared on the front page of newspapers across the nation, including the *Abilene (TX) Reporter-News*, *Billings (MT) Gazette*, *Charleston (WV) Daily Mail*, *Waterloo (IA) Daily Courier*, and *Long Beach (CA) Independent Press Telegram*.

16 The *New York Times* reported eight hundred at the church and twelve hundred at the reception.

17 Anthony, *Camera Girl*, 280, 291–92; Goodman, *Kennedy Mystique*, 28; "Notables Attend Senator's Wedding," 1, 25; and "The Senator Weds," *Life*, September 28, 1953, 45–46, 48.

18 Gertrude Joch Robinson suggests that women appear in the news only when "they have an important husband, have beauty, were victimized, have political significance, are performers in the arts or athletics, show ability as homemakers or hold 'first woman' status." Gertrude Joch Robinson, "Women, Media Access, and Social Control," in *Women and the News,* ed. Laurily Keir Epstein (New York: Hastings House, 1978), 90.

19 Faehmel, *College Women in the Nuclear Age*, 56–57; and Eugenia Kaledin, *Mothers and More: American Women in the 1950s* (Boston: Twayne, 1984), n.p., 17–18, 75–77.

20 Bradford, *America's Queen*, 120.

21 Michael Beschloss, *Jacqueline Kennedy, Historic Conversations on the Life of John F. Kennedy: Interviews with Arthur J. Schlesinger, Jr., 1964* (New York: Hyperion, 2011), 35.

22 Carl Sferrazza Anthony, *As We Remember Her: Jacqueline Kennedy Onassis in the Words of Her Family and Friends* (New York: HarperCollins, 1997), 110.

23 Kenneth P. O'Donnell and David F. Powers, with Joe McCarthy, *"Johnny We Hardly Knew Ye": Memories of John Fitzgerald Kennedy* (1970; Boston: Little, Brown, 1972), 142. Ted Sorensen also noted that Jackie's presence "always augmented the crowds." Theodore C. Sorensen, *Kennedy* (New York: Harper & Row, 1965), 106.

24 Beschloss, *Jacqueline Kennedy, Historic Conversations on the Life of John F. Kennedy*, 8–9.

1 Susan Douglas, *Where the Girls Are: Growing Up Female with the Mass Media* (New York: Random House, 1994), 38.

2 Christopher Andersen, *Jackie after Jack: Portrait of the Lady* (New York: William Morrow, 1998); Sarah Bradford, *America's Queen: The Life of Jacqueline Kennedy Onassis* (New York: Penguin, 2000); Tina Cassidy, *Jackie after O: One Remarkable Year When Jacqueline Kennedy Onassis Defied Expectations and Rediscovered Her Dreams* (New York: itbooks, 2012); Kitty Kelley, *Jackie Oh!* (Secaucus, NJ: Lyle Stuart, 1978); Edward Klein, *Just Jackie: Her Private Years* (New York: Ballantine, 2009); Barbara Leaming, *Jacqueline Bouvier Kennedy Onassis: The Untold Story* (New York: St. Martin's Press, 2014); Barbara A. Perry, *Jacqueline Kennedy: First Lady of the New Frontier* (Lawrence: University Press of Kansas, 2004); and Donald Spoto, *Jacqueline Bouvier Kennedy Onassis: A Life* (New York: St. Martin's Press, 2000).

3 Carl Sferrazza Anthony, *Camera Girl: The Coming of Age of Jackie Bouvier Kennedy* (New York: Gallery Books, 2023); Alice Kaplan, *Dreaming in French: The Paris Years of Jacqueline Bouvier Kennedy, Susan Sontag, and Angela Davis* (Chicago: University of Chicago Press, 2013); William Kuhn, *Reading Jackie: Her Autobiography in Books* (New York: Doubleday, 2010); and Greg Lawrence, *Jackie as Editor: The Literary Life of Jacqueline Kennedy Onassis* (New York: Thomas Dunne Books, 2011).

4 Benjamin C. Bradlee, *Conversations with Kennedy* (New York: Norton, 1975); Thomas Brown, *JFK: History of an Image* (Bloomington: Indiana University Press, 1988); Michael J. Hogan, *The Afterlife of John Fitzgerald Kennedy: A Biography* (New York: Cambridge University Press, 2017); Paul B. Fay Jr., *The Pleasure of His Company* (New York: Harper & Row, 1966); Evelyn Lincoln, *My Twelve Years with John F. Kennedy* (New York: David McKay, 1965); Pierre Salinger, *With Kennedy* (Garden City, NY: Doubleday, 1966); Arthur M. Schlesinger Jr., *A Thousand Days: John F. Kennedy in the White House* (New York: Houghton Mifflin, 1965); and Theodore Sorensen, *Kennedy* (New York: Harper & Row, 1965).

5 Jo Burr Margadant, "Introduction: Constructing Selves in Historical Perspective," in *The New Biography: Performing Femininity in Nineteenth-Century France*, ed. Jo Burr Margadant (Berkeley: University of California Press, 2000), 7.

6 David Greenberg, *Nixon's Shadow: The History of an Image* (New York: Norton, 2003), xii.

7 Alice Kessler Harris, "Why Biography?," *American Historical Review* 114 (June 2009): 630.

8 Barbara Hinckley, *The Symbolic Presidency: How Presidents Portray Themselves* (New York: Routledge, 1990), 4–5, 7; and Barbara Perry, *Jacqueline Kennedy: First Lady of the New Frontier* (Lawrence: University Press of Kansas, 2004), 4, 17.

9 Daniel Boorstin, *The Image; or, What Happened to the American Dream* (New York: Atheneum, 1962), 8–9, 12, 61, 65; Stuart Hall, "Culture, the Media, and the 'Ideological Effect,'" in *Mass Communication and Society*, ed. James Curran, Michael Gurevitch, and Janet Woollacott (1977; Beverly Hills: Sage, 1979), 340–42; and Joshua Meyrowitz, "The Life and Death of Media Friends: New Genres of Intimacy and

Mourning," in *American Heroes in the Media Age*, ed. Susan J. Drucker and Robert S. Cathcart (New York: Hampton Press, 1994), 63–66.

10 Suzanne Pingree and Robert P. Hawkins "News Definitions and Their Effects on Women," in *Women and the News*, ed. Laurily Keir Epstein (New York: Hastings House, 1978), 117–23; Leon V. Sigal, "Defining News Organizationally: News Definitions in Practice," in *Women and the News*, ed. Laurily Keir Epstein (New York: Hastings House, 1978), 109–15; Laurily Keir Epstein, "Introduction," in *Women and the News*, ed. Laurily Keir Epstein (New York: Hastings House, 1978), ix, xii–xiii; and Gaye Tuchman, *Making News: A Study in the Construction of Reality* (New York: Free Press, 1978), 47–48. See also Ellis Cashmore, *Celebrity/Culture* (Oxford: Routledge, 2006), 20–22; and Karen Sternheimer, *Celebrity Culture and the American Dream: Stardom and Social Mobility* (New York: Routledge, 2011), 153.

11 Maurine H. Beasley, *First Ladies and the Press: The Unfinished Partnership of the Media Age* (Evanston, IL: Northwestern University Press, 2005), xvii–xviii, 6–7; Patricia Bradley, *Women and the Press: The Struggle for Equality* (Evanston, IL: Northwestern University Press, 2005), xx, 231; Kathryn Cramer Brownell, *Showbiz Politics: Hollywood in American Political Life* (Chapel Hill: University of North Carolina Press, 2014), 4–5, 8–11; Dustin Harp, *Desperately Seeking Women Readers: U.S. Newspapers and the Construction of a Female Readership* (Lanham, MD: Lexington Books, 2007), 24–49; Pippa Norris, "Introduction: Women, Media, and Politics," in *Women, Media, and Politics*, ed. Pippa Norris (New York: Oxford University Press, 1997); Tuchman, *Making News*, 47–52; and Gaye Tuchman, "Women's Depiction by the Mass Media," *Signs* 4 (Spring 1959): 528–42.

CHAPTER I. CAMPAIGN WIFE

1 Donald Wilson, "John Kennedy's Lovely Lady," *Life*, August 24, 1959, 75–80.

2 Maurine Beasley, *First Ladies and the Press: The Unfinished Partnership of the Media Age* (Evanston, IL: Northwestern University Press, 2005), xviii, 6–7; Gil Troy, *Mr. & Mrs. President: From the Trumans to the Clintons* (1997; Lawrence: University Press of Kansas, 2000), ix, 3–5, 15–18; and Betty Boyd Caroli, *First Ladies: From Martha Washington to Michelle Obama*, 4th ed. (New York: Oxford University Press, 2009), xxi.

3 W. J. Rorabaugh, *Kennedy and the Promise of the Sixties* (New York: Cambridge University Press, 2002).

4 Clifford Geertz, *The Interpretation of Cultures* (2000; New York: Basic Books, 1973), 319; and Barbara Hinckley, *The Symbolic Presidency: How Presidents Portray Themselves* (New York: Routledge, 1990), 5–7.

5 Michael Beschloss, *Jacqueline Kennedy, Historic Conversations on the Life of John F. Kennedy: Interviews with Arthur J. Schlesinger, Jr., 1964* (New York: Hyperion, 2011), 39.

6 Theodore Sorensen, *Kennedy* (New York: Harper & Row, 1965), 120–21.

7 Beschloss, *Jacqueline Kennedy, Historic Conversations on the Life of John F. Kennedy*, 58–59.

8 Barbara Welter, "The Cult of True Womanhood, 1820–1860," *American Quarterly* 18 (Summer 1966): 151–74. On expected differences between men and women of this era, see also Eugenia Kaledin, *Mothers and More: American Women in the 1950s* (Boston: Twayne, 1984), n.p., 18.

9 Anthony, *Camera Girl*, 287–88.

10 Sorensen, *Kennedy*, 120; and Carl Sferrazza Anthony, *As We Remember Her: Jacqueline Kennedy Onassis in the Words of Her Family and Friends* (New York: HarperCollins, 1997), 110. JBK's misgivings also are reported in Sarah Bradford, *America's Queen: The Life of Jacqueline Kennedy Onassis* (New York: Penguin, 2000), 123.

11 Beschloss, *Jacqueline Kennedy, Historic Conversations on the Life of John F. Kennedy*, 54.

12 Troy, *Mr. & Mrs. President*, ix.

13 Troy, *Mr. & Mrs. President*, 42–43.

14 Beasley, *First Ladies and the Press*, 70, 1–4, 8, 24–25, 61–71; and Troy, *Mr. & Mrs. President*, 61, 66, 69–72, 12, 24–25.

15 Pierre Salinger, *With Kennedy* (Garden City, NY: Doubleday, 1966), 303–4; Sorensen, *Kennedy*, 37–38; Bradford, *America's Queen*, 122; and Anthony, *As We Remember Her*, 116.

16 Women, of course, were active in party politics, the labor movement, civil rights, and broader efforts to obtain equal rights across sex. Dorothy Sue Cobble, Linda Gordon, Astrid Henry, *Feminism Unfinished: A Short, Surprising History of American Women's Movements* (New York: Norton, 2014), 37–47. See also Susan Lynn, "Gender and Progressive Politics: A Bridge to Social Activism of the 1960s," in *Not June Cleaver: Women and Gender in Postwar America, 1945–1965*, ed. Joanne Meyerowitz (Philadelphia: Temple University Press, 1994), 103–27.

17 Laura (Cecial Berquist) Knebel, interview with Nelson Aldrich, December 8, 1965, John F. Kennedy Oral History Collection (JFK Presidential Library: Boston, Massachusetts), www.jfklibrary.org.

18 Stephanie Coontz, *A Strange Stirring: "The Feminine Mystique" and American Women at the Dawn of the 1960s* (New York: Basic Books, 2012); John D'Emilio and Estelle B. Freedman, *Intimate Matters: A History of Sexuality in America* (1988; Chicago: University of Chicago Press, 1997), 302–5; and Jessica Weiss, *To Have and to Hold: Marriage, the Baby Boom, and Social Change* (Chicago: University of Chicago Press, 2000), 5–7, 80–81, 226–29.

19 Bradford, *America's Queen*, 123; and "Crowds Cheered Jackie's Speech in French," *AcadiaParishToday.com*, May 16, 2008, http://acadiaparishtoday.com.

20 Sorensen, *Kennedy*, 132; and Kathryn Cramer Brownell, *Showbiz Politics: Hollywood in American Political Life* (Chapel Hill: University of North Carolina Press, 2014), 156–66.

21 Sorensen, *Kennedy*, 150; Steven Watts, *JFK and the Masculine Mystique: Sex and Power on the New Frontier* (New York: St. Martin's Press, 2016), 57; and Betty Houchin Winfield, "The First Lady, Political Power, and the Media: Who Elected Her Anyway?," in *Women, Media, and Politics*, ed. Pippa Norris (New York: Oxford University Press, 1997), 174. On the enhanced role of family in national politics, see

"The Lavender Scare," *Queer America*, November 27, 2018, https://podcasts.apple.com. On the effectiveness of JFK's image as a family man, see Michael J. Hogan, *The Afterlife of John Fitzgerald Kennedy: A Biography* (New York: Cambridge University Press, 2017), 63; Jon Goodman, *The Kennedy Mystique: Creating Camelot* (Washington, DC: National Geographic, 2006), 105.

22 Bruce Biossat, "Nixon, Kennedy Seek Fast Starts in NH," *Gastonia (NC) Gazette*, February 3, 1960, 4A.

23 Sorensen, *Kennedy*, 133–38; and Brownell, *Showbiz Politics*, 165.

24 Beschloss, *Jacqueline Kennedy, Historic Conversations on the Life of John F. Kennedy*, 67.

25 "Dave Felts Column," *Southern Illinoisian* (Carbondale, IL), February 22, 1960, 4.

26 Anthony, *As We Remember Her*, 113.

27 "Mrs. Kennedy Makes Campaign Debut Here: Has Overflow Crowd," *Wisconsin Rapids Daily Tribune*, March 11, 1960, 1.

28 Relman Morin, "The Petticoat Vote Getters Wow Them," *Telegraph-Herald* (Dubuque, IA), March 23, 1960, 1.

29 Anthony, *As We Remember Her*, 113. Donald Jansen, "Kennedy's Wife Charms Voters," *New York Times*, March 11, 1960, 15.

30 Morin, "The Petticoat Vote Getters Wow Them," 1; and Isabelle Shelton, "Potential First Ladies—III, Mrs. Kennedy Is Beautiful, Talented, Wealthy," *Charleston (WV) Gazette*, March 23, 1960, 14.

31 Fletcher Knebel, "Beauty, Brains, Youth: That's Jackie Kennedy," *Daily Journal Gazette* (Mattoon, IL), February 29, 1960, 8.

32 Brownell, *Showbiz Politics*, 160–61; and Watts, *JFK and the Masculine Mystique*, 55–56, 64–68.

33 Peter Edson, "Washington News Notebook: Southern Conservatives after Johnson; Is Jackie Too Pretty for First?," *Gastonia (NC) Gazette*, March 8, 1960, 4; Gladys Engel Lang, "The Most Admired Woman: Image-Making in the News," *Hearth and Home: Images of Women in Mass Media*, ed. Gaye Tuchman, Arlene Kaplan Daniels, and James Benet (New York: Oxford University Press, 1978), 147–60; Harvey L. Molotch, "The News of Women and the Work of Men," *Hearth and Home: Images of Women in Mass Media*, ed. Gaye Tuchman, Arlene Kaplan Daniels, and James Benet (New York: Oxford University Press, 1978), 180; and Suzanne Pingree and Robert P. Hawkins, "News Definitions and Their Effects on Women," in *Women and the News*, ed. Laurily Keir Epstein (New York: Hastings House, 1978), 116–23.

34 Karal Ann Marling, *As Seen on TV: The Visual Culture of Everyday Life in the 1950s* (Cambridge, MA: Harvard University Press, 1996), 19–45; and Troy, *Mr. & Mrs. President*, 59, 73–76, 89–90.

35 Dustin Harp, *Desperately Seeking Women Readers: U.S. Newspapers and the Construction of a Female Readership* (Lanham, MD: Lexington Books, 2007), 1, 24–26.

36 Shelton, "Potential First Ladies—III," 14.

37 Sorensen, *Kennedy*, 140.

38 Anthony, *As We Remember Her*, 115.

39   "Kennedy, Humphrey Wives Both Active Campaigners," *Walla Walla (WA) Union Bulletin*, May 10, 1960, 16.

40   Claudette Rashid, "Youngest Potential First Lady Gives Candid Interview," *Charleston (WV) Daily Mail*, May 10, 1960, 17.

41   Beschloss, *Jacqueline Kennedy, Historic Conversations on the Life of John F. Kennedy*, 81.

42   Benjamin C. Bradlee, *Conversations with Kennedy* (New York: Norton, 1975), 28.

43   Barbara A. Perry, *Jacqueline Kennedy: First Lady of the New Frontier* (Lawrence: University Press of Kansas, 2004), 53.

44   Beschloss, *Jacqueline Kennedy, Historic Conversations on the Life of John F. Kennedy*, 69–70, 91.

45   John Kenneth Galbraith, *Name Dropping: From FDR On* (New York: Houghton Mifflin, 1999), 127.

46   "Playing the Game," *Burlington (IA) Hawkeye Gazette*, May 1, 1960, 4.

47   Anthony, *As We Remember Her*, 117; Perry, *Jacqueline Kennedy*, 57–58; and Sorensen, *Kennedy*, 178.

48   "Sen. Kennedy's Wife Expecting," *San Raphael (CA) Independent Journal*, July 5, 1960, 14.

49   James McCartney, "Mrs. Kennedy to Make TV Appearances," *Oakland (CA) Tribune*, September 25, 1960, 4.

50   Beschloss, *Jacqueline Kennedy, Historic Conversations on the Life of John F. Kennedy*, 83.

51   "Jacqueline Regretfully Will Remain on Cape," *Lowell (MA) Sun*, July 14, 1960, 16.

52   "Changes Are Made in Appearance of Three Kennedy Family Homes," *Lubbock (TX) Avalanche-Journal*, July 18, 1960, 8B.

53   "Democrats: Life on the New Frontier," *Time*, August 1, 1960, https://content.time.com.

54   Mary Barelli Gallagher, *My Life with Jacqueline Kennedy*, ed. Frances Spatz Leighton (New York: David McKay, 1969), 7, 29, 32, 38–40.

55   Mary Ann Watson, *The Expanding Vista: American Television in the Kennedy Years* (New York: Oxford University Press, 1990), 5–10; and Watts, *JFK and the Masculine Mystique*, 5–7, 47–50, 56–57, 64–65.

56   Gallagher, *My Life with Jacqueline Kennedy*, 43–44.

57   Thomas W. Braden and Joan R. Braden, interview with Dennis J. O'Brien, October 11, 1969, John F. Kennedy Oral History Collection (JFK Presidential Library: Boston, MA), 11–12, 28–29, www.jfklibrary.org.

58   Joan Braden, *Just Enough Rope: An Intimate Memoir* (New York: Villard Books, 1989), 109.

59   Bradford, *America's Queen*, 136; and Perry, *Jacqueline Kennedy*, 61.

60   "Will One of These Five Be First Lady?," *U.S. News and World Report*, February 15, 1960, 54.

61   Marie Ridder and Bob Wells, "Lines Are Now Drawn: It's Pat vs. Jackie," *Pasadena (CA) Independent Star-News*, July 31, 1960, 7.

62   Alicia Hart, "Breakfast Is Essential to Teenage Beauty," *Indiana (PA) Evening Gazette*, August 25, 1960, 16.

63 Andrew Tully, "Jackie Kennedy Has Own Ideas about Hairdo and How to Dress," *El Paso (TX) Herald-Post*, August 24, 1960, 1, 2.

64 Ruth Millett, "Mrs. Kennedy Will Have to Fit into Expected Role," *Biddeford-Saco (ME) Journal*, August 29, 1960, 4.

65 Martha Weinman, "First Ladies—in Fashion, Too?" *New York Times Sunday Magazine*, September 11, 1960, 32.

66 Weinman, "First Ladies—in Fashion, Too?," 131–32.

67 Daniel Boorstin, *The Image; or, What Happened to the American Dream* (New York: Atheneum, 1962), 14–15, 39–40.

68 Nan Robertson, "Mrs. Kennedy Defends Clothes: Is 'Sure' Mrs. Nixon Pays More," *New York Times*, September 15, 1960, 1, 29.

69 McCartney, "Mrs. Kennedy to Make TV Appearances," 4.

70 Nan Robertson, "She Shops like Any Woman, Mrs. Nixon Replies on Clothes," *New York Times*, September 16, 1960, 16.

71 Beasley, *First Ladies and the Press*, 7.

72 George Dixon, "Political Debate Shifts from Dogs to What the Wives Are Wearing," *Butte Montana Standard*, September 22, 1960, 4.

73 Henry McLemore, "What's the Issue in 1960 Campaign," *Pampa (TX) Daily News*, October 6, 1960, 22.

74 "Enough of Fashions, Let's Air the Issues," *Charleston (WV) Gazette*, September 23, 1960, 22.

75 Miles McMillin, "A Petition to Carrie Lee Nelson," *Madison (WI) Capital Times*, September 19, 1960, 32.

76 Maurine H. Beasley, *Eleanor Roosevelt: Transformative First Lady* (Lawrence: University Press of Kansas, 2010), 111–15.

77 JBK claimed authorship of the columns herself. See "Worse on Sidelines Than in Midst of Campaign, Jackie Tells Presswomen," *Republican-Courier* (Findlay, OH), September 20, 1960, 5. See also Melody Lehn, "Jackie Joins Twitter: The Recirculation of 'Campaign Wife,'" *Rhetoric and Public Affairs* 15 (Winter 2012): 667–74.

78 Campaign Wife, Weekly Column, First, September 16, 1960; and Campaign Wife, Weekly Column, September 29, 1960, both in Folder B-2397, "Campaign Wife" by JBK, Box 19, Democratic National Committee, Publicity Division, Press Releases (JFK Presidential Library, Boston, MA).

79 Campaign Wife, Weekly Column, First.

80 Campaign Wife, Weekly Column, September 29, 1960; and Campaign Wife, Weekly Column, October 6, 1960, both in Folder B-2536, "Campaign Wife" by JBK, Box 20, Democratic National Committee, Publicity Division, Press Releases (JFK Presidential Library, Boston, MA).

81 Campaign Wife, Weekly Column, October 13, 1960, Folder B-2637, "Campaign Wife" by JBK, Box 20, Democratic National Committee, Publicity Division, Press Releases (JFK Presidential Library, Boston, MA).

82 Campaign Wife, Weekly Column, November 1, 1960, Folder B-2857, "Campaign Wife" by JBK, Box 21, Democratic National Committee, Publicity Division, Press Releases (JFK Presidential Library, Boston, MA).

83 Dick West, "Lighter Side of Congress," *Leader-Times* (Kittanning, PA), September 21, 1960, 13.

84 "Lovely Aspirants for Role of First Lady," *Life*, October 10, 1960, 4, 150.

85 Gallagher, *My Life with Jacqueline Kennedy*, 50.

CHAPTER 2. FIRST LADY

1 "A New Era Begins," *New York Times*, January 22, 1961, 134; and David Halberstam, "Gay Democrats Jam the Capital," *New York Times*, January 19, 1961, 20.

2 "Women: Jackie," *Time*, January 20, 1961, 18–26.

3 Stephanie Coontz, *A Strange Stirring: "The Feminine Mystique" and American Women at the Dawn of the 1960s* (New York: Basic Books, 2011), 1–3; Susan Douglas, *Where the Girls Are: Growing Up Female with Mass Media* (New York: Random House, 1995), 43–45; and Betty Friedan, *The Feminine Mystique* (New York: Norton, 1963).

4 "'Jackie' in New Role, Has Mixed Feelings," *Defiance (OH) Crescent-News*, January 20, 1961, 3.

5 "'Jackie' in New Role, Has Mixed Feelings," 3; "Jacqueline Kennedy Readies for Role," *Alamogordo (NM) Daily News*, January 12, 1961, 21; Maurine H. Beasley, *First Ladies and the Press: The Unfinished Partnership of the Media Age* (Evanston, IL: Northwestern University Press, 2005), 12, 68, 81–82; Gil Troy, *Mr. & Mrs. President: From the Trumans to the Clintons* (Lawrence: University Press of Kansas, 2000), 73–75; Perry, *Jacqueline Kennedy*, xv; and Robert P. Watson, *The Presidents' Wives: Reassessing the Office of the First Lady* (Boulder, CO: Lynne Rienner, 2000), 110–11.

6 "Jacqueline Kennedy Readies for Role," 21; Letitia Baldridge, *Of Diamonds and Diplomats* (Boston: Houghton Mifflin, 1968), 155–58, 165–67; Maxine Cheshire, with John Grenya, *Maxine Cheshire, Reporter* (Boston: Houghton Mifflin, 1978), 40–41; Anthony J. Eksterowicz and Kristen Paynter, "The Evolution of the Role and the Office of the First Lady: The Movement toward Integration with the White House Office," in *The Presidential Companion: Readings on the First Ladies*, 2nd ed., ed. Robert P. Watson and Anthony J. Eksterowicz (Columbia: University of South Carolina Press, 2006), 215–16; Barbara Perry, *Jacqueline Kennedy: First Lady of the New Frontier* (Lawrence: University Press of Kansas, 2004), 77–79; and Troy, *Mr. & Mrs. President*, 110–13.

7 "Kennedy Family Ready for Big Day," *Oakland (CA) Tribune*, January 15, 1961, 16.

8 Beasley, *First Ladies and the Press*, 82.

9 "The White House Washington: J," *Newsweek*, January 1, 1962, 32.

10 Beasley, *First Ladies and the Press*, 79–85; Michael J. Hogan, *The Afterlife of John Fitzgerald Kennedy: A Biography* (New York: Cambridge University Press, 2017), 43–44; Perry, *Jacqueline Kennedy*, 17, 79–80; and Ted Sorensen, *Kennedy* (New York: Harper & Row, 1965), 381.

11 Gay Pauley, "Reluctant Jacqueline Kennedy Tops 1960 List of 'Best Dressed' Women," *Idaho Free Press* (Nampa, ID), 5.

12 "Jackie Mannequins Propriety Questioned," *Bristol Courier and Levittown (PA) Times*, January 22, 1961, 2; Inez Robb, "Jacqueline's Imitators," *Bakersfield Californian*, January 19, 1961, 33; and Gay Pauley, "Jacqueline Kennedy 'Look-Alikes' Are Big in N.Y. Model Agencies," *Norwalk (OH) Reflector-Herald*, January 17, 1961, 5.

13 "Jacqueline Kennedy Nose Popular Say Plastic Surgeons," *Tipton (IN) Daily Tribune*, January 26, 1961, 3.

14 Eugenia Sheppard, "Jackie Kennedy 'Look' Pops Up All over the World," *Corpus Christie (TX) Times*, January 23, 1961, C1.

15 Pauley, "Jacqueline Kennedy 'Look-Alikes' Are Big in N.Y. Model Agencies," 5.

16 Robb, "Jacqueline's Imitators," 33.

17 "Jackie Mannequins Propriety Questioned," 2.

18 Hogan, *Afterlife of John Fitzgerald Kennedy*, 17.

19 Oleg Cassini, *A Thousand Days of Magic: Dressing Jacqueline Kennedy for the White House* (New York: Rizzoli, 1995), 18, 20, 29–30.

20 "It Was a Long, but Proud Day for Wife of the New President," *New York Times*, January 21, 1961, 11.

21 Cassini, *Thousand Days of Magic*, 22, 26–27, 33, 38; and Mark White, *Kennedy: A Cultural History of an American Icon* (New York: Bloomsbury, 2013), 79.

22 Baldridge, *Diamonds and Diplomats*, 173.

23 Cassini, *Thousand Days of Magic*, 103; and Perry, *Jacqueline Kennedy*, 76.

24 Charlotte Curtis, *First Lady: The Glory, Up-to-the-Minute Story of Jacqueline Kennedy's Life in the White House* (New York: Pyramid Books, 1962), 45–46.

25 Baldridge, *Diamonds and Diplomats*, 214–18; and Pierre Salinger, *With Kennedy* (Garden City, NY: Doubleday, 1966), 317.

26 Hogan, *Afterlife of John Fitzgerald Kennedy*, 17, 39, 46–47.

27 Mary Barelli Gallagher, *My Life with Jacqueline Kennedy*, ed. Frances Spatz Leighton (Philadelphia: David McKay, 1969), 174.

28 Daz and Richard Harkness, "A New First Lady, a New Mood," *New York Times Sunday Magazine*, April 23, 1961, 22, 92.

29 Curtis, *First Lady*, 46.

30 Curtis, *First Lady*, 70; and Jon Goodman, *The Kennedy Mystique: Creating Camelot* (Washington, DC: National Geographic, 2006), 128–29, 142. On the ways in which culture contributed to John Kennedy's overall political vision, see Camille Davis, "The Cultural Politics behind America's Fascination with JFK," *Time*, November 27, 2023, https://time.com. This sense of the White House had been shared by first ladies of the past, as in the case of Dolley Madison, who emphasized the home's symbolic importance. See Catherine Allgor, *Parlor Politics: In Which the Ladies of Washington Help Build a City and a Government* (Charlottesville: University of Virginia Press, 2000), 54, 58–64.

31 Harold C. Schonberg, "Casals Plays at White House: Last Appeared There in 1904," *New York Times*, November 14, 1961, 1, 33; and Curtis, *First Lady*, 70, 72.

32 Salinger, *With Kennedy*, 309–10, 317.

33 Arthur G. Neal, *National Trauma and Collective Memory: Extraordinary Events in the American Experience*, 2nd ed. (Armonk, NY: M.E. Sharpe, 2005), 111.

34 Hogan, *Afterlife of John Fitzgerald Kennedy*, 46–47.

35 John Hellman, *The Kennedy Obsession: The American Myth of JFK* (New York: Columbia University Press, 1997); Hogan, *Afterlife of John Fitzgerald Kennedy*; Perry, *Jacqueline Kennedy*, 4, 17, 83, 111, 133–38; Steven Watts, *JFK and the Masculine Mystique: Sex and Power on the New Frontier* (New York: St. Martin's, 2016); and White, *Kennedy*. For discussion of style more broadly, see Allgor, *Parlor Politics*, 52–54.

36 Alan Petigny, *The Permissive Society: America, 1941–1965* (New York: Cambridge University Press, 2009).

37 Cassini, *Thousand Days of Magic*, 61.

38 "Kennedys Hit the Road: A Visit with Neighbors," *Life*, May 21, 1961, 17.

39 Tania Long, "Ottawa Reacts to Mrs. Kennedy with 'Special Glow of Warmth,'" *New York Times*, May 18, 1961, 12.

40 Baldrige, *Diamonds and Diplomats*, 231; and Hamish Bowles, *Jacqueline Kennedy: The White House Years: Selections from the John F. Kennedy Library and Museum* (New York: Little, Brown, 2001), 117.

41 Cassini, *Thousand Days of Magic*, 61–62; and Sorensen, *Kennedy*, 383.

42 Mark Haefele, "John F. Kennedy, USIA, and World Public Opinion," *Diplomatic History* 25 (Winter 2001): 63–84.

43 Beasley, *First Ladies and the Press*, xviii, 6–7.

44 W. Granger Blair, "Just an Escort, Kennedy Jokes as Wife's Charm Enchants Paris," *New York Times*, June 3, 1961, 7.

45 "The President's Scene Stealer," *Life*, June 9, 1961, 46; and Cassini, *Thousand Days of Magic*, 69.

46 "Parisians Await Mrs. Kennedy: They Talk the Same Language," *New York Times*, May 31, 1961, 5; Blair, "Just an Escort," 7; and "In Paris and Vienna . . . Our New President Sees the Tough Guys," *Life*, June 9, 1961, 42.

47 Nicholas J. Cull, "Projecting Jackie: Kennedy Administration Film Propaganda Overseas in Leo Seltzer's *Invitation to India, Invitation to Pakistan*, and *Jacqueline Kennedy's Asian Journey* (1962)," in *Propaganda: Political Rhetoric and Identity, 1300–2000*, ed. Bertrand Taithe and Tim Thornton (Stroud, Gloucester, UK: Sutton Publishing, 1999), 308–9.

48 Baldrige, *Of Diamonds and Diplomats*, 234, 237; "First Lady Wins Khrushchev, Too," *New York Times*, June 4, 1961, 1; and Perry, *Jacqueline Kennedy*, 86–88.

49 Cull, "Projecting Jackie," 309. For more on the conception of soft power and public diplomacy, see Madeline Jones McAleese, "Jackie Kennedy: The Public Diplomacy of Camelot," November 22, 2016, University of Southern California Center on Public Diplomacy Blog, https://uscpublicdiplomacy.org/blog/jackie-kennedy-public-diplomacy-camelot; Joseph S. Nye Jr., "Public Diplomacy and Soft Power," *Annals of the American Academy of Political and Social Science* 616 (March 2008):

96–99, 103; and Gregory M. Tomlin, *Murrow's Cold War: Public Diplomacy for the Kennedy Administration* (Lincoln: Potomac Books, University of Nebraska Press, 2016), xvii, 123–24.

50 Carol B. Schwalbe, "Jacqueline Kennedy and Cold War Propaganda," *Journal of Broadcasting and Electronic Media* 49 (March 2005): 124.

51 Betty Houchin Winfield, "The First Lady, Political Power, and the Media: Who Elected Her Anyway?," in *Women, Media, and Politics*, ed. Pippa Norris (New York: Oxford University Press, 1997), 174.

52 Curtis, *First Lady*, 130.

53 Hogan, *Afterlife of John Fitzgerald Kennedy*, 34.

54 "Schedule for Mrs. Kennedy's Trip to India and Pakistan," March 7, 1962, Folder PP5/Kennedy, Jacqueline, 1-1-62-3-10-62, Box 705, White House Central Files, Subject File, The Papers of John F. Kennedy (JFK Presidential Library, Boston, MA). Paul Grimes, "India Waits in Curiosity," *New York Times*, March 11, 1962, 43.

55 Troy, *Mr. & Mrs. President*, 122–23.

56 Joan Braden, "An Exclusive Chat with Jackie Kennedy," *Saturday Evening Post*, May 12, 1962, 86.

57 *Jacqueline Kennedy's Asian Journey*, dir. by Leo Seltzer (Washington, DC: United States Information Agency, 1962).

58 Clint Hill, with Lisa McCubbin, *Mrs. Kennedy and Me: An Intimate Memoir* (New York: Gallery Books, 2012), 130.

59 Hill, *Mrs. Kennedy and Me*, 136.

60 Government of India, Overseas Communication Service, March 24, 1962, Folder PP5/Kennedy, Jacqueline, 3-11-62-4-30-62, Box 705, White House Central Files, Subject File, The Papers of John F. Kennedy (JFK Presidential Library, Boston, MA).

61 Paul Grimes, "India Nobles Fete First Lady after Sail on a Princely Yacht," *New York Times*, March 18, 1962, 38.

62 Paul Grimes, "Most Magic Two Weeks," *New York Times*, March 27, 1962, 12.

63 Donald Wilson to Lawrence F. O'Brien, November 7, 1962, Folder PP5/Kennedy, Jacqueline, 5-1-62-12-10-62, Box 705, White House Central Files, Subject File, The Papers of John F. Kennedy (JFK Presidential Library, Boston, MA).

64 Walter P. McConaughy to Jay Gildner, April 6, 1962, Folder PP5/Kennedy, Jacqueline, 3-11-62-4-30-62, Box 705, White House Central Files, Subject File, The Papers of John F. Kennedy (JFK Presidential Library, Boston, MA).

65 Hill, *Mrs. Kennedy and Me*, 149.

66 Cull, "Projecting Jackie," 308, 312–13; Schwalbe, "Jacqueline Kennedy and Cold War Propaganda," 120–22; and Tomlin, *Murrow's Cold War*, 127.

67 Nicholas Cull, *The Cold War and the United States Information Agency: American Propaganda and Public Diplomacy, 1945–1989* (New York: Cambridge University Press, 2008), xv.

68 Schwalbe, "Jacqueline Kennedy and Cold War Propaganda," 120–22; Tomlin, *Murrow's Cold War*, 126–27, 128; and Cull, "Projecting Jackie," 309.

69 Cull, *Cold War and the United States Information Agency*, 208.

70 Alex Dreier, ABC Network, Commentary, March 28, 1962, Folder PP5/Kennedy, Jacqueline, 3-11-62-4-30-62, Box 705, White House Central Files, Subject File, The Papers of John F. Kennedy (JFK Presidential Library, Boston, MA).

71 Schwalbe, "Jacqueline Kennedy and Cold War Propaganda," 123.

72 Bowles, *Jacqueline Kennedy*, 140–55.

73 "Jackie Leaves Mark on India and Pakistan," *Life*, March 30, 1962, 24–35.

74 Braden, "An Exclusive Chat with Jackie Kennedy," 87.

75 Joanne Meyerowitz, "Beyond the Feminine Mystique: A Reassessment of Postwar Mass Culture, 1946–1958," in *Not June Cleaver: Women and Gender in Postwar America, 1945–1965*, ed. Joanne Meyerowitz (Philadelphia: Temple University Press, 1994), 231, 237. As Meyerowitz suggests, media celebrated women's domestic and nondomestic pursuits—"sometimes even in the same sentence."

76 Article for *American Weekly*, p. 5, Press files: coverage: Articles by Mrs. Kennedy, Box 17, Pamela Turnure Files, Series 1.1.2, Jacqueline Kennedy Onassis Personal Papers (JFK Presidential Library, Boston, MA).

77 J. B. West, with Mary Lynn Kotz, *Upstairs at the White House: My Life with the First Ladies* (New York: Coward, McCann & Geoghegan, 1973), 192–94.

78 West, *Upstairs at the White House*, 131.

79 Perry, *Jacqueline Kennedy*, 97. Salinger, *With Kennedy*, 305.

80 Bess Furman, "First Lady Plans Report on 'Finds,'" *New York Times*, February 4, 1961, 8.

81 Bess Furman, "Refurnishing Planned," *New York Times*, February 24, 1961, 1, 11.

82 Press Release, "The White House," February 23, 1961, 1–3; Press Release, "Background Information for News Media," February 26, 1961; and Press Release, "White House China Room," March 1961; Press Release, March 29, 1961; Press Release, July 4, 1961, all in Folder: Press files: releases: 1961: February–July, Box 17, Pamela Turnure Files, Jacqueline Kennedy Onassis Personal Papers (JFK Presidential Library, Boston, MA),

83 Hugh Sidey, "The First Lady Brings History and Beauty to the White House," *Life*, September 1, 1961, 57, 63.

84 James A. Abbott and Elaine M. Rice, *Designing Camelot: The Kennedy White House Restoration* (New York: Van Nostrand Reinhold, 1998), 21–24.

85 Perry, *Jacqueline Kennedy*, 112; Sidey, "First Lady Brings History and Beauty to the White House," 62; and West, *Upstairs at the White House*, 241.

86 Perry, *Jacqueline Kennedy*, 124–27; Betty Boyd Caroli, *First Ladies: From Martha Washington to Michelle Obama*, 4th ed. (New York: Oxford University Press, 2009), 229; and Mary Ann Watson, *The Expanding Vista: American Television in the Kennedy Years* (New York: Oxford University Press, 1990), 142–43. The idea for the televised tour came from CBS executive Blair Clark. White, *Kennedy*, 45.

87 Perry, *Jacqueline Kennedy*, 126. *A Tour of the White House*, dir. by Franklin J. Schaffner, February 14, 1962, BS, NBC, ABC, accessed at www.dailymotion.com. Folder: Press Files: Coverage: Television and film: CBS Show of the White House (2 of 2), Transcript, White House Tour, 5, Pamela Turnure Files, Jacqueline Kennedy Onassis Personal Papers (JFK Presidential Library, Boston, MA).

88 Beschloss, *Jacqueline Kennedy, Historic Conversations on the Life of John F. Kennedy*, xxix.

89 Sally Bedell Smith, *Grace and Power: The Private World of the Kennedy White House* (New York: Random House, 2004), 256; and Watson, *Expanding Vista*, 143.

90 Jean Warren Hight to Mrs. Kennedy, February 14, 1962, Messages of congratulations, Folder 2: CBS, T.V. show, February 14, 1962; Margaret V. Knudsen to Mrs. Kennedy, February 15, 1962; Betty Rockwell to Mrs. John F. Kennedy, February 15, 1962; Roy M. Frisbe to Mrs. Kennedy, February 15, 1962; Dr. and Mrs. Maxwell Fields to Mrs. John Kennedy, February 16, 1962, Messages of congratulations, Folder 1. CBS, T.V. show, 14 February 1962; and Mr. and Mrs. James Argodales to Jackie Kennedy, February 15, 1962, all in Messages of congratulations, Folder 2: CBS, T.V. show, February 14, 1962, all in Mary Gallagher Files, Jacqueline Bouvier Kennedy Onassis Personal Papers (JFK Presidential Library, Boston, MA), www.jfklibrary.org.

91 P. K. Kufrin to Mrs. Jacqueline Kennedy, February 16, 1962; Harry Karrass to Jacqueline Kennedy, February 15, 1962, Messages of congratulations, Folder 1. CBS, T.V. show, February 14, 1962; Mame E. Goodell to Mrs. John F. Kennedy, February 15, 1962; Mr. and Mrs. Louie J. Ayoub to Mrs. John F. Kennedy, February 15, 1962; and Jimmy McHugh to Mrs. Kennedy, February 16, 1962, all in Messages of congratulations, Folder: 2. CBS, T.V. show, February 14, 1962, all in Mary Gallagher Files, Jacqueline Bouvier Kennedy Onassis Personal Papers (JFK Presidential Library, Boston, MA), www.jfklibrary.org.

92 "Mrs. JFK—Real TV Pro," *New York Daily News*, n.d.; Jack Iams, "Tour of White House," *New York Herald Tribune*, February 16, 1962; "Tour of the White House Makes Fascinating Hour," *New York Daily News*, February 16, 1962; and "Blessings on This House," *Boston Globe*, February 16, 1962, all in Messages of congratulations, Folder: 2. CBS, T.V. show, February 14, 1962, Mary Gallagher Files, Jacqueline Bouvier Kennedy Onassis Personal Papers (JFK Presidential Library, Boston, Massachusetts), www.jfklibrary.org; and "The First Lady and the White House," *Newsweek*, September 17, 1962, 71.

93 Tomlin, *Murrow's Cold War*, 124; Transcription of White House Tour, pages 5–6, Folder: Press files: Coverage: Television and film: CBS show of the White House (2 of 2), Box 21, Pamela Turnure Files, Series 1.1.2. Jacqueline Kennedy Onassis Personal Papers (JFK Presidential Library, Boston, MA); and Memo from United States Information Agency to Pierre Salinger, June 31, 1962, Folder PP5/Kennedy, Jacqueline, 1-1-62-3-10-62, Box 705, White House Central Files, The Papers of John F. Kennedy (JFK Presidential Library, Boston, MA). See also Karal Ann Marling, *As Seen on TV: The Visual Culture of Everyday Life in the 1950s* (Cambridge, MA: Harvard University Press, 1996), 242–83; and Elaine Tyler May, *Homeward Bound: American Families in the Cold War* (New York: Basic Books, 1988), 10–16.

94 Joan Braden, *Just Enough Rope: An Intimate Memoir* (New York: Villard Books, 1989), 108–9; Hogan, *Afterlife of John Fitzgerald Kennedy*, 34–37; and Victor Lasky, *JFK: The Man and the Myth* (New York: Macmillan, 1963), 570–71.

95 Memo from United States Information Agency to Pierre Salinger, June 31, 1962, Folder PP5/Kennedy, Jacqueline, 1-1-62-3-10-62, Box 705, White House Central Files, The Papers of John F. Kennedy (JFK Presidential Library, Boston, MA).

96 Norman Mailer, "An Evening with Jackie Kennedy: More or Less at Home in Your White House," *Esquire*, July 1, 1962, 57–61; Vaughn Meader, *The First Family* (New York: Fine Recording Studio, 1962); and Watson, *Expanding Vista*, 55, 143–44.

97 Gallagher, *My Life with Jacqueline Kennedy*, 159.

98 Sarah Bradford, *America's Queen: The Life of Jacqueline Kennedy Onassis* (New York: Penguin, 2000), 188–89, 231; and Perry, *Jacqueline Kennedy*, 84, 92.

99 Bradford, *America's Queen*, 182; and Maxine Cheshire, "They Never Introduce M. Boudin," *Washington Post*, September 9, 1962, F1; and Maxine Cheshire, "The Green Room Carpet Magically Comes and Goes," *Washington Post*, September 12, 1962, C1.

100 "How the Public Rates the Nation's First Lady," *US News and World Report*, October 8, 1962, 28. On other polls, see Watson, *Presidents' Wives*, 154–55.

101 Beasley, *First Ladies and the Press*, 6–7.

CHAPTER 3. WIDOW

1 William A. Mindak and Gerald D. Hursh, "Television's Functions on the Assassination Weekend," in *The Kennedy Assassination and the American Public: Social Communication in Crisis*, ed. Bradley S. Greenberg and Edwin S. Parker (Stanford, CA: Stanford University Press, 1965), 132.

2 Michael J. Hogan, *The Afterlife of John Fitzgerald Kennedy: A Biography* (New York: Cambridge University Press, 2017), 50.

3 Barbie Zelizer, *Covering the Body: The Kennedy Assassination, the Media, and the Shaping of Collective Memory* (Chicago: University of Chicago Press, 1992), 61–62.

4 "World Toasted First Lady, but Now It Weeps for Her," November 23, 1963, from United Press International, in *Oh, no! Oh, no! Four Tragic Days: As Reported by "The Milwaukee Journal"* (Milwaukee, WI: Milwaukee Journal, 1963), 2.

5 Hogan, *Afterlife of John Fitzgerald Kennedy*, 90.

6 A sampling of newspapers featuring the image of Hill and Jacqueline Kennedy atop the presidential limousine include the *Chattanooga (TN) News–Free Press*, *Atlanta Journal*, *Evening Press* (Binghamton, NY), *Springfield (IL) Daily News*, and *Berkshire (MA) Eagle*. See *91 American Newspaper Front Pages: Recording Nov. 22-23-24-25* (New York: KMR Publications, 1963[?]), 18, 19, 25, 30, 37.

7 A sampling of newspapers featuring the image of Jacqueline Kennedy standing witness to LBJ's swearing in include the *Tulsa (OK) Daily World*, *Winston-Salem (NC) Journal*, *Muncie (IN) Star*, *Albuquerque (NM) Journal*, and *Florida Times Union* (Jacksonville, FL). See *91 American Newspaper Front Pages*, 42, 43, 48, 49, 51; and Frances Lewine, "Mrs. Kennedy's Farewell Borne with Bravery," *Corpus Christi (TX) Times*, November 23, 1963, 7.

8 Kenneth P. O'Donnell and David F. Powers, with Joe McCarthy, *"Johnny, We Hardly Knew Ye": Memories of John Fitzgerald Kennedy* (1970; Boston: Little, Brown, 1972?), 39.

9 Maurine Beasley, *First Ladies and the Press: The Unfinished Partnership of the Media Age* (Evanston, IL: Northwestern University Press, 2005), 72; and Mark White, *Kennedy: A Cultural History of an American Icon* (New York: Bloomsbury, 2013), 91.

10 Hogan, *Afterlife of John Fitzgerald Kennedy*, 77.

11 Clint Hill, with Lisa McCubbin, *Five Days in November* (New York: Gallery Books, 2013), 112.

12 For examples of mention of the Chanel suit, see Preston McGraw, "Widow Helps Put JFK onto Litter," *Tulsa (OK) Daily World*, November 23, 1963, 1, in *91 American Newspaper Front Pages: Recording Nov. 22-23-24-25*, 42; "Lyndon Johnson Assumes Office of President," *Hamilton (OH) Journal*, November 23, 1963, 1; and "World Toasted First Lady, but Now It Weeps for Her," 2.

13 Cathy Horn, "Jacqueline Kennedy's Smart Pink Suit, Preserved in Memory and Kept out of View," *New York Times*, November 14, 2013, www.nytimes.com.

14 Hogan, *Afterlife of John Fitzgerald Kennedy*, 79.

15 "Jacqueline Seeks Courage to Tell Children," *St. Paul (MN) Dispatch*, November 23, 1963, 1, in *91 American Newspaper Front Pages: Recording Nov. 22-23-24-25*, 54.

16 Zelizer, *Covering the Body*, 4–5, 64–66. See also John Hellmann, *The Kennedy Obsession: The American Myth of JFK* (New York: Columbia University Press, 1997), 91. On the image of the Kennedy family, and especially JFK as a family man, see Hogan, *Afterlife of John Fitzgerald Kennedy*, 63, 66; and White, *Kennedy*, 79.

17 See Frank Cormier, "Suspect Once Renounced Country," *Salina (KS) Journal*, November 24, 1963, 4; and Arthur Everett, "A Day of Gloom Started with Bright Enthusiasm," *Corpus Christi (TX) Times*, November 23, 1963, 7. In subsequent interviews, she claimed to have said, "Mr. President, *you can't say Dallas doesn't love you.*" Some articles, drawing from Dallas UPI reporting, attributed the sentiment to Jacqueline Kennedy. See, for example, Preston McGraw, "For Jackie the Tears Come Late," *Arizona Republic* (Phoenix, AZ), November 23, 1963, 1; and "Remarked Dallas Was Friendly before Shooting," *Lebanon (PA) Daily News*, November 23, 1963, 7.

18 "A Brave and Gracious Lady," *Bangor (ME) Daily News*, November 28, 1963, in *88th Congress, 2D Session, Senate Document No. 59, Memorial Addresses in the Congress of the United States and Tributes in Eulogy of John Fitzgerald Kennedy Late a President of the United States. Compiled under Direction of the Joint Committee in Printing* (Washington, DC: United States Government Printing Office, 1964), 46–47.

19 "World Toasted First Lady, but Now It Weeps for Her," 2; and "Jacqueline Seeks Courage to Tell Children," 54.

20 "Jacqueline Seeks Courage to Tell Children," 54. Other articles also emphasized her reluctance but willingness to participate in her husband's political efforts. See Marjorie Hunter, "Kennedy's Wife Kept Composure," *New York Times*, November 23, 1963, 9.

21 Stuart Hall, "Culture, Media, and the 'Ideological Effect,'" 315–48 in *Mass Communication and Society*, ed. James Curran, Michael Guravitch, and Janet Woollacott (1977; Beverly Hills: Sage, 1979), 343–46; and Pippa Norris, "Introduction," in *Women, Media, and Politics*, ed. Pippa Norris (New York: Oxford University Press, 1997), 2.

22 "World Toasted First Lady, but Now It Weeps for Her," 2.

23 "An American Heroine," *Southern Pines (NC) Pilot*, November 28, 1963, in *Memorial Addresses in the Congress of the United States and Tributes in Eulogy of John Fitzgerald Kennedy Late a President of the United States*, 99.

24 *Lebanon (PA) Daily News*, November 23, 1963, 7.

25 Preston McGraw, "Mrs. Kennedy Clings to Husband in Death," *Wisconsin State Journal (Madison, WI)*, November 23, 1963, 1.

26 "Jacqueline Seeks Courage to Tell Children," 54.

27 "Jackie Must Inform Caroline, John Jr.," *Clarion-Ledger* (Jackson, MS), November 23, 1963, 1, in *91 American Newspaper Front Pages: Recording Nov. 22-23-24-25*, 47.

28 "A Moment of Madness," *Long Beach (CA) Independent-Press-Telegram*, November 24, 1963, in *Memorial Addresses in the Congress of the United States and Tributes in Eulogy of John Fitzgerald Kennedy Late a President of the United States*, 29.

29 "Jacqueline Seeks Courage to Tell Children," 54.

30 Thomas B. Ross, "Among Sorrow, the Strength to Carry On," *Chicago Sun-Times*, December 29, 1963, in *Memorial Addresses in the Congress of the United States and Tributes in Eulogy of John Fitzgerald Kennedy Late a President of the United States*, 829.

31 Frances Lewine, "Jacqueline Kennedy's Courage, Dignity Matchless Memorial to Her Husband," *North Adams Massachusetts Transcript*, December 3, 1963, 7.

32 Hogan, *Afterlife of John Fitzgerald Kennedy*, 88–89.

33 Hill, *Five Days in November*, 194–95, 219–20.

34 Ross, "Among Sorrow, the Strength to Carry On," 829; Hellmann, *Kennedy Obsession*, xi–xii, 146; Barbara Hinckley, *The Symbolic Presidency: How Presidents Portray Themselves* (New York: Routledge, 1990), 4–7; Hogan, *Afterlife of John Fitzgerald Kennedy*, 78, 83–92; and Arthur G. Neal, *National Trauma and Collective Memory: Extraordinary Events in the American Experience*, 2nd ed. (Armonk, NY: M.E. Sharpe, 2005), 30–31, 108–11.

35 Hogan, *Afterlife of John Fitzgerald Kennedy*, 78, 87. See also Thomas Brown, *JFK: History of an Image* (Bloomington: Indiana University Press, 1988), 3; and W. J. Rorabaugh, *Kennedy and the Promise of the Sixties* (New York: Cambridge University Press, 2002), 226.

36 Hill, *Five Days in November*, 167–74, 196–208; and Lewine, "Jacqueline Kennedy's Courage, Dignity Matchless Memorial to Her Husband," 7.

37 Hill, *Five Days in November*, 215–25, 227. After the receiving line, she joined in a birthday celebration for her son, John Jr. Hill, *Five Days in November*, 228–29.

38 Thomas Brown, *JFK: History of an Image* (Bloomington: Indiana University Press, 1988); and Hellmann, *Kennedy Obsession*.

39 Rick Du Brow, "Nation Indebted to Jacqueline," *Monroe (LA) News-Star*, November 26, 1963, 8-A.

40 "For Gallantry," *Worth-Palos (IL) Recorder*, November 28, 1963, in *Memorial Addresses in the Congress of the United States and Tributes in Eulogy of John Fitzgerald Kennedy Late a President of the United States*, 470.

41 "Why Such Tragic Hate?," *Stanly News & Press* (Albemarle, NC), November 29, 1963, in *Memorial Addresses in the Congress of the United States and Tributes in Eulogy of John Fitzgerald Kennedy Late a President of the United States*, 80.

42 Ruth Lee, "The Way It Looks to Me," *Springfield (GA) Herald*, November 29, 1963, in *Memorial Addresses in the Congress of the United States and Tributes in Eulogy of John Fitzgerald Kennedy Late a President of the United States*, 447.

43 Eugenia Kaledin, *Mothers and More: American Women in the 1950s* (Boston: Twayne, 1984), n.p., 18–19.

44 "Woman's Portion: To Bear Tragedy," *Delaware County (PA) Times*, December 3, 1963, 8.

45 "A Portrait of Courage," *Lewiston (ME) Evening Journal*, November 26, 1963, in *Memorial Addresses in the Congress of the United States and Tributes in Eulogy of John Fitzgerald Kennedy Late a President of the United States*, 45.

46 *Portland Oregonian*, November 26, 1963; and *Mount Olive (NC) Tribune*, n.d., both in *Memorial Addresses in the Congress of the United States and Tributes in Eulogy of John Fitzgerald Kennedy Late a President of the United States*, 507 and 116.

47 "An Aristocrat," *Somerset (PA) Daily American*, November 26, 1963, 7.

48 "An American Heroine," 99.

49 "Hail and Farewell," *New Beacon* (Provincetown, MA), November 27, 1963, in *Memorial Addresses in the Congress of the United States and Tributes in Eulogy of John Fitzgerald Kennedy Late a President of the United States*, 719.

50 "The Kennedy Tragedy," *Nantucket (MA) Inquirer and Mirror*, n,d., in *Memorial Addresses in the Congress of the United States and Tributes in Eulogy of John Fitzgerald Kennedy Late a President of the United States*, 721.

51 "The Strength of Conviction," *Greensboro (NC) Times*, November, 28, 1963, in *Memorial Addresses in the Congress of the United States and Tributes in Eulogy of John Fitzgerald Kennedy Late a President of the United States*, 89.

52 "Jacqueline Kennedy Lived like Chapter in a Book," *Florence (SC) Morning News*, December 1, 1963, 8A.

53 Lewine, "Jacqueline Kennedy's Courage, Dignity Matchless Memorial to Her Husband," 7.

54 "The Strength of Conviction," 89.

55 Joanne Meyerowitz, "Beyond the Feminine Mystique: A Reassessment of Postwar Mass Culture, 1946–1958," in *Not June Cleaver: Women and Gender in Postwar America, 1945–1965*, ed. Joanne Meyerowitz (Philadelphia: Temple University Press, 1994), 231–32, 235–36. Ruth Rosen noted this emphasis on individualism as a hallmark of media coverage of feminism in the early 1970s. See Ruth Rosen, *The World Split Open: How the Modern Women's Movement Changed America* (New York: Penguin Books, 2000), 303.

56 C. D. Jackson, "A Letter from the Publisher," *Life*, December 6, 1963, B1.

57 *The Audiences of Nine Magazines: Their Size and Characteristics* (Minneapolis, MN: Cowles Magazines, 1955). For more on the power of *Life*, see James L. Baughman, "Who Read *Life*? The Circulation of America's Favorite Magazine," in *Looking at "Life" Magazine*, ed. Erica Doss (Washington, DC: Smithsonian Institution Press,

2001), 41–51. For magazines' reach, see Carolyn Kitch, *Pages from the Past: History and Memory in American Magazines* (Chapel Hill: University of North Carolina Press, 2005).

58 "Letters to the Editor," *Life*, December 13, 1963, 23.

59 Dora Jean Hamblin, "Mrs. Kennedy's Decisions Shaped All the Solemn Pageantry," *Life*, December 6, 1963, 48.

60 "The Family in Mourning," *Time*, December 6, 1963, https://content.time.com. See also Barbara Leaming, *Mrs. Kennedy: The Missing History of the Kennedy Years* (New York: Free Press, 2001), 346.

61 "In Her Time of Trial," *Newsweek*, December 6, 1963, 30–32.

62 Hamblin, "Mrs. Kennedy's Decisions Shaped All the Solemn Pageantry," 48.

63 "A Profile in Family Courage," *Saturday Evening Post*, December 14, 1963, 32d.

64 Hellmann, *Kennedy Obsession*, 136, 146; and Hogan, *Afterlife of John Fitzgerald Kennedy*, 103.

65 Hogan, *Afterlife of John Fitzgerald Kennedy*, 103; and White, *Kennedy*, 90–91.

66 Hellman, *Kennedy Obsession*, 146.

67 Hon. Milton R. Young, of North Dakota; Hon. Jacob K. Javits, of New York; and Hon. Hale Boggs, of Louisiana, in *Memorial Addresses in the Congress of the United States and Tributes in Eulogy of John Fitzgerald Kennedy Late a President of the United State*, 49–50, 134, 219.

68 Hon. Warren G. Magnuson, of Washington, inserted address by Mr. Clarence C. Dill, delivered on November 25, 1963, courthouse, Spokane, Washington, in *Memorial Addresses in the Congress of the United States and Tributes in Eulogy of John Fitzgerald Kennedy Late a President of the United State*, 23–24.

69 Hon. John E. Moss, of California and Hon. Edward P. Boland, of Massachusetts, in *Memorial Addresses in the Congress of the United States and Tributes in Eulogy of John Fitzgerald Kennedy Late a President of the United State*, 545, 227.

70 Hon. James O. Eastland, of Mississippi; Hon. Joseph E. Karth, of Minnesota; Hon. Seymour Halpern, of New York; Hon. Roman C. Pucinski, of Illinois; and Hon. Harlan Hagen, of California, in *Memorial Addresses in the Congress of the United States and Tributes in Eulogy of John Fitzgerald Kennedy Late a President of the United State*, 51, 390, 254, 305, 473.

71 Hon. Joe Skubitz, of Kansas; and Hon. John C. Watts, of Kentucky, in *Memorial Addresses in the Congress of the United States and Tributes in Eulogy of John Fitzgerald Kennedy Late a President of the United State*, 467, 382.

72 Kenneth E. Foote, *Shadowed Ground: American's Landscape of Violence and Tragedy* (1997; Austin: University of Texas Press, 2003), 8.

73 Neal, *National Trauma and Collective Memory*, 30–31.

74 Hon. Roland V. Libonati, of Illinois, in *Memorial Addresses in the Congress of the United States and Tributes in Eulogy of John Fitzgerald Kennedy Late a President of the United States*, 528–29.

75 William Manchester, *The Death of a President: November 20–November 25* (New York: Harper & Row, 1967), 249.

NOTES

76 Fred I. Greenstein, "Young Men and the Death of a President," 172–92 in *Children and the Death of a President: Multi-Disciplinary Studies*, ed. Martha Wolfenstein and Gilbert Kliman (Garden City, NY: Doubleday, 1965), 186.

77 Greenstein, "Young Men and the Death of a President," 187.

78 Theodore H. White, "For President Kennedy: An Epilogue," *Life*, December 6, 1963, 158–59.

CHAPTER 4. SINGLE WOMAN

1 Ellen Fitzpatrick, *Letters to Jackie: Condolences from a Grieving Nation* (New York: HarperCollins, 2010), xvii.

2 "Jacqueline Kennedy Thanks the Nation, January 14, 1964," YouTube, www.youtube.com/watch?v=oJhAkD8LGwg.

3 Fitzpatrick, *Letters to Jackie*, 116–18, 120–21.

4 Fitzpatrick, *Letters to Jackie*, 119, 159, 169, 240.

5 Fitzpatrick, *Letters to Jackie*, 61, 40–41, 115, 120, 177.

6 Fitzpatrick, *Letters to Jackie*, 80.

7 Fitzpatrick, *Letters to Jackie*, 83, 116, 224, 234, 257, 111, 176–77.

8 Fitzpatrick, *Letters to Jackie*, 267.

9 Fitzpatrick, *Letters to Jackie*, 240.

10 Katherine J. Lehman, *Those Girls: Single Women in Sixties and Seventies Popular Culture* (Lawrence: University Press of Kansas, 2011), 238.

11 "Jackie to Observe 1 Year of Mourning," *Women's Wear Daily*, December 13, 1963, 17.

12 Harriman Jamis, "The First Man Jackie's Cried Over—Since Dallas!," *TV Radio Mirror*, March 1966, 82; and Jacqueline Kennedy, "These Are the Things I Hope Will Show How He Really Was," *Life*, May 29, 1964, 32.

13 Kennedy, "These Are the Things I Hope Will Show How He Really Was," 32–33.

14 Kennedy, "These Are the Things I Hope Will Show How He Really Was," 34B.

15 Laura Bergquist, "A Lonely Summer for Jacqueline," *Look*, November 17, 1964, 45.

16 Kennedy, "These Are the Things I Hope Will Show How He Really Was," 34B.

17 Bergquist, "A Lonely Summer for Jacqueline," 45.

18 Fitzpatrick, *Letters to Jackie*, 201.

19 Bergquist, "A Lonely Summer for Jacqueline," 45.

20 *Look*, JFK Memorial Issue, November 17, 1964, 36.

21 Bergquist, "A Lonely Summer for Jacqueline," 45.

22 Simeon Booker, "How JFK Surpassed Abraham Lincoln," *Ebony*, February 1964, 27; and E. Fannie Granton, "The Lady in Black," *Ebony*, February 1964, 81, 86.

23 Irving Shulman, *"Jackie!" The Exploitation of a First Lady* (New York: Trident Press, 1970), 31, 41–42. See also Karen Sternheimer, *Celebrity Culture and the American Dream: Stardom and Social Mobility* (New York: Routledge, 2011), 154.

24 Shulman, *"Jackie!,"* 93.

25 Shulman, *"Jackie!,"* 23. See also Anthony Slide, *Inside the Hollywood Fan Magazine: A History of Star Makers, Fabricators, and Gossip Mongers* (Jackson: University Press of Mississippi, 2010), 184–85, 195, 202–3.

26 Shulman, *"Jackie!,"* 94–95, 181–82, 186–87.

27 Shulman, *"Jackie!,"* 130–38, 129.

28 Slide, *Inside the Hollywood Fan Magazine*, 171–72, 182.

29 "The Courtship of Jack and Jackie," *Photoplay*, March 1964, 52, 101–3.

30 "The Courtship of Jack and Jackie," 103–4.

31 Maureen Honey, "The 'Celebrity' Magazines," in *New Dimensions in Popular Culture*, ed. Russell B. Nye (Bowling Green, OH: Bowling Green University Popular Press, 1975), 61, 64.

32 Ed DeBlasio, "What Jackie Prays for Now: An Unforgettable Story," *TV Radio Mirror*, April 1964, 88, 89, 90, 91.

33 "How a Mother Hides Her Tears: Jackie's Struggle to Teach the Children Why Kennedys Don't Cry," *TV Radio Mirror*, March 1964, 48, 94; and Honey, "The 'Celebrity' Magazines," 64.

34 Shulman, *"Jackie!,"* 13, 41, 178, 192.

35 "How a Mother Hides Her Tears," 96; and Honey, "The 'Celebrity' Magazines," 64, 68, 75–76.

36 Leslie Valentine, "Jackie's Newest Heartbreak," *TV Radio Mirror*, September 1964, 45–46, 78.

37 Leslie Valentine, "The Love Jackie Doesn't Want—But Needs!," *Photoplay*, September 1964, 78, 77.

38 Honey, "The 'Celebrity' Magazines," 69–70.

39 Valentine, "The Love Jackie Doesn't Want—But Needs!," 77.

40 Shulman, *"Jackie!,"* 130, 41.

41 Susan Douglas, *Where the Girls Are: Growing Up Female with the Mass Media* (New York: Random House, 1994), 68–69; Hilary Radner, "Introduction: Queering the Girl," in *Swinging Single: Representing Sexuality in the 1960s*, ed. Hilary Radner and Moya Luckett (Minneapolis: University of Minnesota Press, 1999), 2, 12, 21, 30; and Jennifer Scanlon, *Bad Girls Go Everywhere: The Life of Helen Gurley Brown* (New York: Oxford University Press, 2009), 65–69, 70–71, 172–73.

42 Lehman, *Those Girls*, 1–4, 237–38; Radner, "Introduction," 15; and Scanlon, *Bad Girls Go Everywhere*, 150–55, 159–65.

43 Readership was divided along lines of education and employment. The only homogenizing factor of *Cosmopolitan* readership was its location in "large metropolitan areas." Scanlon, *Bad Girls Go Everywhere*, 159.

44 Thomas Frank, *The Conquest of Cool: Business Culture, Counterculture, and the Rise of Hip Consumerism* (Chicago: University of Chicago Press, 1997), 118–23.

45 Jim Hoffman, "The Indecent Attacks on Jackie," *Photoplay*, January 1965, 22, 74; and Honey, "The 'Celebrity' Magazines," 68, 71.

46 Hoffman, "The Indecent Attacks on Jackie," 74.

47 Shulman, *Jackie!*, 192, 191, 193–94; and Slide, *Inside the Hollywood Fan Magazine*, 204.

48 Leslie Valentine, "You're Going to Have a New Daddy," *TV Radio Mirror*, March 1965, 34–35, 91–92.

NOTES

49 Leslie Valentine, "How Jackie Handles a Mother's Greatest Problem," *TV Radio Mirror*, October 1965, 50, 87, 88.

50 Jae Lyle, "The Man Bobby Protects Jackie From—And Why!," *Photoplay*, July 1965, 49, 100.

51 Leslie Valentine, "How Jackie Is Raising the Children: Would Jack Approve?," *Photoplay*, September 1966, 48, 51, 74.

52 Shulman, *Jackie!*, 181–82. See also John Fiske, *Reading the Popular* (Boston: Unwin Hyman, 1989), 10; and Stuart Hall, "Culture, Media, and the 'Ideological Effect," in *Mass Communication and Society*, ed. James Curran, Michael Guravitch, and Janet Woollacott (1977; Beverly Hills, CA: Sage, 1979), 315–48, 346.

53 Valentine, "How Jackie Is Raising the Children: Would Jack Approve?," 74.

54 Fred O'Brien, "We Find Three Men Jackie Can Marry," *Photoplay*, October 1967, 60–61, 87–88.

55 George Carpozi Jr., "Jackie, Marry Me!," *TV Radio Mirror*, November 1967, 39, 76–77.

56 George Carpozi, "The Night Jackie Said 'Yes' to Harlech," *Photoplay*, June 1968, 62–63, 86–88; and Kay Wendell, "The Man Jackie Travels With," *Photoplay*, February 1968, 67.

57 Wendell, "The Man Jackie Travels With," 69, 70.

58 Wendell, "The Man Jackie Travels With," 74.

59 Carpozi, "The Night Jackie Said 'Yes' to Harlech," 87, 88.

60 George Carpozi Jr., *The Hidden Side of Jacqueline Kennedy* (New York: Pyramid Books, 1967), 208–9.

61 John Corry, *The Manchester Affair* (New York: Putnam's, 1967), 17–19.

62 Corry, *Manchester Affair*, 22–24, 27–31, 39–40.

63 Corry, *Manchester Affair*, 47, 71–76, 80–81; and Tom Wicker, "In the Nation: William Manchester's Sponsors," *New York Times*, December 27, 1966, 34.

64 Corry, *Manchester Affair*, 50–81.

65 Carpozi, *Hidden Side of Jacqueline Kennedy*, 224–28; Corry, *Manchester Affair*, 83–89, 91, 93, 102–3, 125–26, 128–29; and Brown, *JFK*, 7–8.

66 Corry, *Manchester Affair*, 91; and William Manchester, *Controversy and Other Essays in Journalism, 1950–1975* (Boston: Little, Brown, 1976), 27.

67 Carpozi, *Hidden Side of Jacqueline Kennedy*, 224–28; and Corry, *Manchester Affair*, 98–99, 188, 48.

68 Corry, *Manchester Affair*, 131–34; and Manchester, *Controversy and Other Essays in Journalism*, 39.

69 John Corry, "The Manchester Papers," *Esquire*, June 1967.

70 Corry, *Manchester Affair*, 160–64, 169, 7.

71 Corry, *Manchester Affair*, 172–74.

72 Carpozi, *Hidden Side of Jacqueline Kennedy*, 227–28; and Corry, *Manchester Affair*, 97–98.

73 Corry, *Manchester Affair*, 36–37.

74 Corry, *Manchester Affair*, 176–77; and Manchester, *Controversy and Other Essays in Journalism,* 60, 64.

75 Corry, *Manchester Affair*, 172.

76 William Manchester, *The Death of a President: November 20–November 25* (New York: Harper & Row, 1967), 185–86, 290–94, 309–10, 322–23, 347, 429.

77 Manchester, *Death of a President*, 347–48, 351, 407, 415, 427–28, 463–64, 517, 529, 547, 606.

78 Manchester, *Death of a President*, 294, 347, 351, 562, 624.

79 "Statements by Mrs. Kennedy, Look and Harper & Row on Book Dispute," *New York Times*, December 15, 1966, 36; "Texts of Documents Filed by Lawyers for Mrs. Kennedy in Move to Block Book," *New York Times*, December 17, 1966, 18; and "Texts of Statements on Accord on Kennedy Book," *New York Times*, January 17, 1967, 25.

80 "The Nation," *New York Times*, December 25, 1966, E1.

81 Tom Wicker, "In the Nation: William Manchester's Sponsors," *New York Times*, December 27, 1966, 34.

82 Corry, *Manchester Affair*, 222; and Manchester, *Controversy and Other Essays in Journalism*, 69–70.

83 George Carpozi, "Jackie: What She Took out of the Book!," *Photoplay*, March 1967, 8, 26, 28–29, 94.

84 Corry, *Manchester Affair*, 179; and Manchester, *Controversy and Other Essays in Journalism*, 72.

85 Carpozi, *Hidden Side of Jacqueline Kennedy*, 231–32, 237, 238; and Sam Kashner, "A Clash of Camelots," *Vanity Fair*, August 31, 2009, www.vanityfair.com.

86 Corry, *Manchester Affair*, 172.

87 Leslie Valentine, "Is Jackie Wasting Her Life?," *Photoplay*, April 1968, 26, 66.

88 Wendell, "The Man Jackie Travels With," 54. Arthur Neale has written that John Kennedy, after his death, no longer was regarded in "rational" terms. The same might be said for considerations of his widow. Arthur G. Neal, *National Trauma and Collective Memory: Extraordinary Events in the American Experience*, 2nd ed. (Armonk, NY: M.E. Sharpe, 2005), 109, 111.

89 Valentine, "Is Jackie Wasting Her Life?," 26, 66, 69.

CHAPTER 5. FALLEN QUEEN

1 Alan Levy, "Jackie Kennedy: A View from the Crowd," *Saturday Evening Post*, March 11, 1967, 19–23, 23.

2 Fred Sparks, *The $20,000,000 Honeymoon: Jackie and Ari's First Year* (New York: Dell, 1970), 228.

3 "'Tonight You'll Die!' How Jackie Faced a Madman," *TV Radio Mirror*, February 1965, 98, 99. See also "Jackie Kennedy: Why She Nearly Drowned," *Photoplay*, August 1967, 52–53, 83–84; "Oh God, How Much Longer Must I Hurt the People I Love?," *Photoplay*, November 1966, 60–61, 87–88; and Sparks, *The $20,000,000 Honeymoon*, 227–29. See also Sarah Bradford, *America's Queen: The Life of Jacqueline Kennedy Onassis* (New York: Penguin, 2000), 322–23.

4 Bradford, *America's Queen*, 329–34. See also Carl Sferrazza Anthony, *As We Remember Her: Jacqueline Kennedy Onassis in the Words of Her Family and Friends* (New York: HarperCollins, 1997), 242.

5 "From Camelot to Elysium (via Olympic Airways)," *Time*, October 25, 1968, https://content.time.com.

6 Ellis Cashmore, *Celebrity/Culture* (Oxon, UK: Routledge, 2006), 20–22; Karen Sternheimer, *Celebrity Culture and the American Dream: Stardom and Social Mobility* (New York: Routledge, 2011), 153; and Gaye Tuchman, *Making News: A Study in the Construction of Reality* (New York: Free Press, 1978), 47–48.

7 Pippa Norris, "Introduction," in *Women, Media, and Politics*, ed. Pippa Norris (New York: Oxford University Press, 1997), 1–2, 7; and Jack Levin, Amita Mody-Desbareau, and Arnold Arluke, "The Gossip Tabloid as Agent of Social Control," *Journalism Quarterly* 65 (Summer 1988): 514–17.

8 Jae Lyle, "The Man Bobby Protects Jackie From—And Why!," *Photoplay*, July 1965, 99–100.

9 Eve Pollard, *Jackie* (London: Macdonald, 1969), 132, 128–29, 151. This language also appeared in Paul O'Neil, "For the Beautiful Queen Jacqueline, Goodbye Camelot, Hello Skorpios," *Life*, November 1, 1968, 23; and "From Camelot to Elysium (via Olympic Airways)."

10 *(An Intimate Look at the World's Foremost Lady) The New Jackie* (New York: Capital Publications, 1970), 30, 67; and O'Neil, "For the Beautiful Queen Jacqueline, Goodbye Camelot, Hello Skorpios," 23. This idea of JBK "borrowing" husbands also appeared in "From Camelot to Elysium (via Olympic Airways)."

11 Pollard, *Jackie*, 129–30 *(An Intimate Look at the World's Foremost Lady) The New Jackie*, 9.

12 Mary Van Rensselaer Thayer, *Jacqueline Bouvier Kennedy* (New York: Doubleday, 1961), 104.

13 Muriel Singer, "Why Ethel Wants Her to Wed—and Bobby Doesn't!," *Photoplay*, July 1968, 58–59, 88–89.

14 Fred O'Brien, "We Find Three Men Jackie Can Marry," *Photoplay*, October 1967, 58–61, 87–89.

15 Bradford, *America's Queen*, 323–26.

16 Sparks, *$20,000,000 Honeymoon*, 27–28.

17 Sparks, *$20,000,000 Honeymoon*, 28; and Pollard, *Jackie*, 151.

18 Bradford, *America's Queen*, 334; and Pollard, *Jackie*, 150.

19 "How Jackie Kept Onassis from Her Own Sister! (A TV Radio Mirror Exclusive!)," *TV Radio Mirror*, February 1969, 42–45, 92, 94.

20 Sam Kashner and Nancy Schoenberger, *The Fabulous Bouvier Sisters: The Tragic and Glamorous Lives of Jackie and Lee* (New York: HarperCollins, 2018), 118.

21 Pollard, *Jackie*, 145.

22 Helen Thomas, *Dateline: White House* (New York: Macmillan, 1975), 34.

23 J. Randy Taraborrelli, *Jackie, Janet, and Lee: The Secret Lives of Janet Auchincloss and Her Daughters Jacqueline Kennedy Onassis and Lee Radziwill* (New York: St. Martin's, 2018), 206–9. See also "From Camelot to Elysium (via Olympic Airways)."

24 Sparks, *$20,000,000 Honeymoon*, 15–17.

25 Pollard, *Jackie*, 145–46.

26 Bradford, *America's Queen*, 332–33.

27 Pollard, *Jackie*, 151.

28 Bradford, *America's Queen*, 332–33; and Kashner and Schoenberger, *The Fabulous Bouvier Sisters*, 161–63.

29 Marilyn Bender, "Mrs. John F. Kennedy to Wed Onassis," *New York Times*, October 18, 1968, 1, 32.

30 Bender, "Mrs. John F. Kennedy to Wed Onassis," 32.

31 Bender, "Mrs. John F. Kennedy to Wed Onassis," 32.

32 "From Camelot to Elysium (via Olympic Airways)."

33 On the relationship between *Women's Wear Daily* and Jacqueline Kennedy, see Barbara Perry, *Jacqueline Kennedy: First Lady of the New Frontier* (Lawrence: University Press of Kansas, 2004), 58, 65; and Sparks, *$20,000,000 Honeymoon*, 97.

34 "The Widows Mite," *Women's Wear Daily*, October 18, 1968, 4. See also Kashner and Schoenberger, *Fabulous Bouvier Sisters*, 165–67.

35 "That Wedding," *Women's Wear Daily*, October 21, 1968, 4.

36 "From Camelot to Elysium (via Olympic Airways)."

37 "From Camelot to Elysium (via Olympic Airways)."

38 Pollard, *Jackie*, 146.

39 Gaye Tuchman, *Making News: A Study in the Construction of Reality* (New York: Free Press, 1978), 47–48. See also Ellis Cashmore, *Celebrity/Culture* (Oxford: Routledge, 2006), 20–22; and Sternheimer, *Celebrity Culture and the American Dream*, 153.

40 Maxine Cheshire, with John Greenya, *Maxine Cheshire, Reporter* (Boston: Houghton Mifflin, 1978), 44, 46, 27, 40–41.

41 Cheshire, *Maxine Cheshire, Reporter*, 47.

42 Cheshire, *Maxine Cheshire, Reporter*, 67, 56–57.

43 Cheshire, *Maxine Cheshire, Reporter*, 57.

44 Cheshire, *Maxine Cheshire, Reporter*, 57.

45 Cheshire, *Maxine Cheshire, Reporter*, 59, 64–65. On the limited nature of press access to the ceremony and celebration, see also Alvin Shuster, "'Very Happy' Mrs. Kennedy and Onassis Married," *New York Times*, October 21, 1968, 1, 51.

46 Cheshire, *Maxine Cheshire, Reporter*, 60–65.

47 Cheshire, *Maxine Cheshire, Reporter*, 67, 68.

48 Maxine Cheshire, "Priceless Jewels Jackie's Wedding Gift," *Charleston (WV) Gazette*, October 25, 1968, 25.

49 O'Neil, "For the Beautiful Queen Jacqueline, Goodbye Camelot, Hello Skorpios," 24. For discrepancy on Onassis's age, see Shuster, "'Very Happy' Mrs. Kennedy and Onassis Married," 1, 51.

50 Pollard, *Jackie*, 151.

51 "From Camelot to Elysium (via Olympic Airways)."

52 Harriman Janis, "Now It Can Be Told! Daddy Didn't Want His Little Girl to Be a Kennedy: Why Onassis Was the Kind of Man He Wanted for Her," *Photoplay*, May 1969, 80.

NOTES

53 O'Neil, "For the Beautiful Queen Jacqueline, Goodbye Camelot, Hello Skorpios," 24, 19.

54 "From Camelot to Elysium (via Olympic Airways)." See also Pollard, *Jackie*, 129.

55 Pollard, *Jackie*, 151.

56 "From Camelot to Elysium (via Olympic Airways)."

57 O'Neil, "For the Beautiful Queen Jacqueline, Goodbye Camelot, Hello Skorpios," 20.

58 Janis, "Now It Can Be Told!," 54; and Angela Wilson, "Jackie and Onassis Necking," *Photoplay*, February 1969, 37, 92.

59 "From Camelot to Elysium (via Olympic Airways)."

60 Chrys Haranis, "Behind the Wedding Headlines 'Jack's Warning to Her *against* Onassis,'" *TV Radio Mirror*, January 1969, 78.

61 "From Camelot to Elysium (via Olympic Airways)."

62 O'Neil, "For the Beautiful Queen Jacqueline, Goodbye Camelot, Hello Skorpios," 23.

63 "That Wedding," 4.

64 O'Neil, "For the Beautiful Queen Jacqueline, Goodbye Camelot, Hello Skorpios," 20.

65 "From Camelot to Elysium (via Olympic Airways)."

66 Janis, "Now It Can Be Told!," 54.

67 Haranis, "Behind the Wedding Headlines 'Jack's Warning to Her *against* Onassis,'" 79.

68 *(An Intimate Look at the World's Foremost Lady) The New Jackie*, 51.

69 "That Wedding," 4.

70 Bradford, *America's Queen*, 337.

71 Cheshire, *Maxine Cheshire, Reporter*, 57.

72 Bradford, *America's Queen*, 336–37.

73 Pollard, *Jackie*, 130, 147, 146.

74 Sparks, *$20,000,000 Honeymoon*, 24.

75 Pollard, *Jackie*, 148.

76 Haranis, "Behind the Wedding Headlines 'Jack's Warning to Her *against* Onassis,'" 79.

77 Bradford, *America's Queen*, 337.

78 Haranis, "Behind the Wedding Headlines 'Jack's Warning to Her *against* Onassis,'" 79.

79 Pollard, *Jackie*, 152.

80 *(An Intimate Look at the World's Foremost Lady) The New Jackie*, 52.

81 Pollard, *Jackie*, 148.

82 Steven Erlanger, "Letters from Jacqueline Kennedy to the Man She Didn't Marry," *New York Times*, February 8, 2017, www.nytimes.com.

83 Helen Thomas, *Dateline: White House* (New York: Macmillan, 1975), 36.

CHAPTER 6. JET SETTER

1 "Jackie At 40," *Women's Wear Daily*, July 9, 1969, 4, 6.

2 "Jackie At 40," 4–6.

3 "Public Opinion on Jacqueline Kennedy," *Women's Wear Daily*, January 4, 1968, 4–5.

4 Susan Sheehan, "Jackie's Day Life! Night Life! Love Life!," *TV Radio Mirror*, November 1970, 76.

5   "Jackie At 40," 4.

6   Fred Sparks, *$20,000,000 Honeymoon: Jackie and Ari's First Year* (New York: Dell, 1970), 210–11.

7   Sparks, *$20,000,000 Honeymoon*, viii–ix.

8   Sheehan, "Jackie's Day Life!," 78.

9   Sparks, *$20,000,000 Honeymoon*, 49.

10 Sparks, *$20,000,000 Honeymoon*, 52–53.

11 Sparks, *$20,000,000 Honeymoon*, 64–66.

12 Eve Pollard, *Jackie* (London: Macdonald, 1969), 148.

13 Sparks, *$20,000,000 Honeymoon*, 65.

14 "That Wedding," *Women's Wear Daily*, October 21, 1968, 4.

15 Jeane Dixon, *Kennedy Confidential: The Complete Unbiased Story* (Washington, DC: Metro Publishers, 1969), 69.

16 Christian Cafarakis, with Jacques Harvey, translated from French by John Minahan, *The Fabulous Onassis: His Life and Loves* (New York: William Morrow, 1972), 122–23, 132.

17 Cafarakis, *Fabulous Onassis*, 135.

18 Cafarakis, *Fabulous Onassis*, 139.

19 Sparks, *$20,000,000 Honeymoon*, 183.

20 Cafarakis, *Fabulous Onassis*, 127–32.

21 Cafarakis, *Fabulous Onassis*, 129.

22 "Onassis Marriage Contract Said to Have 170 Clauses," *New York Times*, November 1, 1971, 32.

23 "Jackie's Lonely Nights in Her Bedroom," *TV Radio Mirror*, June 1970, 90.

24 Cafarakis, *Fabulous Onassis*, 128; Sparks, *$20,000,000 Honeymoon*, 172.

25 Sarah Jones, "Did Jackie Get Onassis Back into Her Bedroom?," *Photoplay*, February 1972, 82, 122, 124, 126, 128. See also Sara Evans, *Tidal Wave: How Women Changed America at Century's End* (New York: Free Press, 2003), 3, 128–29.

26 Edie Ellis, "Jackie and Onassis Necking," *Photoplay*, February 1969, 36–37, 44–47, 90–93.

27 "The Eye," *Women's Wear Daily*, December 4, 1968, 8; "Maria Callas: Jackie, I Will Never Give Up Onassis. Never!," *TV Radio Mirror*, March 1971, 60–61, 68; Geri Carre, "Onassis and Maria Callas Kiss," *Photoplay*, April 1970, 57, 90; "Daddy O Steps Out," *Women's Wear Daily*, June 19, 1974, 1; Leslie Valentine, "How Jackie and Onassis Live Their Lives in Separate Rooms," *TV Radio Mirror*, May 1969, 38–39; "The Eye," *Women's Wear Daily*, June 2, 1970, 10; and "Daddy O in Paris Alone," *Women's Wear Daily*, January 21, 1969, 10.

28 Bradford, *America's Queen*, 352–53; and "Intimate! Behind Jackie's Letters of Love! Her Trip to Mexico with a Married Man! What His Wife Says!," *TV Radio Mirror*, May 1970, 30–32, 80.

29 "The Eye," *Women's Wear Daily*, June 2, 1970, 10; and "Jackie and Ari Divorce Rumors Getting Stronger," *Doylestown Daily Intelligencer*, October 7, 1974, 18.

30 *(An Intimate Look at the World's Foremost Lady) The New Jackie* (New York: Capital Publications, 1970), 14–18.

31 "Facts behind Nude Pics," *Photoplay*, March 1973, 50–51, 90, 104–5; "Jackie O: Fashion's Odyssey," *Women's Wear Daily*, June 12, 1972, 4–5; "Jackie Has Her Face Lifted to Keep Young!," *PhotoTVLand*, January 1971, 18–19, 38–39. "O Those Ruffles," *Women's Wear Daily*, July 15, 1971, 1. "Jackie's Last Stand . . . on the Mini," *Women's Wear Daily*, September 24, 1970, 1; "The Eye," *Women's Wear Daily*, June 23, 1972, 8; Marian Rossi, "Jackie Buys See-through Blouse to Please Husband," *Photoplay*, December 1969, 91; and Liz Smith, "The Jackie Nobody Knows," *National Star*, April 13, 1974, 7–10.

32 Sheehan, "Jackie's Day Life!," 78.

33 Rossi, "Jackie Buys See-through Blouse to Please Husband," 91.

34 Dixon, *Kennedy Confidential*, 69.

35 Pat Barnes, "The Guiding Light behind That Book Sheds Some Rays," *Women's Wear Daily*, July 3, 1969, 3.

36 Evelyn Lincoln, *My Twelve Years with John F. Kennedy* (New York: David McKay, 1965); Pierre Salinger, *With Kennedy* (Garden City, NY: Doubleday, 1966); Arthur Schlesinger, *A Thousand Days: John F. Kennedy in the White House* (New York: Houghton Mifflin, 1965); and Theodore C. Sorensen, *Kennedy* (New York: Harper & Row, 1965).

37 Maud Shaw, *White House Nanny: My Years with Caroline and John, Jr.* (New York: New American Library, 1966).

38 Mary Barelli Gallagher, *My Life with Jacqueline Kennedy*, ed. Frances Spatz Leighton (New York: David McKay, 1969), 7, 29–32, 323.

39 Gallagher, *My Life with Jacqueline Kennedy*, 44–54.

40 Gallagher, *My Life with Jacqueline Kennedy*, 36.

41 Gallagher, *My Life with Jacqueline Kennedy*, 19, 44–45, 54, 205.

42 Gallagher, *My Life with Jacqueline Kennedy*, 38–39.

43 Gallagher, *My Life with Jacqueline Kennedy*, 50.

44 Gallagher, *My Life with Jacqueline Kennedy*, 97, 131, 159, 172, 205.

45 Gallagher, *My Life with Jacqueline Kennedy*, 172.

46 Gallagher, *My Life with Jacqueline Kennedy*, 33.

47 Gallagher, *My Life with Jacqueline Kennedy*, 206, 217–19.

48 June Weir, "The Gallagher Report," *Women's Wear Daily*, September 9, 1968, 72.

49 Barnes, "The Guiding Light behind That Book Sheds Some Rays," 3.

50 "Jackie Kennedy . . . Clothing Her Blind Spot," *Women's Wear Daily*, September 4, 1969, 1.

51 Dixon, *Kennedy Confidential*, 68–69.

52 Gallagher, *My Life with Jacqueline Kennedy*, 172, 173.

53 Gallagher, *My Life with Jacqueline Kennedy*, 395.

54 Weir, "The Gallagher Report," 72.

55 Galella v. Onassis, 353 F. Supp. 196 (S.D.N.Y. 1972), 1–2, 4; Max H. Seigel, "Faulty Charge against Mrs. Onassis Admitted," *New York Times*, February 23, 1972, 35; and Lesley Oelsner, "The Cloudy Galella-Onassis Case," *New York Times*, March 20, 1972, 33.

56 *Galella v. Onassis*, 12; and Max H. Seigel, "Editor in Onassis Case Reports Galella Tried to Hide Evidence," *New York Times*, March 2, 1972, 12.

57 *Galella v. Onassis*, 12, 20, 9. This testimony was reported also in Max H. Seigel, "Mrs. Onassis Cites Galella 'Harassing,'" *New York Times*, March 7, 1972, 32.

58 *Galella v. Onassis*, 35, 48. See also Max. H. Seigel, "Mrs. Onassis Cites 'Blackmail' Card," *New York Times*, March 9, 1972, 34.

59 "Testimony Given by Mrs. Onassis," *New York Times*, February 17, 1972; and *Galella v Onassis*, 9.

60 *Galella v. Onassis*, 8; and Max H. Seigel, "U.S. Judge Bars Photographer from Going Near Mrs. Onassis," *New York Times*, July 6, 1972, 18.

61 *Galella v. Onassis*, 4.

62 *Galella v. Onassis*, 7.

63 *Galella v Onassis*, 31.

64 *Galella v Onassis*, 49.

65 *Galella v Onassis*, 28; and Oelsner, "The Cloudy Galella-Onassis Case," 33.

66 "The Most Famous American Paparazzo," *Esquire*, March 1972, https://classic.esquire.com.

67 "One Man's Running Battle with Jackie," *Life*, March 31, 1972, 64.

68 "One Man's Running Battle with Jackie," 64.

69 "One Man's Running Battle with Jackie," 65.

70 Ron Galella, *Jacqueline* (New York: Sheed and Ward, 1974), 5.

71 Galella, *Jacqueline*, 19.

72 Galella, *Jacqueline*, 34.

73 Cafarakis, *Fabulous Onassis*, 150, 153.

74 Bradford, *America's Queen*, 378; Tom Goldstein, "Law Firms Sues Onassis over Photography-Case Fee," *New York Times*, December 22, 1973, 27; and "$235,000 Offered by Mrs. Onassis to Settle Lawsuit," *New York Times*, December 28, 1973, 31.

75 "Alexander Onassis, Only Son of Magnate, Dies of Injuries," *New York Times*, January 24, 1973, 44; and John Corry, "Onassis Said to Have Planned Divorce, Provided $3-Million for Widow in Will," *New York Times*, April 12, 1975, 13.

76 "Aristotle Onassis Is Dead of Pneumonia in France," *New York Times*, March 16, 1975, 1; and Frank Brady, "Jackie and Ari," *Saturday Evening Post*, December 1, 1977, 135.

77 "An Intimate Look at the Merry Widow," *Photoplay*, July 1975, 40; and Bradford, *America's Queen*, 370–72.

78 Corry, "Onassis Said to Have Planned Divorce, Provided $3-Million for Widow in Will," 1.

79 Brady, "Jackie and Ari," 135; Nicholas Gage, "Mrs. Onassis Said to Get 20 Million in a Pact with Christina Onassis," *New York Times*, September 20, 1977, 1, 9; Bradford, *America's Queen*, 374–76; and Jack Anderson and Les Whitten, "Jackie and Ari: Pre-Nuptial Contract," *Washington Post*, April 14, 1975, C23. JKO actually received $26 million, the additional $6 million paying the taxes she would owe on the sum.

80 Brady, "Jackie and Ari," 135.

CHAPTER 7. PROFESSIONAL

1 Mary Thom, ed., *Letters to "Ms.," 1972–1987* (New York: Henry Holt, 1987), 201; and "Gloria Steinem on Jacqueline Kennedy Onassis," *Ms.*, March 1979, 46, 47.

2 "Gloria Steinem on Jacqueline Kennedy Onassis," 47.

3 "Gloria Steinem on Jacqueline Kennedy Onassis," 47.

4 "Gloria Steinem on Jacqueline Kennedy Onassis," 47.

5 Paul Goldberger, "City's Naming of Grand Central as a Landmark Voided by Court," *New York Times*, January 22, 1975, 1, 39.

6 Tina Cassidy, *Jackie after O: One Remarkable Year When Jacqueline Kennedy Onassis Defied Expectations and Rediscovered Her Dreams* (New York: itbooks, 2012), 118–19; and Angela Serratore, "The Preservation Battle of Grand Central," *Smithsonian Magazine*, June 26, 2018, www.smithsonianmag.com.

7 Gregory F. Gilmartin, *Shaping the City: New York and the Municipal Arts Society* (New York: Clarkson Potters, 1995), 402–5.

8 Cassidy, *Jackie after O*, 122.

9 Cassidy, *Jackie after O*, 122–23.

10 "Celebrities Ride the Rails to Save Grand Central," *New York Times*, April 17, 1978, D9.

11 John Belle and Maxinne R. Leighton, *Grand Central: Gateway to a Million Lives* (New York: Norton, 2000), 24.

12 "Tower over Grand Central Barred as Court Upholds Landmarks Law," *New York Times*, June 27, 1978, A1.

13 William Kuhn, *Reading Jackie: Her Autobiography in Books* (New York: Doubleday, 2010), 66.

14 Gilmartin, *Shaping the City*, 406.

15 Sam Roberts, *Grand Central: How a Train Station Transformed America* (New York: Grand Central Publishing, 2013), 187.

16 Lee Dembart, "Snug Harbor Arts Center Is Backed," *New York Times*, April 7, 1977, 86; Fred Feretti, "Arts and Politics Create a New Cultural Center," *New York Times*, November 5, 1977, 18; C. Gerald Fraser, "West 42d St. Theater Row Begins $9.6 Million Phase 2; Part of Redevelopment," *New York Times*, October 9, 1980, 17; Joan Harting, "Another O-pening," *Women's Wear Daily*, November 14, 1977, 24–25; "Jackie O in Focus," *Women's Wear Daily*, October 6, 1978, 1, 4; Sally Rinard, "Eye View," *Women's Wear Daily*, November 16, 1977, 18; and Joyce Wells, "On Their Toes," *Women's Wear Daily*, May 6, 1980, 1, 12.

17 "Jackie Joins Viking as Consulting Editor," *Sarasota (FL) Herald Tribune*, September 17, 1975, 4.

18 Greg Lawrence, *Jackie as Editor: The Literary Life of Jacqueline Kennedy Onassis* (New York: Thomas Dunne Books, 2011), 10–11; and Stephen Birmingham, "The Public Event Named Jackie: 'Better Than Any Other Famous Woman in History (including Garbo), She Has Mastered the Art of Managing Her Celebrity,'" *New York Times Magazine*, June 20, 1976, 17.

19 Lawrence, *Jackie as Editor*, 9; and Birmingham, "The Public Event Named Jackie," 10.

20 Art Buchwald, "Hiring Jackie as Editor," *Idaho State Journal* (Pocatello, ID), October 2, 1975, 4; and Steinem, "Gloria Steinem on Jacqueline Kennedy Onassis," 47, 50.

21 Lawrence, *Jackie as Editor*, 58.

22 Lawrence, *Jackie as Editor*, 31–34; Birmingham, "The Public Event Named Jackie," 18; and Steinem, "Gloria Steinem on Jacqueline Kennedy Onassis," 50.

23 Lawrence, *Jackie as Editor*, 38–44.

24 Thomas Hoving, *Making the Mummies Dance: Inside the Metropolitan Museum of Art* (New York: Simon & Schuster, 1993), 392.

25 Hoving, *Making the Mummies Dance*, 394–95.

26 Joyce Maynard, "Jacqueline Onassis Makes a New Debut," *New York Times*, January 14, 1977, 10.

27 "Jacqueline Kennedy Onassis Talks about Working," *Ms.*, March 1979, 50-51.

28 Hugh Sidey, "The First Lady Brings History and Beauty to the White House," *Life*, September 1, 1961, 56.

29 "Jacqueline Kennedy Onassis Talks about Working," 51.

30 Lawrence, *Jackie as Editor*, 61–63; and John Leonard, "Presidents in Trouble," *New York Times*, October 10, 1977, 27.

31 Deirdre Carmody, "Mrs. Onassis Resigns Editing Post," *New York Times*, October 15, 1977, 36.

32 Bradford, *America's Queen*, 388–89; Lawrence, *Jackie as Editor*, 64.

33 Carmody, "Mrs. Onassis Resigns Editing Post," 1.

34 Liz Smith, "Jackie Mad, Quits Viking in Huff over Unread Book," *Colorado Springs (CO) Gazette Telegraph*, October 18, 1977, 11A.

35 Ellen Goodman, "Jacqueline Onassis: Tripping on Her Past," in *Close to Home* (New York: Simon and Schuster, 1979), 64–65.

36 Goodman, "Jacqueline Onassis," 65.

37 "Jacqueline Kennedy Onassis Talks about Working," 51.

38 "Jacqueline Kennedy Onassis Talks about Working," 51–52.

39 Thomas Brown, *JFK: History of an Image* (Bloomington: Indiana University Press, 1988), 72–76; Traphes Bryant, with Frances Spatz Leighton, *Dog Days at the White House: The Outrageous Memoirs of the Presidential Kennel Keeper* (New York: Macmillan, 1975), 35, 37–40; Michael J. Hogan, *The Afterlife of John Fitzgerald Kennedy: A Biography* (New York: Cambridge University Press, 2017), 179–83; Kitty Kelley, *Jackie Oh!* (Secaucus, NJ: Lyle Stuart, 1978), 117–33; Thomas C. Reeves, *A Question of Character: A Life of John F. Kennedy* (New York: Free Press, 1991); Nelson Thompson, *The Dark Side of Camelot* (Chicago: Playboy Press, 1976), 35–60; Steven Watts, *JFK and the Masculine Mystique: Sex and Power on the New Frontier* (New York: St. Martin's Press, 2016), 69; and Garry Wills, *The Kennedy Imprisonment: A Meditation on Power* (Boston: Little, Brown, 1982).

40 "Kennedy Friend Denies Plot Role," *New York Times*, December 18, 1975, 1; and Judith Exner, *My Story*, as told to Ovid Demaris (New York: Grove Press, 1977), 5–8.

41 Exner, *My Story*, 86–94.

42 Exner, *My Story*, 97–98.

43 Exner, *My Story*, 100–103.

44 Exner, *My Story*, 128–29.

45 Exner, *My Story*, 131–32, 147–48.

46 Exner, *My Story*, 197, 218–22.

47 Exner, *My Story*, 240–41.

48 Exner, *My Story*, 249–52.

49 Stephen Dunleavy and Peter Brennan, *Those Wild, Wild Kennedy Boys!* (New York: Pinnacle Books, 1976); and Tony Sciacca, *Kennedy and His Women* (New York: Manor Books, 1976).

50 Sally Quinn, "Each to Blame, Judith Exner Says of Her Affair with JFK," *Modesto (CA) Bee*, June 29, 1977, A3; and "Exner-JFK Saga Draws Little Interest," *San Antonio (TX) Express*, May 17, 1977, 11.

51 Dave Clemens, "No Comment from Jackie on JFK's 'Other Women,'" *Anderson (IN) Herald*, January 1, 1976, 11.

52 *The Greek Tycoon*, directed by J. Lee Thompson (Universal Pictures, 1978).

53 Roger Ebert, Review of *The Greek Tycoon*, Roger Ebert.com, May 15, 1978, www.rogerebert.com.

54 Mel Watkins, "Negative Tone of 'Jackie Oh' Is Irritating," *Hutchison (KS) News*, March 10, 1979, 4A.

55 Watkins, "Negative Tone of 'Jackie Oh' Is Irritating," 4A.

56 Rudy Maxa, "They Write, They Talk," *Kenosha (WI) News*, May 22, 1979, 6.

57 Hedrick Smith, "Graceful Salutes, Skirting Conflicts," *New York Times*, October 21, 1979, 1; and Arthur M. Schlesinger, *Journals, 1952–2000*, edited by Andrew Schlesinger and Stephen Schlesinger (New York: Penguin, 2007), 478.

58 Terence Smith, "Carter and Kennedy Share Stage at Library Dedication," *New York Times*, October 21, 1979, 1.

CHAPTER 8. ICON

1 Carl Sferrazza Anthony, *As We Remember Her: Jacqueline Kennedy Onassis in the Words of Her Family and Friends* (New York: HarperCollins, 1997), 355; and Robert D. McFadden, "Jacqueline Kennedy Onassis Dies of Cancer at 64: Widow of President Spent Final Days at New York Home," *New York Times*, May 20, 1994, A1.

2 Frank Rich, "The Jackie Mystery: A Good Cry, but for Whom?," *New York Times*, May 26, 1994, A23.

3 Rich, "The Jackie Mystery," A23.

4 Carolyn Kitch, *Pages from the Past: History and Memory in American Magazines* (Chapel Hill: University of North Carolina Press, 2005), 64.

5 Rich, "The Jackie Mystery," A23.

6 Edward Klein, *Farewell, Jackie: A Portrait of Her Final Days* (New York: Viking Press, 2004), x.

7 Sarah Bradford, *America's Queen: The Life of Jacqueline Kennedy Onassis* (New York: Penguin, 2000), 436–37; and Klein, *Farewell, Jackie*, 11–16, 73, 79–80.

8   Robert D. McFadden, "Jacqueline Kennedy Onassis Has Lymphoma," *New York Times*, February 11, 1994, B3.

9   Arthur M. Schlesinger, *Journals, 1952–2000*, edited by Andrew Schlesinger and Stephen Schlesinger (New York: Penguin, 2007), 761–62.

10 Anthony, *As We Remember Her*, 349, 352–53.

11 Nadine Brozan, "Chronicle," *New York Times*, March 9, 1994, B4; and McFadden, "Jacqueline Kennedy Onassis Has Lymphoma," B3.

12 Schlesinger, *Journals, 1952–2000*, 763.

13 Lawrence K. Altman, "Death of a First Lady: No More Could Be Done, Mrs. Onassis Was Told," *New York Times*, May 20, 1994, B10.

14 "Facing Death with Dignity," *Cedar Rapids (IA) Gazette*, May 21, 1994, 8A.

15 Robert D. McFadden, "Fond Adieu to Jacqueline Onassis, at Her Home," *New York Times*, May 23, 1994, B1–2.

16 "Family Friends Maintain a Mournful Vigil in Manhattan," *Janesville (WI) Gazette*, May 22, 1994, 2.

17 Steve Fainaru and Michael Kranish, "Jacqueline Bouvier Kennedy Onassis, 1929–1994: Onassis to Be Buried Monday; Resting Place Next to JFK at Arlington Set," *Boston Globe*, May 24, 1994, in *First Lady Jacqueline Kennedy Onassis, 1929–1994: Memorial Tributes in the One Hundred Third Congress of the United States* (Washington, DC: US Government Printing Office, 1995), 121.

18 McFadden, "Fond Adieu to Jacqueline Onassis, at Her Home," B1–2.

19 *First Lady Jacqueline Kennedy Onassis, 1929–1994*, 61–63.

20 Special Tribute by Senator Edward M. Kennedy, St. Ignatius Loyala Church, New York City, May 23, 1994, in *First Lady Jacqueline Kennedy Onassis, 1929–1994*, 58.

21 Special Tribute by Senator Edward M. Kennedy, 58–60.

22 Schlesinger, *Journals, 1952–2000*, 769.

23 Kitch, *Pages from the Past*, 69.

24 Kitch, *Pages from the Past*, 71.

25 Kitch, *Pages of the Past*, 86.

26 Joshua Meyrowitz, "The Life and Death of Media Friends: New Genres of Intimacy and Mourning," in *American Heroes in the Media Age*, edited by Susan J. Drucker and Robert S. Cathcart (New York: Hampton Press, 1994), 63, 66. See also Richard Schickel, *Intimate Strangers: The Culture of Celebrity in America* (1985; Chicago: Ivan R. Dee, 2000), 4.

27 Meyrowitz, "The Life and Death of Media Friends," 76.

28 Michael Olesker, "Onassis' Image Anchored, and Haunted, a Nation," *Baltimore Sun*, May 22, 1994, www.baltimoresun.com.

29 Olesker, "Onassis' Image Anchored, and Haunted, a Nation."

30 Peggy Noonan, "America's First Lady," *Time*, May 30, 1994, in *First Lady Jacqueline Kennedy Onassis, 1929–1994*, 126–28.

31 Pete Hamill, "A Private Life Defined by Wit, Compassion," *Newsday Magazine*, May 22, 1994, in *First Lady Jacqueline Kennedy Onassis, 1929–1994*, 105.

32 Hon. Benjamin A. Gilman, of New York, and Hon. Corrine Brown, of Florida, in *First Lady Jacqueline Kennedy Onassis, 1929–1994*, 41, 34.

33 Olesker, "Onassis' Image Anchored, and Haunted, a Nation." On the erasure of Onassis, see also Wayne Koestenbaum, *Jackie under My Skin: Interpreting an Icon* (New York: Farrar, Strauss, Giroux, 1995), 9.

34 Noonan, "America's First Lady," 126–28.

35 Noonan, "America's First Lady," 126–28.

36 Noonan, "America's First Lady," 126–28.

37 Hon. Russell D. Feingold, of Wisconsin, in *First Lady Jacqueline Kennedy Onassis, 1929–1994*, 9–10.

38 Hon. Howell Heflin, of Alabama, in *First Lady Jacqueline Kennedy Onassis, 1929–1994*, 13–14.

39 Hugh Sidey, "Once, in Camelot," *Time*, May 30, 1994, in *First Lady Jacqueline Kennedy Onassis, 1929–1994*, 126.

40 Hon. Joseph R. Biden, of Delaware, in *First Lady Jacqueline Kennedy Onassis, 1929–1994*, 12.

41 Joe Fitzgerald, "Jacqueline Kennedy Onassis, 1929–1994: Classy First Lady Won Over Even This Diehard Republican," *Boston Herald*, May 20, 1994, in *First Lady Jacqueline Kennedy Onassis, 1929–1994*, 92.

42 Stephanie Coontz, *The Way We Never Were: American Families and the Nostalgia Trap* (New York: Basic Books, 1992).

43 Daniel Marcus, *Happy Days and Wonder Years: The Fifties and Sixties in Contemporary Cultural Politics* (New Brunswick. NJ: Rutgers University Press, 2004), 3–4, 122–24.

44 "Death Reunites Former First Lady, Slain Husband," *Colorado Springs Gazette Telegraph (from Chicago Tribune)*, May 24, 1994, A3.

45 David Shribman, "Her Lasting Gift Was Majesty," *Boston Globe*, May 20, 1994, in *First Lady Jacqueline Kennedy Onassis, 1929–1994*, 88.

46 Hon. Carolyn B. Maloney, of New York, in *First Lady Jacqueline Kennedy Onassis, 1929–1994*, 46–47.

47 Hamill, "A Private Life Defined by Wit, Compassion," 105.

48 Ellen Goodman, "Jackie Was a Model of Dignity to the End," *Boston Globe*, May 22, 1994, in *First Lady Jacqueline Kennedy Onassis, 1929–1994*, 47; and Noonan, "America's First Lady," 126–28.

49 R. W. Apple Jr., "Death of a First Lady: The Overview; Jacqueline Kennedy Onassis Is Buried," *New York Times*, May 24, 1994, in *First Lady Jacqueline Kennedy Onassis, 1929–1994*, 118.

50 Hamill, "A Private Life Defined by Wit, Compassion," 105.

51 Hon. Howell Heflin, of Alabama, in *First Lady Jacqueline Kennedy Onassis, 1929–1994*, 12.

52 Ellen Goodman, "Jackie Was a Model of Dignity to the End," 47.

53 Marcus, *Happy Days and Wonder Years*, 155–65.

54 Anthony, *As We Remember Her*, 328, 344.

55 President William J. Clinton, Statement delivered from the White House, in *First Lady Jacqueline Kennedy Onassis, 1929–1994*, 55–56.

56 First Lady Hillary Rodham Clinton, in *First Lady Jacqueline Kennedy Onassis, 1929–1994*, 57; and Anthony, *As We Remember Her*, 347.

57 First Lady Hillary Rodham Clinton, in *First Lady Jacqueline Kennedy Onassis, 1929–1994*, 57; and Kay M. Knickrehm and Robin Teske, "First Ladies and Policy Making: Crossing the Public/Private Divide," in *The Presidential Companion: Readings on the First Ladies*, 2nd ed., ed. Robert P. Watson and Anthony J. Eksterowicz (Columbia: University of South Carolina Press, 2006), 241–49.

CONCLUSION

1 Michael Beschloss, *Jacqueline Kennedy, Historic Conversations on the Life of John F. Kennedy: Interviews with Arthur J. Schlesinger, Jr., 1964* (New York: Hyperion, 2011), xiv.

2 Beschloss, *Jacqueline Kennedy, Historic Conversations on the Life of John F. Kennedy*, xv.

3 Beschloss, *Jacqueline Kennedy, Historic Conversations on the Life of John F. Kennedy*, xv.

4 Beschloss, *Jacqueline Kennedy, Historic Conversations on the Life of John F. Kennedy*, xiv.

5 Beschloss, *Jacqueline Kennedy, Historic Conversations on the Life of John F. Kennedy*, xvii.

6 Beschloss, *Jacqueline Kennedy, Historic Conversations on the Life of John F. Kennedy*, xviii.

7 Beschloss, *Jacqueline Kennedy, Historic Conversations on the Life of John F. Kennedy*, 141.

8 Beschloss, *Jacqueline Kennedy, Historic Conversations on the Life of John F. Kennedy*, 325–27, 330.

INDEX

Page numbers in italics indicate Photos.

Bouvier, Jacqueline: as apolitical, xiv–xv, 13; courtship and engagement of, xi–xiii, 133; in France, x–xi; as "Inquiring Camera Girl," xi, 45, 239; as public figure, ix–xix; at Smith College, x; smoking of, ix; as "Society Girl," xii; at the Sorbonne, xi; at University of Grenoble, xi; at *Washington Times-Herald*, xi. *See also* Kennedy, Jacqueline Bouvier; Onassis, Jacqueline Kennedy

Bouvier, Janet (mother). *See* Auchincloss, Janet

Bouvier, John "Black Jack" (father), 13–14, 185–86

Bouvier, Lee (sister). *See* Radziwill, Lee

Bowdoin, Aileen, xiv–xv

Braden, Joan, 18; on JBK international trips, 69–70, 75, 77; JFK presidential campaign and, 32–34, 42; Rockefeller, N., and, 32

Bradford, Sarah, 174; *America's Queen* by, 3, 289n6; on JKO, 190, 191–92

Bradlee, Ben, 26–27, 181; on AO, 190

Bradlee, Tony, 27

Brando, Marlon, 145

Brandon, Mable H. "Muffie," 237

Brown, Corrine, 270

Brown, Helen Gurley, 138–39

Brynner, Yul, 74

Buchwald, Art, 236

Burrows, Barbara Baker, xvii

Cafarakis, Christian: on AO possible divorce, 223–24; on *Christina*, 197, 200; on JKO marriage contract, 200–202, 204

Callas, Maria, 175, 205; *The Greek Tycoon* and, 250, 252

"Calling for Kennedy," 33, 44, 45

Camelot: as imagined reality, 9; JBK on, 114–15, 116; JKO and, 185, 195, 200, 208, 213, 230, 244, 257, 259, 272, 273, 276; as national memory, 191

Camera Girl (Anthony), 4

"Campaign Wife," 33, 42–45, 296n77

Canada, 63–65

Capote, Truman, 181

Carano, Steve, 55–56

Carmody, Deirdre, 241

Carpozi, George, Jr., 149–53, 156

Carrozza, Bernadette, 215

Carter, Jimmy, 255–57

Casals, Pablo, 61

Cassidy, Tina, 4

Cassini, Oleg, 39, 57–59, 65, 68; in Canada, 62–63, 64; in India, 75

Castro, Fidel, 244

Cates, Robert, 125

Catholic Church: JFK in, 1, 18, 20; Kennedy wedding at, xv

Cavafy, C. P., 264

Center of Photography, 234

Central Intelligence Agency (CIA), 244

Charleston (WV) Gazette, 41

Cheshire, Maxine, 90, 145; on AO, 190; on Onassis wedding, 180–84

Chicago Daily News, 158

Chicago Tribune, 274–75

Christina, 198; Cafarakis and, 197, 200; elegance of, 176; JBK on, 171–72, 173; JKO and, 189; JKO wedding and, 177, 183; at Skorpios, 177

Christopher, Sybil Burton, 188

Church Committee, 244–45, 247

CIA. *See* Central Intelligence Agency

CK. *See* Kennedy, Caroline

Clinton, Bill, 265, 277–78, 279

Clinton, Chelsea, 265, 278

Clinton, Hillary, 265, 277–79

Clurman, Harold, 145

"Coffee for Kennedy," 33

Coizart, Andre de, 66

Collingwood, Charles, 83–84, 87, 89

Colombia, 83

Colorado Springs Gazette Telegraph, 274–75

Committee to Save Grand Central, 231

Helene (housekeeper), 200
Hellman, John, 116
vanden Heuvel, William, 174
The Hidden Side of Jacqueline Kennedy (Carpozi), 150–51
"High Hopes," 33
Hill, Clint, 70, 94, 303n6
Hobby, Oveta Culp, 32
Hoffman, Jim, 140, 141–42
Hogan, Michael, 62, 116
Hoover, J. Edgar, 247
horses: Bouvier, Jacqueline, and, ix; JBK and, 12; in JFK funeral, 103; of JKO, 236, 262; in Pakistan, 70, *71*
Hoving, Thomas, 237–38
"How a Mother Hides Her Tears . . . ," in *TV Radio Mirror*, 134–35
"How Jackie Is Raising the Children," in *Photoplay*, 146–48
Humphrey, Hubert, 20, 25
Humphrey, Muriel, 21–22
Hyannis Port, xi, 15, 30, 33, 37, 43, 46, 50, 101, 114, 128, 133, 199, 236

inauguration of JFK, 2, 48; Exner and, 247
"The Indecent Attacks on Jackie," in *Photoplay*, 140–41
India: Cassini in, 75; Eisenhower, D., in, 70; Galbraith in, 69; *Invitation to India*, 72, 73, 74; JBK in, 69–77, *76*; Taj Mahal, 75, *76*, 77
"Inquiring Camera Girl," at *Washington Times-Herald*, xi, 45, 239
Insider's Newsletter, 23
international guests, to White House, 60–61
Interview, 3
In the Russian Style, 237, 238–39
Invitation to India, 72, 73, 74
Invitation to Pakistan, 72, 73, 71
Italy, JBK in, 90
"Ithaka" (Cavafy), 264

Jackie (Larrain), 3
Jackie (Pollard), 170
Jackie after O (Cassidy), 4
Jackie and Jack (Andersen), 3
Jackie as Editor (Lawrence), 4
Jackie Oh! (Kelley), 3, 254–55
"Jackie's Lonely Nights in Her Bedroom," in *TV Radio Mirror*, 203–4
"Jackie's Newest Heartbreak," in *TV Radio Mirror*, 136
Jackson, C. D., 111, 113
Jacqueline (Galella), 222
Jacqueline Bouvier Kennedy Onassis (Leaming), 3
Jacqueline Bouvier Kennedy Onassis (Spoto), 3
Jacqueline Kennedy (Perry), 3–4
Jacqueline Kennedy's Asian Journey, 74
James Cassidy (fictional character), 249–53
JBK. *See* Kennedy, Jacqueline Bouvier
JFK. *See* Kennedy, John F.
JKO. *See* Onassis, Jacqueline Kennedy
John F. Kennedy Memorial Edition, of *Life*, 111–12
John F. Kennedy Presidential Library, 127–28, 130, 153, 154; JKO and, 230, 255–57, *256*; Warnecke and, 149
Johnson, Lady Bird, 12; JBK and, 85, 113
Johnson, Lyndon: after JFK assassination, 94–96, *95*; at JFK funeral, 104; Manchester on, 155; as senator, 12, 45, 48
Jokelson, Paul, 112
Jones, Sarah, 204
Joris, Victor, 194
Just Jackie (Klein), 3

Kaplan, Alice, 4, 192
Kardashian, Kim, 3
Karrass, Harry, 85
Karth, Joseph, 118
Kelley, Kitty, 3, 254–55

Kennedy, Caroline (CK): AO and, 183, 184; at AO funeral, *225*; birth of, 52; Galella and, 214–23; JBK as single woman and, 128; JFK assassination and, 100–101; at JFK funeral, 104; on JKO, 281–83; in *Life*, 46; marriage of, 261; nurse for, 31, 46, 78; nurse of, 46, 78, 146, 209, 210; at Onassis wedding, 175, 183, 184; playing with, 12; RFK and, 170; Secret Service for, 168, 214; Shaw and, 46, 78, 146, 209, 210; White House departure from, *122*; in *WWD*, 167. *See also* motherhood

Kennedy, Edward "Teddy," 170; at AO funeral, *225*; at JFK funeral, 104, *105*; at JKO funeral, 264–65, 277–78; at John F. Kennedy Presidential Library, 256–57; Onassis, A., and, 172; on Onassis wedding, 175; *Shall We Tell the President?* and, 240

Kennedy, Ethel, xi, 195; JBK and, 170–71; on Onassis wedding, 175–76

Kennedy, Jacqueline Bouvier (JBK): African Americans and, 131; AO and, 172–73, 175; as apolitical, 51–52, 99–100; in Austria, 67–68; beauty of, 22–24, 26, 38, 46, 66; as best dressed, 55; Camelot and, 9, 114–15, 116, 185, 191, 195, 200, 208, 213, 230, 244, 257, 259, 272, 273, 276; in Canada, 63–65; on *Christina*, 171–72, 173; Democratic National Convention and, 29, 30, 141; divorce possibility of, 49, 247; domestic side of, 14; fashion of, 4, 26, 31–32, 36–43, 50, 54–59, 62–63, 65–66, 132, 211; as first lady, 48–91, *63*, *64*; foreign language fluency of, 24, 28, 35, *67*; in France, 65–66, *67*; Gallagher, M., and, 208, 209–13; hairstyle of, 32, 36, 37, 39, 43, 55, 56; horses and, 12; in India, 69–77, *76*; international guests and, 60–61; international trips of, 65–70, *71*, 74–76, 90; in Italy, 90; JFK assassination and, 2–3, 92–123, *93*,

95, 281–84; JFK funeral and, 96–98, 101–5, *105*, 112, 113–14; JFK presidential campaign and, 11–47, *34*; Johnson, Lady Bird, and, 85, 113; Kennedy, Ethel, and, 170–71; Kennedy family and, 49–50; on *Life* cover, 63, 65; *Life* on, 210; "Look-Alikes" of, 55–56; Manchester and, 154–62; motherhood of, 78, *79*; mourning year by, 123, 126–27, 130; at National Theater, *63*; New Frontier and, 62, 68; Nixon, P., and, 35–36, 38–42, 45–46; at Nobel Prize Winner's Dinner, *64*; in Pakistan, 69–77, *71*; parties of, 59–60, 62; as political asset, 18, 28, 46; pregnancy of, 28–30, 39; press secretary of, 53, 54; public approval of, 90–91; public relations staff for, 53–54; Secret Service and, 70, 160; as single woman, 124–65; smoking by, 21; social secretary of, 53–54, 59, 61; speeches by, 26; spending by, 36, 38, 39, 40, 199, 211; stillborn baby of, 29; symbolic power of, 14–15; at Taj Mahal, 75, *76*, 77; on *Time* cover, 48–51, 56–57; wedding of, xv–xvii; White House departure from, *122*; White House restoration and, 51–52, 58, 59–60, 78–82, 240; as widow, 92–123. *See also* Onassis, Jacqueline Kennedy

Kennedy, Joan, 172

Kennedy, John, Jr.: AO and, 183; at AO funeral, *225*; birth of, *79*; Galella and, 214–23; JBK as single woman and, 128; JFK assassination and, 100–101; at JFK funeral, 104; at JKO funeral, 264; on JKO's death, 258; Manchester and, 157; nanny of, 78; at Onassis wedding, 175; RFK and, 170; Secret Service for, 168, 214; White House departure from, *122*; in *WWD*, 167. *See also* motherhood

Kennedy, John F. (JFK): African Americans and, 131; at Arlington National

Cemetery, 103, 104, 119; autopsy
of, 98; Camelot and, 9, 114–15, 116,
185, 191, 195, 200, 208, 213, 230, 244,
257, 259, 272, 273, 276; in Catholic
Church, 1, 18, 20; Church Committee
and, 244–45, 247; as congressman, xi;
courtship and engagement of, xi–xiii,
133; *The Death of a President* and,
155–62, 241; at Democratic National
Convention, 20; divorce possibility of, 49, 247; Exner and, 244–48;
extramarital sexual relationships of,
3, 244, 245–48; family man image of,
20; in France, *67*; funeral of, 96–98,
101–5, *105*, 112, 113–14; Gallagher,
M., and, 31; Harlech, Lord, and, 151;
inauguration of, 2, 48; JKO and, 191–
92, 199–200, 208–9, 243–44, 248–49,
281, 283–84; at National Theater, *63*;
New Frontier of, 61, 62, 68, 259, 272,
274; at Nobel Prize Winner's Dinner,
64; *Portrait of a President* about, 154;
presidency of, 48–91; presidential
campaign of, 11–47, *34*; *Profiles in
Courage* by, 110, 135–36; reelection
to senate, 15; Senate Caucus Room
speech by, 17; as senator, xii–xix,
15, 19; as "The Senate's Gay Young
Bachelor," xii, xiv; *TV Radio Mirror*
on, 144–45; wedding to, *xvi*
Kennedy, John F. (JFK), assassination of, 1,
274, 281–84; *Baltimore Sun* on, 268–69;
Bergquist after, 129, 130–31; CK and,
100–101; JBK and, 2–3, 92–123, *93*, *95*,
281–84; JKO and, 268–72; Johnson,
Lyndon, after, 94–96, *95*; Kennedy,
John, Jr., and, 100–101; *Life* on, 112, 114;
Newsweek on, 112; RFK and, 101; *Saturday Evening Post* on, 113; Schlesinger
and, 281–84; Secret Service at, 94; *Time*
on, 112, 269–72; UPI on, 100
Kennedy, Joseph, Sr., xv, 30; JBK and, 50;
on possible JFK-JBK divorce, 48

Kennedy, Patrick Bouvier, 101, 114, 129;
AO and, 173
Kennedy, Robert F., xi; on JBK as single
woman, 136; JFK assassination and,
101; at JFK funeral, 104, *105*; JFK
presidential campaign and, 15–16, 29–
30; John Kennedy Presidential Library
and, 128; presidential campaign of, 141;
Tippitt and, 113
Kennedy, Robert F. (RFK): AO and, 172;
assassination of, 168, 173; fan magazines
on, 145–46, 169–70; as JBK protector,
145–46; JFK presidential campaign and,
32–34; Manchester and, 154–55, 159–60;
Photoplay on, 169–70; presidential
campaign of, 141, 171
Kennedy, Rose, 30; fashion of, 38–39; in
JFK campaigns, 289n8; on Onassis
wedding, 175–76
Kennedy Confidential (Dixon, J.), 199–200
Kessler-Harris, Alice, 6–7
Khrushchev, Nikita, 66; Nixon, R., and, 87
Khrushchev, Nina, 66
King, Ed, 26
King, Martin Luther, 174
Kitch, Carolyn, 259, 266
Klein, Edward, 3, 262
Knebel, Fletcher, 22
Knickerbocker, Suzy, 188
Koch, Ed, 234
Kuhn, William, 4, 234, 236–37

Ladies' Home Journal, 131; on JKO, 212
"The Lady in Black," in *Ebony*, 131
Larrain, Pablo, 3
Lasch, Christopher, 275
Lawrence, Greg, 4
Leaming, Barbara, 3
Lebanon (PA) Daily News, 100
Lee, Ruth, 108
Leonard, John, 240–41
"A Letter from Joanne," 28
Levy, Alan, 166–67

Prix de Paris, of *Vogue*, x, xi
Profiles in Courage (Kennedy, John F.), 110, 135–36
Pucinski, Roman C., 118

Quinn, Anthony, 249–53, *250*

Radziwill, Lee (sister), x, 69; AO and, 173, 176; divorce of, 176
Radziwill, Stanislaw "Stash," 176
Rashid, Claudette, 26
Reading Jackie (Kuhn), 4, 236–37
Reggie, Edmund M., 19
Reilly, David, 189–90
Remember the Ladies, 237
Reynolds, Debbie, 157
RFK. *See* Kennedy, Robert F.
Rich, Frank, 258–61
Ridder, Marie, 35–36
Robb, Inez, 55
Robinson, Ethel M., 126
Robinson, Gertrude Joch, 290n18
Robinson, Hugh B., Jr., 125
Rockefeller, Nelson, Braden, Joan and, 32
Rockwell, Betty, 85
Rokacz, Joseph, 264
Roosevelt, Eleanor (ER), 13, 25; JBK and, 148; "My Day" of, 42; political activism of, 17; public relations of, 53
Roosevelt, Franklin: funeral of, 103; New Deal of, 44
Rosen, Ruth, 306n55
Rosselli, John, 244–45
Rubenstein, Mala, 194–95
Ruby, Jack, 113
Rutherford, Janet, 29, 149; in *Photoplay*, 167

sable underwear, 39, 40, 42, 49
Sachs, Hans, 112
Salinger, Pierre, 18, 53, 90; on JBK and international guests, 61; on JBK parties, 59; on JKO, 208; Manchester and, 154; after White House television tour, 88

Saturday Evening Post, xii, xiv, 167; on JBK after JFK assassination, 113; on JBK international trips, 69; "The National Sport of Watching Jackie Kennedy" in, 166
Sauer, Marie, 180, 181
Save Grand Central Station, 230–34
Schlesinger, Arthur, 15–16, 27, 115; JFK assassination and, 281–84; on JKO, 208; on JKO's, 265; JKO's non-Hodgkin's lymphoma and, 262, 263; at John F. Kennedy Presidential Library, 256
Schlossberg, Edward, 261
Schonberg, Harold C., 61
Schwalbe, Carol B., 68, 74–75
Screenland, 131
Secret Service: for CK, 167–68, 214; JBK and, 70, 160; at JFK assassination, 94; at JFK funeral, 104; for JKO, 214; for Kennedy, John, Jr., 167–68, 214
Seltzer, Leo, 73
Senate Caucus Room speech, by JFK, 17
Sex and the Single Girl (Brown), 138–39
Shall We Tell the President? (Archer), 240–43
Shaw, Maud, 46, 78, 146, 209, 210
Sheehan, Susan, 195–96, 207
Shelton, Isabelle, 22, 24
Shribman, David, 275
Shriver, Sargent, 101
Shulman, Irving, 132–33, 137–38, 142, 148
Sidey, Hugh, 272–73
Simmons, Patti, xiii
Sinatra, Frank, 33
single woman: African Americans and, 131; Democratic National Convention and, 141; discotheque as, 140–41; fan magazines as, 131–42, 144–46, 148–50, 162–63; fashion as, 132; JBK as, 124–65; Manchester and, 154–62; motherhood as, 128, 134–35, 141, 143–44, 146–49, *147*, 153; mourning year by, 126–27, 130; parties as, 153; Secret Service and, 160; as single woman, 124–65; Smith, E., and, 141, Warnecke and, 149–50. *See also* Bouvier, Jacqueline

ABOUT THE AUTHOR

KAREN M. DUNAK is Professor and Arthur G. and Eloise Barnes Cole Chair of American History at Muskingum University in New Concord, Ohio.